Bedfordshire Historical Record Society

2025

THE BEDFORDSHIRE
HISTORICAL RECORD SOCIETY

Contact details for the Society are on its website
http://www.bedfordshirehrs.org.uk

THE PUBLICATIONS OF THE BEDFORDSHIRE
HISTORICAL RECORD SOCIETY
VOLUME 99

ROMAN CATHOLICISM IN BEDFORDSHIRE 1700–1900

The Other Non-Conformists

Peter Doyle

THE BEDFORDSHIRE HISTORICAL RECORD SOCIETY

THE BOYDELL PRESS

First published 2025

A publication of
Bedfordshire Historical Record Society
published by The Boydell Press
an imprint of Boydell & Brewer Ltd
and of Boydell & Brewer Inc.
website: www.boydellandbrewer.com

Our Authorised Representative for product safety
in the EU is Easy Access System Europe – Mustamäe tee 50,
10621 Tallinn, Estonia, *gpsr.requests@easproject.com*

ISBN 978-0-85155-086-2

ISSN 0067-4826

Details of previous volumes are available from
Boydell & Brewer Ltd

A CIP record for this book is available
from the British Library

Contents

Illustrations

Tables

Foreword

Every family has a story to tell. The family of the Church is no different. By reflecting on our past we become more aware of our identity and confident to work for a secure future. A living church must not forget that past and the people who laboured to help it grow from the last years of persecution to the beginnings of social acceptance. There was little scope for heroism or the spectacular in the service to others provided by clergy and laity in Bedfordshire, and most of them were little known, but all in their own way were striving for the same thing. I am delighted that Peter Doyle has prepared this history of Catholicism in Bedfordshire, 1700–1900, and feel sure that those who join me in reading it will be encouraged and grateful for the tremendous witness of those who have gone before us, clergy, religious and lay faithful. *Ad multos annos!*

David
Right Reverend Dr David J Oakley
Bishop of Northampton

Acknowledgements

By the early 1700s in Bedfordshire, Catholicism was generally regarded as foreign and, fortunately, rare. This account sets out to show how it grew and extended, albeit slowly, over the next two hundred years or so. In researching this history I have enjoyed both kind support and considerable practical help from a range of people whom I would like to take this opportunity to thank.

First of all my thanks go to the Right Reverend Dr David Oakley, Bishop of Northampton, for writing the foreword to this whole study.

Throughout, the Rev. Brin Dunsire, Diocesan Information Manager and Archivist, was extremely helpful, ever ready to share his extensive knowledge of the diocese and its archives and generous with his time and advice. Without his continued support the study would never have been completed. Much of the work involved in organising and transcribing the original documents has been done by Mrs Margaret Osborne, Diocesan archivist from 1984 to 2008, building mainly on the extensive researches of the late Fr Collins (1915–96). I would also like to acknowledge the help I have received from the new archivist, Mr Ayodeji Anthony. Copyright in all this material belongs to the Northampton Diocesan Archives, and I am very grateful for permission to use and quote from those archives in this study.

I am also grateful to my fellow members of the BHRS Editorial Group for their warm and even enthusiastic support of the project throughout the years of preparation: Nicola Avery, Stuart Antrobus, Bob Ricketts and James Collett-White. Special thanks are due to James Collett-White, former county archivist, whose critical eye and extensive knowledge of the history and archives of the county of Bedfordshire have been of great value. His reading of an early version of the work enabled me both to avoid errors and to include valuable detail. Stuart Antrobus has been generous with advice on possible sources and in reading the completed version. Outstanding, however, has been the advice and assistance of the General Editor, Nicola Avery, whose meticulous attention to detail and work on the final version of the study and its illustrations have been truly invaluable.

Staff at Bedfordshire Archives were always helpful, especially on the records of the seminary and orphanage at Shefford, and in providing copies of illustrations and photographs.

The second part of the volume consists of official mission and parish registers for Bedfordshire, kept informally in the early years and formally after the restoration of the hierarchy in 1850. It is unusual to have such a complete set of early records that illuminate the activities of the priests stationed at Shefford when so little is known about them personally. I am grateful to Canon Keenan for permission to reproduce the post-1860 registers of Bedford's first mission in Midland Road and to copy the photograph of Canon Warmoll its founder, to Fr John Danford at Leighton Buzzard, and to Canon Noonan at Shefford for the copy of the window to Mrs Lyne Stephens and for his general support of the whole project.

Finding a suitable map for inclusion in the volume was not easy since the period it covered ran from before the canal age to the height of the Victorian railway age. I am grateful to Bedfordshire Archives for filling the gap so well. Special thanks are due to Tim Hedges for his expert photography, especially of the stained glass windows and nineteenth-century portraits. Thanks also to Barbara Tearle for alerting me to the work of Tony Hadland on the parallel establishment of Catholicism in Oxford over the same period. Photos of the bishops of the period appeared in Derek Lance's history of the diocese, *The Returning Tide*. Mr Frank Tierney has been helpful in supplying some early Shefford material from his collection, especially some fine pictures of the church and orphanage. My thanks also go to Biggleswade Historical Society for the copy of the early photo of the Catholic church in the town.

I am very grateful to previous authors and archivists without whose labours this study could not have been undertaken – in particular the late Jack Robbins for his *John Priestley Warmoll, Apostle of Bedford* volume; also the various editors of BHRS volumes, especially Anne Allsopp, Patricia Bell and David Bushby. Any errors or shortcomings are entirely my own.

The whole enterprise has taken much longer than anticipated, due mainly to the closing of record offices and archives during covid restrictions. One can only hope that the longer maturation has enabled a healthier product to be the result. Certainly that could not have been even envisaged without the active support of my wife, Barbara, to whom I owe so much.

Abbreviations

AAW	Archives of the Archbishop of Westminster
BA	Bedfordshire Archives
BCH	*British Catholic History* (formerly *Recusant History*)
BHRS	Bedfordshire Historical Record Society
BL	British Library
BM	British Museum
CRS	Catholic Record Society
CUP	Cambridge University Press
GM	*The Gentleman's Magazine*
JEH	*Journal of Ecclesiastical History*
NDA	Northampton Diocesan Archives
ODCC	*Oxford Dictionary of the Christian Church*
ODNB	*Oxford Dictionary of National Biography*
PCC	Prerogative Court of Canterbury
Propaganda	*Congregatio de Propaganda Fide*: The Roman Congregation for Propagating the Faith
RH	*Recusant History*
SCH	*Studies in Church History*

Primary and secondary sources

The principal archival source for the history of Roman Catholicism in Bedfordshire is the Northampton Diocesan Archives. This contains both original sources from the eighteenth and nineteenth centuries, and a range of secondary materials, mostly unpublished although some have been written up in article form. This applies particularly to the extensive researches carried out by Fr Gerald Albert Collins, which form an extraordinarily rich source in their own right. A meticulous and critical scholar, he compiled a large number of carefully written mission histories, catalogues and other invaluable work which he deposited in the diocesan archives.[1]

For all of the period under review in this study, the Roman Congregation for Propagating the Faith (*Congregatio de Propaganda Fide*, referred to usually as Propaganda; established in 1622) was the main Roman body responsible for the various Catholic missionary territories across the world and for those long-established areas where the Catholic church was by law not allowed to have its regular administrative organisation of dioceses and bishops.[2] Its Roman archives are divided into several distinct collections and sub-sections; those dealing with the British Isles between the seventeenth and early twentieth centuries are remarkably complete, containing official and unofficial materials, reports, letters from bishops, clergy and laity, and copious statistics. It was in practice the ultimate authority in ecclesiastical affairs in England and Wales in the years under review in this study; it is perhaps surprising the amount of contact with it that was maintained.[3]

The Archives of the Archbishop of Westminster are another central source of official papers, Roman correspondence, visitation reports and occasional records of individual bishops, including some of those with responsibility for Bedfordshire.

Bedfordshire Archives is an important source particularly for the records of the orphanage and, to a lesser extent, the seminary located in Shefford.[4] It also contains microfilms of some later parish registers.

The Catholic Record Society was founded in 1904; its volumes (published annually, with occasional breaks, since 1905 and now digitised), are an invaluable help to the historian of post-reformation Catholic history in England and Wales. In addition to its regular Records Series, the Society publishes occasional monographs. The Society also publishes a twice-yearly journal *British Catholic History* (now published by CUP), previously published as *Recusant History, A Journal of Research*

1 Born in October 1915, he was ordained at the English College in Lisbon in 1943. He was secretary to Bishop Leo Parker in the early 1950s, and also served at various times as Cathedral Administrator, Chancellor and Vicar General of the diocese. Retiring in July 1987, he pursued his passion for historical research. He died in July 1996.

2 Now the Congregation for the Evangelisation of Peoples.

3 A large number of the relevant Propaganda archives may be consulted in the National Archives, Dublin.

4 BA, X627, Records of St Francis Boys Home, Shefford.

in Reformation and Post-Reformation Catholic History in the British Isles (1957–2014), for the results of the latest scholarship on the history of Catholicism.

A number of Bedfordshire Historical Record Society volumes have been very useful, especially for the social, economic and religious background to the period. Particular mention should be made of the volumes by Chris Pickford: *Bedfordshire Churches in the Nineteenth Century*.[5] These deal solely with the Church of England parish churches in the county, but are very useful for the general ecclesiastical background. Other volumes that have been very useful are the two works by David Bushby: 'The Ecclesiastical Census, Bedfordshire, March 1851'and *The Bedfordshire Schoolchild: Elementary Education before 1902*.[6] A full bibliography is to be found below, pp. 223–32; particularly useful has been the general coverage of the period in Joyce Godber, *History of Bedfordshire 1066–1888* (Bedford, 1969; repr. 1984), and Patricia L. Bell, *Belief in Bedfordshire* (Bedford, 1986).

A very useful secondary source, published anonymously to mark the centenary of the establishment of the Diocese of Northampton, is *Centenary Book of the Diocese of Northampton, 1850–1950* (London, 1950). While this was attributed to 'Anon.', it was almost certainly by Michael Trappes-Lomax (1900–72), author of a number of studies of Catholic history.

Something should be said here about the sources of information about the Catholic clergy. Basic biographical details may be found in two extensive lists of the clergy: Dominic Aidan Bellenger OSB (ed.), *English and Welsh Priests 1558–1800* (Downside Abbey, 1984), and Charles Fitzgerald-Lombard OSB (ed.), *English and Welsh Priests 1801–1914* (Downside Abbey, 1993); both of these are invaluable in tracing and identifying individual priests. Bellenger gives a very useful summary account of the English colleges abroad (principally those at Douai, Rome and Lisbon) and their re-establishment in England at the end of the eighteenth century at Ushaw in County Durham, and St Edmund's at Ware in Hertfordshire; a college was also opened at Oscott, near Birmingham, in 1793.[7] Fitzgerald-Lombard stresses the importance of the annual *Catholic Directory* as the 'only regularly published national record' of English and Welsh clergy from the late eighteenth century onwards; he claims that it is 'the longest running periodical on any subject in Britain, if not in the world'.[8] It started in the eighteenth century as the *Ordo Recitandi Officii Divini* for the clergy; this was joined in 1793 by *The Laity's Directory for Church Services*, which ran annually for almost fifty years, eventually becoming *The Catholic Directory and Annual Register for the Year 1838*. By the end of our period, in 1901, its full title was *The Catholic Directory. Ecclesiastical Register and Almanac for the Year of Our Lord 1901. The Sixty-fourth Annual Publication* (published by Burns & Oates Ltd, London).[9] It is referred to here as *The Catholic Directory*. Fitzgerald-Lombard also provides a very useful bibliography of general works on the history

5 BHRS, vol. 73 (Bedford, 1994), vol. 77 (Bedford, 1998), vol. 79 (Bedford, 2000), vol. 80 (Bedford, 2001).

6 BHRS, vol. 54 (Luton, 1975), pp. 109–92 and BHRS vol. 67 (Bedford, 1988) respectively.

7 Dominic Aidan Bellenger, *English and Welsh Priests 1558–1800* (Downside Abbey, 1993), pp. 6–7.

8 Charles Fitzgerald-Lombard, *English and Welsh Priests 1801–1914* (Downside Abbey, 1993), pp. viii–ix.

9 It is now published online.

of Catholicism in the period, as well as specialist ones on the colleges, individuals, the post-1850 dioceses, and the religious orders.[10] Still useful in this context is John Kirk, *Biographies of English Catholics in the Eighteenth Century* (London, 1909).

Finally, as an indispensable printed source of clerical biographies, used by both Bellenger and Fitzgerald-Lombard, mention must be made of Godfrey Anstruther's four volumes: *Seminary Priests: 1, Elizabethan 1558–1603* (Ware and Ushaw, 1968); *2, Early Stuarts 1603–1659* (Great Wakering, 1975); *3, 1660–1715* (Great Wakering, 1976); *4, 1716–1800* (Great Wakering, 1977).[11] One of his principal sources for priests who studied in the English College in Rome was the two volumes of the so-called *Liber Ruber*, or student registers, covering the years 1579–1783; edited by Wilfrid Kelly, these were published as *Liber Ruber Venerabilis Collegii Anglorum de Urbe Annales Collegii, I. A.D. 1579–1630*, CRS, vol. 37 (Leeds, 1940) and *II. A.D. 1631–1783*, CRS, vol. 40 (Leeds, 1943).

10 Fitzgerald-Lombard, *English and Welsh Priests*, pp. 347–58.

11 He also left manuscript notes for two later volumes, covering 1800–1900; see Fitzgerald-Lombard, pp. viii, 347.

Introductory notes

Organisation of the church

Between 1700 and 1850 the Catholic church in England and Wales was organised in districts (four to begin with, eight from 1840) instead of dioceses; this reflected the fact that it was regarded by the Roman authorities as a missionary territory not settled or secure enough to have a normal hierarchical structure. Each of these districts had a vicar apostolic in charge; he was in episcopal orders and had the personal title of 'bishop' but did not enjoy the full rights of a normal diocesan bishop. They came under, and were expected to report regularly to, the Roman Congregation of Propaganda (see above, p. xi). Again reflecting their missionary status, the districts were not sub-divided into geographical parishes, but into missions that were more or less rigidly demarcated according to the strength of Catholicism in the area; where Catholics were few they might be served by a 'riding missionary' rather than a locally resident priest. A substantial number of Catholic gentry and aristocratic families had their own chaplains who might or might not also serve the local community, more or less independently of the vicars apostolic, although the latter had gradually increased and imposed their authority by the 1840s. After 1850 the Catholic Church in England and Wales was divided into twelve dioceses and one archdiocese (Westminster), each with a fully canonical bishop in charge and each fully divided into a number of parishes (though, confusingly, these were still called missions; technically they did not become parishes until 1918).

Secular and regular clergy

It might be helpful to explain the difference between the secular and the regular or religious clergy. Traditionally, the former lived and worked 'in the world', attached to a parish and under the control of a diocesan bishop, while the latter lived apart, normally in a monastery or friary, following a particular 'rule' (e.g. Franciscans, Benedictines) and often referred to as 'monks'. In England after the Reformation these distinctions became somewhat blurred and regular clergy were to be found working singly as chaplains to the gentry or running missions. They were independent of the vicars apostolic/bishops, owing obedience instead to their religious superiors. (Although it did not happen in Bedfordshire, this independence could be a cause of serious conflict as the vicars apostolic/bishops sought to impose their authority over all the clergy working under them. The situation was finally settled, in favour of the bishops, in 1881.)

Original documents

Extracts from relevant documents and accounts are incorporated in the text. Mission registers (baptismal, marriage, or death/burial) are reproduced in full.

Episcopal authority in Bedfordshire, 1688–1900

From 1688 the Catholic Church in England and Wales was divided into four districts, each with its own vicar apostolic in episcopal orders and addressed as bishop. (As they could not be given English or Welsh place-names in their titles, they were given place-names of defunct ancient sees, usually in North Africa or the Middle East.) The districts were later renamed the Northern, the Midlands, the Western and London. Bedfordshire came within the London District. In 1840 the four districts were subdivided into eight, again each with its own vicar apostolic, with the addition of the Eastern, Lancashire, Yorkshire and Welsh districts. This change led to Bedfordshire becoming part of the Eastern District.

In 1850 a major reorganisation led to the establishment of twelve dioceses, each with its own bishop, and one archdiocese, Westminster, with an archbishop. One of the new dioceses was that of Northampton, which covered the counties of Bedford, Buckingham, Cambridge, Huntingdon, Norfolk, Northampton and Suffolk.

All appointments were made by the Roman Congregation of Propaganda, chosen usually from three names provided by the existing vicars apostolic or bishops.

Table 1. Episcopal authority in Bedfordshire, with the year of appointment, 1688–1880[1]

1688–1840: District of London	
1688	John Leyburne
1703	Bonaventure Giffard
1734	Benjamin Petre
1758	Richard Challoner
1781	John Talbot
1790	John Douglas
1812	William Poynter
1827	James Yorke Bramston
1836	Thomas Griffiths

1840–1850: Eastern District	
1840	William Wareing

1850–1900: Diocese of Northampton	
1850	William Wareing
1858	Francis Kerril Amherst
1880	Arthur Riddell

1 Brian Plumb, *Arundel to Zabi. A Biographical Dictionary of the Catholic Bishops of England and Wales (Deceased), 1623–1987*, North West Catholic History Society (Wigan, 1987), with biographical notes on each bishop; W. Maziere Brady, *The Episcopal Succession in England, Scotland and Ireland A.D. 1400–1875* (Rome, 1876–7; repr. London, 1971), 3 vols.

Bedfordshire c. 1800
Map of the principal settlements and connecting trunk roads c.1770–1830
(courtesy of Bedfordshire Archives, based on BA Z54/84)

Chapter 1

Introduction and religious background

At the beginning of the eighteenth century, the starting point of this study, Bedfordshire had a total population in the region of a little over 40,000; this was set to rise over the coming century to about 63,400. This population was split between the county town of Bedford, a number of smaller towns such as Luton, Dunstable, Biggleswade and Ampthill, and a substantial number of villages and hamlets. As in neighbouring largely agricultural counties, aristocrats were still dominant in society and politics – the Duke of Bedford at Woburn, Viscount Torrington at Southill, the Earl of Ossory at Houghton Conquest (bought from the Catholic Conquest family who had been there for centuries)[1] and the Lords St John of Bletsoe among others; whatever national role they may have played at various times, 'each noble family was the centre of its own little constellation of local gentry and clergymen.'[2] These gentry families, such as the Whitbreads, Osborns, Pyms, Orlebars, Monoux, Burgoynes and several others, came from a variety of backgrounds: some were of ancient lineage, some had prospered more recently in the legal profession, others through marriage or trade (perhaps in London) or just good fortune and inheritance. Some continued to trade, some built new country mansions and patronised the arts, all were proud of their local standing and the roles they performed in keeping society peaceful and, as they saw it, increasingly prosperous.

That prosperity was evident in various ways. Market towns thrived: most of them experienced a rise in population of over 40% by the 1770s, as communications improved, with a key development of navigation along the Great Ouse and Ivel river systems, and improved roads (including Watling Street) that allowed regular long-distance carriers and coaching links to London and the north. Bedford, for example, was able to control the important coal trade because of its position on the Ouse, and among its leading citizens were a number of coal merchants; another trade that flourished in the town at the time was brewing.[3] Good communications could make all the difference to a settlement's development compared with its perhaps larger neighbours; so, for example, Shefford, with one of the smallest populations

1 See BA, RO5, Conquest Bury Estate, for an extensive archive with an excellent introduction by Margaret McGregor: daughters became nuns in Cambrai and Paris, sons studied in Douay; serious financial problems led to the family moving to Irnham, Lincolnshire, a strong Catholic centre, in the 1730s, and the sale of their Bedfordshire estates in 1740; the male line died out in 1761.

2 Joyce Godber, *History of Bedfordshire 1066–1888* (Luton, 1969), p. 302. One of the St John family died in Florence, having become a Catholic; a codicil to his will, dated 1739, made several bequests to Catholic causes in Italy; see BA, J1255–6, Codicil to will of Oliver St John, esquire, made at villa of Prattelina, Florence.

3 Godber, *History of Bedfordshire*, p. 322.

(about 400), was thriving because of its river and road links. What industry there was, was of the kind one would expect in an agricultural county and developed principally to meet local needs: straw plaiting, brick-making (both to develop later into national concerns) and brewing. The county as a whole, however, remained essentially untouched by the changes taking place in other parts of the country that were experiencing the beginnings of industrialisation.

With regard to religious organisation across the county, the Church of England formed part of the widely spread Diocese of Lincoln and in the early years of the century was visited pastorally by the bishop, or his representative the archdeacon, about every three years. Returns made in connection with these visitations provide useful information on the state of the national church at the start of the eighteenth century. At this time there were some 125 parish churches in the county, plus a very small number of chapelries (for example, at Shefford and Heath and Reach).[4] Incumbents (and their congregations) varied, of course, in their devotion to their duties. Regular attendance at church by the people seems to have been low; a number of clergy were pluralists, others were non-resident (at one point late in the century none of Bedford's five incumbents was resident) or else provided the minimum by way of services. But one has to be careful here not to judge by later expectations (including those of nineteenth-century evangelicals), and to recognise that the colourful and wayward were much more likely to feature in the records than the hard-working and devoted. It does seem, however, that a vicar's commitment to and care for the poor and afflicted earned him a much higher reputation than his devotion to what might be called his liturgical duties. Perhaps it was always so in the minds of the majority of the people; belief may exist without formal practice.

Given that it was Bunyan's county, it was only to be expected that there was a strong Non-conformist presence. Around 1700, perhaps 25% of the county's population owed some allegiance to Dissenting or Non-conformist religious groups, primarily Baptist, Congregationalist (Independents) and the Society of Friends (or Quakers). Their membership was not geographically determined as it tended to be generally in the Church of England: the Bunyan Meeting in Bedford, for example, had members from Blunham and Gamlingay, while the members of the Luton Baptist Meeting were as likely to be from Hertfordshire as Bedfordshire. There were strong congregations meeting regularly, especially in Bedford, Luton, Southill, Blunham and Carlton, along with other smaller ones elsewhere in the county. Differences over doctrine, church discipline, or ministerial practice could lead to divisions and the setting up of new congregations as distinct churches: after all, 'Independent' was the result of conviction and a source of pride. New congregations could also result from an increase in numbers – by 1725 both Blunham and Gamlingay had become separate and independent churches; in general these older Dissenting churches seem not to have been particularly evangelistic in gathering new members, although a growth in membership was a regular feature.

Legal disabilities remained in place against Dissenters, although there was no active persecution after the Test and Corporation Act of 1689. While they could now have their own buildings and worship openly, they were barred from studying

4 See the listings in Pickford, *Bedfordshire Churches in the Nineteenth Century*, BHRS, vol. 73, vol. 77, vol. 79, vol. 80 and his 'General Introduction' in BHRS, vol. 73, pp. viii–xi.

at the universities, running schools and becoming members of parliament. Where reported by the Anglican clergy in episcopal returns or reports it was not infrequently in belittling or dismissive terms. In 1717, for example, the incumbent of Streetly, reporting to the bishop about non-conformity, wrote, 'We have nothing of that Naturr (*sic*) in our Parish, and hope we never shall', while his opposite number in Melchbourne said he had two Dissenting families in his parish, but did not know 'what Sect they belong to, neither do they know themselves.'[5]

This more or less steady-state situation was to change remarkably with the birth and development of Methodism – what a recent writer refers to as an important moral, cultural and political influence in the county, with an emphasis on 'the spiritual authenticity of emotion and personal experience'.[6] It experienced a quite remarkable growth over the next hundred years, so that by 1851 Methodism in its various forms was the largest of the Dissenting congregations in the county and was stronger in Bedfordshire than in any other county except Cornwall.[7] In general, one of the features of Protestant non-conformity was its division into sects and individual congregations, a tendency that increased over the years and led to a multiplicity of Non-conformist communities of the elect in Bedfordshire by the mid-nineteenth century.[8]

This Protestant presence and progress, whatever some of its shortcomings may have been, makes the weakness of the Roman Catholic situation only too obvious – often dependent on the support of gentry or other key local families, with concomitant decline and failure as their fortunes waned or they moved away. Severe anti-Catholic laws were still on the statute book and outbreaks of active persecution occurred from time to time. So, for example, the rebellions of 1715 and 1745 strengthened anti-Catholic attitudes and caused active persecution in certain areas. Pro-Stuart attitudes, however, were not entirely restricted to Catholics, as was clear from the Atterbury Plot of 1722–3: there were still some Anglicans who believed the Stuarts were the legitimate rulers of the country. Few of them took to rebellion, of course: while they might raise a glass to the Stuart cause, they were not prepared to draw a sword or cock a pistol in its support.[9] What might be called 'constitutional Jacobitism' existed, certainly down to the mid-century; it was strongest in English and Irish Catholic centres on the Continent and not restricted to having the Stuart monarchy restored in England. Anti-Catholicism, however, was the dominant attitude throughout the country amongst all classes, though lessening somewhat in its severity as the century progressed.[10]

5 See Patricia Bell (ed.), *Episcopal Visitations in Bedfordshire 1706–1720*, BHRS, vol. 81 (Woodbridge, 2002); also Edwin Welch (ed.), *Bedfordshire Chapels and Meeting Houses: Official Registration 1672–1901*, BHRS, vol. 75 (Bedford, 1996). 1717 quotations from W. M. Wigfield (ed.), 'Recusancy and Nonconformity in Bedfordshire. Illustrated by Select Documents between 1622 and 1842', BHRS, vol. 20 (Aspley Guise, 1938), pp. 145–229; at pp. 208–11.

6 Jonathan Rodell, *The Rise of Methodism: A Study of Bedfordshire 1736–1851*, BHRS, vol. 92 (Woodbridge, 2014), p. xvii.

7 *Ibid.*, pp. xix, 157–8.

8 *Ibid.*

9 Apparently, in Bedfordshire, Sir Humphrey Monoux of Wootton, a non-Catholic squire, was one such armchair Stuart supporter; see Godber, *History of Bedfordshire*, p. 306.

10 Adam Morton, 'Anti-Popery', in James E. Kelly and John McCafferty (eds), *The Oxford History of British and Irish Catholicism* (Oxford, 2023), 5 vols; vol. 2, pp. 278–91.

While estimates of numbers are uncertain, the trend of recent research is to reject the traditional picture of a slowly declining Catholic body, keeping itself apart from the rest of society in some sort of shadowy half-life as though waiting for a nineteenth-century renaissance. One recent study has argued that generally there was

> a complex web of relationships that linked Catholics below the rank of gentry to their neighbours … it is evident that, if separation was the characteristic of some of the gentry, integration was the model at parish level, in secular and community affairs at least … In this way they were more similar to the Protestant dissenters than might be thought; their Catholicism did not exist in isolation, but was part of the culture of their time and location.[11]

It seems that 'the virtues of civic society were at last beginning to triumph over religious hatred'.[12] The first fruit of this gradual change in attitudes was the Relief Act of 1779 (which ironically resulted in the serious anti-Catholic Gordon Riots of the following year). The second Relief Act of 1791 allowed the building of Catholic chapels (though without bell-towers and having to be unlocked during services). Agitation for further emancipation led eventually to the Catholic Emancipation Act of 1829, which to all intents and purposes removed all the remaining anti-Catholic legislation from the statute book and allowed Catholics to share full civic rights and duties as citizens. It has to be stressed in this context that the principal motivation behind these legal liberalisations was the state of affairs in Ireland, not England.

Across the country as a whole Catholic organisation at this time was straightforward and minimal. England and Wales as a whole were divided into four districts (London, Midland, Western and Northern), each with a Rome-appointed bishop in charge (more accurately, a vicar apostolic, since these districts were not established as canonical dioceses). Bedfordshire was in the London District. The vicars apostolic jointly had an agent in Rome who was the channel for their reports, requests and complaints, and for correspondence from Rome. Much of this correspondence went by way of the vicar apostolic of London and may be found in the current Westminster Archives (see p. xi), though individual vicars apostolic, clergy and even laity could also make their own approaches.

Not all the clergy serving in England, however, came under the authority of the vicars apostolic. Members of religious orders ('religious' or 'regulars' such as the Jesuits and Benedictines) who were serving as missioners (and in some areas they made up over half of the clergy), came under their own superiors and were zealous in keeping as independent as possible. There were frequent and sometimes bitter rows between the two sets of missioners, and in some cases between rival sets of their lay supporters. There is even some evidence that the civic authorities were happy to

11 Marie B. Rowlands (ed.), *English Catholics of Parish and Town 1558–1778: a joint research project of the Catholic Record Society and Wolverhampton University*, CRS, Monograph 5 (London, 1999), p. 233.

12 J. A. Hilton, *The Cockpit of Conscience: Society, Politics and Religion in Stuart Lancashire 1603–1714* (Carlisle, 2020), pp. 150–1. Gabriel Glickman, *The English Catholic Community 1688–1745: Politics, Culture and Ideology* (Woodbridge, 2009), highlights the growing confidence of Catholic authors to enter into public debate on key issues and no longer be 'silent spectators' either culturally or politically.

see the Catholic clergy expend their energies in such quarrels.[13] The matter was not settled finally until the Roman document, *Romanos Pontifices*, of 1881.

What priests there were had been trained abroad in one of a number of continental seminaries, chiefly at Douay and Rome. No territorial parishes existed in England for these priests to serve; instead, they might be chaplains to gentry or aristocratic families and so provide services for local Catholics, or 'riding priests' serving a scattered flock, or, in areas where Catholicism was more established (e.g. Lancashire), they might serve as resident priests in more or less established 'missions'. As a result of the turmoil caused by the French Revolution, the English continental seminaries had to relocate to England: by the beginning of the nineteenth century priests for the English mission would be trained mainly at Ushaw (near Durham), Ware (in Hertfordshire) or Oscott (near Birmingham) – though some of the continental links were re-established after the Revolutionary Wars, especially in Rome, Lisbon and Spain.[14]

After the restoration by Rome of a Catholic hierarchy of bishops for England and Wales in 1850, Bedfordshire became part of the Diocese of Northampton. Apparently some had argued for the diocese to be centred on Cambridge as being geographically a better choice, but Northampton had been the centre of the former Eastern District and was chosen instead.[15] It was the largest of the thirteen new dioceses in area, covering seven counties, but probably contained the lowest or second-lowest number of Catholic people and clergy. Bishop Wareing's report to Rome in 1854 painted a generally sad picture of his diocese, with few churches, few priests and too great distances between its scattered Catholics.[16]

It is not possible to get precise figures for the different dioceses; one indicator is the 1851 national religious census that reported the numbers at church on a particular Sunday in March 1851. According to this, the Diocese of Plymouth had the fewest Catholics at Mass on that day (2,492), with Northampton second lowest (3,092) and Shrewsbury third (10, 284 – though 9,000 of these were in Cheshire with bustling Birkenhead, leaving a mere 1,230 for its seven other counties). By way of comparison, Liverpool had over 69,000 and Salford over 33,000. No wonder Bishop Brown of

13 See, for example, J. C. H. Aveling, 'The Eighteenth-Century English Benedictines', in Duffy, *Challoner and His Church*, pp. 152–73; also Maurice Whitehead, 'The English Jesuits and Episcopal Authority: The Liverpool Test Case, 1840–43', in *RH*, vol. 18 (October, 1986), pp. 197–219.

14 On the period from the late sixteenth to the mid-nineteenth centuries, John Bossy, *The English Catholic Community 1570–1850* (London, 1975) is essential reading; it provides a much more positive approach to the survival and subsequent growth of the Catholic community than traditional accounts had suggested. The most recent studies of the whole period are collected in James E. Kelly and John McCafferty (eds), *The Oxford History of British and Irish Catholicism* (2023); for this study see particularly Liam Chambers (ed.), 'Relief Revolution, and Revival, 1746–1829', vol. 3, and Carmen M. Mangion and Susan O'Brien (eds), 'Building Identity', vol. 4.

15 Derek Lance, *The Returning Tide: Northampton Diocese 1850–2000* (Northampton, 2000), p. 2; John Charmley, 'East Anglia in the Victorian Diocese of Northampton 1850–1901', in Francis Young (ed.), *Catholic East Anglia: A History of the Catholic Faith in Norfolk, Suffolk, Cambridgeshire and Peterborough* (Leominster, 2016), pp. 155–79.

16 F. J. Devany, *The Faithful Few: A History of Norfolk Roman Catholics 1559–1778*, 2nd ed. (Norwich, 2010), pp. 161–3, quoted in Young, *Catholic East Anglia*, p. 159.

Shrewsbury could speak of his 'desolate diocese', a description echoed in 1858 by Northampton's second bishop, Francis Kerril Amherst, who wrote of his diocese being 'destitute and in sad want'.[17] A few years later, in 1863, Amherst appointed the Rev. John Priestley Warmoll to Bedford to see if the town could support a Catholic mission; this was the start of a slow renewal in the town and of a gradual acceptance of Catholics into general society there. Catholicism remained very much a minority interest, however, and there could still be opposition if its adherents strayed into what were considered to be either too-much outward show or attempts to claim equality.[18]

This study ends in 1900, by which time Catholicism was firmly established in Bedfordshire, the previous twenty-five years or so having witnessed a modest growth in the establishment of a Catholic presence throughout the county. By the turn of the century missions existed in Bedford, established with a resident priest in 1863 and a fine permanent church from 1874; in Luton, established in 1884 with a house chapel, and a full public chapel and resident priest in 1897; and in Leighton Buzzard, with a resident priest and house-chapel by 1895 and a permanent 'iron chapel' by 1897. By far the oldest establishment, however, was in Shefford; it may have been part of a 'riding mission' in the 1720s, with a house chapel in the 1760s and a purpose-built church in 1791; after a very short break in the mid-nineteenth century the mission had been re-established in 1868 and the town also became the site of a diocesan theological college and a Catholic orphanage. It is this revival in the rural parts of the county in the eighteenth century that marks the starting point of this study.[19]

I have given this study the sub-title of 'The Other Non-conformists'. This might appear fanciful to some, and certainly Catholics in the two centuries under review would not have accepted it as a meaningful descriptor of how most of them saw themselves – they were, they were sure, the *only* true religious community in the country. Yet the phrase has a validity; indeed, Bossy stated that his principal aim was to ensure that the Catholic community 'ought properly to be considered a branch of the English non-conforming tradition'.[20] There is also another issue – that of continuity; what similarities, beyond those of the basic religious tenets of belief, were there between the English Catholic community of 1700 and that of 1900? Non-conformists were given to division almost by their very nature (how far would Wesley recognise late nineteenth century varieties of Methodism?) – did this apply to Catholics as well? Bossy argued that the Catholic church in England and Wales was radically different ('fundamentally transformed' was his phrase) after 1850;[21] if this is true, the transformation surely lay not in radical divisions but in coalescence and the gradual imposition, and acceptance, of unity.

17 There are serious problems of interpretation with the 1851 census; obviously, total numbers were higher than these attendance figures; see Philip Hughes, 'The English Catholics in 1850', in G. A. Beck (ed.), *The English Catholics 1850–1950* (London, 1950), pp. 47–51.

18 On Bishop Amherst, see Stewart Foster, '"In sad want of priests and money": Bishop Amherst at Northampton 1858–1879', in *RH*, vol. 25, no. 2 (October, 2000), pp. 281–93.

19 See *Catholic Directories* for the foundation dates of various missions.

20 Bossy, *The English Catholic Community*, pp. 7, 385.

21 *Ibid.*, p. 5. Recently it has been suggested that historians have failed to assess what it was like to 'be, think and feel' Catholic individually rather than institutionally. See Simon Ditchfield's review in *BCH*, vol. 36, vol. 4 (October, 2023), p. 474; evidence for such an examination does not seem to exist for Bedfordshire.

It was not that there were no public disagreements, some of them serious. The quarrels over *The Rambler* (a Catholic periodical supported by liberal converts to Catholicism) in the 1860s, for example, the beginnings of what became known as 'Liberal Catholicism' in the 1880s, and the condemnation of Anglican Orders in the 1890s – there were enough disagreements here to persuade the bishops to issue a cautiously negative pastoral letter in 1900.[22] Cardinal Manning had earlier described Northampton as the 'dead diocese'[23] and certainly, major events and developments, positive and negative, affecting the English Catholic Church as a whole, seem to have made little impression locally, though no doubt readers of the extensive Catholic press would have been fully aware of them. It is important, however, in assessing local progress to remember the low starting point, especially in Bedfordshire, which may well have had the lowest Catholic population of any county across England at the start of the period in 1700: there were different ways of achieving and measuring progress.

22 See V. Alan McClelland, 'The Formative Years, 1850–92', in McClelland and Hodgetts, *From Without the Flaminian Gate: 150 Years of Roman Catholicism in England and Wales 1850–2000* (London, 1999), pp. 1–20; on the 1900 pastoral letter, see pp. 155–6.
23 See p. 103.

Chapter 2

Catholicism in early eighteenth-century England

The reigns of King William III and Queen Anne saw some of the harshest anti-Catholic legislation enacted in England, a result of the 1688 Revolution and of fears of attempts at a Jacobite restoration. Among these laws mention may be made of the penalty of perpetual imprisonment for any Catholic priest convicted of exercising priestly functions (milder, admittedly, than the Elizabethan penalty of hanging, drawing and quartering); the charge of high-treason against anyone attempting to reconcile a person to Catholicism; exclusion from all offices of profit or trust in the state, including commissions in the armed forces; a general permission for Protestant next-of-kin to disinherit a Catholic heir, while forbidding Catholics to inherit or purchase land; the imposition on Catholics of a double land tax, and the confiscation of any property or funds left to Catholic clergy. Furthermore, Catholics were forbidden to keep arms, could not practise as barristers, doctors or school masters, could be dispossessed of a horse worth more than £5, and were liable to be fined for having their children educated abroad.[1] Moreover, it was not just a case of forbidding certain external activities or imposing legal obligations: the oath that might be tendered to anyone seeking office implied a full interior acceptance of Protestant belief:

> I A.B. do solemnly and sincerely, in the presence of God, profess, testify and declare, that I do believe that in the Sacrament of the Lord's Supper there is not any Transubstantiation of the Elements of Bread and Wine into the Body and Blood of Christ at or after the Consecration thereof by any Person whatsoever: And that the Invocation or Adoration of the Virgin Mary, or any other Saint, and the Sacrifice of the Mass, as they are now used in the Church of Rome, are superstitious and idolatrous.[2]

The oath went on to deny that the pope had any power to dispense from its terms anyone who had subscribed; moreover, it was to be understood as its words would commonly be understood by English Protestants. Clearly there was to be no room for casuistical (still less Jesuitical) manoeuvrings. It remained on the statute book in one form or another into the nineteenth century: as late as 1835 the Rev. John

1 The best summary of anti-Catholic legislation in the early years, with references to the relevant acts of Parliament, is Basil Hemphill OSB, *The Early Vicars Apostolic of England 1685–1750* (London, 1954), pp. 86–9, and for the eighteenth century, J. Anthony Williams, 'Change or Decay? The Provincial Laity 1691–1781' in Eamon Duffy, *Challoner and His Church: A Catholic Bishop in Georgian England* (London, 1981), pp. 27–54. See also Tony Hadland (ed.), *From Country House Catholicism to City Church: The Registers of the Oxford Catholic Mission 1700–1875*, Oxfordshire Record Society, vol. 75 (Oxford, 2023), pp. 20–4 for a list of the relevant statutes.

2 Stat. 2 (1678), in Wigfield, 'Recusancy and Nonconformity', p. 214.

Baxter, a Dissenting Minister of Ravensden, 'took and subscribed the oath ... (and) the Declaration against Popery required by 1 William and Mary C.18'.[3]

Fears of a re-imposition of Popery were fed by rumours of an invasion by the Catholic Pretender which occurred intermittently in the first half of the eighteenth century. Sometimes they had only a short life, but were taken seriously by the authorities: in March 1708, for example, one led to the calling out of the militia at Newport Pagnell, with some confiscation of Catholics' horses and weapons in line with current Orders in Council, and the Lord Lieutenant of Buckinghamshire urging local JPs to implement anti-Catholic legislation. The scare was over in a month – and, interestingly, the horses and weapons were returned (with a note that, in any case, the horses were too old for military use and some of the guns were rusty!). There are, perhaps, indications of local leniency (or, perhaps, just carelessness) in complaints that the lists of Catholics had not been drawn up clearly enough and needed to be re-done. Similar confiscations took place again twice in 1715, along with the arrest of the 'persons of disaffected Papists'.[4]

It is true that many of the heaviest of the anti-Catholic laws and restrictions were increasingly ignored as the eighteenth century progressed, and magistrates seemed in many cases to be unwilling to enforce them, especially once the fears of Jacobitism diminished. Yet they remained on the statute book for most of the century and could occasionally be invoked. For example, Bishop Bonaventure Giffard, from 1703–34 vicar apostolic of the London District (which included Bedfordshire), spent four separate spells in prison and frequently had to change his lodgings for fear of arrest. In 1714 he reported that he had had to move no fewer than fourteen times in five months, including a spell in a 'poor garret' in the Venetian ambassador's house; he added that 'three private persons' were the cause of his troubles, two of them actually ordained priests whose immoral lives had become a scandal.[5] Some years earlier, writing in the third person, Giffard had described how he had escaped trial:

> on the 8th December he was to have had his trial, and as he could expect nothing else but to be condemned to Hurst Castle or some remote prison for his life ... thereunto had settled all his little affairs relating to others. But the night before the trial was to be, there came to him several persons of all states and conditions, who told him that they having consulted together, twas (*sic*) the unanimous judgment and advise (*sic*) of all that he should not appear, but rather forfeit his recognizance ... having no time to consult others, or to reason things within himself, he was forced to yeald (*sic*) to the advise (*sic*) then given. Next morning therefore he withdrew into a private solitude.[6]

3 *Ibid.*, p. 225.

4 Anthony G. Petti (ed.), *Recusant Documents from the Ellesmere Manuscripts*, CRS, vol. 60 (St Albans, 1968).

5 The Very Rev. E. Estcourt M.A., F.S.A. and John Orlebar Payne, *The English Catholic Nonjurors of 1715: Being a Summary of the Register of Their Estates, with Genealogical and Other Notes* (London, 1885), pp. xiii–xv. Edgar E. Estcourt (1816–84), a convert from Anglicanism and a canon of the Birmingham Diocese, died before the volume was completed. His co-editor was John Orlebar Payne, presumably related to the leading Protestant Bedfordshire Orlebar family of Hinwick House, Podington, Bedfordshire. A convert to Catholicism, he lived in Highgate, London. He was responsible for the writing and publication of the book, Estcourt for the research; he also contributed to some of the early CRS *Miscellanea* volumes.

6 Hemphill, *The Early Vicars Apostolic of England*, p. 46.

The seriousness of the situation is clear from a letter from Bishop Witham, vicar apostolic of the Midland District, written a few months later, stressing the danger Giffard had been in, a danger not yet removed. According to Witham, only Giffard's staunch friends, including, interestingly, 'some in government', had saved him from 'perpetual imprisonment without any possibility of relief'. Priests, he believed, were in more than ordinary danger and any communications with Rome would, if discovered, have caused fresh persecution. Witham himself was obliged to 'scamper about and often to change lodgings and seek hiding holes'. Among other dangers he noted was action by 'miscreant Apostate Catholics' (who coveted the informant's substantial reward of £100), which could lead to perpetual imprisonment, which not even the queen could commute. The laws were more likely to be enforced in London than in the provinces.[7]

For most of the population, anti-Catholicism just became a routine reaction – for example some thirty years later in the diary of Elizabeth Brown of Ampthill: she was a Quaker, and most of her diary is about Meetings, but it also contains references to 'the gross errors of the Papists'.[8] There was a continuing market for anti-Catholic sermons – see, for example, John Barker, *Popery the great Corruption of Christianity. A Sermon Preached at Salters Hall, January 9, 1734–5*, 4th ed. (London, 1735): the preacher claimed that the Catholic missionary effort succeeded in corrupting 'the meanest people especially'.[9]

What internal picture of these Catholics can we see, apart from their strictly legal position and occasional outbursts of anti-Catholicism? How far could Catholics be incorporated in, or be part of, their local secular communities, as were Protestant non-conformists? To some extent there was a Catholic community, or a number of mini-communities, with people gathering for worship and devotions. In Turvey in 1767, for example, there were twenty-nine Catholics (including twelve under 15), while in Shefford there were twenty-one (with seven under 15); no doubt these 'centres' were also used by some of the small numbers of Catholics from nearby villages.[10] Shared persecution and exclusion by others could also, of course, create a sense of community as well as internal cohesion of belief and practice. Anti-popery was the default position of the great majority of the population, breaking out from time to time into active persecution and anti-Catholic legislation – but for most of the people for most of the time it was just an accepted and expected feature.

It appears that despite these constraints the number of Catholics in England and Wales began to increase, after a period of stagnation and even decline between about 1650 and 1700.[11] This period was important for the establishment of the four vicars apostolic in 1688 – each a bishop and each with a defined district: this meant that under their admittedly limited episcopal control organised missionary labour could be successfully deployed, and might operate, especially in urban areas, without aristocratic or gentry patronage. This allowed pastoral visitations, the conferring

7 *Ibid.*, pp. 46–8. The £100 was the standard reward for informing on Catholic clergy.

8 Joyce Godber, 'Elizabeth Brown of Ampthill, 1778–91', in *Some Bedfordshire Diaries*, BHRS, vol. 40 (Streatley, 1960), entry for 6/17 March 1779.

9 Quoted in Eamon Duffy, '"Poor Protestant Flies": Conversions to Catholicism in Early Eighteenth Century England', in *SCH*, vol. 15 (Oxford, 1978), pp. 289–304, at p. 293.

10 See 1767 returns, pp. 32–3.

11 Bossy, *The English Catholic Community*, pp. 278–9.

of confirmation and some control over the clergy; Catholics could attend Mass in urban centres, such as Bath and Durham. Overall, it appears that in the eighteenth century the number of Catholics across the country was holding its own and probably increasing in some places, despite some pessimistic reports and later rather negative historical accounts; overall the population may have risen to about 80,000 by the 1780s.[12]

A minor though indicative action by the vicars apostolic involved the reduction of the large number of holy days in the calendar, so that Catholic congregations could approximate more closely with the rest of society and adopt similar working patterns. Catholic practice in this regard had become so complicated and, one may say, casuistical in avoidance tactics, that the vicars apostolic took the initiative and reduced the number of non-working holy days eventually to ten, a pattern that Rome agreed to in 1777.[13]

It has been argued that the impact of post-1700 anti-Catholic legislation as a brake on growth was less effective than new spiritual initiatives were as a growth factor.[14] Especially important here were the devotional works of John Gother (?1654–1704) and, later, those of Bishop Challoner (1691–1781), published openly and readily available, at least to the minority who could read. A re-vitalised secular clergy developed a missionary spirit and Challoner showed what active organisation could achieve, while his extensive visitation records show that 'the ideal was at least coming within measurable distance of realisation'.[15] Clergy and people could take

> spiritual sustenance from the increasing and better-organised availability of the Mass, the sacraments, catechetical instruction and Catholic schooling in England, as well as from the writings of Challoner … and Gother … whose Instructions were both practical and edifying.[16]

One has to be careful here, however: London and some other urban areas, along with northern areas such as Lancashire, were exceptional both in terms of numbers and in the freedom to practise allowed to Catholics – and even there it was a somewhat fragile freedom. There is little sign of a markedly renewed missionary enthusiasm in, for example, Christopher Taylor at Shefford; certainly conscientious and committed to providing decent facilities for his scattered flock, he showed few if any signs of an evangelical revival. Anthony Williams' point about the growth of the Catholic community from the early eighteenth century onwards is interesting in this context: it was not necessarily a sizeable increase in numerical terms among Catholics, but a definite increase in confidence as they went about their religious practice.[17]

Greater confidence may also be found as a factor in a more limited sector of Catholic life, that of scholarly publications contributing to eighteenth-century Enlightenment debates in Britain and continental Europe. This is to question the former accepted view, summed up in the judgment that the century was a good time

12 Still the most trustworthy account of a difficult area of research is in Williams, 'Change or Decay? The Provincial Laity 1691–1781', pp. 26–31.
13 Bossy, *The English Catholic Community*, pp. 119–21.
14 *Ibid.*, p. 286.
15 *Ibid.*, p. 287.
16 *Ibid.*, p. 125.
17 Williams, 'Change or Decay? The Provincial Laity 1691–1781', p. 33.

for Catholic music but a poor one for Catholic thought.[18] Glickman has shown that there were English Catholic authors concerned with such international issues as the separation of state and church, and universal religious toleration, questions of increasing importance across a number of countries as the century progressed. He may, perhaps, have exaggerated the extent of Catholic involvement in the life of eighteenth century Britain, but his central point is a valid one.

Moreover, it is clear that the English continental colleges were themselves no intellectual backwaters. It has been apparent for some time that they were 'thoroughly modern … and scientifically up-to-date' in their teaching, with courses in astronomy, optics and applied physics. The philosophy course at Douay, for example, has been described as 'anti-scholastic … with an element of critical doubt' and modern logic more in favour than former metaphysics.[19]

A question of more immediate importance for the generality of English Catholics was the role of the aristocracy and gentry in supporting the pastoral ministry of the clergy between, say, 1750 and the early 1800s. Their role had been essential in keeping Catholicism alive during the worst years of persecution and while there is no doubt their importance was declining, it would be a mistake to regard it as having passed altogether. As Mullett has argued, there was no rapid and certainly no complete transition from what he calls a 'rural-patronal-peasant' pattern of Catholicism to an 'urban-bourgeois-proletarian' one; aristocrats and gentry were still important, and in some areas essential, to the development of that community. We must certainly not write off all these patrons as somehow anti-intellectual examples of a traditional hunting, shooting and fishing type. While what might be called the chaplaincy model of the gentry/aristocratic support of earlier years was doubtless diminishing, the support itself certainly continued, although in a different form. In Bedfordshire, for example, as we will see later, while there was a marked absence of traditional support after about 1740, later Catholic establishment and expansion was heavily dependent on gentry and aristocratic money, old and new.[20]

It is important, however, to note Mullett's point that while to some extent this might be seen as a period of calm and social involvement after the earlier years of persecution, 'the tolerance of the English people depended indeed upon the maintenance by English Catholics of a modest and unthreatening demeanour … (including) low rates of activity on the part of priests and their practical invisibility as such.'[21]

18 Thomas Clancy quoted in Gabriel Glickman, *The English Catholic Community*, p. 6; see also pp. 4–18, 252–7.

19 See David Beales, *Prosperity and Plunder: European Catholic Monasteries in the Age of Revolution, 1650–1815* (Cambridge, 2003); also, for the general picture Ulrich L. Lehner, *The Catholic Enlightenment: The Forgotten History of a Global Movement* (Oxford, 2016). On the curriculum in the Catholic colleges, Joseph P. Chinnici, *The English Catholic Enlightenment: John Lingard and the Cisalpine Movement, 1780–1850* (Shepherdstown, WV, 1980), esp. pp. 4–8.

20 Michael Mullett, *Catholics in Britain and Ireland, 1558–1829* (London, 1998), pp. 141, 146–7; he gives a range of examples, including Preston, Leeds and Bristol, to illustrate the variety of experiences in passing from full gentry patronage to its ending or being shared with middle-class Catholics. See also in this context Chinnici, *The English Catholic Enlightenment*, pp. 12–13, for the development of a type of Catholic congregationalism between the later 1700s and about 1840.

21 Mullett, *Catholics in Britain and Ireland*, p. 144.

Clearly, a balance is needed in assessing the risks involved in being a Catholic at the time and the impact this had on Catholics' mentality and societal relationships. The threat of legal action was always there and could become a reality from time to time, but it was not by any means incessant. Ordinary economic relationships obviously necessitated mixing and even socialising. This would normally lead to some friendships, even inter-marriage. There might be joint service on parish bodies, involvement in local charities perhaps, and so on. While this was no doubt true for most places most of the time, the urban mob could be excited by the determined anti-Catholic rabble-rouser, so that high-ranking Catholic ecclesiastics needed to keep eyes and ears open constantly for possible persecution. Rowlands' conclusion is a fair one:

> there was both tradition and change, prejudice and toleration, separation and integration, danger and security, and individuals managed these contradictions as best they could, responding to changing pressures in different ways from day to day.[22]

Away from the larger urban centres, much would depend on the outlook and reactions of the local Anglican clergy. A key area where this was true was that of burials, and it is clear that some were quite willing to allow local Catholic burials to take place in their churchyards and even in some cases to allow Catholic prayers to be said over the grave.

This underlines the danger in describing or seeking a Catholic 'body' or 'community' as a whole at this time. There was, indeed, a rainbow of reactions to the various legal and social situations in which Catholics found themselves, ranging from the ultra-conservative to the liberal/enlightened. Such variations are well illustrated between the clerical worlds of Rev. Robert Banister, as shown in his correspondence with his nephew Rev. Henry Rutter, and that of the scholarly Rev. John Lingard, though all three were working in the North.[23]

Support for the Catholic clergy

This raises the issue of how secular priests at the time were supported in areas or missions where there was no Catholic family of substance and where the local Catholics were unlikely to be able to provide sufficient in offerings to do so. 'Riding priests', especially, would have needed some sort of external funding, apart from the small number who may have had their own family money. A document from c.1705 is interesting in this context. After listing the various aristocratic and gentry Catholic families up and down the country who could support a chaplain or local priest, it looks at those areas where such support was non-existent and Catholics 'of the lower rank' predominated. Such congregations, the writer continued, were looked after by a priest from 'the Clergie', as, for example,

> At Woolverhampton (*sic*) [where] the Clergie maintains a priest to help that Town & the parts adjacent; his flock was a hundred souls … At Newcastle a Clergie

22 Rowlands, *English Catholics of Parish and Town*, p. 348.

23 See Leo Gooch (ed.), *The Revival of English Catholicism: The Banister-Rutter Correspondence 1777–1807* (Wigan, 1995), and Peter Phillips, *John Lingard: Priest and Historian* (Leominster, 2008).

> priest is also maintained to help that town and the poor people in the country about …

It is clear from the various examples given that 'the Clergie' here refers not to individual priests but to a common association or fund, set up to assist priests who could not rely on the support of sufficient local Catholics. Moreover, these funds (there were different ones across the country) were established almost entirely by the priests themselves – it had become the custom for priests to contribute to them while alive or to leave bequests to them when they died. The above document continued:

> 'tis moreover the common practice among the Clergie priests, when they dye (*sic*), to leave what little they have towards the maintenance of priests in such places as most want help … The same is done in several other parts of England where the number of Catholicks is considerable: so that all England over the main body of the Catholicks depend chiefly on the Clergie.[24]

Clearly, mention of funds, administered locally or on a county or district basis, raises the issue of the origin of those funds and their practical organisation. Relevant here is an institution that had been established in the early seventeenth century, known as the Old Chapter (later the Old Brotherhood). This consisted of a dean and twenty canons who would assist the (single) bishop in the task of administering the church in England and Wales, and would rule when the bishop died, recommending to Rome a successor. As matters worked out, there was no bishop (more correctly, no vicar apostolic) for over fifty years, until 1685; then in 1688 the number was increased to four, each responsible for a district: the London District, the Northern District, the Midlands District and the Western District; each district consisted of a number of counties, with Bedfordshire in the London District. With the establishment of these four districts, the Old Chapter lost its canonical role and became an honorary body. However, it kept what had become a most important practical responsibility: the provision of financial assistance to its clerical members. It is remarkable, given the severe penalties attached to being a priest, that as early as 1630 a chapter fund had been set up to this end, with contributions from the clergy themselves and a small number of lay benefactors. It is not clear how these monies were distributed, although we know that some of the donations to the fund were intended to support a priest in a particular neighbourhood. The general benefits of having the funds increased into and throughout the eighteenth century and a principal concern was that a better distribution could be made towards supporting priests in their old age. The existence of these various funds assisted, unintentionally, in lessening the dependence of the secular clergy on aristocratic and gentry patronage and perhaps helped to provide a more even provision of service across the country.[25] Their meetings also provided

24 Michael Gandy, *Catholic Missions and Registers 1700–1880*, vol. 2, *The Midlands and East Anglia* (London, 1993), pp. 1–5; this is a reprint of J. Williams, 'The Distribution of Catholic Chaplaincies in the Early Eighteenth Century', in *RH*, vol. 12, no. 1 (1973–4), pp. 42–8. The original author of the list is unknown, presumably a contemporary secular priest. 'Clergy' in this context refers solely to the secular or missionary clergy and does not include regulars such as the Jesuits and Benedictines.

25 Bossy, *The English Catholic Community*, pp. 243–5; Hemphill, *The Early Vicars Apostolic of England*, p. 162, fn. 1.

occasions for local clergy, often isolated in their pastoral work, to meet together and share mutual support.

After 1688, one of the tasks of the four new vicars apostolic and their successors was to bring order to a somewhat disorganised situation relating to these funds and their distribution. Most secular priests appear to have joined up to one of the funds when they began their active ministry, unless they had their own private income or were serving as chaplains to the gentry; in Bedfordshire, for example, where the number of Catholics was too small to support a priest, we know that Stephen Robinson and John Barnewall were dependent on the fund until the Noddings family of Shefford left money for the purpose.[26] An important achievement was to get the clergy to accept the obligation to support the funds financially; according to Bossy, 'this achieved the ideal of being both relatively painless and relatively profitable'.[27] In the London District, for example, the fund grew sufficiently for Bishop Challoner to be able to pay a 'salary' of £20-£40 a year to priests working in the less fashionable and poorer areas of the city; he was also able to support a number of charitable works from the same source.[28] Recent research has highlighted Challoner's business and financial acumen, enabling him to manage a substantial range of funds and support a wide range of causes, social as well as religious.[29]

In the 1820s Bishop Poynter of the London District was able to provide a yearly income of £25 to a priest who had to retire through ill health.[30] Overall, the existence of the funds suggests a degree of organisation one might not have expected at the time.

The size of the Catholic body

In the early eighteenth century there was no accurate estimate of how many Catholics there were in England and Wales; numbers seem normally to have been exaggerated, certainly in the popular mind. There now appears to have been a steady increase, say from 60,000 in 1700 to 70,000 by the 1780s. Growth was more noticeable in urban areas and accelerated towards the end of the century in centres such as Birmingham, Newcastle-on-Tyne, Liverpool, Manchester and other Lancastrian towns – and, of course, London. In all these centres, the increase was due in a large extent to Irish newcomers.[31] Mainly rural counties were a different matter. Some recent estimates for Bedfordshire put the number towards the end of the seventeenth century as low as forty Catholics for the county as a whole and suggest that there was little change over the next century, although this may well be an underestimate. Some attempts

26 See pp. 41–4.

27 Bossy, *The English Catholic Community*, p. 248.

28 *Ibid.*, pp. 248–9.

29 See Giada Pizzoni, 'The English Catholic Church and the Age of Mercantilism: Bishop Richard Challoner and the South Sea Company', *Journal of Early Modern History*, vol. 24 (2020), pp. 111–35. I am grateful to Mr Frank Tierney for this reference.

30 Peter Phillips (ed.), *The Diaries of Bishop William Poynter, V.A. (1815–1824)*, CRS, vol. 79 (London, 2006), pp. 215–16. For brief notes on these funds, see Godfrey Anstruther, *Seminary Priests: 1660–1715*, vol. 3 (Great Wakering, 1976), p. ix; *Seminary Priests: 1716–1800*, vol. 4, p. viii.

31 Mullett, *Catholics in Britain and Ireland*, p. 140.

were made in the early eighteenth century by the bishops of Lincoln (whose Anglican diocese included Bedfordshire) to establish the numbers more precisely through the returns made as part of their Episcopal Visitations in 1706, 1709, 1712, 1717 and 1720.[32]

These returns were part of incumbents' answers to a set of questions sent out to parishes by the bishop. As might be expected the amount of information given varies from incumbent to incumbent, but the general impression from reading all the returns is that they were on the whole carefully compiled. In some cases the numbers of Dissidents and Papists are given as 'families', at other times as individuals. Individual names are only given if the Catholic is the patron of the parish with the right of appointment (there was just a single example of this in Bedfordshire).

The great majority of parishes (including all those in Bedford) in the 1706, 1709 and 1712 returns report no Papists or 'reputed papists'. The returns for 1717 and 1720 rarely mention them; the episcopal letters instigating the returns after 1709 do not ask for the number of Papists, presumably because it was thought there were not enough of them to constitute any danger. While there was no explicit enquiry about Catholics in 1717 or 1720, some returns do include references to them: for example, the Bedfordshire returns for 1717 show eight Catholic families in the whole county, five of which were in Turvey (see Table 2 below), two in Eaton Socon and a single person in Roxton; almost certainly this was an under-estimate for the county.

It is worth having a closer look at the Campton cum Shefford returns for 1706, 1709 and 1712, as Shefford later became the county's only Catholic centre. Overall, the episcopal returns show that few people in the Anglican communities had been confirmed and there appears to have been a generally low level of religious practice. In 1709, for example, of the seven hundred or so people in the parish (the figure given in the return), only fifty received communion at Easter and it was noted that 'great numbers seldom or never receive at all'; these low levels seem to have been taken for granted, though there were extra services on festivals and fast days (not specified), as well as in Lent on Wednesdays and Fridays. There were reckoned to be about twenty-two Dissenting families in all; it was claimed that they used to meet regularly but had recently become less regular and met less often. In Shefford itself, an Anglican service was held once a month. Much the same picture emerges from the later reports of 1717 and 1720, with the 'Sacrament of the Lord's Supper' generally celebrated four times a year.

Bell gives some estimated totals for the numbers of Roman Catholics in the county.[33] In 1742, when Bishop Challoner carried out confirmations at Turvey, she reckons there were thirty-five at Turvey and a further twenty or so at Chawston and Shefford. As confirmation was a rare event, people might well have travelled in from elsewhere – perhaps even from outside the county borders. Bell mentions some individual families – the Hunts of Chawston, for example, and the Conquests of Houghton Conquest. We know that the last of the Conquests left for Irnham in 1733. John Higgins, a Catholic, lived in the Turvey Abbey farmhouse in the late eighteenth century. Also in Turvey, the Brand family lived in the Mordaunt's

32 See Bell, *Episcopal Visitations in Bedfordshire* for the full text of these returns. For a more general study see Wigfield, 'Recusancy and Nonconformity', p. 159.

33 Patricia Bell, *Belief in Bedfordshire* (Bedford, 1986), pp. 62–3.

Table 2. Bedfordshire parishes listing known Catholics, 1706–20

Campton cum Shefford	Given its later importance for a Catholic presence in the county it is surprising it does not figure in any return. Shefford was a 'chapelry' or a 'chapel of ease' in the parish of Campton. In 1717: it had a 'private school' where the children are instructed in Church Catechism and 'are brought pretty duly to Church'.
Carlton	In 1706: one poor family of 'reputed papists'. In 1709: two 'reputed Papists'.
Chalgrave	In 1706: the patron, Capt. Potts (aet. 78), was a Catholic. He did not exercise his right of patronage. His wife and his 'man' were also Papists. They are not mentioned in later reports.
Chawston	*see* Roxton
Eaton Socon	In 1709: one Papist, and four occasional conformists (unclear – the four were not necessarily Papists). In 1717: two reported Papists.
Houghton Conquest	In 1706: one 'Recusant', Mr Benedict Conquest, a gentleman and patron; he did not exercise right of patronage. In 1709: one Papist family. In 1712: one Papist family. In 1717/20: none.
Pulloxhill	In 1706: one Papist, 'a Boarder, named Mary Major'.
Roxton	In 1717: one family of the 'Church of Rome'. In 1720: none.
Turvey	In 1706: three Papist families. The Earls of Peterborough are noted as not resident – they had formerly had a seat there (see below regarding the 3rd Earl). In 1709: of c.660 souls, seventeen are Papists. In 1712: no mention. In 1717: five Roman Catholic families reported. In 1720: no mention of Catholics in the (extremely brief) return.

house (see pp. 28–9); Winifred Brand died in 1745. One report says that Mass was said at Turvey Abbey by a priest from Weston Underwood in neighbouring Buckinghamshire. According to Bell, none of these groups or families lasted in the county into the second half of the century.

The mention of Chawston in the Bedfordshire list above is of some interest in this context of possible Catholic centres of growth. A hamlet in the parish of Roxton, its manor house had been in the hands of the Hunt family from the fifteenth century. In the early seventeenth century two-thirds of the estate had been sequestered, but Thomas Hunt, a recusant Catholic, compounded for its restoration in 1653. By 1700 half the manor was in the hands of John Cufaude, the Catholic husband of Anne Hunt; five years later the whole manor was in the hands of Mary Hunt, a spinster. A gentlewoman, Elizabeth Hunt, was buried at Roxton in 1718. For some reason the whole of the manor passed to the Metcalfe family. In 1719 the Rev. Edward Hunt, a Catholic priest (alias Colebeck, described in the records as 'of Bedfordshire'; probably ordained in 1679, he died in 1726), made a will that left money to his nieces Anne Fincham and Mary Hunt and also mentioned John Cufaude. He desired that the remainder of his property and goods should go towards establishing 'a small fund', the profits of which should go towards the member of secular clergy to help the poor around Chawston in Bedfordshire 'in case he has no sufficient subsistence; otherwise to be disposed of where the Bishop for the time being shall judge necessary'.[34] Hunt himself appears to have ministered mainly in Hampshire, and there is no evidence of a priest having been resident in Chawston.

Obviously, a Catholic presence could be over-dependent on individual families and their necessarily unsecure futures. At Houghton Conquest about 1725 a Mrs Conquest gave a gold and silver pyx to the Benedictines, but the family shortly moved to Lincolnshire. At Turvey the third Earl of Peterborough married a Catholic, Mrs Robinson, in 1722; she maintained a chapel there (presumably with a chaplain). After the Earl's death in 1735 she continued to maintain the chapel, though she no longer resided there: in 1742 Bishop Challoner confirmed twenty-five people there (not all, of course, necessarily from the immediate area) and found a total congregation of thirty-five. Its main supporters were the Brand family, living in Turvey Abbey; but they died out in 1745 and the chapel closed.

In this context, about 1718 the Hon. Rev. Richard Howard (1687–1722, fourth son of Lord Thomas Howard, Duke of Norfolk) vicar apostolic elect and coadjutor designate to Bishop Giffard of the London District, sent a memorial to the Roman agent to report both on the persecution being suffered by English Catholics and the general state of Catholicism as he saw it.[35] The early part of the memorial is a complaint about the burden of the extra taxation laid on Catholic families after 1700: this, he claimed, had led to some of them giving up their faith. Others could no longer afford to keep a priest as family chaplain, and so several priests were currently unemployed. It is important to note, however, that his main complaint dealt with internal Catholic matters. In the London District, a number of Irish missionaries, both Secular and Regular, were apparently causing scandal and giving the Catholic mission a bad reputation: it was necessary, he claimed, for the Roman authorities to come up with an effective remedy and get them to return to their own country. Such anti-Irish sentiments were not new: an earlier report to Rome had attacked the number of Irish priests in London,[36] especially the members of religious orders, who were giving the vicar apostolic and English priests 'great displeasure' and causing damage to every missionary endeavour. It is interesting that later in the century Bishop Challoner was still complaining about them: 'we have no want of them here: and daily experience too many scandals from those of that nation'.[37] Howard's memorial ends on a slightly more optimistic note, at least as far as Catholic numbers were concerned:

> it has become clear how little true sense of Religion the Protestants show in their religious practice, just as they show uncertainty regarding the principles of their belief. In many people this has caused disgust … together with a desire to learn about that faith which the Nation at one time gave up to become engulfed in so

34 AAW, B 1536, Challoner's Ledger; Anstruther, *Seminary Priests: 1660–1715*, vol. 3, pp. 108–9; Fr Gerald Albert Collins, 'An Ancient Catholic Mission: Shefford, Beds 1762–1869', in the NDA (unpublished typescript), pp. 5–6, on the Hunt family, referencing Victoria County History: *Bedfordshire* vol. III.

35 AAW, Z 73–5, Mayes' Roman Agency; Z 74 (1712–20), no. 102: 'Memorial on the State of Catholics in England'.

36 Dated a year or so earlier: AAW, Z 74, no. 81.

37 Quoted in Duffy, *Challoner and His Church*, pp. 15–16.

great a confusion of beliefs. Hence many have been reconciled to the ancient Faith, especially those of the lower and middling orders; but very many others, especially the wealthy, are held back so as not to be exposed to the danger of loss and increased taxation … The lack of public chapels in London is notorious, and those that are open are so crowded that every day it is necessary to rescue from the throng someone half-suffocated: so much so that Catholics cannot fulfil their sacred obligations without some danger to their lives.

Though the Irish were cast as the worst offenders with respect to clerical indiscipline, the English clergy caused their own problems, particularly in London; Bishop Challoner was to complain about clerical drunkenness, neglect and scandal – as he said, 'a bad priest seldom goes to hell alone'.[38] The great majority of the clergy, of course, were innocent of such charges and carried out their duties in an effective and reasonably exemplary way. But it is probably true to say that the districts were too large for effective episcopal control and the effective deployment of resources.

Overall, then, while the first half of the eighteenth century was a period of gradual moving away from active persecution and legal prohibitions, any signs of growth in the Catholic body remained a cause of concern to many Protestants and they would find it particularly worrying if that growth seemed to be the result of evangelical endeavour. This raises the question of the leadership of the Catholic body and its effectiveness in these conditions.

Bishop Challoner

The key figure among the leaders of English Catholics in the mid-eighteenth century was Bishop Richard Challoner (1691–1781). A young convert to Catholicism, he had studied at the English college in Douai in the Netherlands. After ordination, and some years teaching in the seminary, he moved to London, with its Catholic population of about 20,000, and found there his true vocation as a missionary priest, ministering especially to the poor and the 'middling sort'. The church in the capital, however, unlike elsewhere in the country, was not without its splendour, and many of the capital's Catholics had access to the half-dozen or so embassy chapels with their clergy, baroque setting and full liturgical services.[39]

Perhaps surprisingly, throughout his life Challoner was a prolific writer of spiritual works (and some works of controversy). It has been claimed that one should never take any of this extensive work as his own original material, but that is to miss the point. In the interests of saving souls the message alone mattered and his presentation of that message, in print or sermon, was straightforwardly without frills or compromise. His classic prayerbook, *The Garden of the Soul*, served generations of Catholics for both instruction and devotion and he has rightly been called the

38 Quoted in Duffy, *Challoner and His Church*, p. 15.

39 Eamon Duffy, 'Richard Challoner 1691–1781: A Memoir', in Eamon Duffy (ed.), *Challoner and His Church*, pp. 1–26, at pp. 8–9. Also Mullett, *Catholics in Britain and Ireland*, on Challoner, pp. 152ff; *ODNB* entry. The classic nineteenth century biography by Edwin H. Burton, *The Life and Times of Bishop Challoner, 1691–1781* (London, 1909), 2 vols, is still useful, especially for its documentation.

'Georgian architect of Victorian Catholicism'.[40] All this marked a new apostolate, indicating both a relaxation in practice of the penal legislation and a growing confidence on the part of the Catholic leadership, clerical and lay. Duffy gives the example of a successful London woollen-draper, William Mawhood, a Catholic, whose diaries over these years give us a picture of a thriving and open Catholic milieu with charitable activities organised by middle class trustees (not unlike those of contemporary Non-conformists). We get an intriguing picture of clerical pastoral activity from Kirk's brief account of the Rev. Christopher Piggot, a London priest who died in 1735: he formed 'a community of converted gentlewomen' who, among other good works, spent large sums of money annually maintaining several poor Catholic families in the capital; he was 'most laborious' among the poor in Southwark.[41]

Challoner became auxiliary vicar apostolic of the London District in 1741, succeeding to the full role in 1758 (a post he held until his death in 1781). When he left London to visit the rural parts of his district he found a quite different situation regarding Catholic observance. He expected all his clergy to share and practise his evangelical sentiments. In London he was able to organise regular clerical conferences in which to persuade his priests to follow his ideals. This was not possible in rural areas where clergy were often geographically isolated and the bishop had to rely on his visitations to improve clerical performance if this had fallen below his high ideals. This is not to imply that there was any serious laxity among them, rather more it was a matter of the acceptance of the status quo, with no particular evangelical drive to take advantage of the more relaxed atmosphere that Catholics enjoyed, though one should not presume either that that relaxation necessarily existed in more isolated rural areas.

In September 1742, as we have already seen, he was at Weston Underwood in Buckinghamshire to carry out a visitation there and in neighbouring Bedfordshire. Weston Underwood, a seat of the wealthy recusant Catholic Throckmorton family, had about 200 Catholics; the rest of Buckinghamshire about 100, Bedfordshire fewer than that. He confirmed sixty people at Weston Underwood on 5 September and on the next day crossed into Bedfordshire to Turvey, confirming fifty-five people from Turvey, Shefford and Chawston (and perhaps elsewhere). Challoner was nothing if not conscientious in carrying out these visitations and confirmations. Between 1749 and 1751 he was in the area again, though his notes on these visits are not as thorough as earlier. Overall numbers seem to be much as before; as one might expect, there were small variations up and down across the counties.[42]

Some years later, in 1773, in response to a request from Propaganda in Rome, the four English and Welsh vicars apostolic sent in detailed reports of their districts. We do not know what lay behind Propaganda's unusual request; perhaps it was to do with the imminent suppression of the Jesuits, who were very active as missioners in parts of England and Wales, although no similar request appears to have been made

40 Mullett, *Catholics in Britain and Ireland*, p. 152. Bossy's chap. 15, 'The Heart of the Matter', *The English Catholic Community*, is excellent on the role and development of *The Garden of the Soul* and other prayerbooks.

41 Duffy, *Challoner and His Church*, pp. 8–9; John Kirk, *Biographies of English Catholics in the Eighteenth Century. By the Rev. John Kirk, D.D., being part of his projected continuation of Dodd's Church History* (London 1909), p. 184.

42 Burton, *The Life and Times of Bishop Challoner*, vol. 1, pp. 203ff, 295, 299.

of other areas where the Jesuits were active. All that the Propaganda's letter said was that it had been a long time since it had received detailed information on the state of the four districts. Whatever the reasons for the request the four vicars apostolic sent in detailed replies.

After a full and generally favourable report on the conditions of the Catholic presence in London, where he reckoned there were no more than twenty thousand Catholics in a total population of 'hundreds of thousands', Challoner turned to conditions elsewhere. He thought that the state of religion outside London was 'much sadder' and the number of Catholics mostly very small. He went on to describe conditions in the ten counties that constituted his vicariate; Bedfordshire was the ninth and easily disposed of: 'In the county of Bedfordshire, scarcely a hundred Catholics, with one missioner.' Regarding missioners in general, he reckoned that altogether there were about 120 priests in his vicariate, fifty-five of them seculars, the remainder members of religious orders – an interesting statistic, meaning the majority of the clergy did not come directly under his control but owed obedience in the first place to their religious superiors. This divided loyalty and the disputes it could lead to were to trouble the English and Welsh mission for over a century, principally over claims for autonomy on the part of the regular clergy.

On the whole, Challoner reported favourably on the state of his clergy who were working conscientiously in the face of anti-Catholic opposition, especially outside London; he was, of course, reporting to Rome and unlikely to paint too critical a picture: most of the priests, apart from foreigners and the ever-troublesome Irish, he wrote,

> behave in an exemplary way. Some, especially in London, work very hard in the Lord's vineyard and bear considerable fruit in the conversion of souls. But outside London conversions are rarer due to the iniquity of our laws and the opposition of magistrates and ministers of religion, who often arouse serious persecution against both the priests who reconcile some people to the Church and the Proselytes themselves: for conversions of this sort, which in London with its huge population often go unnoticed by magistrates and ministers, in the smaller towns and villages are immediately known to everybody and excite the anger of opponents against Catholics.

He was also at pains to allay any fears the Roman authorities might have about the orthodoxy of the people's beliefs and practices (though, again, not those of the Irish or foreigners):

> our native Catholics, of whom the greater part have undergone severe persecution for the Catholic faith for two hundred and more years, are zealous in their reverence and obedience towards the Holy Apostolic See and in the orthodox faith, and are most loyal to the Holy See; therefore they are accustomed to abhor greatly any unholy novelties of belief. They are also most commendable for the uprightness of their way of life and their devout practice of religion. That we affirm only about the English, not about foreigners or the Irish living in London, whose irregular and depraved way of life repeatedly gives grave scandal to our native Catholics.

There follow here sections about the Catholics in North America, the West Indies and other colonies, which came under Challoner's nominal jurisdiction; where the Jesuits were the priests in charge, he reported, matters were in a generally good state; elsewhere, where there were Irish priests, the state of religion was generally lamentable, especially in Jamaica, Barbados, Antigua, etc. Again, the generally anti-Irish sentiment is noteworthy. Challoner signs off the report, 'Your most obedient servant, Richard, bishop of Debra, Vicar Apostolic, London 10 September 1773'.[43]

Whatever political or social events and developments were affecting the general English Catholic body during Challoner's years as vicar apostolic, his main responsibility in his own eyes was to ensure that Catholics were up to the mark spiritually. Deeply conservative in outlook, with a touch of anti-intellectualism, he shared none of the intellectual and leisured pursuits of some of the rural clergy and domestic chaplains to the gentry: with a dedication to Tridentine orthodoxy in doctrine and discipline,[44] and infused by an eighteenth-century evangelical fervour, he was truly a missionary to every class of Catholic, poor or rich, urban or rural. His means were preaching, writing, the provision of a pastorally-minded clerical workforce, and regular visitation of his district. While not a creative thinker, and borrowing much from earlier writers, both English and Continental, he created an English Catholic Evangelical model that was to last well into the next century and beyond, and be a major factor in the development of a common devotional culture among English and Welsh Catholics.[45] By the last quarter of the eighteenth century what a recent scholar has termed a 'period of reform and consolidation' was taking place in both English and Irish Catholicism. The developments were not, of course, uniform but the foundations had been laid for future growth.[46]

How far these developments helped to create or foster a Catholic community is a matter of interpretation. Is there any sense in which the disparate groups of believers – recusant gentry families, Lancashire and Yorkshire middling and lower classes, Londoners of diverse social standing and nationality – can be seen as a community? At one level, in their daily lives Catholics shared in local communities with their non-Catholic neighbours, as Sheils has claimed about the earlier period,

> Borrowing and lending to each other, witnessing each other's wills and legal documents, and inter-marrying to a degree, in the face of opposition from their priests ... As with dissenters, non-gentry Catholics were to be found in the families of better-off farmers and craftsmen as well as among the poor.[47]

43 The original report, in Latin, is in the Propaganda archives, reference: Fondo di Vienna, sett.–ott. 1773. It is printed in full with commentary in J. H. Whyte, 'The Vicars Apostolic' Returns of 1773', in *RH*, vol. 9, no. 4 (January, 1968), pp. 205–14. Challoner's unfavourable statements about the Irish clergy were in line with strong anti-Irish statements from earlier in the century – see Hemphill, *The Early Vicars Apostolic of England*, pp. 76, 99.

44 i.e. as laid down by the Council of Trent, 1545–63; used subsequently to refer to generic reform inspired by the spirit of the Council though not legislated for in so many words.

45 Mullett, *Catholics in Britain and Ireland*, pp. 154–9. See Mary Hardy, 'The seventeenth-century English and Scottish reception of Francis de Sales. An Introduction to a Devout Life', in *BCH*, vol. 33, no. 2 (October, 2016), pp. 228–58; also on spiritual writings, Duffy, '"Poor Protestant Flies": Conversions to Catholicism in Early Eighteenth Century England', pp. 289–304.

46 Peter Phillips, 'Catholic Belief and Practice', in *The Oxford History of British and Irish Catholicism*, vol. 3, ed. Liam Chambers, *Relief, Revolution, and Revival, 1746–1829*, pp. 122–41, at p. 146.

47 See his 'Religious Divisions in the Localities: Catholics, Puritans and the Established Church before the Civil Wars', in Edward Vallance et al. (eds), *Faith, Place and People in early*

Yet in the very important fundamental area of having a set of key beliefs in common and sharing whenever possible in joint religious practices, sometimes with possibly dangerous consequences, they were part of a distinctive religious grouping. While, as we have seen, there was no guarantee of the permanency of such groupings, surely while they lasted they gave the participants a sense of being part of something bigger than their own perhaps small gathering. When, for example, Challoner visited Turvey and confirmed a group of local Catholics from there and other parts of the county and elsewhere, how did they know of the arrangements? Who invited them and were those to be confirmed prepared in any way for their reception of the sacrament – and if so, by whom? Do these practicalities not suggest at least the existence of some sharing of information and a means of communication, an embryonic form of community?[48]

modern England: Essays in memory of Margaret Spufford (Woodbridge, 2018), pp. 29–42, at pp. 30–1.

48 William Sheils, 'Catholics and their Neighbours in a Rural Community: Egton Chapelry 1590–1780', in *Northern History*, vol. 34 (Leeds, 1998), pp. 117–43; see p. 40 for Joy Rowe's work on Norfolk; also, Williams' 'Change or Decay? The Provincial Laity 1691–1781'. It may be worth noting here the warning quoted by a recent writer, 'the search for communities of the mind may ascend to levels of vagueness as yet undreamed of'; see A. R. Muldoon, 'Recusants, Church-Papists, and "Comfortable Missionaries"', in *Catholic Historical Review*, vol. 86, no. 2 (April, 2000), pp. 242–57.

Chapter 3

Moving slowly towards liberation

As we have seen, London was exceptional in the size of its Catholic population, its embassy chapels open to the public and providing a full Catholic liturgy for all, at the same time experiencing a stricter enforcement of the anti-Catholic laws than was generally experienced elsewhere. The second half of the eighteenth century saw limited steps towards easing the legal restrictions on Catholic practice and the end of practical persecution. Such limited liberation was, of course, welcomed by Catholics and became a spur for campaigns to obtain full equality before the law; it was not to be a straightforward passage or one without occasional serious setbacks.

It is worthwhile here to look at the prestigious *Gentleman's Magazine*. This had been founded in 1731 as a literary journal; it often reprinted pieces from other journals of the day and commented regularly on general news. It illustrates the prevailing anti-popery sentiment: a piece from 1735, quoting from 'Free Briton', gives a typical statement:

> It has been the Merit of the Protestant Dissenters, that they never allowed the Church of Rome to be a True Church: and 'tis as impossible to reconcile the Ideas of a True Church and an Idolatrous Church, as the Worship of God and the Worship of Idols.

The same issue also claimed that there were 10,000 Catholic priests active in London![1]

Not surprisingly, 1745 with its Stuart threat brought a resurgence of explicit anti-Catholic material that had seemed to be receding in the immediately preceding years. For example, notices of books published that year listed seventeen titles under the heading 'Political and Anti-papistical Publications'; some of these were most obviously anti-Catholic, for example, *Popery Confuted by a Jew* (1/–); *The opposition between Christianity and Popery* (1d.); *The pope's scourge; or an exact portraiture of a popish pretender* (3d.). Publishers used anti-Jacobite fears to dig out and re-publish anti-Catholic materials or to publish new titles: 'Just published (Price 4/6): The Conformity between modern and ancient CEREMONIES: Wherein is proved, by incontestable Authorities, that the Ceremonies of the Church of Rome are entirely derived from the Heathen … Now first translated into English from the original French, printed at Leyden in the Year 1667.' (Printed for E. Cave, at St John's Gate.)[2]

This theme was repeated in a piece taken from *The Westminster Journal*, reprinted in October 1745 and entitled, 'Pagan and Popish Idolatry equally gross'. This claimed that converts to Roman Catholicism were expected to accept pagan practices such as

1 This magazine ran from 1731–1922; Samuel Johnson served as its editor for a time. See *The Gentleman's Magazine* (*GM*), January 1735, vol. 5, pp. 5, 47.

2 *GM*, April 1745, vol. 15, pp. 224.

incense, holy water, lamps and candles, votive gifts (especially pictures and statues), and recommended its readers to consult a recent book, *The Conformity between the ancient (Pagan) and the modern (Popish) ceremonies* (this could well have been the book already mentioned above).[3]

Any stick, no matter how broken, could be an anti-Catholic weapon. The November edition carried a long account, again taken from *The Westminster Journal*, of the trial and condemnation of Galileo. The same issue also carried a quite detailed account of an English Protestant woman in Portugal who had been whipped, tortured and burned (though not to death) by the Inquisition; the events were 'solemnly affirmed by the English consul' – they had occurred in 1706.[4] The October issue reported that Catholics were being accused of arson in various parts of the country: in particular, farmers' stocks had been burned, while 'his Majesty's bakehouse in Dover' had also been destroyed.[5]

Not surprisingly, the fears of what would happen if the Young Pretender came to power in 1745 were clearly spelled out:

> ... final bondage and the inquisition; monks and fraud triumphant, conscience oppress'd, the bible banished, popery and flames in fashion, and protestants burn'd, or their bodies secured at the expence of their faith and their souls. Here is a catalogue of woes, dreadful ones, yet not all. Behold them, Britons, abhor them, and prevent them!

The author was now in full swing:

> A Popish government and a Protestant parliament are a contradiction: they are fire and water to each other. A Popish parliament in a Protestant country, is equally impossible ... The most furious papists are his [ie the Young Pretender's] keenest emissaries, the most active to poison and pervert protestants: the grossest papists, almost savages, are armed for him, and for our destruction.[6]

Such sentiments were not limited to the popular press. The following is an extract in the same issue from a speech in Parliament in October 1745:

> I shall not say, Sir, that all the Jacobites are for arbitrary Power; but I am sure that the Consequence of their succeeding in their Scheme, would be the establishment of it; and as for the Papists, if they understand the Religion they profess, they must be for arbitrary Power; for their Religion can be supported by nothing but Ignorance or arbitrary Power: In former Ages it was supported by Ignorance, and now that Veil is pretty well removed, it can be supported by nothing but Inquisitions and arbitrary Rule; we may therefore suppose, if the Papists amongst us should ever get the Government into their Hands, they would establish a despotick (*sic*) Sway, in order to restore the Religion they profess.[7]

The magazine did not need the 1745 Stuart threat to justify an anti-Catholic stance. An earlier report that year had focused on the Catholic missions in Malabar: these

3 *GM*, October 1745, vol. 15, p. 548.
4 *GM*, November 1745, vol. 15, pp. 584–6 and pp. 582–3 respectively.
5 *GM*, October 1745, vol. 15, p. 555.
6 Extract from *The General Evening Post*, 2 November 1745, reprinted in *GM*, November 1745, vol. 15, p. 580.
7 *Ibid.*, pp. 600–1.

were marked, it claimed, by the 'pomp and grandeur' so beloved by Roman Catholics, with their priests riding about on elephants, employing Negro clerics who were ignorant and incapable of explaining the Gospel to infidels, and using catechists who taught that Mary was greater than Jesus, while all the time running a profitable trade in relics.[8]

Such public fears in 1745 also prompted the re-publication of previously published materials and of out-of-date documents that might serve to heighten or justify those fears. The longest of such documents appears to be that published by Charles Cosin in 1745, with a second edition in 1746. The list of propertied Roman Catholics and non-jurors (but see note about non-jurors below) for each county had originally been drawn up in 1715 by Cosin's father, who had been Secretary to the Commissioner for Forfeited Estates, presumably to help deal with the Stuart threat of that year and as a means of raising taxes. It gave the names of Catholic landowners in each county and listed the value of their property. His son's edition was the first to be published, a substantial and detailed book of 170 pages.[9]

A completely revised edition of the list was published by two Catholic editors in the nineteenth century, the Very Rev. E. Estcourt M.A., F.S.A, and John Orlebar Payne. They were probably moved by the re-publication of Cosin's original text in 1862. They pointed out that Cosin's list contained many errors and for some reason had omitted no less than a quarter of all the Lancashire names as well as some names from other counties; he had also, they claimed, omitted the genealogical and other notes, now included. Their main comment, however, was that the names included were the names of those who had registered their estates in accordance with the law of 1715, passed with a view to possibly imposing additional taxation on the Catholics.

'Roman Catholics' are not mentioned by name after the first line and there are no references to 'papists' or 'papistry'; the attention is all on rebellion, with phrases such as 'unnatural rebellion', 'rebellious insurrection' in the North; also mentioned is 'a need to protect the Protestant interest of the Kingdoms'. Yet the only people named throughout were Catholics – no Protestant non-jurors were included.

The title page of the book lays out clearly its purpose and origin in 1715, attributing the information in it to James Cosin:

> The Names of the Roman Catholics, Nonjurors, and others, who refus'd to take the Oaths to his late Majesty King George. Together with their Titles, additions, and Places of abode; the Parishes and Townships where their Lands lay and the Names of the then Tenants or Occupiers thereof; and the annual valuation of them as estimated by themselves.
>
> Transmitted to the late Commissioners for the Forfeited Estates of England and Wales after the unnatural Rebellion in the North, in the Year 1715. As appears from the Returns of the Clerks of the Peace for the several Counties, pursuant to an Act of Parliament made for registering their estates in the first year of the Reign of his said late Majesty.

8 *GM*, April 1745, vol. 15, pp. 197–9.

9 Charles Cosin, *The Names of Roman Catholics, Nonjurors, and others, who refus'd to take the oaths to his late Majesty King George* (London, 1745; repr. for John Russell Smith, London, 1862). The following text is that of Cosin's 1745 edition, with author's additional notes, mainly from Estcourt and Payne (eds), *The English Catholic Nonjurors of 1715*.

> Taken from an original Manuscript of a Gentleman, who was the Principal Clerk to the Accomptant-General's Office, belonging to the said Commissioners and now Published with a Generous View to promote and serve the true Protestant interest of these Kingdoms.
> James Cosin.

On the same page are the details of publication of the second edition by Charles Cosin in the year 1746:

> Great Britain. Commissioners and Trustees for the Forfeited Estates
> London: G. Woodfall; T. Lister, 1746
> By Charles Cosin
> Second Edition
>
> LONDON
>
> Printed for G. Woodfall, at the King's-Arms, Charing-Cross, and T. Lister, at the Bible, without Temple-Bar, 1746

Not surprisingly, the book carries a dedication to the king, George II:

> TO THE KING
>
> Most Gracious Sovereign,
> The following List, which was carefully collected by my deceased Father, when he acted as Secretary to the Honourable Commissioners, for forfeited Estates, appointed in the Reign of your Royal Father, after that unnatural Rebellion in the Year 1715, is on this occasion most humbly presented to your Majesty, by
> SIR,
> Your Majesty's most dutiful Subject,
> Charles Cosin[10]

There follows a general introduction, linking the present publication to the earlier attempts to gather the required information, pointing out that no action had been taken against those who had refused to co-operate with the inquiry and how they all had been allowed to benefit from the peaceful rule that had resulted from the accession of George I:

> To The Publick
>
> The following LIST of Estates, which was collected by Authority in the Year 1715, is published at this Time, with no other View, but to assist the Magistrates, and other Officers, who shall happen to be instructed with the Execution of such Orders of Government, as either have already been, or may hereafter be issued, for suppressing the Growth and unhappy Effects, of the present rebellious Insurrection in the North; which, its (*sic*) hoped, will caution the Possessors of such Estates, at this Juncture, carefully to keep within the Bounds, of their known Duty, to our Gracious Sovereign King GEORGE, and his rightful Government over them, unto which it is conceived, they will find themselves, more especially obligated, if they only please to observe that many of them (who in the said Year neglected to give in such a particular Account of the Value of their respective Estates, as was then under severe Penalties required of them by Law) were never as yet, called upon to answer for such Neglect, but gently permitted to go on quietly, and to partake equally with their Fellow-Subjects, of all that Lenity and special Effects,

10 Cosin, *The Names of the Roman Catholics, Nonjurors, and others*, p. 9.

> of a mild Administration in Government, which these Kingdoms have peacefully enjoyed, ever since the most joyful and happy accession of his late Majesty King GEORGE the First to the Throne.
>
> N.B. The Estates which appear to have been registered, but not valued, belong to such as neglected their Duty, in complying with the legal Orders of the Government at that Time.[11]

In the two pages that follow is an alphabetical list headed 'CONTENTS of the Counties', which summarises the values given for each county. (Two cities are included separately in the list, Lincoln and Worcester.) Bedfordshire comes first; the total value of its named estates is given as £998. 5. 3; this is one of the smaller amounts: Durham, for example, was valued at £12,330; Kent £6,606; Lancashire £13,123; on the other hand, the Cambridgeshire total was only £501 and Carnarvon a mere £167.4s. The grand total value is £358,194. 5. 3¾. The owners of the various estates were not necessarily resident in the counties where their estates are listed. After these two pages comes the main part of the work, and the page numbering starts again. It is worth noticing that while the heading covers 'Roman Catholics, Nonjurors and others', in fact all the names given are of Roman Catholics.

> THE NAMES OF THE ROMAN CATHOLICS, NONJURORS, and others. who refused to take the Oaths to his late Majesty, King George
>
> BEDFORD

Magdalen Giffard, of the Parish of St Giles in the Fields, Middlesex, Spinster:	
Estate at Roxton, late in possession of John Fincham, Esq.	£133.0.0
George Heneage of Lainton in County Lincs, Esq	£210.0.0
Robert Kilby of Soulderne in Oxfordshire, Esq.	£ 96.0.0
Christian Brand	£ 80.0.0
Susanah Brand	
Winifred Brand all of Turvey	
Margaret Brand and	
Mary Brand	
Bryan Hinde of Irnham in co. of Lincs	£154.5.9½
Benedict Conquest of Houghton, Esq.	£283.19.6
Henry Stonor of Stevington, Gent.	(blank)
Edmund Lewkenor of Easebourne in co. of Sussex, Gent.	£ 40.0.0

It is possible to reconstruct something of these people and families from other sources, from information not contained in Cosin's original list.[12]

Magdalen Giffard was a daughter of Walter Giffard of Chillington, Staffordshire, a leading Catholic family that counted a number of priests among its members and a bishop, Bonaventure Giffard of the Midland District, 1688–1734.

Bryan Hinde, surprisingly, was a Catholic priest, one of forty listed overall, along with three Catholic bishops – surprising given their illegal status at the time. Hinde was a Douay student ordained in 1682; he served as priest at Irnham about 1702 and died in 1724:[13] he is described as 'trustee' of the estate at Roxton, Bedfordshire,

11 Cosin, *The Names of the Roman Catholics, Nonjurors, and others*, pp. 11–12.
12 Added from Estcourt and Payne (eds), *The English Catholic Nonjurors of 1715*.
13 *Ibid.*, p. 241.

which belonged to John Cuffaud, whose wife was related to the Catholic Hunts of Chawston.[14]

Robert Kilby held an estate at Turvey along with one at Souldern(e); he died without issue in 1757.[15]

The five Brand sisters lived in Turvey, spinster-daughters of Thomas and Margaret Brand; they are listed also as having property in Carlton, Bedfordshire, and in Essex and Shropshire (the list here adds their mother, Margaret). There were also two sons, Peter and Thomas. The family feature in the Turvey parish registers; the death of Margaret, the mother, in 1718 is noted in the Weston Underwood registers: 'a septuagenarian. A person of very holy life. She left one (*sic*) son and five daughters.'[16]

Benedict Conquest came from Houghton Conquest: the male line of this recusant Catholic family became extinct with the death of his son at Irnham, Lincolnshire, in 1753. His daughter married into the Arundell family.

The very ancient and wealthy recusant Stonor family with its principal estate at Stonor in Oxfordshire, and extensive holdings elsewhere, held the barony of Camoys, a title restored to them in 1839 after being in abeyance since the sixteenth century. This Henry Stonor died in 1739 and according to Estcourt and Payne was buried at Steventon.[17] The Cosin list gives 'Stevington' as the place of burial, but Estcourt and Payne's 'Steventon' is much more likely to be correct: Steventon was a village in Berkshire (now in Oxfordshire after boundary changes in the 1970s).[18]

Edmund Lewkenor, along with his wife Elizabeth and his brother Anthony, held an estate at Carlton. He came from an ancient landed family of Easebourne (*sic*), Sussex, just north of Midhurst.

While panic over the 1745 Stuart invasion was understandable, it is clear that a basic anti-Catholic sentiment was never far away from the popular mind. It surfaced again just twenty years later in 1767, a year that saw the conviction at Croydon assizes of John Baptist Maloney from Ireland for the offence 'of exercising the functions of a popish priest' – he was jailed for life, though this was later commuted to perpetual banishment in 1771. In the same year fifteen priests were prosecuted, along with nine teachers, while four Mass-houses in London were temporarily closed. It may be that it was some elements of the London press that lay behind the pressure for action: the *St James Evening Post* had run such a campaign and in 1766 had repeatedly called on the bishops to compile lists of the papists in their dioceses, accusing them of neglecting their duty in this matter. Various such attempts had, indeed, been made from 1660 onwards: in the eighteenth century these had taken place in 1706, 1714, 1715, 1743 and 1744, not to mention the thousands of partial lists made by individual incumbents.[19]

14 See reference to *GM*, July 1788, vol. 58, p. 575. There are some minor genealogical notes about the family at Irnham, see Edmund Knight, 'Family Notes of the Knights of Lincolnshire', *Miscellanea IV*, in CRS, vol. 4 (London, 1907), pp. 261–3.

15 Estcourt and Payne (eds), *The English Catholic Nonjurors of 1715*, p. 214.

16 *Ibid.*, pp. 1, 59, 225.

17 *Ibid.*, p. 2.

18 Robert Julian Stonor OSB, *Stonor. A Catholic Sanctuary in the Chilterns from the Fifth Century till Today* (Newport, Mon., 1951).

19 See Bell, *Episcopal Visitations in Bedfordshire*. These returns throw a useful light on the state of the parish churches, and include some dismissive and insulting attitudes to

We have an account of related events at this time in the voluminous notebooks of the Rev. William Cole, rector of Bletchley, Buckinghamshire, from 1753–67. He was a well-known antiquary – and a friend of the Rev. Alban Butler and other Catholic priests, including Fr Christopher Taylor, later of Shefford.[20] He reported how the newspapers had called on archbishops and bishops to compile diocesan lists of Papists and wrote of an 'energetic campaign in the press against Catholics'. As part of this, the Bishop of London had written to his clergy in 1765:

> The visible increase of Papists in the Cities of London and Westminster … (is) a matter of serious Reflection to all, who wish well to the Safety and Happiness of this Protestant Country … [He calls for] a more particular Zeal and Attention at a Time when … the Emissaries of the Romish Church … appear to have forgot, that there are Bounds, which our Constitution has set to the Exercise of their Religion.

It is not altogether clear what had caused this re-awakening of suspicions about Catholic influence; Challoner referred to it as a 'kind of persecution, raised by some of the bishops under the pretence of stopping the growth of popery'.[21] Whatever lay behind it, it was strong enough to move the bishops to take concerted action to discover just how strong Catholicism actually was across the country, perhaps hoping that the figures would show that the anti-Catholic outcry was unjustified.[22]

The Anglican bishops wrote to their parish clergy in 1767, ordering them to answer a set of questions about the extent of 'papistry' in their parishes. Cole gives us both the letter of the Bishop of Lincoln and the questions that incumbents had to answer:

> I received a few days ago a letter from the Lord Archbishop of Canterbury acquainting me with His Majesty's pleasure, in consequence of an address presented to him in the House of Lords about the 22nd of May last, that I should in his Majesty's Name require from all parochial clergy in my diocese as correct and complete lists as can be obtained, of the Papists or reputed Papists within each of their respective parishes, distinguishing their sexes, ages and occupations; and how long they have been there resident; which lists his Majesty will order to be laid before the House of Lords on the first day of the next session of Parliament. In obedience to these commands I write this to desire that you would pay due attention to this needful work …
>
> John Lincoln Buckden, July 28, 1767

The short questionnaire was straightforward, with five main queries. Answers were to be returned by 'Michaelmas at the latest':

> Query 1. What is the number of Papists or reputed Papists in your parish of Bletchley?
>
> Answer – *number.*

Non-conformist practice, which seems to have been seen not infrequently as a greater threat to the established church than Catholicism.

20 BL Add Mss 5811, Notebooks of Rev. William Cole, 1714–82, ff. 132v–135v: he thought at one stage of converting to Roman Catholicism. He left 100 volumes of antiquarian notes, now in the British Museum.

21 Mullett, *Catholics in Britain and Ireland*, p. 145.

22 On the growth of a *de facto* toleration of Catholics in the years after 1745, see Adam Morton, 'Anti-Popery', in *The Oxford History of British and Irish Catholicism*, vol. 2 (Oxford, 2023), pp. 170–88, at pp. 185–6.

Query 2. How many are there of each sex?
Answer – males, *number*
females – *number*
Query 3. Of what age do you apprehend them to be, viz–
How many are under 15? – *number*
How many are above 15 years? – *number*
Query 4. How many are persons of family or estate? – *number*
How many are servants? – *number*
How many subsist by trade? – *number*
by farming? – *number*
by other occupations? – *number*
Query 5. How many of them have been resident in the parish under two years? – *number*
How many above that time? – *number*[23]

These 1767 detailed returns have been published in full by E. S. Worrall.[24] Later 1780 returns have not been published in detail, but figures from them are available as diocesan totals, and are useful for the purposes of comparison.[25] The total number of Catholics in Bedfordshire came to sixty-nine (not counting four infants under two years of age). Of these, none were 'of family' or had estates. Forty were listed as having 'other occupations' – i.e. not servants, nor in farming nor trade.

It is interesting in the light of future developments that of the sixty-nine, twenty-one (31.3%) were from Campton with Shefford (not counting one infant); while twenty-eight (41.8%) were from Turvey (again not including one infant). Almost 75% came from these two parishes. Of the rest, only Biggleswade (six), Woburn (four), Bedford (three) and Potton (two) had more than a single Catholic (see Table 3, below).

The totals from neighbouring counties have been added here for the sake of comparison. If one compares the total for Bedfordshire with those in neighbouring counties (in all cases omitting infants under two years of age) we can see that while Bedfordshire did not have the smallest number of Catholics, it was well within the bottom range; the differences across the counties were notable, though nothing like the range across the whole of the country: in the neighbouring Diocese of Ely (including Cambridge) only seven Catholics were listed, while the Diocese of Chester (including Lancashire) had 25,139. Unusually across the counties, only one entry in Bedfordshire gives the full names of those listed. This is the return for Wo(o)burn. The four listed were servants of the Duke of Bedford – two cooks, one lady's maid and a hairdresser. All four were over fifteen years of age. They have unusual names and were, perhaps, French:

> John Gaittait and Nicholas Perthold: cooks to the Duke of Bedford; John Francis Perrier: hairdresser; Agnes Faynard: her Grace's woman.

No 'papist/popish priest' is listed as resident in the county; there may, of course, have been one visiting reasonably frequently from a neighbouring county

23 Cole's own reply: there were no Papists or reputed Papists in his parish of Bletchley, Buckinghamshire.

24 E. S. Worrall (ed.), *Returns of Papists 1767*, CRS Occasional Publications, no. 2 (np, 1989), 2 vols. The first volume covers only the Diocese of Chester, including Lancashire with its high numbers; the second volume, the other counties, including Bedfordshire on pp. 74–5.

25 See Williams, 'Change or Decay? The Provincial Laity', p. 31, n. 29, for what he calls 'tentative' totals.

Table 3. Catholic returns for Bedfordshire and comparative counties, 1767

BEDFORDSHIRE												
		Sex		Age		Rank					Resident	
								Subsist by				
Parish		**M**	**F**	**Under 15**	**Above 15**	**Of family or have estates**	**Servants**	**Trade**	**Farming**	**Other occupations**	**Under 2 years**	**Above 2 years**
Ampthill	1	1			1			1				1
Bedford, St Paul	3	3			3			3				3
Biggleswade	7	4	3		7			2		5		7
Campton with Shefford	22	10	12	7	15		2	6		14	1	21
Clifton	2	1	1		2		2					2
Eaton Socon	1		1		1					1		1
Harrold	1	1			1					1		1
Potton[1]	2	2		2			2				2	
Staughton, Little	1	1		1					1			1
Turvey	29	16	13	12	17		6	4		19	1	28
Wooburn	4	3	1		4		4					4
Total	**73**	**42**	**31**	**19**	**54**		**6**	**16**	**1**	**40**	**4**	**69**

[1] There appears to be an error in the Potton return: the 2 in the 'Under 2 years' column should be in the 'Above 2 Years' column, giving the final altered totals.

No. of Papists in:		Sex		Age		Rank					Resident	
								Subsist by				
		M	F	Under 15	Above 15	Of family or have estates	Servants	Trade	Farming	Other occupations	Under 2 years	Above 2 years
Lincs	957	474	483	281	676	41	141	98	184	493	80	877
Leics	218	105	113	79	139	5	20	48	71	74	14	204
Bucks	330	140	190	117	213	13	28	19	24	256	19	311
Beds	73	42	31	19	54		16	16	1	40	6	67
Herts	27	13	14	6	21		5	3		19	4	23
Hunts	37	17	20	10	27	5	8	2	1	21	6	31
Total	**1642**	**791**	**851**	**512**	**1130**	**54**	**218**	**186**	**281**	**903**	**129**	**1513**

(e.g. Buckinghamshire and Weston Underwood), or a 'riding priest' from elsewhere. In Cambridgeshire, with its very low number of Catholics, there was at Sawston one gentleman (aet. 34) and one 'reputed popish priest' (aet. 73), who had been resident for thirty years (from at least 1730 until his death in 1776). This raises the issue of family chaplains: the priest in question was a Jesuit, Fr John Champion, long-time chaplain to the Huddlestons of Sawston (an ancient recusant family). He was a scholar whose secular interests were 'literary, scientific, sporting, musical and antiquarian' – apparently a typical gentleman-cleric of the period and friend of the above mentioned Rev. William Cole, who described him as a 'worthy Jesuit, and a very learned, modest and sweet-tempered man'. He was active as the Jesuit Superior in East Anglia for seventeen years, but there is no evidence of any particular local missionary endeavour outside the family, though we may assume local Catholics attended services in the family chapel at least from time to time.[26] One has to be careful, however, in assessing his influence and impact: the enmity between the Jesuits and the secular clergy had become ingrained and by this time was just an accepted part of English clerical life; he might have been as pastorally active as any other family chaplain could be without being acknowledged in general clerical records. His 'quiet backwater' image (similar to that of Rev. Christopher Taylor at Shefford in some ways – see below) compares oddly with the picture of busy pastoral activity in contemporary London, supported and indeed inspired as it was by spiritual and controversial writings and pastoral initiatives.

After the episcopal initiative and organisation of the 1767 exercise, it is strange that no official use of these detailed returns appears to have been made at the time: they were laid before the House of Lords at the beginning of the next parliamentary session, but not mentioned in the king's speech nor apparently on any subsequent public occasion locally or nationally. Perhaps it was just part of what Williams refers to as 'an Anglican propensity for papist-counting', part of a 'toothless vigilance'.[27] This unimportance has been mirrored in most of the historical accounts of the period that ignore or barely notice the census, yet it does give us a detailed and mainly accurate picture of the state of Catholicism in the mid-eighteenth century, a picture not otherwise available.

Also, surprisingly, there appears not to have been any explicit link between this census and the first relaxation of the anti-Catholic laws brought in a few years later by the Relief Bill of 1778. We must assume that the census at least showed that there were insufficient Catholics across the country to cause civil trouble and justify further persecution. In the move towards some relaxation of the anti-Catholic laws, more weight seems to have been given to threatened wars with France and in North America, with the subsequent need to recruit Catholics to the armed forces from Scotland and Ireland by offering some freedom of conscience.[28]

26 T. G. Holt, 'An eighteenth century chaplain: John Champion at Sawston Hall', in *RH*, vol. 17, no. 2 (October, 1984), pp. 181–8.

27 Duffy, *Challoner and his Church*, p. 33.

28 See Robert Kent Donovan, 'Sir John Dalrymple and the Origins of Roman Catholic Relief, 1775–1778', in *RH*, vol. 17, no. 2 (October, 1984), pp. 188–96; Nigel Abercrombie, 'The First Relief Act', in Duffy, *Challoner and his Church*, pp. 174–93. Burton (*The Life and Times of Bishop Challoner*, vol. 2, pp. 183ff), does not mention the 1767 census in his otherwise good account; neither does Wigfield, 'Recusancy and Nonconformity in Bedfordshire'.

Whatever the effect, if any, of the census, the legal situation of Catholics was improving, though slowly. A few years later, in 1771, when the Hon. and Rev. James Talbot, vicar apostolic (coadjutor to Bishop Challoner from 1759), was indicted to appear on a charge of exercising the office of a bishop and for saying Mass, he was acquitted; the court used Lord Mansfield's decision that there had to be written proof that the accused was a priest before such a charge could even be heard – clearly, the court sided against the malicious informer. In practice, this largely stopped the activity of such informers, although Challoner himself was indicted; the charge against him was withdrawn by the informer, presumably for fear of counter charges.

For those Catholics who took their religion seriously, there was at the time more regular provision of Mass and, interestingly, a useful book and pamphlet trade. Gother's and Challoner's publications provided a whole library of devotional, instructional and apologetic works and not just for the leisured upper-classes. As Duffy has claimed, Gother's was a piety aimed at 'ordinary men and women'; no matter how busy people were they could find Christ in their everyday lives:

> The Tradesman may find him in his Shop, the labourer at his work, the Porter in the streets … the Servant in the Kitchen … and the Afflicted in all their Distress. [The priest should be] indefatigable in study … a vigilant pastor, a zealous preacher, a constant catechizer, in visiting the sick constant …[29]

It was a world away from the age of active persecution and the lives of domestic chaplains to the wealthy. Gother died in 1704; the sixteen volumes of his spiritual writings, published posthumously and covering every aspect of the spiritual life, especially that of the laity, shaped the domestic piety of English Catholics for more than a century.[30]

Recent historians of Catholicism in these years of waning persecution have sought to determine how Catholics felt and reacted in their everyday lives. The occasional outbreak of active persecution was not, perhaps, the main issue, terrible though its effects might be for individuals. Overall, there was the constant background of awareness of one's doubtful legal standing, and consequent vulnerability, as second-class (at best) citizens, and a continuing struggle to have the Mass and the sacraments available regularly. This inner world of Catholicism was not, however, uniform and its membership included both idealists and realists; when it came to questions of integration; much depended on where one lived.[31]

Whatever Enlightenment intellectuals and idealists might urge in the way of toleration and free religious enquiry, however, anti-popery had been for too long a deep element in English society for it just to fade away or to be overcome by rational

29 Quoted in Duffy, *Challoner and his Church*, pp. 2–3.

30 Judith Champ, *The Secular Priesthood in England and Wales: History, Mission and Identity* (Oscott, 2016), pp. 51–2. See also W. Maziere Brady, *The Episcopal Succession in England, Scotland & Ireland A.D. 1400–1875* (Rome, 1876), 3 vols; new edition with introduction by A. F. Allison (London, 1971): on Challoner and Talbot, vol. 3, pp. 164–78. Williams' 'Change or Decay? The Provincial Laity', pp. 27–54, gives a very balanced overview.

31 See the excellent overview by Francis Young, 'Surveying a field come of age', in *BCH*, vol. 36, no. 2 (October, 2022), pp. 204–21; this is a detailed discussion of Robert E. Scully and Angela Ellis, *A Companion to Catholicism and Recusancy in Britain and Ireland: From Reformation to Emancipation* (Leiden/Boston, 2022).

argument. Telling in its own way was the fact that Richard Burns' *The Justice of the Peace and Parish Officer*, a practical handbook for local officials detailing all the legislation against Catholics, remained in use and went through fifteen editions between 1755 and 1785. Open and public conversions from Roman Catholicism among the gentry or nobility continued to make public news. While such converts might be received politically and socially by their peers, they continued to be regarded as aliens and so untrustworthy by the majority of their compatriots. Part of this resulted from a firm belief that people in the United Kingdom could be either loyal citizens or committed Catholics owing allegiance to a foreign power, but not both.[32] According to Defoe, Catholicism had become 'the universal Scarecrow … the Spectre with which the Nurses fright the Children'.[33]

Yet there were some encouraging signs of a more liberal atmosphere and Challoner felt emboldened to question the government's approach to a major social problem of the day on the grounds that it would be unintentionally unfair to Catholics. At issue was the Marriage Act of 1753 which required all marriages (except those of Jews and Quakers) to be performed in the local Anglican church by an Anglican minister.[34] While there was general acceptance that the aim of the legislation was beneficial, in that it would end the widespread evil of clandestine and bigamous unions, Challoner objected to the ruling that all marriages had to take place in an Anglican church and according to the Book of Common Prayer: this, he argued, would force Catholics to take part in a Protestant service against their consciences. He went on to claim that his co-religionists acknowledged, gratefully,

> the lenity of the present government in their regard and their known averseness to persecution … [and so it] will not be unwilling to admit of some qualification in the bill by which R. Catholics (*sic*) might be exempted from the necessity of going to church to be married, or at least from going through the whole service appointed in the Common prayer book … lest otherwise they should be exposed, merely for not going against their consciences, to the dreadful consequences of having their marriages annulled and their children bastardized …

Furthermore, Challoner was even willing that Catholics might be required to have the banns announced and to register their marriages in the local parish church in public with witnesses; he wanted, in other words, for the couples to go through a Catholic form of marriage as their main celebration and so receive the sacrament of matrimony as laid down by canon law. Not surprisingly, his appeal got nowhere and Catholics were subject to the Act's requirements until changes were introduced in the 1830s. No doubt it was because of the Act that the priest in Shefford, the Rev. Christopher Taylor, only celebrated one marriage in his twenty-six years there, and his successor, Rev. John Potier, none at all in ten years.[35]

32 See the useful discussion in Alexander Lock, 'Catholicism, Apostasy and Politics in Late Eighteenth-century England: the case of Sir Thomas Gascoigne and Charles Howard, Earl of Surrey', in *RH*, vol. 30, no. 2 (October, 2010), pp. 275–98.

33 Quoted in Williams, 'Change or Decay? The Provincial Laity', p. 49.

34 One could avoid some of the Act's demands by obtaining a licence (for a fee) from the bishop or archdeacon; the calling of banns, for example, was unpopular with many of the better off. (I am grateful to James Collett-White for information here.)

35 See John Bossy, 'Challoner and the Marriage Act', in Duffy, *Challoner and His Church*, pp. 126–36; Bossy makes it clear that not all Challoner's fellow bishops and clergy agreed with

The first step towards formal Catholic emancipation was the Relief Act of 1778. This allowed Catholics to purchase and inherit land legally and removed the right of Protestant relatives to disinherit them. Furthermore, Catholic bishops and clergy were henceforth free from persecution by informers and Catholics were allowed to run schools. The Act laid down that an oath of loyalty to the king had to be taken by Catholics over the age of twenty-one, but although this involved disavowal of any papal deposing power and the denial of any civil authority that Rome might supposedly claim, it no longer involved explicitly anti-Catholic sections. Reminiscent of earlier controversies was the Act's denial of any dispensing power that might supposedly allow Catholics to take such an oath verbally while not accepting it mentally. When consulted about it by Rome, Challoner accepted the oath attached to the Act: having considered it carefully and prayerfully, he wrote, he could not discover in it 'anything contrary to Faith and good morals' and so thought it advantageous to religion to encourage as many Catholics as possible to take it 'without scruple'; he added that he believed the other bishops felt the same. He also issued a pastoral letter, requiring his priests and their congregations to pray for the king by name, for Queen Charlotte and the royal family, as part of the Christian duty owed by all to their sovereigns. For all his strictness in moral matters, he was willing to go as far as possible to get his co-religionists to show publicly that they could be loyal subjects and 'good citizens'. The Act was passed by both Houses without a division.[36]

Given the general antithetical attitudes to Catholics, it is not surprising that the Act did not go unquestioned. The most striking example of opposition was the Gordon Riots of 1780. These started as an attempt in June 1780 to present to Parliament a petition to have the Relief Act repealed; a mob led by Lord George Gordon, leader of the 60,000 strong Protestant Association, got completely out of control and during the night Catholic chapels and houses were destroyed (including the embassies of Sardinia and Bavaria, where Catholics had been accustomed to hear Mass). The violent rioting and disturbances lasted for about a week and were only finally quelled by the deployment of 10,000 soldiers. Gordon was tried for treason but acquitted; sixty-two rioters were sentenced to death, twenty-five of whom were executed; in all, 285 people were killed in the riots.

The London riots were far and away the most serious and alarming of the second half of the century, but other urban Catholic communities also witnessed violent anti-Catholic outbursts. In the case of Preston, in 1768, the town's Catholic chapel in Friargate had been 'plundered and violated' by a mob – an occurrence quite out of character with the general acceptance of a strong Catholic presence in the town. For its part, Bath had usually enjoyed a toleration fitting its standing as a popular fashionable resort, but after the 1778 Act there were 'scenes of pillage … a re-enactment' of the London riots.[37]

his conciliatory approach to the government. The Act did not apply in Ireland. Interestingly, the only marriage recorded as celebrated by Taylor was a mixed one, in September 1804; see the registers for that date below.

36 Burton, *The Life and Times of Bishop Challoner*, vol. 2, p. 206; for the oath's wording, see pp. 293–4.

37 Mullett, *Catholics in Britain and Ireland*, pp. 146ff. See the good summary in Jenny Uglow, *The Lunar Men: The Friends who made the Future, 1739–1810* (London, 2003), pp. 338–9; for Challoner in hiding, see Duffy, *Challoner and His Church*, pp. 23–4. Also, Mullett for

It was not just the 'mob' who objected to the Act. On a different level altogether, but significant in its own way, was an editorial comment in *The Gentleman's Magazine*. The editors wrote in the strongest terms against the riots which, they claimed, had been initiated

> by a set of miscreants … assuming the character of men heated with zeal for their religion … (who) proceeded to commit the most horrible acts of unprovoked desolation that are to be met with in any history.

They went on to say, however, that while they had favoured the repeal of the worst of the penalties against Catholics in a truly 'enlightened manner', they had now to issue a warning:

> The Papists, elated with the favours that had been granted to them, instead of prudently and thankfully enjoying the blessings of freedom from penalties that were judged hard to be borne, began to abuse their new privileges, and to extend them beyond what the law allowed …

The language here is interesting. While Catholics had campaigned for what they had seen as their 'rights', the editors wrote in terms of 'favours' and 'privileges'. They went on to claim that while the position of Catholics under the law was still not one of full equality, they, the Catholics, were abusing the freedom that had been granted under the Act and leading Protestants were becoming alarmed:

> while still left subject to many prosecutions for propagating their religion, which they very unwisely disregarded and became apparently more earnest than ever, in preaching, teaching, visiting the sick, and making proselytes, to the no small scandal of many pious divines of the Established Church, whose duties they usurped, and to whose characters they did not always pay due regard. To this it was owing, as we have been credibly informed, that an Establishment of worthy Protestants was established with a view only to endeavour by legal means to obtain security against the abuse of the law that had passed in favour of Catholics, but not to deprive them of the benefits of it.[38]

Not all the rioters, of course, had acted from purely religious motives. There were elements of economic motivation; it was largely the property of the well-to-do that suffered attack and this, no doubt, explains the initial reaction of the *Gentleman's Magazine* editors. There were also anti-Irish factors at play.[39] Overall, however, there is no doubting the massive and frightening 'anti-popery' element at the root of the riots; it was Catholic chapels across London that were destroyed, including some of the embassy chapels where London Catholics had attended religious services, while the aged Bishop Challoner only just escaped the attention of the mob, fleeing to a Catholic country house in Finchley.

Just as long traditions served to determine the reactions of Protestant anti-Catholicism, so also among some Catholics there could still be an attitude of

Preston in 1768 – but this was not typical of the attitudes towards Catholics in many northern towns (Mullett, *Catholics in Britain and Ireland*, pp. 146ff); see Williams, 'Change or Decay? The Provincial Laity' on Bath.

38 *GM*, June 1780, vol. 50, p. 265.

39 Duffy, *Challoner and his Church*, p. 24.

apprehension or fear of persecution, even after the beginnings of official toleration; as the Catholic apologist the Rev. Joseph Berington wrote in 1780:

> Shall I sit down satisfied, because the good humour of a magistrate chooses to indulge me; whilst there are laws of which any miscreant has daily power to enforce the execution? My ease, my property and my life are at the disposal of every villain … To-morrow his humour may vary, and I shall then be obliged to hide my head in some dark corner or to fly from this land of boasted liberty … [a condition leading] to such anxious and dreadful uncertainty.[40]

The overall impact of this initial lifting of anti-Catholic legislation was, however, positive and it encouraged Catholic leaders to start campaigning for further liberalisation (this was what lay behind Berington's complaint, above). Challoner could still be despondent about the general 'great decay in piety and religion' among his flock, but that was a reaction to what he saw as their lack of individual spirituality, not their place in society. The leadership in these campaigns was in the main lay, not clerical, and that lay element was provided by gentry and aristocracy; as has been said, it was the old leadership in a new cause. The body set up to negotiate with the government over the second bill was chaired by Lord Petre of Essex who accepted the role only because the Duke of Norfolk was not available, repeating the role of upper-class and aristocratic laymen that had been behind the first bill, when over a hundred of the 130 signatories to the 'loyal subscription' preceding it had been from ancient landed families.[41]

The campaigning was successful and led to the passing of the second Relief Act in 1791: 'An Act to relieve upon Conditions and under restrictions the persons therein described from certain penalties and disabilities to which Papists or persons professing the Popish Religion are by Law subject'. Its principal benefit was that it allowed the building of public chapels and their use for religious services, as long as they were legally registered, unlocked during the services and had no bells (see below for its effect in Bedfordshire). This was a very important development since having a physical chapel provided a focus for shared interest and even a source of local pride, and perhaps most of all the locus for a resident priest with the possibility of building some sort of local community: having 'our' chapel avoided much of the dependence on a particular family or patron. Although Bossy argues that as early as 1700 or so 'post-Reformation Catholicism had developed denominational characteristics similar to those of the dissenting churches',[42] the likeness seems exaggerated as long as Catholics could not practise in their own public chapels. As we have seen, there has been a good deal of discussion recently among historians about the existence or otherwise of Catholic communities; having their own chapel at least made it easier for such communities to develop and provided a visible presence for them in a locality.[43]

40 See David Butler, 'The Catholic London District in the Eighteenth Century', in *RH*, vol. 28, no. 2 (October, 2006), pp. 245–68, at p. 246.

41 Mullett, *Catholics in Britain and Ireland*, pp. 142, 216.

42 Quoted in William Sheils, 'Religious Divisions in the Localities: Catholics, Puritans and the Established Church before the Civil Wars', in Trevor Dean (ed.), *Faith, Place and People in Early Modern England: Essays in Honour of Margaret Spufford* (Woodbridge, 2018), p. 34.

43 See for example, Joy Rowe for Norfolk: 'The 1767 Census of Papists in the Diocese of Norwich: The Social Composition of the Roman Catholic Community', in David Chadd (ed.),

The 1791 Act also had its restrictive clauses. It required priests to take an oath of loyalty before a clerk of the peace, though it is not clear how regularly this was imposed in practice – there are examples of its being required in the 1820s. The Act also forbade the wearing of clerical dress in public, and left some severe exclusions for Catholics on the statute book. Money could not be left for 'superstitious practices' (i.e. the saying of Mass and bequests to Catholic charities, including education); Catholics could not become judges or king's counsels, sit as MPs or even vote in parliamentary elections. Moreover, they were still forbidden to hold commissions in the armed forces or any office of trust under the crown, while Catholic peers could not take their seats in the Lords. The legal position of Catholic schools was unclear, while Catholic marriages still had to be celebrated in Anglican churches. Catholic leaders, however, were emboldened to continue their campaigning by the Act and also by the positive attitude of the government to French Catholic clergy, large numbers of whom fled to England during the Revolution with full support from the British government and some of whom worked as parish clergy here; even those strange beings known as nuns began to appear from their continental hideaways.

Whether we should talk of Catholic communities in this period or not, it is certain that the regular presence of a priest was essential to the survival of Catholicism in a locality. The Relief Acts of 1778 and 1791 allowed priests to exercise their roles without hindrance. Joy Rowe has shown how the focus of Catholic life shifted in Norfolk and Suffolk during the mid-eighteenth century and was re-aligned around places where a priest said Mass regularly. As we have seen, there were ways of supporting that priest financially where the people were not able or numerous enough to do so (see pp. 13–15), and this could be particularly important in the case of rural areas. It is certainly not that the traditional gentry support disappeared; rather it tended to change in character. There was now the genuine possibility of Catholics being able 'to worship undisturbed with their priest' in their own chapel.[44] These developments were relevant to what was happening in Bedfordshire in the eighteenth century.

Religious Dissent in East Anglia III (Norwich, 1996), pp. 187–234. Attached to her article are thirty-two pages of named Catholics throughout the county – an amazing list, parish by parish, which she calls a 'demographic source second to none, in consideration of the Catholic community of Norfolk and Suffolk', p. 190.

44 Rowe, 'The 1767 Census of Papists in the Diocese of Norwich', pp. 197–8.

Chapter 4

Shefford, 'a cheerful and pleasantly situated town'

As we have seen, the 1767 returns provide what is most likely to be an accurate census of the number of Catholics in Bedfordshire. This gives twenty-one Catholics (plus one infant) in Shefford, and twenty-eight in Turvey (again with one infant). While the latter number was no doubt the result of Turvey's connections with Weston Underwood, one might ask why it was Shefford that went on to become the county's only Catholic centre for almost a hundred years. It had had no substantial Catholic presence, as Turvey had had earlier in the century and where Challoner had chosen to visit to confer confirmation.[1] The development of a Catholic presence in Shefford may have been helped by the fact that the town was not a parish but technically a dependent chapelry of Campton, and so had no resident Church of England clergyman or active parish council. It was the smallest market town in the county with a population of about 400 (the next smallest was Harrold, with 700, while Leighton Buzzard had about 1,500) in the early years of the eighteenth century. Though small, Shefford had its market renewed in 1713 and a little later benefited from the improved Bedford to Hitchin road. According to Godber, it had a strong concentration of fellmongers (preparers of hides) and tanners. Some educational work took place in the town, for we find schoolmasters there in the eighteenth century, though there is no evidence of any endowments for education. Also important was the availability of transport links in the form of good turnpike roads – Harrold and Toddington did not have these – Shefford and Potton (also with populations under 1,000) did. Its position on a navigable river also helped its development as an important transport centre, especially for coal.[2]

A description of the town in the later eighteenth century in *The Merchants Miscellany and Complete Compendium* is interesting:

> Shefford, 8m. S: a small town, pleasantly situated between two rivulets, over each of which there is a good bridge; and the town is rendered cheerful, by being the thoroughfare to Bedford. It has no church, but a chapel of ease to Campton.
>
> 'Tradesmen, etc': Brewer, malsters, sadler, fell-monger, hatter, glazier, plumber, wagon owner, physician, two surgeons and four inn owners.
>
> Market on Fridays. Fairs: January 23rd, Easter Monday, May 19th & October 10th. Coach from Bedford daily. Wagon to London Tuesdays & Fridays to the Windmill, St. John Street.[3]

Its growth as a Catholic centre was almost certainly accidental. It was home to the Noddings family. According to a strong Catholic tradition they were intimately

1 W. M. Wigfield (ed.), 'Recusancy and Nonconformity', p. 159.

2 Godber, *History of Bedfordshire*, pp. 333–4.

3 J. F. Henington, *The Merchants Miscellany and Complete Compendium, containing a mercantile state and public view of the county of Bedford for 1785* (Bedford, repr. 1885), p. 17.

linked into the beginnings and development of a Catholic revival in the county in the early years of the eighteenth century, providing a room for a priest to say Mass in regularly. King, in an early history of Catholicism in Bedfordshire, says:

> Shefford is more interesting to Catholics as having been from time immemorial a centre of Catholicity, and, indeed until comparatively recent times, the only centre of Catholicity in the whole county of Bedford. The early history of the mission is shrouded in obscurity, but there is a tradition that Shefford has ever been a rallying place for Catholics, and a place where occasionally a priest was found and Mass was said … it is quite certain that there were Catholics resident in Shefford quite at the beginning of the last century, notably a family of the name of Noddings.[4]

The Noddings were not a family of standing in the ordinary sense, though they appear frequently in the parochial records for almost two centuries before this, usually described as malsters, sometimes as butchers.[5] Immediately relevant to our account is William Noddin(g)s who married Susanna Barford, in November 1697. Their six children were William (bapt. May 1701, died June 1719); Susanna (bapt. July 1703, md. 1733); John (bapt. Dec. 1706, died Aug. 1776); Elizabeth (bapt. June 1711, died June 1781); Mary (bapt. June 1714, died Jan. 1715); and Mary (bapt. March 1715, died Oct. 1783). Susanna Noddings, the mother, died on 15 April 1730; the father, William, a butcher, on 3 October 1743. King goes on to describe their tombstones in nearby Campton churchyard: both carry the traditional Catholic prayer, 'Give to him (her), O Lord, eternal rest, and let perpetual light shine unto him (her). May he (she) rest in peace. Amen.' He argues that these inscriptions, in a Protestant churchyard, provide evidence that their Catholicism must have been known and accepted, and ends by saying that it was in their house (a public house and butcher's) that for many years Mass had been celebrated.[6] It is, however, entirely possible, even likely, that these prayers were added later by their children.

We know that William's will was proved by his two daughters Elizabeth and Mary in the Probate Court of the Archdeacon of Bedford on 15 October 1743; it nominated them joint executors and residuary legatees in equal shares. Amongst other bequests, he left to his daughter, Susanna, 'a fourth part of my household goods now standing in my house at Shefford'.[7] Shortly after his father's death, John Noddings, at a Court of the Manor of Shefford with Campton, on 12 October 1743, was recognised as the son and heir of William Noddings, late of Campton, and therefore entitled to hold 'All that messuage or tenement … in Shefford … in the occupation of John Noddings'.[8] John had previously been named as juror for Shefford in 1740, 1741 and 1742,[9] a post his father had held in the 1730s as well as being one of the trustees of an ancient fund held in trust for the poor of the parish and distributed through the church-wardens and overseers of the parish of Campton. All the available evidence shows a family fully involved in local life, if sometimes on the wrong side of the law: between 1744 and

4 H. E. King, *An Ancient Catholic Mission and its Modern Development* (Shefford, 1896, repr. 1918), p. 5.

5 See Collins, 'An Ancient Catholic Mission', pp. 2–3 for early history, and *Campton cum Shefford*, Bedfordshire Parish Register Series, vol. 52 (Bedford, 1982).

6 This account is repeated in Burton, *The Life and Times of Bishop Challoner*, vol. 1, p. 204.

7 BA, ABP/W1743/62, Will of William Noddings of Campton Kiln …1743.

8 Collins,' 'An Ancient Catholic Mission', p. 9.

9 *Ibid.*

1761 John Noddings, butcher, and two others were regularly charged with 'blowing and puffing up veal which they offer for sale'.[10]

Despite the strong tradition linking the family to Catholicism, there are no references in any of this material to local Catholics or the Catholic church. There can, of course, be a problem with Catholic wills at this time: bequests that involved leaving money for what were still legally 'superstitious practices', such as the saying of Mass and offering prayers for the dead, were forbidden and liable to be declared invalid. To avoid this, often the real intentions of the will-maker were contained in a separate 'spiritual will', while the legal will was made out to legatees who could be trusted to carry out the deceased's true (Catholic) intentions.

John did not make a secular will and there is no evidence of a spiritual one. When he died, in 1776, Letters of Administration were granted to his spinster sisters, Elizabeth and Mary as his next of kin.[11] At the Manorial Court on 26 October 1776, Mary and Elizabeth were recognised as heirs to John and lawful owners of 'a cottage or tenement in Shefford'.[12] In Bishop Challoner's papers there is a mention of the address of a John Noddings of Shefford; unfortunately, the reference is undated, but the inference is clear.[13]

Elizabeth died a spinster in June 1781, also intestate. Letters of Administration were granted in the Court of the Archdeacon of Bedford on 14 March 1782 to Mary as next of kin; she took an oath to declare that her sister's personal effects had amounted to £300 and upwards.[14] The manorial court in 21 October 1783 also recorded Elizabeth's death, adding that the messuage and tenement in Shefford descended to Mary and her heirs.[15] Finally, Mary, also a spinster, made her will on 5 June 1781: in this,

> she did give and devise unto John Courtenay Throckmorton of Weston Underwood ... all and singular my real and personal estate whatsoever and wheresoever subject to the payment of just debts ... and lastly I appoint the said John Courtenay Throckmorton sole executor ...'.

She died in October 1783 and the will was proved by John Throckmorton on 9 November 1783, following her burial at Campton.[16] This is probably an example of the habit already mentioned of not detailing specifically Catholic bequests because of legal prohibitions.

The Throckmorton involvement here is interesting. John Courtenay Throckmorton was the eldest son of George and grandson of Sir Robert Throckmorton, fourth Baronet, of Weston Underwood in Buckinghamshire. This wealthy family had a long recusant tradition, keeping a Catholic chaplain and providing Mass for their family and neighbourhood in their attic chapel. Sir John became fifth Baronet on his grandfather's death in 1791; he was one of a group of English Catholic nobility and gentry campaigning for a further relief bill for Catholics in the late 1780s.[17] Mary's true intention is clear from Throckmorton's later letter to Bishop Douglass (26 July 1802):

10 *Ibid.*

11 PCC, PROB. 6/1776/152, Estate of John Noddings, d. August 1776.

12 Collins, 'An Ancient Catholic Mission', pp. 8–9.

13 AAW, Z 71, Undated list of addresses in Challoner's hand.

14 Collins, 'An Ancient Catholic Mission', p. 9.

15 *Ibid.*

16 PCC, PROB. 11/1110/575, Will of Mary Noddings, d. October 1783.

17 He became a militant member of the extreme Catholic group known as the Cisalpine Club, keen to diminish the power of the papacy and advocating the election of bishops by the laity;

> In compliance with your desire I have looked over the Deed of Trust of Mrs Noddings of Shefford and find that the payment of rent and profits … bequeathed to me are directed to be paid to Mr John Barnewall during his life and after his death to his successor or successors so long as he or they shall continue to reside at Shefford. This clause I apprehend precludes all power to remove the fund to any other place.[18]

John Barnewall was a Catholic priest of the London District, of Irish origin.[19] He died in 1782 after working for some years in the Midlands on what was called the 'riding mission' – a sort of roving placement that included north Bedfordshire; he was certainly doing this work in 1764 and for some time was stationed at King's Cliffe in Northamptonshire. Mary Noddings' deed would imply he was resident at least for a time in Shefford; we know he was buried at King's Cliffe in the same grave as his brother Anthony, also a priest, who had died in 1778.

This Noddings legacy was obviously a basic factor in the establishment of the Shefford mission. There were some initial legal problems regarding the estate, with some uncertainty about the extent of the property and monies and mortgages involved. John Throckmorton was involved in legal negotiations in June 1785, as also were the Rev. Mr Willacy, and Bishop James Talbot (1726–90), at one stage a priest of the London District and then Challoner's co-adjutor from 1759, succeeding as vicar apostolic in 1781. The involvement of these leading figures can only indicate the importance attached to the Shefford mission and the legacy.[20]

The question remains about the links between the Noddings family and Catholicism. It is possible that the traditional account of the elder members being Catholics and providing facilities for Mass in Shefford is correct, although there is no positive evidence of the parents' Catholicism. There is no doubt that the three children, John, Elizabeth and Mary were Catholics in later life, but if, as was quite possible, they were converts, then when and under what influences their conversions occurred remains unknown. There were some links with the strongly Catholic Throckmorton family of Weston Underwood; perhaps a priest from there said Mass in a Noddings property in Shefford and the conversion of the children, and even of their parents or at least one of them, resulted from his ministry. Alternatively, the family was already Catholic and offered the priest a place to say Mass. Fr Collins, in his detailed account, stated definitively that the parents were not Catholic; for once his certainty seems misplaced.

It would help to support the traditional account of the Shefford mission's history and the earlier involvement of the Noddings family, if there were evidence of any Catholic clergy based or working in the area earlier in the century. Three have been suggested: Thomas Whitaker (he appears to have regularly used his alias Martin, even in his will), James Angel, and John Poulton. In his authoritative history, Anstruther links all three with Shefford in Bedfordshire.

Thomas Whitaker (1702–78) of London was ordained in 1729 and was confessor to the English Benedictine nuns in Brussels before moving to Shefford by November

Bernard Ward, *The Dawn of the Catholic Revival in England 1781–1803* (London, 1909), vol. 1, pp. 112–21; vol. 2, p. 40.

18 AAW, Douglass III.L.35, Bp John Douglass, VA London District, 1790–1812.

19 Collins, 'An Ancient Catholic Mission', pp. 16–17.

20 AAW, 'A' Series, vol. 42, nos 159, 160, 162–4, Letters re Shefford Mission 1783–85.

1738. Anstruther has him also looking after Hyde End and Newbury in Berkshire, until at least 1742; in 1743 he moved to Woolhampton, also in Berkshire, where he died in 1778.[21] James Angel (1720–75) was ordained in 1745; he came to England in the same year and worked at Fawley, Berkshire, and at Shefford from 1747–50. He died at East Hendred in 1775.[22] John Poulton was the third priest suggested: his family were from Desborough in Northamptonshire. A Franciscan friar, he became Provincial in 1737 and died in London in 1748. Anstruther includes him as a secular priest and mentions some uncertain connections with Shefford.[23] Neither the *Liber Ruber* nor Kirk,[24] however, mention a Bedfordshire connection for any of these three priests and it is now clear that the normally reliable Anstruther was entirely mistaken in connecting them with the county: the Shefford they worked in was in Berkshire, more accurately known as Great Shefford, or West Shefford, near Newbury and Hungerford – this is the obvious explanation for the references above to Fawley, Hyde End, Woolhampton, etc.

If none of them served in Bedfordshire, can we say who the first resident priest was? The evidence points to Stephen Robinson, born in 1716 in Tuscany and ordained in Rome in 1744. His true surname was Vezzosi: he was the son of Michael Vezzosi of Florence and Ann Robinson (some sources give her name as Robertson). The family were strong Stuart supporters and it had been through the influence of Prince Charles Stuart that the family's three sons had been accepted into the Venerable English College in Rome (technically they would otherwise have been excluded as of non-English birth and parentage). After ordination Stephen served for a time as chaplain to the English nuns at Hooghstraet in the Low Countries before coming to England. According to Anstruther, he was in Shefford in 1773 at the latest, and perhaps as early as 1761 when he joined the common fund of the English secular clergy.[25] He died in 1781 and was buried in Campton; in the burial register under 12 February 1781 he is described as 'a Roman Catholic priest'.[26] Collins argues that Robinson must have at least been in England in 1757 when, according to the Lincoln's Inn register he had baptised a child of the Dixie family. A Mary Dixie was one of the witnesses to Mary Noddings' will in 1781, and appears from time to time in the Shefford registers as a god-parent or sponsor.[27]

Some questions remain about Robinson: when did he begin ministering at Shefford, and why? Did he have connections with the Dixie family or the Noddings? Did he live with the Noddings from the beginning – or had there been an earlier priest who did so or who served there from elsewhere? We have no registers for the period of

21 For Anstruther, see Introduction, Primary and secondary sources (p. xiii); this is *Seminary Priests: 1716–1800*, vol. 4, p. 298.

22 *Ibid.*, p. 5.

23 *Ibid.*, p. 221.

24 See Introduction, Primary and secondary sources (p. xiii).

25 Wilfred Kelly, *Liber Ruber Venerabilis Collegii Anglorum de Urbe, Annales Collegii, II. A.D. 1631–1783*, CRS, vol. 40 (Leeds, 1943), p. 194.

26 *Campton cum Shefford*, Bedfordshire Parish Register Series, vol. 52, p. 158.

27 See for example 1797, on p. 162. She was related to the Bower family of Shefford, the other witness to the will. On the Lincoln's Inn registers, see Claud Reginald Lindsay (ed.), 'Catholic Registers of Lincoln's Inn Fields Chapel, London', in *Miscellanea XI*, CRS, vol. 19 (London, 1917), pp. 202–368 at p. 215.

his ministry other than the single entry in the Lincoln's Inn register. It is an additional pity that we do not have any evidence of his general views, given the very strong Jacobite background and involvement of his family.

As already noted, Robinson was succeeded by the Rev. John Barnewell (1781–82), to whom Mary Noddings left her property; then there is a gap and apparently no resident priest for a few years. Again, we have no registers covering his short ministry.

One might well ask at this stage how many Catholics there were in Bedfordshire for these priests to minister to. We have seen that the detailed report of 1767 had listed a total of seventy-three in the county (sixty-seven over the age of two, with six infants); Shefford and Campton were listed as having twenty-two, while Turvey had twenty-nine. A few years later, in 1773, Bishop Challoner had reported to Rome that there were 'scarcely a hundred Catholics' in the county, served by a single missioner – near enough to the 1767 figure.[28] It is, then, rather strange to find that Challoner's successor, Bishop Talbot (1781–90), in his report to Rome in 1786, should say:

> In the county of Bedford there is only a single priest who lists only three Catholics, but I hope he will soon list many more. This is a recent foundation made by a wealthy Catholic who lived there with his two unmarried sisters; he left his total inheritance by his will to this pious foundation.[29]

As we have seen, the three Noddings siblings were dead by this time (the last, Mary, had died in 1783), and so it is not clear who Talbot's 'three Catholics' were – perhaps members of the Dixie and Bower families. And what had happened to Challoner's 'scarcely a hundred'? To add to the confusion, the Rev. Christopher Taylor, who had moved to Shefford as minister in 1786, later wrote that at the time of his arrival there were only five or six Catholics in the parish, but that the number had increased to twenty by the time of his writing in 1791. There may be some confusion in these figures between the number of Catholics in Shefford and the number in the county as a whole; his 'parish' included Hitchin as well. Moreover, as the county was without a resident priest for a time, Catholics may well have gone elsewhere to attend Mass – for example, across the county boundary to Weston Underwood. Whatever the case, Taylor was confident enough to go to the expense and labour of building a dedicated chapel in the town as soon as possible after it became legal to do so in 1791. He was to serve in Shefford until his death in 1812, while the chapel he built was to last for almost a hundred years. While he was not the first resident priest in the town, he might justly be regarded as the founding father of the Catholic presence there.[30]

28 AAW, Challoner to Propaganda, 10 September 1773 (in Latin). See J. H. Whyte, 'The Vicars Apostolics' Returns of 1773', in *RH*, vol. 9, no. 4 (January, 1968), pp. 205–14.

29 AAW, 'A' Series, vol. 42, no. 88, Bp Talbot to Rome; in Latin (author's translation).

30 His chapel was one of the earliest post-reformation chapels in the country, apart from those that had been part of gentry or noble households or the embassy chapels in London. A few public chapels had been opened before the legislation of 1791; the earliest appears to have been that in Little Crosby, near Liverpool, opened in 1720. Liverpool itself had a purpose-built public Catholic chapel in 1759, replacing one burned down by the mob; the Bar Convent in York opened a public chapel in 1769; the chapel at Lulworth, opened in 1786, claims to be the oldest public chapel in the country.

Chapter 5

The national context and issues of legal equality

The Union with Ireland after 1800 increased Catholic demands for more relief. There were various attempts at getting Relief Bills through Parliament so that Catholics might enjoy, as Bishop Poynter, vicar apostolic of the London District, put it, 'an equal participation in the rights, privileges and immunities of the British Constitution'. A petition of 1810, for example, contained five resolutions, the fifth of which stated,

> That the English Roman Catholics … are firmly persuaded that adequate provision for the maintenance of the civil and religious establishments of this kingdom may be made consistently with the strict adherence on their part to the tenets and discipline of the Roman Catholic religion; and that any arrangement of this basis of mutual satisfaction and security and extending to them the full enjoyment of the civil constitution of their country will be met with their grateful concurrence.[1]

There was, however, a major and bitter split among the Catholics themselves, with the main point at issue being whether the British government should have any say, even a right of veto, in the appointment of Catholic bishops. Bishop Milner strongly and vociferously opposed any such concessions by his fellow Catholics, refusing to sign the petition and siding with the Irish bishops to oppose Poynter and those English Catholics who were willing to allow it for the sake of gaining general British support for Catholic emancipation.[2] The Rev. John Lingard, a well-known member of the secular clergy, for example, had suggested that before Rome made a particular episcopal appointment a list of candidates might be sent to the government for vetting; only when cleared should it then go to Rome for a final decision. A further petition to Parliament in 1813 was refused by the speaker of the Commons as causing too much strife among Catholics and so it was stopped at the committee stage – Milner had even sent a pamphlet to MPs saying that the petition ran counter to Catholic discipline, a point welcomed, no doubt, by those opposed to any further emancipation.[3]

1 Phillips (ed.), *The Diaries of Bishop William Poynter*, p. 9. Poynter (1762–1827) became co-adjutor in the London District in 1803 and succeeded as vicar apostolic in 1812; he died in 1827. Two recent studies in the new *Oxford History of British and Irish Catholicism*, vol. 3, are particularly relevant to this chapter: Michael Mullett, 'Catholics in the United Kingdom, 1800–1820', pp. 67–84 and Thomas Bartlett, '"The Abominable Catholic Quest". Catholic Emancipation, 1820–1829', pp. 85–103.

2 Rev. John Milner (1752–1826), served in Winchester for twenty-seven years, before becoming vicar apostolic of the Midland District in 1803; he was a noted and very strong-minded controversialist.

3 Rev. John Lingard (1771–1851), a renowned historian; a former pupil of Poynter and unofficial leader of the more liberal clergy. The best modern biography is Phillips, *John*

Francis Young makes the interesting point that this division between the Catholic groupings was not just political: it had theological and cultural elements as well. Those in favour of concessions played down (and even openly rejected) the role of the miraculous in popular Catholic devotion, the veneration of images and what were deemed inappropriate Italianate excesses and superstition – if nothing else, they argued, all this only played into the hands of Protestant anti-Catholic propagandists. Milner and his supporters, on the other hand, looked on such scepticism as disloyalty to the Catholic traditions that their forebears had fought and suffered for over the centuries, and several steps too far towards political appeasement and rationalism.[4]

Both Milner and Poynter were in Rome in 1814–15 to put their separate cases, a journey interesting in its own right at such a troubled time, indicating as it did a self-confidence in their position as leaders at home and an acknowledgement of the possibility of gaining further government liberalisation. Though there was still obvious anti-Catholicism in England, the Roman authorities had a generally favourable view of the country, especially given English support for the pope against Napoleon. Cardinal Consalvi was well received when he visited London for the (premature) peace celebrations in 1814.[5] Poynter was convinced the government would grant emancipation if Catholics went about it in the right, sensitive way. Early in 1815, Cardinal Litta was also encouraging:[6] Poynter should outline the full case for emancipation and how it might be achieved. Poynter agreed and produced a very long letter (over 5,000 words) to the Cardinal, which he summarised himself thus:

> I drew up a long statement of the case of the English Catholics, in which I expressed all that they suffer in civil and religious respects from the Penal Laws, and the objects of this petition. Next I stated fully and clearly the prejudices of the Protestants ... Then I showed how from these prejudices the Protestants naturally called for some securities, observing that their call for securities was supported by the practice of other countries, a-Catholic (*sic*) as well as Catholic. I then exposed the differences of opinions that exist among Catholics on the subject of what are called securities, every part of which arose from the facts I had stated in the first part.[7]

This, however, was a somewhat inadequate summary of his lengthy letter, and in particular omitted any reference to the vexed issue of so-called ‘securities’ or guarantees to the British government that the loyalty of Catholic bishops could be relied on.[8]

Lingard, Priest and Historian; see also Peter Phillips (ed.), *Lingard Remembered: Essays to Mark the Sesquicentenary of John Lingard's Death*, CRS, Monograph 6 (London, 2004).

4 See Francis Young, ‘Bishop William Poynter and exorcism in Regency England’, in *BCH*, vol. 33, no. 2 (October, 2016), pp. 278–97.

5 Ercole Consalvi (1757–1824), Cardinal Secretary of State; an able diplomat, staunchly anti-Napoleon and pro the divine right of kings. See *ODCC*.

6 (1756–1820); Prefect of the Congregation of Propaganda and hence officially in charge of the English mission. There are extensive references to him in Phillips, *The Diaries of Bishop William Poynter*.

7 Bernard Ward, *The Eve of Catholic Emancipation, Being the History of the English Catholics during the First Thirty Years of the Nineteenth Century* (London, 1912), vol. 2, p. 123.

8 There is a copy of the document (unpaginated) in the Foreign Office Archives. Mr Cooke, an Under-Secretary at the Foreign Office, had been sent to Rome to seek papal support against

In the original document Poynter had gone to some lengths to explain how the pope might assure the government on this point, listing what he saw as a principal Protestant objection to further Catholic emancipation: the pope might well be in league with England's enemies and any correspondence between him and English bishops might easily become 'a means of communicating with the enemies of Britain', especially if any of the bishops happened to be foreigners.

We are clearly back here in the old accusations of English Catholics necessarily having a dual or divided loyalty between their church and their country. Poynter went on, at some length, to suggest how the pope might re-assure the British government in a formal letter that these fears were groundless: in particular, he could promise never to appoint any bishop who should not be a British subject. Indeed, any candidate recommended for appointment should have a certificate of loyalty issued by the government:

> Such a certificate, which does not seem to interfere with any ecclesiastical rights, might be easily obtained, if, before the election, ... the names of several Priests were sent, privately ... to the King's Minister, with a request, that he would please to state, whether the King has any objection to make to the loyalty, or the peaceable disposition of any of them ... [Thence three names] might be chosen as might be presented or recommended to the Supreme Pontiff.

Despite Poynter's arguments, internal divisions among the Catholic leaders remained and the general peace after 1815 meant less priority had to be given to securing peace in Ireland: Catholic affairs no longer had the same importance. This rather uneasy calm did not last, however, and Daniel O'Connell's rise to power in Ireland brought the issue of Catholic emancipation to the fore again.[9] Hints that the government might be willing to grant some reform in return for Catholic co-operation caused outbursts of intense anti-Catholicism. For example, Dean Phillpotts, later bishop of Exeter, wrote at length to Wellington to make clear unchanging Protestant objections to the Catholic ideal and practice of priesthood. To make his case he quoted the Council of Trent; a class book used at Maynooth college; the writings of Rev. Joseph Berington and the Catholic Bishop Baines, among others. He concluded his letter by stating that Roman Catholic claims about the powers of their priests were nothing less than blasphemous, for the people were taught to have complete faith in their clergy and so relieve themselves of all personal responsibility, including in political questions, especially in Ireland: priestly authority was supreme.[10] For his part, the bishop of Chester wrote that he had the strongest objections to any recognition of a Roman Catholic hierarchy or of any suggestion that their clergy should be paid by the government (a suggestion made to ensure their loyalty in Ireland): this would only be a recognition of their 'corrupt tenets' and a danger to the constitution and the Church of England.[11] Such arguments were common fare among Protestant writers of the time.

Napoleon; Poynter had a number of meetings with him there, which presumably is why there is a copy of the document in the National Archives; see Phillips, *The Diaries of Bishop William Poynter*, pp. 42–3.

9 He was to become the famous and successful Irish nationalist leader (1775–1847).

10 *Despatches, Correspondence, and Memoranda of Field Marshall Arthur Duke of Wellington, K.G.*, edited by his son The Duke of Wellington, K.G., vol. 4 (London, 1873), pp. 386–91.

11 *Ibid.*, vol. 5, pp. 350–1.

Wellington, though personally opposed to any liberalisation of anti-Catholic laws, appears to have taken a balanced view of the whole question in a real politik fashion. In August 1828 he replied to Lord Bathurst, who had suggested that Wellington might deal directly with the pope over the Irish question, that any direct dealing with the pope was out of the question and would only create 'all sorts of difficulties' since the Church of England would have great and 'well-founded' objections to any such action; Wellington himself believed the government could manage without doing so. When the Roman Catholic archbishop of Armagh wrote to him in December 1828 concerning the vexed issue of the appointment of Roman Catholic bishops and suggesting a possible way of the government having a say in such appointments, Wellington replied, sending his good wishes, but seeing no prospect of a settlement – 'passions are so raised' that it would be better to 'let it go into oblivion' for a while and then see if the admittedly great difficulties might be sorted out later. There had, indeed, been petitions for and against the proposed changes, but those anti far outnumbered those pro, by 720 to 220.[12] There were echoes here of Poynter's letter to Cardinal Litta: objections, he thought, were not so much based on principle as on practical politics. But as with Milner and many of the Irish bishops then, there were those who opposed any compromise in such matters – and this included King George IV himself who stood firmly by his anti-Catholic coronation oath and in 1829 threatened to abdicate if Wellington went ahead with a Catholic Emancipation Bill.

Despite such strong opposition, and some monster anti-Catholic petitions, in the end Wellington's pragmatism prevailed over his personal deep anti-Catholicism, and he even persuaded the king to assent to the bill, in April 1829.[13] Technically it did not grant complete equality: no member of the royal family could legally marry a Roman Catholic, while no Roman Catholic could become Lord Chancellor (constitutionally the 'conscience of the monarch') or Regent. None of these restrictions seemed to worry British Catholics overmuch, but others were of greater significance. The Act disenfranchised most Irish voters by raising the value of the property qualification five-fold. It also forbade English Catholic bishops from using the name of towns or cities in their titles where there was already a Church of England see. Members of religious orders were forbidden to wear their religious habits in public. Overall, the Act may be seen as a piece of practical political manoeuvring rather than one resulting from any principled commitment to religious toleration.[14]

Of course, as in previous cases, the passing of a controversial act of parliament did not change the opinions of those who had vociferously opposed giving any further legal freedoms to the Catholics, and anti-Catholicism was too ingrained at all levels of English society for a smooth passage to full toleration and acceptance – even though some Dissenters in the country were largely in favour of the 1829 Act as a step in

12 *Ibid.*, vol. 5, pp. 308–9, 326. For petitions see Bartlett, 'The Abominable Catholic Quest', p. 102.

13 For a lively, detailed account see Antonia Fraser, *The King and the Catholics: The Fight for Rights 1829* (London, 2018). See also Phillips, *John Lingard: Priest and Historian*, especially chapter 4, for some of the controversies in the lead up to the Act. Sir Robert George Throckmorton was the first English Catholic to be elected an MP, in 1831; see Marshall and Scott, *Catholic Gentry in English Society*, p. 248.

14 Phillips, *John Lingard. Priest and Historian*, pp. 245–7, 287. For a summing up see Bartlett, 'The Abominable Catholic Quest', pp. 102–3.

the direction of religious equality. Anti-popery, however, continued as a feature of election addresses in the 1830s in Bedford. The recent historian of Methodism in the county cites Captain Frederick Polhill, one of the MPs for the borough, who went in for 'repeated tub-thumping about the Catholic threat' during the parliamentary campaigns of 1832 and 1837.[15] Attention was, however, beginning to shift from Rome to closer to home: for many, perhaps the majority, Tractarianism and Ritualism were becoming twin bugbears within the established church, while its reforming bishops were attempting, and in the case of Bedfordshire meeting with some success, to implement a move towards more effective episcopal control and care. The transfer of the county from the Diocese of Lincoln to that of Ely in 1837 should be seen as a positive development here.[16]

While anti-Catholicism continued, the legislation of 1829 did have important effects for English Catholics. At a basic level it left them free of any government interference, real or feared, and able to attend to the pressing problems that increasing numbers and urbanisation were creating for them. Additionally, they could now take some part in civic life and try to counter the effects of continuing local anti-Catholic prejudices. Across the country as a whole, the four English and Welsh vicars apostolic were free to develop their own much needed pastoral initiatives in public. Basic to such development was a re-organisation of the four districts, which by the 1830s were obviously too large to allow for proper oversight and the effective deployment of clerical resources. The vicars apostolic hoped that along with an increase in their number from four to eight there would be a change in their standing, to get their authority more fully accepted by their clergy and to impose greater control and some degree of uniformity of practice.

As a key first step, in 1838 they sent to Rome for approval their *Statuta Provisoria* ('Forward-looking Statutes'). These proposed that they should effectively become bishops, led by an archbishop, and each assisted by a vicar general. On the important question of the appointment or replacement of vicars apostolic, they suggested that the pope should choose from a terna (list of three nominees) drawn up by either the chapter of the district concerned or by the vicars apostolic. It is of interest to note here that the long and difficult negotiations over such appointments in the lead up to the 1829 Act seemed to have been forgotten. If implemented, these 1838 proposals would have largely satisfied the demands of many of the Catholic clergy to be involved in the administration of their districts and in the appointment of their leaders.[17]

After an initial favourable reception in Rome the vicars apostolic hesitated to implement the proposals, principally because of a lack of funds and a shortage of qualified priests able to provide proper administration. This delay, coupled with some differences of detail among the vicars apostolic themselves, led to exasperation in

15 See Rodell, *The Rise of Methodism*, pp. 201, 204. For an interesting example of such ingrained anti-Catholicism in a country rector, see John Skinner, Howard and Peter Coombs (eds), *Journal of a Somerset Rector 1803–1834*, 2nd rev. ed. (Bath, 1971); it is clear that the Rev. Skinner automatically signed any anti-Catholic petition offered him in the 1820s and early 1830s.

16 Bell, *Belief in Bedfordshire*, pp. 122–3. Bedfordshire retained its position as an archdeaconry.

17 Richard J. Schieffen, *Nicholas Wiseman and the Transformation of English Catholicism* (Shepherdstown, US, 1984), pp. 79ff. Text in Ward, *The Dawn of the Catholic Revival in England*, vol. 2, pp. 244–5.

Rome. The situation was not helped by the fact that the English agent in Rome during the negotiations was Mgr Nicholas Wiseman, rector of the English College; unfortunately, for various reasons he was not fully trusted by the English vicars apostolic. While there was no doubting his enthusiastic commitment, he had a fairly low opinion of the abilities and character of most of the English secular clergy, thinking them too 'measured and almost cold' in their pastoral commitment. He saw himself ideally as a roving missionary, inculcating warmth and enthusiasm to revivify the English Church, hardly an approach to endear him to the general body of the clergy or the vicars apostolic. For his part, Pope Gregory XVI did not trust the vicars apostolic, partly because of their determination to curb the role of the Regulars, but also because of what seemed to be unnecessary delays in implementing the changes.[18] The Holy See had been willing to leave administrative details to them, but stepped in when they seemed unable to proceed.

1840 was a key year in the general re-organisation of the Catholic Church in England and Wales, with eight districts replacing the original four. These smaller districts and the increase in the number of vicars apostolic from four to eight made administration easier and more effective. The new Eastern District included Bedfordshire and Buckinghamshire, both formerly under London, and stretched north to Lincolnshire and east to Norfolk and Suffolk; although still very extensive, it was more of a geographical unit than the former London District had been.

A momentous change for the English Catholic Church came in 1850 with the restoration of the hierarchy: this established thirteen dioceses to replace the former eight districts, each with a bishop with full canonical rights, a chapter of canons and various diocesan officials (at least where there were enough priests to fill the posts). Rome's decision here was a recognition of the maturity that had been achieved by the Catholics of England and Wales, as well as of the hard work of the vicars apostolic in coping with an increasingly urban and industrialised constituency.

As the new dioceses took the names of English or Welsh towns or cities, led by an archbishop of Westminster, this was seen across the nation as a direct threat to the Protestant constitution and led to the Ecclesiastical Titles Bill of 1850, forbidding any Catholic diocese from taking the name of an already existing Anglican one. In practice the legislation was already out-of-date: the Emancipation Act of 1829 had forbidden Catholic dioceses from taking the names of their Anglican counterparts, and so the thirteen dioceses named in the papal decree of 1850 had been given alternative titles.[19] There was an outburst of active anti-Catholicism, strengthened by the indiscretion of a triumphalist announcement by Nicholas Wiseman, the newly appointed cardinal-archbishop of Westminster. His public letter, 'From Out the Flaminian Gate'[20] seemed to justify Protestant suspicions that the whole issue was

18 Schieffen, *Nicholas Wiseman and the Transformation of English Catholicism*, pp. 72–89.

19 So, for example, Salford had been chosen instead of Manchester, Westminster and Southwark instead of London, Shrewsbury instead of Chester, Beverley (in 1878 divided into Leeds and Middlesbrough) instead of York; there was no Anglican bishopric of Liverpool at the time.

20 Schieffen, *Nicholas Wiseman and the Transformation of English Catholicism*, chapter 10. The title related to the custom requiring Catholic bishops not to write pastoral letters addressed from Rome, the papal see; even if actually written there, they had to be sent as though from outside the city gates.

somehow a papal move to impose Catholicism on the nation. There were, almost inevitably, protest meetings up and down the country, including one in Bedford in November 1850, which attracted people from around the county.[21] Public opposition was to a large extent whipped up by the government, inspired in part by political considerations: it took attention away from its political difficulties and provided what was hoped would be a national bonding against the old enemy. The outburst was, fortunately, short-lived and there was nothing like the Gordon Riots outbreak or even those of the pre-1829 years.

The Catholic bishops (most of whom had been vicars apostolic) settled into their new roles and had no difficulty in being accepted as leaders by their clergy and people. Overall, it would be difficult to over-estimate the importance of these 1850 changes, in themselves a sign of developing maturity as well as providing a platform for further growth. Effective leadership however, here as in any context, would depend as much on personal ability as on legal status and could not be taken for granted.

21 See, for example, Richard Morgan (ed.), *The Diary of a Bedfordshire Squire (John Thomas Brooks of Flitwick, 1794–1858)*, BHRS, vol. 66 (Bedford, 1987).

Chapter 6

Ups and downs in Bedfordshire

So much for what might be called the high politics of the situation. At ground level, it is necessary to retrace our steps. While Bishop Poynter, as vicar apostolic of the London District, was involved in matters nationally and was recognised in practice by the government as 'head' of the Catholics in England, he was also active as vicar apostolic across his district, including Bedfordshire. His diaries are an invaluable source for both sides of his ministry.[1] We also have some of his reports to Rome on the state of his district. For example, in July 1814, while he was visiting Rome, he wrote a report that included Bedfordshire, where there was one mission at Shefford with a resident missionary, serving thirty-five Catholics. Another report towards the end of 1815 gave the same numbers for the county.[2] From his diaries we learn that he visited Shefford at the end of May 1821, and confirmed there (unfortunately, no names are listed); he was also involved in appointing clergy there in 1824.[3] Clearly, by the early years of the nineteenth century a mission was fully established in Shefford, with a properly appointed resident priest, and pastoral visitations by the local bishop. We need to retrace our steps to understand how these developments had taken place.

As we have seen, there are difficulties in drawing up a list of the clergy, if any, who served at Shefford in the first half of the eighteenth century (see pp. 44–6). Bedfordshire Catholics were few in number and there were no obviously wealthy patrons, so it is most likely that the clergy funds (see pp. 13–15) were used to support whoever resided there. It is possible of course that members of the Noddings family were already supporting a priest in Shefford; we know that Christopher Taylor later had an annual income of about £70 from the Noddings' legacy. We do not know whether the family had also been supporting two earlier priests who definitely served there in the second half of the century, the Rev. Stephen Robinson and the Rev. John Barnewall; both of them had joined the fund when starting on the English mission.

Sometime in the late 1770s and/or early 1780s, there was almost certainly a resident priest in Shefford, the Rev. John Barnewall (according to Bellenger, from Ireland), who had been named as Mary Noddings' legatee. He had died in February 1782 and the mission was left without a resident priest until 1786. It is possible that during these years it was served for at least some of the time by visiting priests from Old Hall Green, Hertfordshire, one of whom was probably the Rev. James Willacy; as well as being the missioner there he was the headmaster of Old Hall Green School,

1 See pp. 47–9.

2 Details from Brady, *The Episcopal Succession in England, Scotland and Ireland*, vol. 3, pp. 187–9.

3 Phillips, *The Diaries of Bishop William Poynter*, pp. 207, 244, 247.

a preparatory school established in 1767 for young boys who would then proceed to one of the English colleges abroad.[4]

Willacy was to be involved in negotiations over the Shefford properties before a new resident priest was appointed, trying to sort out the Noddings' bequests, mortgages and property holdings. It is of some interest that the agent used in these negotiations was a layman named Joseph Cole, of Shefford, who appears to have been a sort of land manager.[5] He also had dealings with Sir John Throckmorton, described as 'an attorney at law' of South Audley Street, London, and a member of the wealthy Throckmorton family of Weston Underwood. Cole acted as agent for a number of families – he was surveyor for the Wrest Park estates, for example, and the Pyms of Sandy, as well as being a schoolmaster, and a skilled map-maker.[6] He may well have been a Roman Catholic, or at least very supportive of the clergy; was he related, perhaps, to the Anglican clergyman of the same name in the area? (see p. 30).

The first priest resident in Shefford for whom we have substantial information was Christopher Taylor (1730–1812), alias Nicholson (his mother's name). He was educated at the English College, Rome, where he gained a reputation as a linguist and scholar of some note before leaving for the English mission in 1760. After a short spell in Surrey his principal posting had been in Thorndon Park, near Brentwood in Essex, where he served from 1762–86, eventually moving to Shefford in August 1786.[7] He comes across as a type of gentleman-scholar not unknown in the eighteenth century, perhaps more especially among family chaplains. He did key work, however, in establishing the Shefford mission, building a chapel and refurbishing the Noddings' house in the High Street as his presbytery; one of the bedrooms had served as a public chapel for some years. He was a friend of Sir George Osborn of Chicksands (who had the right of appointment to the local Anglican living) and benefitted from being able to use Sir George's library.[8] We also have some business letters to the vicar apostolic and others dealing with disputed funds and the refurbishments of buildings.[9]

There is little evidence of any great missionary fervour or 'evangelical' outlook on his part, although one has to be careful in making such judgements given the lack of evidence and his age. It would also be unfair to compare his activity with that of missioners in other parts of the country who were serving in much longer established missions and with larger Catholic populations.[10] Cunningham makes the valid point that recent research leads us to question 'the common image of the passive country chaplain of the eighteenth century'.[11]

4 Ward, *The Dawn of the Catholic Revival in England*, vol. 1, pp. 40–1.

5 AAW, 'A' Series, vol. 42, nos 159, 160, 'Letters re Shefford Mission'.

6 Godber, *The History of Bedfordshire*, pp. 358, 364.

7 The sacramental registers that he kept during his time in Thorndon still exist. NDA, Notes on the Baptismal Register of the Catholic Chapel of Thorndon Park, nr Brentwood, Essex (unpublished typescript), p. 1.

8 Bell, *Belief in Bedfordshire*, p. 63.

9 See AAW, 'A' Series, vol. 42, nos 159, 160, 162–65, 'Letters re Shefford Mission'.

10 See, for example, on Simon Bordley in Lancashire: Jack P. Cunningham, 'Fr Simon Bordley: eighteenth-century recusant priest, schoolmaster and trader in "two-legged cattle"', in *BCH*, vol. 36, no. 3 (May, 2023), pp. 280–308; see also the discussion in Bossy, on how the missionary outlook of the clergy changed during the eighteenth century and into the nineteenth: Bossy, *The English Catholic Community*, pp. 264ff.

11 *Ibid.*, p. 282.

As we have seen, Taylor was responsible for building the first custom-built Catholic chapel in the county – legally permitted by the second Relief Act of 1791 – justifying it on the grounds that his flock had increased from 'five or six' on his arrival to 'above twenty' in 1791. His letter of that year to the vicar apostolic seeking permission to build throws some light on his outlook and approach:

> I am now verging hastily towards my grave, having already passed my grand climacteric,[12] and, though unable to enjoy the comforts which an old worn-out missionary might have expected, yet I hope that my rallying spirits will enable me to smooth my passage off this stage, and that charity will prompt me to place the future general good of my brethren in Jesus Christ in the primary corner of my heart. ... Behold one reason why I wish to see a chapel erected in the market town of Shefford, and as I find no money reserved for this purpose, I mean to turn beggar in my old age (with your Lordship's leave), but I fear with no very great success, as I hear that a late rage for chapel building has tired our rich ones.

He believed that the existing Catholic buildings in the town (mainly the former Noddings house and shops) were too dilapidated to raise any money from a sale, and went on to justify building a chapel where there were only a handful of Catholics:

> You seem to imagine that I have no congregation, but this is no reason why a chapel should not be built. People open shop in order to procure custom. My flock is small, I allow, but more numerous (thank God) than when I quitted Essex for Bedfordshire; in fact, it is too big for my bedchamber. ... We hope for more, with heaven's blessing, but that chiefly depends upon Him Who alone can view the number of His own elect. We are placed in a country swarming with jarring sectaries, where much good may be done with the divine grace. Shefford is the only place of Catholic worship in the whole Province, and, as a tolerable foundation is affixed thereto, it is a pity that Shefford should want its public chapel.[13]

The standing of Catholics in the town was, he believed, very important. In an earlier letter of 1788, shortly after his appointment to Shefford, he had pointed out the general poverty of his position, arguing for more support:

> This infant place requires a peculiar attention, as being the only one in the County; and amidst a great variety of Sectaries. A decent appearance among them is absolutely necessary, and this cannot be kept up without a considerable expense.[14]

The chapel was built at the rear of the former Noddings property and was approached through a narrow passage off the main street, so it was not visible to passers-by. It was one of the earliest chapels in the country built after the Relief Act and was one of only a small number built in places that had a very small Catholic population. Unfortunately, there seems to be no account of the furnishing or decoration of the chapel; presumably it possessed a full range of essential altar fittings (candlesticks were thought of at the time to be a peculiarly Catholic thing) and vestments. Certainly where we do have detailed information (e.g. family

12 He was probably sixty-three.

13 'tolerable foundation' refers to the Noddings' legacy that supported a priest there; see his long letter of December 1788, pp. 78–80.

14 *Ibid.*

St George's Chapel, Shefford, dating from c. 1791.
(courtesy of Bedfordshire Historical Record Society)

chapels such as at Weston Underwood), there was no lack of traditional fittings and ornamentation.[15]

It is clear that Bishop Talbot, vicar apostolic since 1781, had seen possibilities for development in the town: he had authorised Taylor to buy additional buildings and land next to the old Noddings' property: two cottages, a barn, a malthouse, a stable, pasture land and a garden, though it was all in such a bad state that Taylor thought it was in need of considerable improvement before any of it could be let profitably.[16] It is interesting that Taylor used some subterfuge at the auction to get this property, because he feared opposition if it were known locally that a Catholic priest was buying land in the town:

> Your remark with respect to my personal interference in the Sale of the premises, next to me, was very just; and considering it in the same light I had engaged Mr Bower to bid to a certain Sum, before I had the honor (*sic*) of acquainting yr. Lordship with it. But having received your instructions in due time, I then engaged a 2nd person (Mr Phips, the Landlord at the George) to advance a little higher, than Mr. Bower had done if in case an Antagonist shd. step in between them. And so it happened. Mr. Bower was supposed to bid for me. He went to a certain height

15 The Shefford chapel was later registered for marriages (in 1838) following thc Marriage Act of 1837 that allowed marriages to be celebrated in Non-conformist chapels, in the presence of a civil registrar, or just in the registry itself. See Welch, *Bedfordshire Chapels and Meeting Houses*, pp. 4, 6, 152. The main pressure for the Act had come from Dissenters. See also Welch, p. 150, for the watercolour of the chapel by Thomas Fisher, dated about 1820. Later in the century it became the sacristy of the new church, see pp. 99–102.
16 AAW, 'A' Series, vol. 42, no. 163, Letter re Shefford Mission.

> and stop'd. In consequence I was thought to have given it up; & the next Bidder was expected to have it; when lo! Mr. Phips went on, as it were for himself, & the Estate was knocked down to us at 152 (*sic*).

While Taylor clearly saw this as a coup, he was quick to point out to the vicar apostolic that there would not be any quick return on the investment:

> Though this is much below the sum your Lordship mentioned, yet you must give me leave to tell you that the Buildings are in much worse plight than imagined. Money must be laid out before they can be said to be dwellable (*sic*). Yet I presume that if the remaining £48 of the 200 (*sic*) were laid out upon them the houses would be habitable indeed, and would bear some rise in rent. We shall know by the 3rd. of Jany. next, whether they can be legally convey'd or not; at which time I could wish to see yr. Lordship at Shefford; with the hope of meeting with yr. Lordship's Approbation.

This property was later to be the cause of a quite amicable but lengthy dispute between Taylor and the bishop – did it (and its eventual income) belong to the mission and its incumbent or to the bishop and his successors? Apart from the legal issue involved and the effect on Taylor's annual income (which was settled as being £74. 8s. – a quite considerable sum for a priest in his position at that time), Taylor lost his fundamental claim; it is clear from the quite complicated documentation that the vicar apostolic saw the issue basically as one of regulation and the imposition of order over his clergy.[17]

Taylor's is the first ministry in Shefford for which we have any parochial registers. They are reproduced below at pages 158–86 and show, amongst other things, the extent of his mission beyond Shefford itself, covering as it did Bedford, Blunham, Biggleswade, Luton and Hitchin (Hertfordshire). He recorded only sixteen baptisms in twenty-four years, none of them from Shefford itself: the baptised were mainly from Hitchin and Blunham. The Clarkson family from Blunham, for example, had ten children confirmed in a single ceremony by Bishop Douglass in 1802. Unfortunately, it appears to be impossible to determine the number of those attending Mass regularly. We can assume, however, that the number of those receiving Holy Communion was low: traditionally in England reception was limited to major feast days; even a fully committed Catholic such as William Mahwood normally received the sacrament only at Easter and Christmas.[18]

As well as a number of business and official letters, we have an interesting personal letter from Taylor, written to a priest friend at Claughton-le-Brock, Garstang, in Lancashire. This was the Rev. John Barrow (1735–1811) known as the 'Old Tar' because he had been press-ganged into the navy for a staggering seven years while travelling home as a student from the English college in Rome. He then returned to the college and was ordained in 1766; he never lost a certain salty roughness of language that he had acquired in the navy, though in Kirk he is also listed as 'of saintly memory'.[19] His original period in Rome had over-lapped with Taylor's years as a student there.

17 *Ibid.*, Letter (no date, but probably 1787).

18 Peter Phillips, 'Catholic Belief and Practice', in *The Oxford History of British and Irish Catholicism*, vol. 3, pp. 123–41, at p. 126.

19 Kirk, *Biographies of English Catholics in the Eighteenth Century*, p. 262.

The letter, dated 16 July 1809 from 'Shefford, Biggleswade', was in reply to Barrow's letter of a few days earlier.[20] The first section of it looks back at the disputes between the northern clergy and the vicars apostolic, in which Barrow had been heavily involved. One of the key issues concerned the setting up of a seminary in England after the closure of the English continental colleges due to the French wars. The letter gives their shared views on the national scene and shows the unsettled state of English Catholicism, and the weakness and difficulties of the vicars apostolic, whom both men criticise strongly. But the main interest of the letter is probably the moving personal picture it gives of their experiences as priests, and their spiritual outlook as they were nearing the end of their lives: as Taylor put it, if they could not meet any more on this earth he hoped they would do so in heaven. Despite this seriousness, Taylor adopted a light touch, referring to Barrow as 'a daring Tar accustomed … to struggle with every species of tempest'; he had brought his ship successfully into port and might now relax.[21] Indeed,

> In a moral sense, we have (both of us) voyaged round the world, and why should not, both, be carefully laid up in dock, like the famous Centurion.

They could both claim to have 'done good' in their lives and should pray for each other:

> Man is an imperfect Being, often wanting aid from his fellow creatures of all descriptions, always wanting grace from his Creator.

Taylor died in June 1812, and was buried at Campton on 8 June; his burial is listed in Campton parish register simply as that of 'the Romish Priest'. His detailed will of 15 July 1808 was proved on 15 June 1812: it has nine sub-sections, as follows:

> The will of Rev. Christopher Taylor of Shefford in the coy (*sic*) of Bedford £10 to Mr. Leigh of Hammersmith 'for the use of the Society of which he is now president'.[22]
>
> [2–7. Individual bequests of small amounts of money, silver and clothing to relatives living in various parts of Yorkshire.]
>
> 8. I give & bequeath to the Mission at Shefford my household furniture bedding sheets table linen and towels together with my whole library excepting the books hereafter to be mentioned. And I also leave to the said Mission all my pictures mass-plate and mathematical instruments excepting some to be hereafter mentioned. With a proviso however that the Incumbent shall for ever lie under the obligation of performing one Obit annually Pro Jacobo et Christophero Taylor sacerdotibus junctis on the 5th day of March or on some other near day as it may best suit him.[23]

20 See pp. 80–1 for the full text of Taylor's letter.

21 For Barrow and various Catholic disputes of the later eighteenth and early nineteenth centuries (e.g. on the setting up of Ushaw College), see David Milburn, *A History of Ushaw College* (Durham, 1964). For background: Gooch, *The Revival of English Catholicism*, esp. pp. 287ff. Brian Charles Foley, *Some Other People of the Penal Times* (Lancaster, 1991) has brief extracts from Barrow's letter to Taylor, pp. 78–9.

22 Probably a reference to a clergy fund.

23 An annual Mass jointly for James and Christopher Taylor, priests.

9. As to my very imperfect manuscript of sermons I commit them to the care of the Rt. Rev. Dr. Poynter of Old Hall Green, Herts in order to be by him inspected revised rejected or edited as he may judge fittest.

Exors. (*sic*) Henry Clarkson of Blunham Beds, Farmer
James Corney jun 479 The Strand, London.

The James Taylor mentioned in section eight was his nephew, also a priest (1761–1806); he had studied in Rome and Douay before ordination in, probably, 1788. He was part of the 'Riding Mission', then chaplain to Lord Shrewsbury and, finally, to the Hales family, near Canterbury. He died on 5 March 1806, 'much respected and beloved' according to Kirk.[24] Unfortunately, there is no trace of the sermons left to Dr Poynter, later bishop of the London District.[25]

It is interesting to get a picture of Shefford itself at this time. Its population was rising steadily: having been about 370 at end of the seventeenth century, by 1801 it was up to 474; over the next fifty years it was to rise by 230%:

1801:	474	1831:	779
1811:	536	1841:	902
1821:	618	1851:	1,115

An account of 1806 gives the number of houses in the town as ninety, with none of them uninhabited, and a total of 107 families making up the 474 census figure. Interestingly, it mentions the Roman Catholic chapel, with John Throckmorton as trustee of 'a small stipend left in trust', but no other details. Bishop Poynter, writing to Rome in 1816 on the state of his district, reported the mission at Shefford as having thirty-five Catholics.[26]

The town's transport links were developed over the half century, with the River Ivel navigation being extended by six miles in 1822 to link it to Biggleswade, and plans for further extensions to Hitchin and Baldock. Coaching links were extensive, with principal daily connections to Bedford, London (five daily services) and Leeds (via Nottingham and Sheffield), as well as twice or three times weekly to Kettering, Potton (via Biggleswade) and Uppingham. The town itself had a weekly market day and three annual cattle fairs, one of which was also a 'large pleasure fair'. The following extract from Pigot & Co's *Directory* for 1827 shows a town that had developed considerably since the eighteenth century (despite the writer's opening few words), and, at least on the surface, would have seemed a promising centre to develop a Catholic presence in central Bedfordshire.

Shefford in 1827:
An inconsiderable market town, and dependent hamlet to the parish of Campton, in the hundred of Clifton. Is (*sic*) 41 miles from London, 9 from Bedford, about 7 from Hitchin (in Hertfordshire) and 5 from Biggleswade. It is situated in a valley, on the river Ivel, which is navigable to its two bridges; and in a decidedly

24 Kirk, *Biographies of English Catholics in the Eighteenth Century*, p. 230.

25 PCC, PROB, 11/1534/298, Will of Rev. Christopher Taylor, d. June 1812.

26 Samuel and Daniel Lysons, *Magna Britannia: being a concise topographical account of the several counties of Great Britain* (London, 1806–22), vol. 1, pp. 63–4; this is the first volume of six, covering Bedfordshire, Berkshire and Buckinghamshire. The brothers were noted antiquaries, with other important publications to their names; see *ODNB*.

> agricultural and fertile part of the county. The town is clean and well paved, the streets wide, and its general appearance bespeaks comfort. The principal trade here is in corn, timber, coal and iron, transmitted by the Ivel to [Kings] Lynn; straw plat (*sic*) also, in the making of which many women and children are employed, is brought in great quantities to the market. The Duke of Bedford is lord of the manor, under him a court leet is holden annually, when a bailiff and constable are appointed.

Inconsiderable in size, perhaps, but clearly a successful trading centre. The *Directory* went on to talk about its religious facilities, though without giving any detail of the services available:

> The places of worship here are the chapel of ease under Campton, another belonging to the Roman Catholics, and one for the methodists (*sic*). The parish church is at Campton, about two miles hence: this church contains the remains of Robert Bloomfield, the author of the 'Farmer's Boy,' and many other beautiful poems, celebrated for their pathos and simplicity: he died at Shefford in 1823. The living of this parish is a rectory, in the gift of Sir John Osborn …

So there was no parish church or resident Church of England clergyman in Shefford, a situation that might help to explain the relatively active Catholic presence there. The account of the town noted that its neighbourhood was 'studded in an interesting and pleasing degree, with numerous seats of the nobility and opulent individuals', and went on to list:

> Chicksands priory, the property of Sir John Osborn, Bart. and residence of T. Potter Macqueen, Esq. M.P; Southill, the seat of W. H. Whitbread, Esq. M.P; West (*sic*) Park, the residence of the Countess de Grey; Henlow Park, the seat of G. N. Edwards, Esq. etc.,

along with seventeen other 'Gentry and Clergy', a list that shows the wide range of people considered to be within Shefford and presumably making up some sort of 'society' locally.[27] The tribute to the poet Robert Bloomfield (1766–1823) is interesting: he had moved to Shefford from London in 1812 to avoid some of the publicity that his poetry had created, but died in 1823 in relative poverty, despite his *The Farmer's Boy* being a major hit, selling 100,000 copies by 1826.[28]

According to the census of 1821 Shefford's population was 618, comprising 296 males and 322 females. In the detailed list of occupations in the *Directory*, eighty-four individuals are named, including eleven women. The wide range of occupations and the transport links witness to the town's relative prosperity and importance. While the stress at this time was clearly on coach travel and the waterways, all was soon to change with the development of the railways. Shefford's first rail link opened in 1857 with the Midland line from Wigston in Leicestershire to Hitchin in Hertfordshire, so that the town was no longer wholly dependent on waterborne and coach traffic. While these continued to be important for a short time, as railway lines and stations multiplied and towns such as Bedford, Biggleswade and Luton were

27 Pigot and Co.'s, *London & Provincial New Commercial Directory, for 1827–8* (London, 1827), pp. 23–4.

28 See Stuart Antrobus, 'Robert Bloomfield (1766–1823): the self-taught rural poet', in BLHA newsletter, *History in Bedfordshire*, vol. 9 (Spring, 2022), pp. 5–8.

linked to London, Cambridge and the North, it was not long before rail became the all-dominant means of transport for both passengers and freight.[29]

It is noticeable that the *Directory's* list of gentry and clergy in Shefford in 1827 contains the name of the Rev. George Rolfe. He was a Catholic priest, resident in the High Street, Shefford, from 1824–38 (see below). We have seen that Christopher Taylor had died in 1812, to be succeeded by the Rev. John Potier (1758–1823), who was sometimes referred to as 'abbé' as though an émigré priest, but he was English, born in London and educated at the English College, Douay. Potier taught for some time at the school at Old Hall Green, Hertfordshire, and was headmaster there in the difficult 1790s when the English colleges abroad had to close because of the French Revolution, and their students escaped to England. St Edmund's College opened at Ware to take in southern students; Potier remained at Puckeridge as local parish priest for seventeen years. Before coming to Bedfordshire he had run a small school there, with just six scholars; this either migrated with him or he opened another one in Shefford. The *Laity's Directory* for 1813 carried an advertisement under the heading 'Shefford, Bedfordshire':

> The Rev. John Potier (removed from Puckeridge, Herts) receives six young gentlemen under 12 years of age. As the design of the school is to accommodate those parents, who are unwilling to expose their children at so tender an age to the inconveniences necessarily attendant on more extensive establishments, and to unite the convenience and comforts of the nursery with the benefits of an early and virtuous education, the young gentlemen will be treated on every occasion with all the kindness and attention which the most affectionate parent can desire.[30]
>
> [An earlier version of this advert had added:] Drawing, Music and Dancing will be charged as extras.

One may assume that this Shefford foundation was similar in aims and methods to the one he had run in Puckeridge, Hertfordshire. In an advertisement for that in the *Directory* for 1793 he had included the daily menu:

> At dinner, two good dishes besides vegetables. Breakfast, milk, milk pottage, or tea and bread and butter, if parents desire it. Supper, bread and butter, or cheese, or sometimes tarts: besides a piece of bread at eleven and four o'clock.[31]

Was this the first Catholic school in Bedfordshire? It is clear that the school was for boarders, not local boys (though the Clarkson boys were probably from the local family). The register names are English – Walmsley, Eccles, Jinks, Gifford, Clark, Cockerrel, Clarkson, Gregson, Ware, Aylett – and represent some of the old Catholic families across the country.

While the Shefford register praises Potier's upright principles, eminent sanctity and unbounded charity,[32] others had more modified judgements:

29 See Godber, *History of Bedfordshire*, pp. 510–19, for a detailed summary of the changes and their effects.
30 *The laity's directory; for the church service on Sundays and Holy Days, for the year of our Lord MDCCCXIII* (London, 1813).
31 *The laity's directory; for the church service on Sundays and Holy Days, for the year of our Lord MDCCXCIV* (London, 1793).
32 Register gives his date of death as 21 March, 1823; see p. 165.

> Mr. Potier's place was always in request by the most respectable people, although Mr. Potier was alone, and an old man, and inactive from age and unacquaintance with exertion.[33]

The last entry by Potier in the parish register was for 1819, over three years before his death; in all he recorded fifteen baptisms, one conversion, no marriages and no deaths – statistics that would seem to support the adverse judgement above. Bishop Poynter reported to Rome in 1814 that the number of Catholics in the parish was thirty-four. The school closed with Potier's death and his pupils transferred to the junior seminary at Oscott, near Birmingham.[34]

There was no immediate successor to Potier at Shefford and the mission was served for a few months by visiting priests, mainly from St Edmund's, Ware. The next resident incumbent was one of the French emigré clergy, the Rev. Claude Sébastien Chabot, who had served in a number of places since his arrival from France, including St Albans and Carshalton, Surrey, where he ran a school. His stay at Shefford was to be short; there is only one entry in the registers by him, a baptism in April 1824. It is not clear why he stayed for such a short time – probably his had only ever been a temporary appointment. Bishop Poynter noted in his diary in July 1824 that Chabot was to leave Shefford in 'a week's time';[35] he served in Epsom, Surrey, until his death in 1853, aged eighty-three.[36] He was one of the small number of exiled French clergy who did not return home but remained to serve in this country.

Chabot was followed by the Rev. George Rolfe: a native of Sheffield (not London, as Anstruther states); born in 1799, he had been ordained at St Edmund's, Ware, in 1823. Appointed to Shefford in November the following year, he soon developed a name as a 'riding priest', seeking out Catholic families across a wide area, including St Albans, Biggleswade, Huntingdon, Stevenage and Baldock, and gaining a reputation for combining 'apostolic zeal with apostolic poverty'.[37] He officiated at eight marriages between 1825 and 1837:

Dec. 2, 1825	Rich. Charles [blank] to Eliza Lawford. Witnesses were Sara Jaspar & Betsy Godfrey	G. Rolfe
May 5, 1827	Mary Sullivan to Geo. Butterfield	G. Rolfe
Jan. 3, 1830	Biddy Esther to Thomas White	G. Rolfe
May 29 1831	Mary Riley to Michael Boyle	G. Rolfe
Jan. 20, 1832	Elisa Banks to James Quinlon	G. Rolfe
April 19 1835	Charlotte Elson to John o Hara Shefford	by me G. Rolfe

33 Collins, 'An Ancient Catholic Mission', pp. 32–3 and note by Rev. Foley, April 1824.
34 Bernard Ward, *The History of St Edmund's College, Old Hall* (London, 1893), pp. 191–2, notes that Potier's house in Shefford, and presumably his school, was 'almost opposite the turning to Standon (vere Stondon), now used as Mrs Cottam's shop'. It also gives an obituary inscription that includes the verse, 'Calm and meek, benevolent and kind, There are but few such left behind'.
35 Phillips, *The Diaries of Bishop William Poynter*, p. 244.
36 Dominic Aidan Bellenger OSB, *The French Exiled Clergy in the British Isles after 1789* (Downside, 1986), pp. 161, 262.
37 Collins, 'An Ancient Catholic Mission'; Phillips, *The Diaries of Bishop William Poynter*, p. 250, later he served in the Diocese of Westminster, dying in 1864.

May 31 1835	Sara Pankers to Wm Murphy Hawkers Hitchin	by me G. Rolfe
May 22 1837	Maria Dillon to Michael Larkins before the witnesses Michael Dempsey & Margaret Hughes	by me G. Rolfe

This list in Rolfe's hand gives only the basic details of the marriages. It was usual to record the names of witnesses and often locations; this seems to have been a summary, compiled sometime later. The number of partners with obviously Irish names is interesting. He also recorded twelve deaths and a huge 111 baptisms – sixteen of them children of travellers, hawkers, and vagrants; only ten were children of Shefford residents: others were from Blunham, Biggleswade, Hitchin, St Neots, Hemel Hampstead, Baldock and Greenfield (Bedfordshire). Bishop Griffiths confirmed in Shefford in October 1835 – eleven of the twenty-one confirmands were from five Shefford families. Again, the number of Irish names is noteworthy:

Confirmed by Illus. & Most Revd. Bp. Griffiths, Sunday 25 October 1835:

Names	Confirm. names	Place of residence
Dillon, Ellen	Mary	Luton
Dillon, Patrick	John	Luton
Mathews, Mary	Margaret	Hitchin
Mathews, James	Michael	Hitchin
Butterfield, Mary	Anne	Hitchin
Close, Margaret	Mary	Hitchin
Murphy, William	Peter	Hitchin
Stocker, Margaret	Mary	St Neots
Riley, Mary	Mary (*sic*)	St Neots
Regan, John	John (*sic*)	Maulden
Burns, Mary	Bridget	Shefford
Caherty, Luisa (*sic*)	Mary	Shefford
Sharp, Margaret	Mary	Shefford
Sharp, Richard	Paul	Shefford
Lawford, Sarah L	Mary Anne	Shefford
Dempsey, Margaret	Mary	Shefford
Dempsey, Michael	Michael (*sic*)	Shefford
Dempsey, Barney	Patrick	Shefford
Delaney, Michael	Joseph	Shefford
Delaney, Elisabeth	Teresa	Shefford
Delaney, Mary Anne	Mary (*sic*)	Shefford

This page stands alone in the register. In the original list, Christian names are given before surnames. There is some confusion in the names of some of the candidates, where the baptismal and confirmation names are the same. There is another list of those confirmed on this date by Bishop Griffiths, vicar apostolic of the London District, in the Westminster archives, in which the names are in different order, but are clearly the same people.[38] The Westminster list does not give places of residence. Along the side of this document is written in Latin: 'the Godfather of these was the Rev. George Rolfe'; it is not clear why this unusual practice was used here.

38 AAW, Bishop Griffiths' Papers, 2/17, p. 177, 'Confirmati apud Shefford, die 25 Oct. 1835'.

We get an interesting insight into Rolfe's ministry from an unusual source – the comments he added to the death registers.[39] They amount in some cases to mini-biographies – so, for example, on 31 January 1829, he commented on Mrs Anna Maria Hughes who had used her considerable money 'almost wholly in the charitable exercises of Religion', including supporting the poor and the mission, which he hoped would benefit from her legacies. (This is followed by an odd statement: 'provided certain people are just & honest' – a reference perhaps to her relatives and probably to the lack of a formal will.) There is also his moving account (on 3 January 1836) of a young Miss Jenks of Oundle, dying of consumption aged twenty-four, and effecting a reconciliation on her death-bed between her divided family: 'may the lessons taught them and me in her death bed produce their fruit in our souls'. Not all was good news, however: on 11 June 1835 he reported in the register being worried about the widow and children of one of the Clarksons who had got into financial problems through no fault of his own: 'God only knows what will become' of them. And there was Mrs Godfrey, the clergy's former house-keeper in Shefford, who died of the dropsy and a 'mental malady', but had received the last sacraments.

Rolfe was confessor to Sir George Throckmorton of Weston Underwood. He left Shefford in February 1838, returning to St Edmund's College in Ware, where he became vice-president, before serving in a number of London churches and being appointed one of the first canons of the new Westminster Archdiocese in 1852. He died in retirement in 1864.

A sure sign of a more formal organisation across their districts was the formal collection of statistics by the vicars apostolic. The first of these that we have for Shefford was completed by Rolfe:

> Reports on state of mission at Shefford [on official printed report sheets; Rolfe's answers are in italics]
> [1837:]
> Number of Souls in Congregation: *about 100*
> .. of Communicants at Easter 1837: *about 20*
> .. of Converts: in 1834 – *2*, in 1835 – *1*, in 1836 –
> .. of Baptized in 1834 – *11*, in 1835 – *12*, in 1836 – *14*
> .. of Children educated by Charity *About 16*
> .. .. by Parents etc.
> .. .. Catechised in Chapel *6*
> .. .. .. in School
> Number of Masses on Sundays & Holidays *1*
>
> What Afternoon or Evening Services? *In Afternoon, Acts of Faith, Hope and Charity and Part of the Psalter – Devotions for Sunday .. Litany of Jesus – Catechism. In the Evening – Litany for a happy death – Butler's Lives (read) – usual night Prayers – Instruction (moral) upon a subject connected with death.*
>
> What Public Instructions in the Chapel? *Sermon in the morning, Catechism in afternoon.*
>
> What opportunities of Confession? *daily.*
>
> *April* 1837. *Geo Rolfe* Apost. Miss

39 See pp. 176–7.

Some idea of the growth of Catholicism in the town may be gained from these statistics. Whereas Christopher Taylor had baptised sixteen people in the twenty-four years he had spent in Shefford, Rolfe had baptised thirty-seven in his last three years. The description of the Sunday afternoon and evening services shows what might be called a normal Catholic devotional life in the mid-nineteenth century, with classics such as Butler's *Lives of the Saints* and, almost certainly, Challoner's *Garden of the Soul.*

Rolfe was succeeded in Shefford by the Rev. Charles Threlfall, but he died of consumption in March 1839, at the early age of thirty-six. His successor was the Rev. Peter Coop (1809–1868), at Shefford from 1839–44; he had been ordained in 1837 after studying in Rome. In his five years in Bedfordshire he recorded the unusually high number of twenty-four baptisms, five marriages and ten deaths, along with at least seven converts. Bishop Griffiths, vicar apostolic of the London District, visited the mission in late 1839, confirming just five local people. While in Bedfordshire Coop published a pamphlet in 1841, *'Reply of Rev. P. Coop M.A., Catholic Priest of Shefford, Beds, to the Sermon and Appendix by Rev. G. McLean M.A. of Bedford, entitled "Christian Freedom and Popish Bondage"'.*[40]

Coop moved to Great Marlow, Buckinghamshire, in 1844; he then served in different missions before retiring to Lancashire, where he died in 1868. Before leaving Bedfordshire, in 1840 he had completed an official return on the state of the local mission (his replies are given here in italics):

State of *Shefford (Beds)* Congregation

Converts in 1837, –	in 1838, *3*	in 1839, *4*
Baptized in 1837, *11*	in 1838, *6*	in 1839, *5*
Children educated in Charitable Schools, January 1840		*5*
Children catechised besides the above, January 1840		*12*
Communicants at Easter 1840		*28*
Souls in Congregation		*40 regular. 31 occasionally*

Collection for "New Chapels" &c. on 14th June, 1840 *£1.. 10s.. 0d.*
enclosed in letter, Forwarded to *Revd. E. Norris V.G. 35 Golden Square London*

Peter Coop Missry. Ap.

Comparison of these statistics with those collected in April 1837 shows that the 1837 total of 'c.100 souls' had dropped to '40 regular, 31 occasionally' (though allowance must be made here for the greater care apparently taken by Coop in providing the figures). Easter communicants had increased from twenty to twenty-eight, while the number of those baptised dropped markedly to five in 1839 compared with an average of about twelve in the earlier years. Catholic children attending charity schools had also dropped markedly from sixteen to five, while the number attending catechism classes in the church had doubled from six to twelve. Finally, over the six years covered by the two reports there had been ten converts to Catholicism, four of them in a single year (1839). Neither return requested information about the number

40 I have been unable to trace a copy of this; it is not in the British Library, Cambridge University Library, nor Northampton Diocesan Archives. On Coop's ministry, see Collins, 'An Ancient Catholic Mission 1762–1869', pp. 37–8, and the registers below, pp. 173–5, 177–8.

of marriages, despite the registration of the chapel for marriages granted in March 1838.[41] Overall, then, a 'steady state' situation, or a slightly optimistic one.

As shown above in the list of those confirmed in 1835 a high proportion of the candidates bore Irish names (probably thirteen out of the total of twenty-one). Generally no indication of nationality is given in the registers, but it is interesting that Canon Freeland, writing much later, talks (rather romantically, perhaps) about what he calls 'the Irish immigration' at this time:

> The Black Swan, landlord Mr John Caherty, must on Sundays, particularly in Summer time, have been the centre of great activity ... They all put up there. The Sheehys and the Fitzgeralds from St Albans, the Mackrollys (?) from St Neots, the Sullivans from Hitchin, together with the Murphys, the Dillons from Luton, and McHughes from Aspley Guise, to say nothing of the Reagans from Maulden. Most of them tramped in, but some of them, in a way, answered the Psalmist's description *Hi in curribus et hi in equis* [these in carriages and these on horseback] and the yard of the Black Swan was filled with shaky conveyances on their last wheels and the stables with infirm quadrupeds on their last legs ... we must except the nag which pranced in from Bedford ... bearing its master, Mr Samuel Boyle, ... who seemed to be something though what he was we have been quite unable to find out. ... together with the Dempseys and the Delaneys of Shefford, pillars of the congregation.

Freeland went on to exempt the landlord from this band of worshippers: as we can see from the registers compiled for 1839, Caherty died from his 'long habit of drinking spirituous liquors'. He also features in the registers as a godfather, in December 1823, presumably with his wife, Louisa Anna, as godmother.[42]

It is of some interest how scattered the homes of these people were; to what extent could they be said to have formed a community? They probably had a strong sense of belonging together, meeting regularly for Mass and perhaps some of them on other occasions such as baptisms. And, of course, they would have mixed with the non-Irish members of the congregation (the majority). There was still a sense of Catholics being different, not accepted by society as a whole, and a lasting sense of persecution was always a key element in creating a sense of community.

The Eastern District

As we have seen, a major organisational change was introduced in England and Wales in 1840, when the Roman authorities increased the number of districts from four to eight.[43] The first vicar apostolic of the new Eastern District, which included Bedfordshire, was Bishop William Wareing.[44] Not long after his appointment he

41 Welch, *Bedfordshire Chapels and Meeting Houses*, p. 152.

42 See registers, pp. 165 and 177. Freeland, ordained in 1885 and attached to the orphanage in Shefford, was writing much later, in the 'St Francis Magazine' of 1919, in an article entitled 'The Ancient Mission of Shefford (From its Registers)'. He cited no precise sources but, as a priest working in the orphanage, one may presume he was using the parish records and his own knowledge of the congregation worshipping there. He moved to Ipswich in 1887; he died in 1940.

43 See pp. 51–2.

44 Born in London in 1794, he was ordained in 1815 and served for a time as vice-president of Oscott College; he was later to become the first bishop of Northampton in 1850, resigning

sent out an appeal to 'The Nobility and Gentry of the Eastern District', in which he lamented the small number of chapels in the district and the clergy having to live on 'a pittance less than that offered to a respectable domestic'.[45] He set up the Eastern District Fund, urging all who could to contribute generously to it and promising an annual report. Two years later he reported that the fund had not been 'a complete success', adding,

> We feel deeply anxious to afford spiritual assistance to some very desolate portions of the counties of Buckinghamshire and Bedfordshire; we'll start by appointing a zealous pastor to open the way into the many destitute and abandoned localities of our District.[46]

Perhaps his appeals were not helped by some of the sentiments he occasionally expressed in his pastoral letters. The Catholic body throughout the country, he claimed in December 1844, was suffering from a 'spirit of independence and opposition to episcopal authority'. The bishops were too often thought to be 'troublesome and importunate', while 'insidious and calumnious (*sic*) misrepresentations' were not infrequent:

> there were some who seem to pride themselves in thwarting and opposing us … [We have been] taunted as easy-livers and inactive … grasping and self-seeking … haughty and domineering …

Coming from members of the Catholic body, he concluded, such sentiments were 'ominous and distressing'.[47] All this seems to have been related to the English bishops as a body and not just to himself.

A few years later, in August 1847, his pastoral letter again spoke of the 'deplorable spiritual destitution of Bedfordshire and Luton'. This was after his appointment to Shefford, in 1844, of the Rev. John Taylor to replace Peter Coop. Taylor, presumably the 'zealous pastor' mentioned above, was a convert from Wesleyanism who had been ordained in 1842. Before moving to Shefford he had served for two years at Barton on Humber, in Lincolnshire. Of the thirty-two baptisms he registered in Bedfordshire before moving to Thetford in 1850, only six were of children from Shefford itself; the rest were from the central and southern parts of the county, as well as Hitchin and Stevenage in Hertfordshire. He recorded only two marriages and one death in his six years in the county. We do not know what he thought of the bishop's description of his watch.

A new diocese

A much greater, and in many ways final, national re-organisation was that of 1850, with the establishment of a full hierarchy of bishops and dioceses across England and Wales. The former Eastern District became the new Diocese of Northampton in 1850,

in 1858. He died in 1865 in East Bergholt, Suffolk, where he had served as a convent chaplain, see Lance, *The Returning Tide*, p. 55.

45 Bishop Wareing's 'Appeal to the Nobility and Gentry of the Eastern District' was dated February 1841: NDA, Coll. A. 3. 19, Pastoral Letters of Bishop Wareing 1840–50. It was reported in *The Tablet*, 27 February 1841.

46 *The Orthodox Journal and Catholic Monthly Intelligencer*, 4 March 1843, p. 135.

47 NDA, Coll. A. 3. 19, Pastoral Letters of Bishop Wareing 1840–50.

although without the counties of Lincolnshire and Rutland, both of which became part of the new Diocese of Nottingham. William Wareing, who became the first bishop of Northampton, has been written off, unkindly but perhaps with some truth, as one of the new bishops who left 'all but no mark' on the history of the restored hierarchy. Like some others of the new bishops, he was unprepared for financial administration. When asked about records of the diocesan finances he replied that he had burned 'whole rooms of papers and documents' because he had a 'hatred of bookkeeping', and anyway could not see that the papers would have any use.[48]

He definitely made a mark in November 1850 when he replied to the national anti-Catholic outcry against the pope's setting up of the Catholic hierarchy earlier that year. His pastoral letter to his clergy and people was reported in the *Illustrated London News*, the *Northampton Mercury*, and the national Catholic press on 16 November. He described the public reaction to the pope's announcement as an

> indignant feeling and violent declaration, a furious onslaught and unscrupulous misrepresentation … exhibiting little short of insanity.

He failed, he said, to understand why the papal action had caused such bitter hatred and ended his letter, diplomatically, by ordering his priests and people to pray for the queen. His reply pre-dated that of Wiseman ('An Appeal to the English People') by a few days; that obviously removed the national attention from the lowly bishop of Northampton.[49]

As required by canon law and accepted practice, the bishop visited Rome, in December 1854, to give a report on the state of his diocese. According to this it contained twenty missions and thirty priests, with perhaps a total of ten thousand Catholics (this appears rather high); for 'fear of profanation' the Sacrament was not reserved in the great majority of these chapels, but in the priest's house. In addition, the bishop claimed that 'almost everywhere' had a school for the teaching of Catholic doctrine; this must have been a reference to Sunday schools, as there most certainly were not anything like that number of day schools. Strangely, the bishop claimed that there were very few Irish Catholics in the diocese. Was this, perhaps, a throwback to the times when Irish clergy were unwelcome in the country, or, more probably, an attempt to show the strength of native English Catholicism? Finally, Wareing reported that he had bought a site for a cathedral (for £673) and had had a design for the building drawn up by Augustus Welby Pugin (who had died in 1852); he was appealing for more funds to start work on it.[50]

48 Schiefen, *Nicholas Wiseman and the Transformation of English Catholicism*, p. 206; Hughes, 'The English Catholics in 1850', in Beck, pp. 42–85, at p. 72; for a somewhat more positive summing up, see Lance, *The Returning Tide*, p. 55. On John Taylor, see Fitzgerald-Lombard, *English and Welsh Priests*, p. 68, and Collins, 'An Ancient Catholic Mission', p. 39.

49 NDA, Coll. A. 3. 18, Pastoral Letters of Bishop Wareing 1840–50.

50 *Ibid.* The cathedral in question was never built. There is a reference to it in Rosemary Hill, *God's Architect: Pugin and the Building of Romantic Britain* (London, 2007), p. 512; she claims Pugin designed the original 1843–44 church, dedicated to St Felix, and later made new designs in 1851, but the bishop was prevented (presumably by his Chapter) from building anymore because of costs. Eventually a cathedral was built in 1863, designed by E. W. Pugin and subsuming Pugin's original building.

Strangely, the figures in the bishop's report do not tally with those in the diocesan records:

1851	26 churches/chapels	27 priests
1852	26	28 ..
1853	25	28 ..
1854	25	28 ..

It is not clear why the bishop should have exaggerated the number of clergy at his disposal (30) but reduced the churches/chapels they had to serve (20). An example, perhaps, of his generally careless approach to statistics.[51]

His whole report has a rather anodyne air about it and certainly does not give a true picture of the struggles he was facing. Perhaps Hughes' summing up of Wareing was true from a national perspective, but he was active across his very large diocese, trying to make the best of an almost impossible situation. As a man of wide vision but limited talent and insufficient resources, he faced a quite unrealistic task but did succeed in laying some of the foundations necessary for future development.

Bedfordshire was not as immediately affected by the establishment of the dioceses in 1850 as some areas. That year, however, did see the appointment of an important new pastor in Shefford to replace John Taylor. The Rev. Patrick John Quinlivan (occasionally spelt Quinlivian) had been born in Co. Clare, Ireland, about 1818, and after studying in France had been ordained priest for the Irish Diocese of Killaloe. He seems to have been in England about 1849, perhaps staying with a priest cousin of the same name in Cambridge and serving at Thetford in Norfolk; there was some talk of his teaching French at Oscott, but instead he was appointed by Bishop Wareing to Shefford. John Taylor, whom he replaced, succeeded him at Thetford, in a straightforward 'swap'.[52] Clearly, attitudes to the employment of Irish priests had changed since Challoner's day. The establishment of 'The Royal College of Maynooth' in Ireland in 1795, to replace most of the continental Irish colleges, and supported by generous funding from the British government, was intended to win over the loyalty of the Irish clergy; whether it did so or not, it certainly helped to make them fully acceptable as pastors in England.

We get an unusually detailed picture of the state of religion in Bedfordshire in the following year, 1851. The government organised a religious census to take place nationally on Sunday, 30 March, the only one ever taken in the country. It aimed to determine the true state of religion in England and Wales amid claims of a sad decline in religious practice and the dangers to society that would ensue. The task of completing the returns was laid on the incumbents of the parishes of all denominations and on the leaders, clerical or lay, of other religious groups; it is not always clear who actually completed the form. The questions asked were relatively straightforward: the name and date of erection of the church or place of worship, the amount of accommodation available, what was referred to as the 'General Congregation' in the morning and the afternoon/evening, and the number at Sunday school; some returns included the average attendances over previous months. A space was left for

51 NDA, Coll. A. 3. 18, Pastoral Letters of Bishop Wareing 1840–50.
52 Collins, 'An Ancient Catholic Mission', p. 41.

Bishop William Wareing (1794–1865), first bishop of Northampton, 1850–58. (courtesy of the Diocese of Northampton)

comments but this was not always used. As Shefford housed the only Catholic church in the county, the incumbent involved was the Rev. Quinlivan.

His return gave fifty Catholics at the morning service, and twenty in the afternoon. He claimed that there had been an average of forty at the morning service over the previous year and twenty in the afternoon, and reckoned there was a total of about one hundred Catholics in the county. Presumably he was counting here only the relatively settled Catholic community and not the widely fluctuating numbers of itinerant Irish, working on the railways or doing seasonal farm work. There was no Sunday school. He signed himself as the 'Roman Catholic Pastor'.

Table 4 below gives a summary of the church returns for the county as a whole and is included here to show the weakness of the position of Roman Catholicism at the time. The statistics are notoriously difficult to interpret exactly, partly because of variations in how different churches interpreted the questions, the fact that we do not have complete returns, and the fact that different denominations put different stresses on attendances at different times of the day (basically, morning or evening, with several Non-conformist congregations putting greater stress on their evening services). In addition, it is clear that in many instances members of a congregation attended their place of worship twice or even three times on a Sunday and the consequent double or triple counting of attendees is usually impossible to unravel. (In working out the percentage of the population attending each place of worship, the total county population is taken as 124,478.)[53] Thirty-three villages out of a total of 120 (27.5%) in Bedfordshire had only a single place of worship (the Church of

53 The figures are taken from those supplied in Rodell, *The Rise of Methodism*, pp. 156–8; 239–41. His figures are an amended version of those in D. W. Bushby, 'The Ecclesiastical Census, Bedfordshire, March 1851' in BHRS, vol. 54 (Luton, 1975), pp. 109–200.

Table 4. Summary of Bedfordshire returns, 1851 religious census

Denomination	Places of worship	Est. attendance	Est. % of population
C. of England	137	36,832	29.6
Baptists	52	16,762	13.5
Independents	18	5,477	4.4
Union	13	4,410	3.5
Quakers	3	152	0.1
Moravians	6	1,324	1.0
Wesleyans	87	20,647	16.6
Matthewsites	2	173	0.1
Latter Day Saints	6	510	0.4
Primitive Methodists	38	4,715	3.8
Temperance Christians	43		1
Wesleyan Reformers	1?	50?	0.2
Bible Christians	1?	150?	–
Catholic Apostolic	1	120	0.1
Roman Catholic	1	60	<0.1
TOTAL	**367**	**91,425**	**73.4**

England). The size of the village was not the determining factor here: some relatively large villages came within this category: Odell (pop. 538); Renhold (pop. 484); Silsoe (pop. 755); Henlow (pop. 970). Rodell groups the Baptists, Independents and Union chapels in his list as 'Dissenters' and those from Moravians to Bible Christians as 'Methodists'; of these, the Temperance Christians, Wesleyan Reformers and Bible Christians combined amount to 0.2% of the total population of the county. Forty-six places of worship made no return; estimates of attendance for these have been included in the above table.

It is interesting that in a separate list at the end of the register about the same time, Quinlivan gave the names of those attending church regularly; they number fifty-two adults and children; unfortunately, the list is undated. It takes up two pages; the comments (given here in italics) were clearly added later.

A List of persons who generally attend the Roman Catholic Chapel Shefford

Henry Lewington
Frances Lewington *R.I.P.*
Lucy Clarke *R.I.P.*
Jn Galliv(n)an *gone*
W Galliv(n)an
Pat. Galliv(n)an *gone*
Jn Higgins & wife & 5/4 children*
Denis Kelly *gone*
Pat. Lane *gone*
John & Mrs Dunne [?]
John Dunne Jnr
Mary Cotton

Elizabeth Thomson
Jane Collen *R.I.P.*
Mrs O'Brien
James O'Brien *gone away*
Margt. O'Brien .. ..
Mrs Sawford (or Lawford?)
John Reid
John Scott *gone*
Michl. O'Sullivan *gone*
Saml. Williams
Charles Allen
James Flynn *gone*
Peter McLaughlin *gone*

[*page 2*]

James Collins *gone*	Mr Howe *gone*
Daniel Collins *gone*	Mrs Howe *gone*
Pat. Bone *gone*	Ellen Sargent
John Scally *gone*	Jn Hunt
James Bowers *gone*	Mrs Bloomfield
William Barker *gone*	John M McKeowne
Patt. Carthy *gone*	Mr McKeowne & wife *R.I.P.*
Patk. Burke *gone*	–
Mich. Dunn *gone*	–
Jn Regan & 4 or 5 children	–
Rosanna Faulkner *gone*	–
Mrs Williams	–
Peggy Hunt *R.I.P.*	–

* 5 crossed out and 4 inserted.

In all, he listed thirty-six baptisms, two deaths, and four marriages during his ministry. He left Shefford (and the diocese) about April 1854, perhaps returning to Ireland.

His successor was William Jerome Poole (1828–67). After finishing his studies in Paris he was ordained by Bishop Wareing in April 1854 and appointed to Shefford in May of the same year. The bishop visited the parish in August, confirming eleven members of the congregation:[54]

Name	In Confirmation	Residence
Higgins, Elizabeth	Mary	Shefford
Higgins, Elizabeth Junr.	Mary	ditto
Higgins, John	Joseph	ditto
Higgins, Emma	Theresa	ditto
Thompson, Betsey	Agnes	ditto
Butterfield, Margaret	Agnes	Hitchin
Butterfield, Ellen	Agnes	ditto
Regan, Thomas	Domnick	Maulden
Regan, Margaret	Agnes	ditto
Regan, Anne	Cecilia	ditto
Regan, Sarah	Agnes	Ditto
		W. J. Poole. Parochus

Notes:

1. The two Butterfield names were originally entered as Chipperfield, but crossed out and replaced by Butterfield; a baby, Jane Chipperfield of Hitchin, had been baptised by Poole in the July.
2. Only four families are represented in the list, with two of them, the Higgins of Shefford and the Regans of Maulden, providing four candidates each; both families feature in Quinlivan's list above, still resident in the parish.
3. It is very unusual to have different members of the same family choosing the same patronal name at their confirmation, and to have five of the nine girls choosing the same name, Agnes. Domnick is as written with underlining.
4. This is the first use in these registers of 'Parochus' ('Parish Priest'); this was technically incorrect as the missions in England and Wales were not canonical parishes.

54 See registers, pp. 182–3. For Poole, see Collins, 'An Ancient Catholic Mission', p. 41.

In all, Poole recorded seven baptisms, with one each from Bedford, Luton, (Old) Warden, Haynes (spelt Hawnes), Cotton End, Shefford and Hitchin. He moved on, probably in July 1855, being appointed to Coldham Cottage, near Bury St Edmunds, the home of the Gage family. In 1862 he left there for King's Lynn, where he died five years later, aged only thirty-nine. The Rev. Francis Cuddon succeeded Poole about July 1855, but stayed for only a year, leaving the diocese for Southwark in mid-1856. He then moved to Westminster, and died at St Patrick's, Soho, in 1880. At Shefford he recorded just two baptisms and one marriage.

A pattern of brief incumbencies was beginning to develop. Cuddon's successor was Canon Henry Joseph Thrower (1824–91) who arrived in Shefford in August 1856. While there he performed eight baptisms, none of them of people from Shefford: there were two travellers, as well as four candidates from Bedford and one each from Luton and Hitchin. In addition, he recorded one marriage (a Luton couple), and four funerals of residents from Bedford, Campton, Hitchin and Shefford. The last of these buried was Frances Lewington, a convert and, according to the glowing account in the register, extremely pious, with 'great faith and devotion' (see the lengthy entry for 19 April 1857, p. 185). A member of the Lewington family had been listed as post-mistress in 1827. Listed as a regular attender in Shefford was Henry Lewington, presumably a relative, perhaps her husband.[55]

Late in 1857 or early 1858 Thrower took the most unusual step of resigning his canonry and leaving the diocese; he moved to Lancashire, in the Diocese of Liverpool, where he died at Lytham in 1891. It is not known why he spent so little time in Shefford or why he left the diocese. He was not alone in taking this step: he was one of four of the chapter's seven canons who left the diocese at this time, all within a very short period; the others were Canon George Rigby, who went to New Zealand; Canon Thomas Fox, who went to Salford; and Canon John Morris, who went to Westminster (where he served as Archbishop Manning's secretary, 1865–67) en route to joining the Jesuits.[56] There are no papers in the diocesan archives to explain these strange departures; they were, obviously, a great blow to a diocese so short of clergy. It is possible they were the result of dissatisfaction and serious disagreement with the ailing bishop.

With Bishop Wareing's resignation in 1858 on grounds of ill-health, the task of coping with these shortages and of developing the diocese fell to the new bishop, Francis Kerril Amherst, consecrated in the July of that year. He has been described as a 'man of different stock and different outlook' from his predecessor and 'in the best possible sense a man of the world as well as a man of God … his horizon was as wide as the Catholic world'.[57] He had been born in London in 1819 into a gentry family with aristocratic connections; when he was ordained in 1846 it was on his own patrimony (i.e. as an independent priest not attached to or supported by any diocesan bishop). For the next seven years he taught at Oscott, spending considerable periods travelling in Europe and the Holy Land. His directly pastoral experience was limited to two years in charge of the mission in Stafford. A few months after becoming bishop he wrote to his sister (a sister superior):

55 See p. 185. For Thrower see Collins, 'An Ancient Catholic Mission', p. 42–3.

56 See lists in Fitzgerald-Lombard, *English and Welsh Priests*, pp. 60 (Thrower), 70 (Rigby), 93 (Fox), 218 (Morris).

57 Quoted in Lance, *The Returning Tide*, p. 56.

Bishop Francis Kerril Amherst (1819–83), bishop of Northampton 1858–79. (courtesy of the Diocese of Northampton)

> My poor diocese is in a most destitute condition, fifty years behind the rest of England. I am in sad want of priests and money. You must pray for us.[58]

He shared with a number of his fellow bishops what might be termed, rather oddly, an optimistic outlook based on a pessimistic view of society: as he put it in 1869,

> the struggle in a few years will be between Catholicity and infidelity, as it is on the Continent – at least in France, Spain and Italy; and though infidelity will carry off a very great number, the sense of the necessity of religion will prevail over a vast crowd of people whose only refuge will be the Church.[59]

That same year he was off to Rome to attend the Vatican Council. Though a convinced supporter of papal infallibility and general authority, he was one of the group of English bishops (probably the majority) who thought it was not an opportune time to define it doctrinally. He was 'much relieved' to be able to leave Rome on grounds of ill-health before the final vote was taken and to return to Northampton, albeit to a life dedicated to coping with the 'many burdens' of administering such a large area 'without an adequate number of clergy or sufficient funds'.[60] It is interesting that in July 1870 his clergy wrote a joint letter supporting the definition; among the signatories were Warmoll and Collis.[61]

58 Foster, '"In sad want of priests and money"', p. 281.
59 Quoted in Alan V. McClelland, and Michael Hodgetts (eds), *From Without the Flaminian Gate*, p. 9; see McClelland on Manning's 'apocalyptic vision', ibid., pp. 7–8.
60 Foster, '"In sad want of priests and money"', p. 281, 289–91.
61 *The Northampton Catholic Magazine*, July 1870. This had been launched the previous year; copies of it are very rare, see Lance, *The Returning Tide*, p. 22; each issue had a section entitled 'Diocesan and Local News, etc.'

He remained as bishop for twenty-one years, resigning in 1879 due to increasing blindness. Given the problems he faced in his diocese, his achievements over that period may well be considered noteworthy:[62]

Table 5. Development of the diocese under Bishop Amhurst, 1858–79

	1858	1879
Missions with a resident priest	25	36
Mass centres	7	22
Other chapels	0	5
Clergy (incl. Religious)	26	44
Convents	3	8
Schools (all ages/types)	2 ?	16

With regard to Bedfordshire, there was a gap in making an appointment to follow Canon Thrower at Shefford for most of 1858, with only one baptism (of a child from Luton) being recorded that year and that by a Jesuit, Fr John Rigby, who was stationed at Boston in Lincolnshire. It is possible that he may have been supplying at Shefford on a regular basis at the time. But the mission there was certainly in decline: it had been serving somewhere between seventy and a hundred Catholics in the 1830s;[63] twenty years later almost all the Irish names had gone from the registers, and in 1859 there are only two entries recorded for the whole year, a baptism (at Bedford) and a funeral (at Hitchin), both in January 1859. However, one has to be very careful here: at this point the registers cease. It is inconceivable that Canon William Thomas Hammond (1828–1900) who was appointed to Shefford about November 1858 and remained there until 1865, would have performed no pastoral ministry there after January 1859, and would not have kept records of that ministry.

Unfortunately, to date no later registers for Shefford have been found. Hammond is recorded as often saying an early Mass there at 7.30 a.m. and then travelling (by rail, one assumes) to say a second Mass at Peterborough at 11 o'clock. In 1865 he exchanged places with the priest at Aston le Walls, Northamptonshire: the Rev. John Duff arrived June/July 1865.[64] But he stayed only until December 1866 when he went to Ramsey, Huntingdonshire. It appears that a number of attempts were made to close the mission in Shefford altogether: Duff reported having only eight people regularly attending Sunday Mass, and the former Irish segment of the congregation had gradually moved away. What probably saved it from closure was the Noddings' foundation for the support of a priest there. Even so, after Duff's departure the mission was without a resident priest; hence the Rev. John Priestley Warmoll at Bedford could claim in a letter of August 1867 to be the only Catholic priest in the whole county.

It was not, however, the end. The arrival in Shefford of the Rev. William Collis (1822–93) was to change everything. A convert from Anglicanism as a young man,

62 For a detailed breakdown of these statistics see Foster, '"In sad want of priests and money"', pp. 288, 292.

63 See returns pp. 65–6.

64 For Hammond and Duff, see Collins, 'An Ancient Catholic Mission', pp. 43–4.

he had a number of secular jobs (including being station master at Peterborough, when he was described as 'handsome and precise and careful'), before being ordained in February 1863.[65] After a brief spell as curate in Warwick Street, London, he moved to Walthamstow, Essex, where part of his brief was to manage St Nicholas' Industrial School for Boys. It is clear from his diaries that part of his duty was to raise money to support the school, so, for example, between May and early June 1864 he visited or lunched with Lady Londonderry, Lady Clifford (twice), Lady Lothian and Sir Charles Clifford. He was to prove a very effective fund-raiser throughout his priestly career.[66] He then moved in 1867 to Finchley, North London, where he looked after St Margaret's House, an Industrial School for Girls. A year later he moved to Costessey in Norfolk to become chaplain to Lord Stafford, but was soon on the move again. When Bishop Amherst wanted to open a Catholic boys' home-cum-orphanage, he saw Collis as its obvious manager in the light of his previous experience. He appointed Collis to Shefford in February 1868 and it appears to have been the priest who, a year or so later, saw the possibility of opening the orphanage there.[67]

There was much to do, however, just to get the mission back into shape. He set to work immediately by launching a national appeal for funds to restore the old chapel:

> it must be a matter of sorrow that any of the old chapels should be falling into ruin, and the faith in consequence banished from places which were the retreats of old Catholics who, a hundred years ago and more, hid themselves, that they might be enabled, unmolested in the practices of their faith, to end their days in peace. On taking possession of the old chapel here, I found it sadly out of repair, a sinking floor and an opening roof; an altar, the furniture of which I could only desire the opportunity of reverently committing to the flames. For the memory of the dear old Catholics, to whom all of us owe so much, I beg that something may be sent me, however small, to cover the costs of repairs and restoration, for which about £100 is required.[68]

His appeals were successful and a few months later he was able to report that the chapel had been renovated and that a number of Catholics 'from a distance' were returning to Sunday Mass, including some who had 'neglected their duties' – although he had had to borrow a decent set of vestments in which to celebrate St George's Day with due solemnity![69] He was, in effect, the second founder of the Shefford mission.

65 See long obituary of him, *The Catholic Times*, 5 May 1893.
66 BA, X627/41, Annual Diary kept by Canon William Collis, 2 May – 7 June, 1864. His diaries are, unusually, double for most years 1863–93, one personal, one for boys entering and leaving. There are occasional gaps – e.g. 1872 and 1873.
67 See pp. 82–5.
68 *The Weekly Register*, 28 March 1868.
69 Collins, 'An Ancient Catholic Mission', pp. 49–50; *The Tablet*, 6 June 1868.

Primary sources for Chapter 6

1. Letters of the Rev. Christopher Taylor of Shefford

Christopher Taylor's letters from the early years of his ministry in Shefford are important in giving us a picture of the various tasks involved in establishing the mission, including securing land and income, and dealing with possible opposition in a strongly Protestant area; especially as before the second Relief Act of 1791 it is clear that Catholics were not completely sure of their position in society. He was an experienced missioner and, to judge from his correspondence with the vicar apostolic, quite a capable businessman. It is also clear that while he was willing to stand up for what he saw as his rights, he accepted fully the authority of the vicar apostolic as the final arbiter in any disagreement.

Letter of 1788[70]

Underlining as in original. Added in a different hand: '2nd. Decr. 1788. Christopher Taylor'

My L(or)d.
Mr. Cooch has finished the affair, & as being skilled in the Law, assures me, that all is safe with respect to the Purchase. His Bill is discharged, which (no doubt) will appear to yr. Lordship, as it did to me, very extravagant. I could not suppress an Exclamation, when I saw it. But, in answer, he observed that yr. Lordship had agreed to have what they call a Fine levy'd. This alone has cost 8. or 9. Guineas which being added to his charges amounts to the Sum of £18. 12s. 6d. I have paid the £2 to make up the purchase money, & also £1. 2s. 3d. being half the duty on the Sale as per conditions. All which amounts to £21. 14s. 9d.

As to the £6. 1s. which your Lordship demands of me, I must beg leave to observe I have a bill upon it for expenses in going to Weston, Hitchin, etc. in order to get the little wreck out of the £200 due from Atkinson to Noddings. Besides, as Mr. Cole, during his very inactive agency, had neglected to receive interest for the said sum, and as the same composition could only be obtained for it as for the Principal, I, being the incumbent, felt myself not well treated by Cole and Atkinson, the interest arising from that money being certainly my property, from the moment I was inducted into Shefford. Nevertheless I was obliged to secure what I could from a Rougue (*sic*), who did not mean to pay a farthing, and so got Mr. Throckmorton to set a lawyer upon him in order to make the best of a bad market. The Account, as delivered to me, I transmitted with the £50 into Mr. Willacy's hand,[71] and, if my memory fails not, I also explained myself to the (*sic*) respect of what I reserved, I mean the £6–1–0. From which account you will find that 3 years (*sic*) interest had been due. And though its composition made but a small sum, yet out of it I took care to pay the lawyer and remit you the £50, which is exactly 5/– in the £ on the £200 bond. – You must

70 AAW, 'A' Series, vol. 43, no. 165, Letters re Shefford Mission.
71 James Willacy, Priest (1738–1805, ord. 1761).

not suppose, my Lord, that I have the least embezzeling (*sic*) spirit about me. But I retain that Esprit d'Eglise (*sic*) which has alwaies (*sic*) said Fundi proventus ad Usufructuarium attinet (*sic*).[72]

Notwithstanding all I have said, as I am ignorant of the real proventus[73] of this place, I am willing to act as your Lordship directs, and shall deduct the £6–1–0 (though much out of pocket) if your Lordship insists upon it. I have already sold out some part of my poor little pittance, and let it all go, in the name o' God (*sic*), provided that the Mission can be ameliorated by it. This infant place requires a peculiar attention, as being the only one in the County; and amidst a great variety of Sectaries. A decent appearance among them is absolutely necessary, and this cannot be kept up without a considerable expense. Your Lordship is not to be told what a many (*sic*) articles are wanted in any style of housekeeping. I have ever found you possessed of a proper idea in that respect; and supposing you had it not, the dearness of all kinds of provisions is sufficient to make us all feel it and feel it severely. This is my case, I do assure your Lordship: But I keep up spirits as much as possible, being well persuaded that I am under an honourable Patron, that will not hurt (*sic*); and to whom I am indebted for many favors (*sic*) done to self and nephew.

I wish your Lordship could find time to come down and give some Orders about my next door ragged premises. I have tried to let the Malting; but in vain. I have done no repairs, except the mending of an old pump. My tenants are all poor people, and the whole of my Rental at present amounts to the vasty (*sic*) sum of 3/1 per week. I must gather my rents every month at furthest, or I shall find all my keys left under their respective doors. Yesterday I received 4/– for 3 weeks at 9d pm (?) from the 10th ult on which day You, Sir, were said to take possession. Being the first time I ever, in my life, received any rent, I spat upon the money by way of hanvel, and may the Alm(ighty). send his Blessing upon it.[74]

I hope my Nephew will have health and do well. He has written me once, & desires some of my books, which I shall send him. My writings (such as they are) he also begs to look at: But as these are my own children, I shall be loath to trust them out of my sight. Besides, they have not finished their education as yet and I should blush to see them abroad in the [world? *Page torn*] and exposed to the ridicule of mankind, like the many unfinished brats, which we have lately seen, and which do but little honour to the pens that produced them. I beg your Lordship's pardon for having trespassed upon your patience so long. Therefore shall conclude (*sic*) with telling you, that you need not to hurry in sending me any Balance. I hope so to economise the money I have yet in hand as to make it last out until I shall have the honour of seeing your Lordship. Meantime remaining yr. Lordship's most hble. & obedt. Servt,

Chr. Taylor

72 Taylor argues here on the basis of ecclesiastical custom that he should enjoy the legal principle of usufruct, i.e. the income of a property belongs to the person who has the right of temporary possession, use and enjoyment of that property.

73 Presumably, the total income.

74 hanvel: Good luck; lucky charm for financial success.

The second Taylor letter in this appendix gives an unusually personal picture of him and one of his clerical friends, the Rev. John Barrow, who was working in Lancashire at the time. Both were nearing the end of their clerical lives. (See pp. 58–9 above for their friendship.)

Letter to John Barrow, 1809

There is no date on the letter itself; the year was added later in another hand.

My dear friend

Your long looked for letter is arrived & has given me much pleasure – the Community is certainly much indebted to your activity, & perseverance wherewith you transacted an affair of that difficulty, which would have tired, or intimidated any one, but a daring Tar, accustomed from his youth to struggle with every species of tempest. Now having brought your Ship into port with a cargo of four times the value of the original Shipment, I congratulate your good fortune, & wish you may live long to enjoy the fruits of your skill, & your labor (*sic*). You see I am alluding to Claughton's foundation, & also to the monies belonging to the rest of your Body.[75] I wish we had had such Agents for our funds in the London district. Had they possessed your knowledge, vigilance, economy, we should not be so poor as we are. Even from my foundation above £1000 was lost thro' inattention, or ignorance. Bp. Talbot, who had the administration of almost every thing, dyed insolvent. You did extremely well to withstand Math. Gibson.[76] The imposition of a mitre does not infuse into what it covers, either the wisdom of the world, or a parsimonious disposition. For this last the Gibsons are none of them famous. With respect to some public monies belonging to your missions, if I do not mistake, they came under my cognizance above 30 yrs agoe (*sic*). They were monies of which Edw. Clifford of Lancaster had been made Trustee by Mr. Skelton,[77] & imprudently. These could not be wrested out of his hands: nor would he pay the interest as it became due. I remember Tom Butler[78] of Hornby desiring me to speak to Ld. Petre of the affair, with a view that his Lordship might mention it to the Clifford family, which he did, & I had a promise from Mr. Clifford of Tixel, that it should be paid. Whether that promise has been fulfilled, or not so, you know best. I suppose it has; for I heard no more of it since. If this my detail has a reference to your very generous transaction, you'll allow me a small degree of merit along with you, tho' no larger in bulk than the widow's mite. I wish I had health, strength, & spirits enabling me to claim it at Claughton. We should then congratulate each other upon the many hairbreadth escapes we have been blessed with, during the chequered scenes of our youthful daies (*sic*), & for the still life we, now, enjoy in years, that make up the full age of man.

75 The secular clergy, see p. xiv above.
76 Bishop Matthew Gibson (1734–90), vicar apostolic of the Northern District, 1780–90; his brother William Gibson was also vicar apostolic (1790–1821); see Plumb, *Arundel to Zabi*.
77 Presumably the Rev. Nicholas Skelton (1691–1766, ord. 1718).
78 Presumably the Rev. Thomas Butler (1743–95, ord. 1761).

In a moral sense, we have (both of us) voyaged round the world, & why should not, both, be carefully laid up in dock, like the famous Centurion. Were I able to beat up your quarters, I wd be sure of meeting with a hearty welcome, & you might be equally sure of having my absolution for your going ahunting. Every one has his hobby-horse. And I cannot see why yours is not safe to ride as any other. Of this I am sure. If Taylor had delighted in no other hobby-horse than that of hunting Taylor would have been more innocent than he, now, is. But we both have a merciful God, who does not wish us to fall even into Purgatory. If we cannot meet any more upon earth I hope we shall meet in heaven. Tho' we ought to acknowledge, & repent of failings, nevertheless, our good works will follow us to plead in our behalf before the throne of him, who desires the salvation of all. We both may say, & without vanity – I have done good. To snuff many midnight lamps for the instruction of our respective congregations, must, certainly, be some balance, in the book of life, against any harmless amusement taken for the sake of bodily health, or mental dissipation. *Non omnia possumus omnes.*[79] Man is an imperfect Being, often wanting aid from his fellow creatures of all descriptions, always wanting grace from his Creator. But I am not to preach thus to one, who has composed hundreds of Sermons. I hope they will be preserved for the benefit of futurity. I have had vanity enough to compile 200, & have bequeathed them to Bp. Poynter to be by him inspected, corrected, rejected, or edited, as he may think proper.

I thank you again for your last kind letter. It breathes sincere friendship to me, & philanthropy to all mankind. Let me have another soon. I must say you have been tardy in sending your last. I expected it long agoe (*sic*); but can make an allowance for indisposition.

The Clarksons[80] were all at Church today, & are all well. Young Henry has been some weeks in Lancashire; & I rather wonder he has not called upon you. I had more to say; but paper only allows me to subscribe my self your most unfeigned friend & servant.

Christr. Taylor.

Oremus pro invicem ut salvemur![81]
[*written in right hand margin vertically:*] Scribe quantum voleris et quam primum possis[82]

79 'We cannot all do everything.'
80 See pp. 58, 62 and 65. Various members of the family feature several times in the Registers.
81 'Let us pray for each other that we may be saved!'
82 'Write as much as you like and as soon as you can.'

2. The re-founding of Shefford mission, 1869

This account is given in full. It is very rare to have such a personal retrospective, illustrating as it does Collis's own outlook and fundamental faith. We see his total commitment, his successful fund-raising methods and, overall, we are given a flavour of his work and achievements well beyond the basic statistics.

The re-founding of Shefford mission in 1869: Canon Collis' account, 1885

It is eighteen years ago – walking by the side of my late Bishop, Dr. Amherst – he proposed to me that I should undertake to establish a school for orphan boys in his diocese. It was a work, he said, very much needed: there were orphan boys scattered about through its great extent, and no school to which they could be sent. I expressed my willingness to do anything he wished. But I imagine the want of means – for he had no money that he could devote to the work – and the difficulty as to the choice of place, prevented at that time anything being determined upon. At all events, shortly afterwards the good Bishop desired me to undertake a mission for which he had great need of a priest. This was in 1867. Twelve months later he wrote to ask if I would take charge of Shefford.

It is here pleasant to record that Shefford was a place I had heard much of since my early Catholic days. I had visited it while yet a layman more than once, many years before. The mission had been established in 1780 or thereabouts,[83] and our Catholic forefathers had here enjoyed quiet and repose, sheltered by the good feeling and good wishes of the inhabitants. But since the passing of the Emancipation Act, the old inhabitants had gradually passed away, and their children had gone elsewhere. The result was that, in 1868, there was not work for a priest, nor sufficient support for the mission. The chapel, priest's house, and adjoining buildings were all falling into a state of extreme dilapidation. There had been no resident priest nor Sunday Mass for more than twelve months. The desolation was complete.

This condition of things had for a long time been a matter of deep regret. I had often heard the late venerated Vicar-General, Dr. Oleron, say he wishes something could be done for 'poor little Shefford,' as he used to call it. These old recollections must have moved me, and I gladly accepted the Bishop's offer.

After I had been at Shefford a little while, it suggested itself – Surely this must be the place designed for the Orphanage the Bishop has need of; and with his permission, I began the foundation on the 11th of April, 1869.

How providentially all had been arranged! The property adjoining the priest's house was freehold: belonging to the mission, and could be made to accommodate forty boys. But there was little else. A large outlay would be required to make the old buildings fit for use: wind and water must be kept out, and for this money would be needed; and of money I had none. I was not dismayed: I heard of good old priests – Alas! now no more – who were astonished at my want of prudence. I never saw it. I was saying to myself – Who is to provide the means? Under whose patronage shall I place the work? Who is to stand before God as the Friend and Patron of this institution? – Who

83 As we have seen in chapter 4, it is not surprising that Collis could not date the start of the mission more precisely.

so fitting as the great S. Francis? – His love of poverty will cause him to smile, for he must be pleased with a beginning like this. I was not mistaken; and so it came to pass, that my anxieties – and I must have had many – quickly disappeared, leaving no impression behind, so that I can scarcely remember their ever having existed.

Then I adopted S. Francis' mode of begging from door to door; this has always been to me a great cross, which has not become less heavy after carrying its weight for fifteen years; S. Francis' prayers have brought a special blessing upon a task so distasteful; and in this way success has been achieved. But I am forestalling. No sooner was it known that this work was to be begun for God and His orphans, than it happened, as I believe it always will, kind friends appeared tendering assistance. One gentleman and members of his family at Northampton raised a sum of three hundred pounds, and a great nobleman, coming of age about that time, sent me two hundred pounds. I mention these because, although larger gifts have since been placed in my hands, none have given me so much surprise and pleasure. In those days my mind had never conceived that such offerings as these would be made. I will state here that this nobleman, his Grace the Duke of Norfolk, in the course of the following ten years, sent to me contributions towards the buildings which amounted to more than two thousand pounds.

I will here relate another incident which touched me much. I must preface by saying that I have the gift, and I am thankful for it, of taking small offerings and even refusals with contentment. In the long course of fifteen years, I can only remember on two or three occasions being annoyed with the result of my application. But on a certain day when I had been soliciting very earnestly one who I knew had the means of giving, and the result of my urgent begging was *two shillings*, I must say I felt annoyed, but no word escaped me. I took the offering and went my way. Shortly after, this person died, and within a few weeks I received a cheque for two hundred pounds – a legacy for the Orphanage. I can't describe my feelings on receiving it. I was very thankful for the gift, very thankful for my silence on the occasion above referred to, but I felt also that at that time I had been wanting in my heart of a right judgement of the donor.

But I must go back to say the old houses were repaired, partition walls knocked down, and by this means a dormitory large enough for twenty boys was obtained. I was obliged to do a bit of building to provide a schoolroom and another dormitory – S. Francis' Dormitory – and this first extension has been carefully preserved, and remains surrounded at this time by the various buildings which constitute S. Francis' Home. In this way provision for forty boys was made. There can be little doubt all was as humble and as poor as it well could be, yet I remember the joy I had when so much had been accomplished, with what satisfaction I walked through the poor old room, and the pleasure I had in the new one. I have had nothing like it since. It seemed as if I could wish for nothing better, and I remember I was not a little surprised when visitors failed to recognise all that was so patent in my eyes.

I must record another special providence. At the time I was doing this work, there resided near me a very worthy lawyer – not a Catholic – who took a great interest in my doings. It happened, as it will happen, when I was making the preparations spoken of above, I discovered that the ground was hardly large enough for our needs and I ventured to inquire of this good man whether it was possible to purchase the adjoining property. He undertook to find this out, and in a short time he let me know the result. The owner would *not* part with it. I thought no more about it, and did my best with the ground at my disposal. On the day the buildings were being inspected previous to the opening of the Home, I had a message from the lawyer, asking me to go over to his office. I went. 'You remember,' he said, 'asking me about the adjoining property?' 'And I remember,' I replied, 'the answer you sent me.' He proceeded, 'The property has been offered to me to-day, and if you like you shall have it.' I at once closed with this generous offer. This good man was a great benefactor to S. Francis' Home. Without this addition it would have been impossible to have made the Orphanage what it has since become.

To my very great regret, my worthy friend died very suddenly, shortly after rendering me this great service. He never had the satisfaction of seeing any portion of the new buildings. But what he did for the Orphanage will not be forgotten in the great day of account. It was nearly two years before I had possession of this property: S. Francis' Home had been opened on the 11th of April, 1870: and by the end of 1873 the work was so far declared a success that it was resolved to commence the rebuilding of the Home.

Looked at to-day this would be thought a great undertaking, but the idea of doing even half so much was not present to me. It could not have been entertained for a moment. My plan was to add to the existing buildings what was most required, and afterwards to replace bit by bit – as the means came to hand – the old tumble-down houses and out-house, with new erections. And not even so much as this could have been determined upon had it not been that God had been preparing for this work a special friend – one whose great interest in the Home, and more especially in its inmates, had been made evident; and of whose liberality – boundless, I might almost call it – I had received by this time abundant proof.

I well remember the day I saw this benefactor for the first time. I was on one of my begging tours, and had walked some miles from the place I was at to his house. He received me with all the kindness and hospitality which is so eminently the characteristic of the fine old English gentleman. This he was to perfection. I told him my tale; he listened attentively, said the work doubtless was a good one, and expressed his approval. But, as he gave me nothing, I came away without an idea that I had had my first interview with one chosen to be the munificent benefactor of S. Francis' Home. This gentleman was the late John Eyston, of Walford (*vere* Welford).[84] His bounty freed me from the debt incurred by the purchase of the adjoining property. Doubtless it was that, having become assured of his interest and friendship, the idea of rebuilding the house came to be entertained, and the work determined upon. The first of the new buildings was commenced upon the ground lately purchased, and from that day this portion of S. Francis' Home has been called after the name of our benefactor – the Eyston Buildings. His bounty, I trust, in this way will be commemorated as long as the Home shall stand.

Before taking leave of him, let me say that though on that first visit he gave me nothing, for the next ten years – alas! his life was not spared longer – I never saw him without his placing in my hands a cheque for a large amount, and this without any solicitation. He never waited to be asked. He had the grace to give as if he was receiving a favour, not conferring one. He always asked to be prayed for, and begged that his bounty might not be made known. He died on the 30th of May, 1882.

[84] See p. 116.

I must now relate that the same wonderful Providence that I have been declaring, as attending the commencement and the continuance of work, accompanied it to its completion. Shortly before Mr. Eyston was removed from this life to his reward, I called for the first time upon a lady whom God had designed to finish S. Francis' Home. The great want required for its completion was a church. It is not necessary to repeat what has been said in former reports of our poor little chapel, and how utterly inadequate it was to accommodate the inmates of the Home and the Catholics of Shefford.

I had made a resolution that I would not commence the building of the church unless I had in hand the money to pay for it. The last fifteen years had made an old man of me, and I had no longer the strength of body required for the labour of raising several thousand pounds. As this was so, I had accustomed myself to the thought that it would not be permitted to me to see the new church. On my second visit to this lady – Mrs. Lyne Stephens – I was led once to say, 'A church is very much needed – it would be a great work to do for God and His orphans. How grateful they would be, and their prayers are of much account before God.' I did not say many more words than are put down here.[85]

Two months afterwards, I was informed this lady had written to the Bishop to say she would build the church. The foundation stone was laid on the Feast of S. Francis, October 4th, 1882, the seven hundredth anniversary of the birth of this great Saint. It was consecrated on July 3rd, 1884, and it was solemnly opened on July 8th, 1884. I must now add that the same noble lady to whose bounty we are indebted for this beautiful church has since, in her goodness, paid the debt on the buildings of S. Francis' Home. She did this, as she most kindly expressed it, that I might be freed from the anxiety that a grave burden of debt must always occasion; and that I might have a little repose after the fatigue of the labour of so many years. Her thoughtful consideration made this great gift doubly welcome. How can I write down what I feel, even if it would be becoming to express it? Works such as these cannot be sufficiently acknowledged by man: their reward must be left to God.

I have engaged in narrating the foundation of the Orphanage, and how it came to pass that I was enabled to rebuild S. Francis' Home and to build the church, but I must not omit to commemorate those numberless benefactors, living and dead, whose names have appeared annually in the subscription list. A large pile of buildings, though much to look at, are of little worth unless filled by the orphans for whose benefit they were designed. In fifteen years the bountiful aims of generous benefactors have enabled me to receive, educate, and dispose of two hundred and seventeen boys; and I pray they may have the reward spoken of by the prophet, – 'that they that aid many to justice, shall shine as the stars for all eternity.'

I must now bring this narrative to an end. I wish I could have done it better; but I trust that all those who have read what I have written, will be induced to agree with me that great things have been done at Shefford: much greater than anything I myself could have brought to pass, and that the praise is due to GOD and S. FRANCIS.

WILLIAM COLLIS

85 Mrs Lyne Stephens, see pp. 100–1.

Chapter 7

Fresh fields and new harvests

In Bedfordshire, as in the country as a whole, the second half of the nineteenth century was generally a period of substantial population growth, as evidenced by the decennial census returns, with Shefford as a clear exception.

Table 6. Bedfordshire population statistics, 1841–1901

	1841	**1851**	**1861**	**1871**	**1881**	**1891**	**1901**
Bedford	9,178	11,693	13,413	16,850	19,533	28,023	35,144
Luton (civil parish)	7,748	12,787	17,821	20,733	26,140	32,401	–
Luton (township)	5,827	10,648	15,329	17,317	–	–	–
Luton (borough)	–	–	–	–	23,960	30,063	36,404
Shefford	902	1,115	1,071	1,182	1,123	1,055	936
Bedfordshire	108,000	124,000	135,000	146,000	149,000	161,000	172,000

Across Great Britain as a whole the population increased from 15.9 million to 32.5 million (104%). As a county Bedfordshire failed to match this rate of increase, rising by approximately 60%, but both Bedford and Luton outstripped it, Bedford rising by 280% and Luton by 370%.[1] It was not just that the urban populations were growing, of course. Larger populations demanded increased opportunities for employment and improved communications. In Bedford this growth in employment came principally in the brewing and engineering sectors, drawing in workers mainly from the county's rural areas.

We have seen how Shefford's population had more than doubled in the first half of the century, reaching a total of 1,115 by 1851 (see p. 60). During that time, however, its Catholic population failed to keep pace and by the 1850s was in quite serious decline. The appointment of Rev. Collis, and his relatively long period of ministry in the town, halted that decline and Shefford became an important Catholic centre again, though more because of its two institutions (the orphanage and seminary) than its general Catholic population. Canon Collis claimed in 1880 that there were 153 Catholics served by the mission at Shefford. Unfortunately, there are no reliable statistics for the size of the Catholic community across the county as a whole.

Meanwhile, given the growth in the population of the county town and its obvious importance, it is not surprising that Bishop Amherst saw Bedford as a place that called for the establishment of its own mission centre. It was, however, a strongly Protestant

1 Anne Allsopp, *The Education and Employment of Girls in Luton, 1874–1924: Widening Opportunities and Lost Freedoms*, BHRS, vol. 84 (Woodbridge, 2005), pp. 2–3.

Canon John Priestley Warmoll, 1885. Founder of the Bedford mission, 1863–85. (courtesy of the Diocese of Northampton)

town, proud of its Bunyan heritage and, according to the 1851 religious census, with one of the highest levels of religious practice in the country.[2] The difficult task of establishing a Catholic presence there was given to the Rev. John Priestley Warmoll, its first resident Catholic priest since the sixteenth century.[3] A convert Anglican clergyman, he was sent to Bedford in 1863, arriving on 24 December, to see if it would be possible to open a Catholic mission there; he was to refer to this later as a 'forlorn hope … to look up the stray Catholics there', of whom about twenty were known.[4]

Among them were the Tandy family, living at the time at 7, Little Grove Place and it was there that he stayed for a few weeks and used his room as a Mass centre. It appears that his first public services were his three Masses on Christmas Day, when a total of fourteen people attended. He was to describe the room he used as a 'crowded room, of eleven feet square'.[5] He soon moved from there and rented the first floor of 48 Offa Street (now 60 Tavistock Street), knocking the two bedrooms into one to form a chapel.[6]

2 On the census see D. W. Busby (ed.), 'The Ecclesiastical Census, Bedfordshire, March 1851', pp. 109–200. On the difficulties of interpretation, see W. S. F. Pickering, 'The 1851 Religious Census – a Useless Experiment?', in *British Journal of Sociology*, vol. 18 (1967), p. 393.

3 A 2004 biography of Warmoll: Jack Robbins, *John Priestley Warmoll, Apostle of Bedford: His Life, Times and Family* (Downham Market, 2004), privately published, gives a detailed account of his work and achievements, as well as of his family background (he was a relative of the famous scientist Joseph Priestley). It has been very useful in drawing up this account.

4 *The Bedfordshire Times*, 16 May 1874; for the names of some of the Catholics concerned see the registers below, pp. 189, 213–14.

5 See the description by Rev. Wrigglesworth, Warmoll's successor in Bedford, quoted in Robbins, *John Priestley Warmoll*, p. 107. It was the traditional custom for priests to celebrate three Masses on Christmas Day; see *ODCC*, p. 281.

6 Warmoll probably already knew the Tandy family; one of its members was the Rev. William Tandy (1807–86) of the Birmingham Diocese, ordained in 1833, a regular correspondent of

His immediate task of getting himself known and established in the town cannot have been helped by the welcome given in April to the great Italian hero Garibaldi as he visited the local Britannia Iron Works. The streets of the town were decorated, ecstatic crowds welcomed his arrival and *The Bedfordshire Times* dedicated a special edition to him as the champion of liberty and tolerance, and the enemy of every sort of despotism including, of course, that of the pope. His reception was such that the authorities, fearing popular outbreaks, cancelled the rest of his planned visits around the country. The Catholic *Tablet* referred to him as a 'foreign adventurer' with no right to the titles of 'liberator and statesman' that he was being given; later it attacked the Anglican bishops for their reception of him. Bishop Ullathorne, Catholic bishop of Birmingham, denounced him as the 'High Priest of the Goddess of Reason'. But Garibaldi remained a popular hero and the market for souvenirs and memorabilia (including biscuits) assured his celebrity status and can only have heightened Bedford's anti-Catholicism.[7]

Given this atmosphere and the tiny number of known Catholics in the area, Warmoll was forced to look outside the town for the funding he needed and to appeal to the wider Catholic community around the country and even beyond. His early begging letters appeared mainly in *The Tablet* and *The Weekly Register*, the two principal Catholic newspapers of the day. The first of these, *The Tablet*, was a weekly founded in 1840 by a Catholic layman, Edwin Lucas. In 1868 its ownership passed to Fr Vaughan, later the cardinal-archbishop of Westminster, but it did not become an official publication. (It is still being published weekly.)

The other paper used by Warmoll for his appeals was *The Weekly Register*, founded in 1849; its full title was *The Weekly Register, A Catholic Journal of Literature, Correspondence and Intelligence*. Like many similar papers, Catholic and otherwise, it had a chequered career and a number of owners; it folded in 1850, but was re-launched five years later as *The Weekly Register and Standard*, run by Henry Wilberforce, a convert to Catholicism. This title lasted until 1863 and was a rival to *The Tablet* which was thought by some to be too Irish and domineering. *The Weekly Register* was more 'liberal' with regard to Catholic doctrines, and willingly printed letters questioning, for example, the wisdom of defining papal infallibility. Eventually, in 1881, Cardinal Manning rescued it from collapse and gave it to Wilfrid Meynell as editor. Despite his imaginative and versatile leadership the paper failed to be a serious rival to *The Tablet*, though it lasted for another eighteen years or so.[8]

Wiseman under whom he had studied at Oscott. The two female members living in Little Grove Place died very shortly after Warmoll's visit: Ellen Monica (a daughter?), in September 1864, aged twenty-nine, and Eleanor Mary in October 1865, aged sixty-one (see death registers, p. 214). Their two gravestones in Bedford cemetery were recently restored; see Adrian Bean (ed.), *Bedford's Victorian Cemetery* (Bedford, 2021?), p. 147, and Robbins, *John Priestley Warmoll*, pp. 113–14. A son (?) Francis features as godfather in the baptism register, 19 February 1865 and 7 March 1868; he later emigrated to Australia.

7 *The Tablet*, April 1864 and *Bedfordshire Mercury*, 16 April 1864. Garibaldi had spent some years in South America, which had earned him the title of 'pirate'. Wiseman preached against him in his Trinity Sunday pastoral letter.

8 See Michael Walsh's short but insightful history, *The Tablet, 1840–1990: A Commemorative History* (London, 1990). He deals with *The Weekly Register* in passing (pp. 14–21). See also Beck, *The English Catholics*, pp. 504–5.

Both papers published general national and international news as well as Catholic news, and had lively letters pages. Even allowing for the purpose of Warmoll's letters and their necessarily sympathetic slant, we can get an insight from them both of the origins of the Bedford mission and of himself as the first resident missioner in what was a strongly Protestant town. It is also interesting that he frequently listed at the end of a letter the donations he had received recently. As early as January 1864, for example,

> 5*l.* for the altar from M.G; 5s. from Winchester; 5s. from a poor servant at Reading; 2*l.* from the congregation at Weston Underwood; 10s. from Anglo-Saxon; 14s. from Eardington; 2s. from Stourbridge.

Given its earlier links with Shefford, the £2 from the congregation at Weston Underwood is interesting.

The benefit of using the national press for his appeals is immediately obvious; other lists mention gifts from all over the country as well as from Ireland. He was obviously a successful beggar: this early letter to *The Tablet* is a good example of his approach.

> Dear Mr. Editor, Again I find myself compelled to beg in your columns, and for God's dear sake, I trust that it may not be in vain, as He knows it is not for myself but for Him.
>
> Although our tiny chapel, consisting of two bed-rooms, is by far too diminutive for our numbers, and although I have not a servant of any kind to wait upon me, yet I feel that to support things even as they are my dear little band of Catholics is already taxed beyond its means.
>
> Once more, after the lapse of centuries, the Sanctuary lamp burns in this town before the Divine Presence, and Jesus in the most Holy Sacrament dwells lovingly as of old, and silently drawing (*sic*) devout souls to visit Him.
>
> Oh! for the love of Him who has given such a gift to men, dear children of Holy Church suffer not the lamp to go out, compel not that Presence to be withdrawn.
>
> You never can estimate the value of the smallest act done for the love of Him. Think on this, and send us *something*, however trifling it may seem, and may our Holy Child, His Immaculate Mother, and St. Joseph, bless you.
>
> Yours etc., JOHN PRIESTLEY WARMOLL, 48 Offa-street (*sic*), Bedford.[9]

Obviously, he had already chosen the name of the new mission. Within a few months he estimated that the number of Catholics attending his small chapel was over 100, creating obvious problems:

> Picture to yourselves, in the midst of this town, where each Protestant sect is amply supplied with its elegant and commodious place of meeting, our poor congregation of the Faithful crowded around the altar of God in an atmosphere already unhealthy and suffocating.[10]

Later in the year this unhealthy atmosphere was beginning to have a practical outcome: in May he cancelled the Sunday evening service 'as we are crammed, squeezed and half-suffocated, so that it would be imprudent to go on with them any longer'. His appeals, fortunately, were still effective:

9 'Mission of the Holy Child and St. Joseph, Bedford', *The Tablet*, 30 January 1864.
10 *The Weekly Register*, 30 April 1864.

> Received with many thanks – L.C., 12s; T.W., 2 *ls*; Torquay, 5s; Dublin Widow's mite, 3s.; Poor Weaver, Blackburn, 6d.; a gold ring; London, W., 2s 6d.; E.J.W. Durrow, 1*l*,1s.; Mary Eliz., 5s.; M. and S.W., Leamington, 2s 6d.; Poor Widow, 2s.; C. Elliott, 5s.

There were, he reported, 'fainting scenes, Sunday after Sunday', and the influx of Irish harvest labourers: 'generous as we know they are with what they have, it is not fresh air or an increase of space' that they bring.[11] It was not all gloom, however. In October of that year he reported a donation of £5 from Lord Edward Howard of Glossop, in response to his press appeals, with permission to use the accompanying letter as he thought best:

> Rev. Sir,
>
> I cannot but think that Bedford, with its present isolated congregation – with more than 14,000 inhabitants – with, no doubt, periodical accession of Irish harvest labourers – its prison – its poorhouse – its five lines of railway – and proximity to the metropolis (thus probably receiving Catholics, who, educated in London schools, wander into the country and become lost), must be well entitled to the possession of a chapel and resident Priest.
>
> I therefore send you for this object a small additional donation, and regret that the demands upon me and the distress of this neighbourhood, prevent my giving more to advance so necessary a purpose.
>
> Yours truly,
>
> E. G. F. Howard[12]

Among other issues that the small number of Bedford Catholics had to cope with, not mentioned by Howard, was the continuing anti-Catholicism in the town. As might be expected, Warmoll's reception was initially unfriendly, to put it mildly, with the long-standing anti-papalism strengthened in the minds of some by the apparent revival of Roman sentiments and practices among the Anglican establishment. Letters to the local press in the 1870s, for example, were as likely to be objecting to ritualism in the Church of England as to the revival of Roman Catholicism, with particular antipathy to the developing practice of auricular confession.[13] Similar fears were also to be found among some of the local Non-conformist meetings, across a range of social groups. The *Labourers' Union Chronicle*, for example, reported from Eversholt that meetings had been held there on a Sunday afternoon and evening, organised by the Protestant Evangelical Mission, and each attended by an average of about 400 people. One of the aims of the occasion was to 'counteract the subtle and wide-spreading influences of popery'.[14]

Warmoll had himself referred to the 'active hostile neighbourhood'. When he had been burying one of his parishioners in March 1865 in the town cemetery 'he was surrounded by a vicious crowd … whose behaviour was outrageous'.[15] But he went

11 *The Tablet*, 15 August 1864.

12 *The Weekly Register*, 8 October 1864, see also Robbins, *John Priestley Warmoll*, p. 119.

13 See for example *The Bedfordshire Times and Independent* for 1876–77: the most frequent topic in the correspondence columns would appear to be the development of ritualism in the Church of England.

14 Nigel E. Agar, *The Bedfordshire Farm Worker in the Nineteenth Century*, BHRS, vol. 60 (Bedford, 1981), p. 182, entry for 16 August 1873.

15 Robbins, *John Priestley Warmoll*, p. 121; see death registers, p. 214, entry for Catherine Huckle.

ahead and in April 1867 applied to the clerks of the peace for a licence to open a place of public worship. The application referred to 'a building adjoining the dwelling house of John P. Warmoll in New Street [presumably Brereton Rd], running out of Midland Road', and registered by John Priestley Warmoll of Bedford, Catholic Priest.[16] Another licence, this time to celebrate marriages in the 'Catholic School Room' in Midland Road, was granted in January 1872, later replaced in April 1878 by the 'Church of the Holy Child and St Joseph in Midland Road'[17]

A letter to the *Weekly Register* of 25 June 1870 from an unknown correspondent picks up the theme of local Protestant antipathy towards Catholics in the town:

> Isolated as we are from the mass of English Catholics … prevented by want of a church from extending the borders of our little fold, looked down upon and scorned by those who are only too eager to crush and destroy us as a congregation, we have no recourse under the providence of God but the kind sympathy and co-operation of our fellow Catholics.

What is very unusual in this letter is the picture it presents of the varied nature of the growing congregation:

> We are a strange combination here of diverse elements and nationalities. On Sunday last I saw a Hindoo and an Irishman bent together before the same altar, while English, French and German hearts were at the same time pouring their tales of sorrow before the throne of Him … whose ear is open to the wail of every creature, no matter from what clime he may derive the accident of his birth. … As every cloud has a silvery lining, we hope that our days of darkness are about to draw to a close …

No doubt a major element in that 'silvery lining' would be the provision of a permanent church building, giving Catholics a public presence and position in the town, with an accompanying respectability to match that of the other local religious bodies, including even the town's ancient parish churches. No one could any longer doubt that they were 'here to stay': it would be a worthy restoring of the glory that in Catholic eyes the town had lacked for centuries. There would no longer be a need for the cautious approach of former times: perhaps the convert clergymen, in particular, played an important part in developing and strengthening this renewed confidence.

For ten years this had been the objective of Warmoll's persistent begging. He had chosen a site in Midland Road, Bedford, for his new church which was to be dedicated to The Holy Child and St Joseph. The architect was Gilbert Blount (1818–76), a keen admirer of Pugin and the designer of a number of Catholic churches, schools and convents around the country. His biographer says that most of his work was carried out for relatives or friends; it is not clear whether Warmoll fell within these categories or not, but since Blount worked on the Catholic school in nearby Wolverton and designed St Edward's Catholic church in Cambridge, Warmoll would certainly have known of his work. It is more likely, however, that the link came through Bishop Amherst: he and his brother were close family friends of Gilbert and the Blount family. Blount was certainly in contact with Warmoll from 1865 (in his diary he

16 See Welch, *Bedfordshire Chapels and Meeting Houses*, p. 36.

17 *Ibid.*, p. 37. See pp. 56–7, for registration of the old Shefford chapel.

refers to him as Mr Priestley Warmoll) and drew up his first plans for a church in the town as early as the following year.[18]

This original plan was for a cluster of buildings (sacristy, presbytery, hall and schools) around a central church with a large bell-tower at its west end: a Catholic enclave in a Protestant stronghold. The first of these to be completed was the chapel-cum-schoolroom (now called the Guildroom); when the bishop visited in February 1866 to administer confirmation (to twenty-two candidates), he also laid the foundation stone of the new building. Mass was first celebrated there in March 1867, followed a month later by the completion of the adjoining presbytery, in Brereton Road, allowing Warmoll to move from the cramped quarters in Offa Street. Work on the church itself, however, was delayed for financial reasons and did not start until 1872. By then the need for something larger than the temporary chapel was obvious: Warmoll claimed that the number of Easter communicants that year was tenfold what it had been in 1864.[19]

The eventual opening of the church in 1874 received full coverage in the national Catholic press and also locally; reactions were very largely positive. In *The Bedfordshire Times and Independent*, for example, the style was described, perhaps a little uncertainly, as 'somewhat after the model of the late period of Early English'; the description continued,

> the nave is exceedingly graceful and bold, though plain and unornamented, and is divided by (*sic*) either aisle by rows of slender columns which carry a lofty roof with very effective clerestory lighted on either side by windows of subdued colouring. The chancel arch is one of the most beautiful features of the design. The sanctuary is the only decorated or ornamental portion of the sacred edifice …

The paper's account went on to describe some of the 'limited ornamentation', which included,

> The chancel arch springs at each end from a bas-relief: one representing St. Gregory teaching children the Chant, while the other is an illustration of St. Cecilia playing a harp … The sanctuary is exquisitely designed and is chastely decorated with Minton's encaustic tiles … The altar rests on miniature columns with marble shafts and the tabernacle is also cut out of marble with much care and delicacy of workmanship, the door being studded with jewels.[20]

For its part, *The Builder* reported that the stone used came from Warrington, near Olney, with Bath stone for the dressings; it thought one of its best features was the chancel's 'groined wooden roof' with bosses representing the Holy Child, the Agnus Dei ('Lamb of God'), the Pelican and the IHS (the accepted abbreviation for the Greek form of Jesus) symbols. Other images below the chancel arch represented

18 For an account of Blount's work based on his diaries, see Philippa Hunter and Richard Barton, 'Gilbert Blount: A Victorian Architect through his diaries', docslib.org, accessed online 22 September 2020. The fullest treatment is in Constance C. McPhee, 'Gilbert R. Blount (1819–1876). Catholic Gothic Revival Architect', a thesis presented to the University of Pennsylvania, for the Degree of Master of Arts, 1987 – a well-documented study based on the Blount archive (now housed at the university) and the architectural press of the day.

19 Robbins, *John Priestley Warmoll*, p. 135.

20 Ran for two weeks, 9 May 1874 and 16 May 1874.

The Church of the Holy Child and St Joseph, Midland Road, Bedford, 1917.
The view shows the exterior of the church on the corner of Midland Road and Brereton Road.
(courtesy of Bedfordshire Archives, Z1306/11/10/1)

Archbishop (later Cardinal) Manning and Bishop Amherst.[21] Coloured marble was used for some of the pillars (kept slender to assist visibility), as well as for the pulpit and baptismal font. All the descriptions mention the 'Stations of the Cross' around the walls; the set had been painted and donated by a French artist, the Marchioness Di Savio, and were a very unusual feature in churches at the time. There was certainly nothing make-shift or temporary about the building, although it was one of Blount's plainer churches, presumably to keep the costs as low as possible. Both Warmoll and Blount would have agreed with Pugin's declaration, 'It is … by parish churches, that the faith of a nation is to be sustained and nourished'.[22]

It was not only the building that struck a positive note. The whole occasion was outstanding; indeed, the local population, including Catholics, probably found it quite amazing, considering the shortness of time that Warmoll had been in the town and the apparently total lack of any Catholic presence there before his arrival. No less a figure than Archbishop Manning preached at the opening Mass and later attended a ceremonial lunch, along with Bishop Amherst and a guest list such as Bedford can rarely have seen, composed of Catholics and non-Catholics: the Earl of Denbigh presided, with fellow guests Lord Walter and Lady Anabel Kerr (responsible for the Lady altar), Mrs Arkwright of Knuston Hall (near Irthlingborough), the Honourable Lady Simeon and her three daughters,[23] Dr Coombs of the Bunyan Meeting,

21 Description in *The Builder*, 19 September 1874.

22 Quoted in Rosemary Hill, *God's Architect*, p. 241.

23 The widow of Sir John Simeon, Bart., a Catholic landowner and MP from Swainton, Isle of Wight, who had died in 1870.

Mr Thomas Shepherd JP and his wife, Mr Alderman Bull, Councillor Mr Horsford, Mr and Mrs Lane of the *Universe* newspaper, Mr E. de Vere Corcoran,[24] Mr Everard Green FSA, M and Mme Schaedelin,[25] Mr and Mrs Eyston,[26] and some members of Warmoll's family. These and the rest of the guests drank the health of the Pope and the Queen and the various notables present. Such a list of guests, and the overall financial support he raised in so relatively short a time, are witness not just to Warmoll's persistence as a fund-raiser but to his, and the bishop's, family and social connections.[27]

Unfortunately, Blount was too ill to attend; he was to die in 1876. The president of the RIBA later summed up Blount, rather dismissively, as having been

> responsible for a small body of interesting but unadventurous works, variable in quality. Whilst he was not in the top flight as a designer, his work often had character – a personal flavour – due to his choice of parts and, at times, the wayward handling of their details …

Financial constraints remained, however: spending on the church was more or less double what Warmoll had estimated – and despite his intensive fund-raising, not all the building work (by the firm of John Watkin of Northampton) could be completed in this first stage, although what was built was impressive enough: the chancel, side chapels (which *The Tablet* called 'perfect gems of Catholic architecture')[28] and two-thirds of the nave; the remainder, planned for 1877, was delayed until 1912 and completed by Blount's successor, A. E. Purdie, who had already carried out some alterations to the altar and reredos in 1889. The planned bell-tower (important for some Pugin disciples to make urban churches stand out from their built-up surroundings) was never completed.[29]

We have a summary of the building costs involved, dating from 1878:

	£	£
Land for church and presbytery	380	
Building presbytery & large room	1,450	
Architect's commission	74	1,904
Building church	3,572	
Architect's commission	185	

24 de Vere Corcoran was a successful shoe manufacturer. He later gave money for a new Sacred Heart side-altar, and left over £6,000 in legacies to the bishop; see Diaries of Bishop Riddell, June 1887 and July 1893, NDA, Box 157. A large collection of Riddell's personal correspondence has recently been acquired by the NDA; as yet it is un-catalogued.

25 A very complimentary report in *The Bedfordshire Times and Independent* for 28 July 1877, p. 6, describes the annual prize day at a preparatory school in Bedford run by Madame Schoedelin, presumably the same lady; it was not a Catholic school. The family name occurs quite frequently in the registers in the 1870s.

26 See p. 116.

27 Robbins, *John Priestley Warmoll*, p. 149, for list of guests. The sermon and speeches are given in full in *The Bedfordshire Times and Independent*; there are reports in all the local papers and *The Tablet*. Various collections on the day raised over £200.

28 9 May 1874.

29 Robbins, *John Priestley Warmoll*, pp. 143–51. See also the *Bedfordshire Mercury*, 12 January 1912.

Clerk of works, salary	200	
Roads and pavement	59	4,016
TOTAL		5,920

Clearly, such costs could not be met by the small contributions raised by Warmoll's letters to the press. One remarkable feature of his fund-raising was how he involved Catholic children. He had decided that they should pay for the altar and sanctuary in the church and sent out appeals accordingly. The response was remarkable and resulted in contributions coming in from rich and poor children across the country and beyond: London, Liverpool, Pantasaph, Ryde, Roscrea, Cork, Dublin, Detroit, Barcelona, Paris, Pau and even the Grand Duchy of Baden. He listed almost 2,000 names of young donors between 1865 and 1874. (The book of names was deposited under the new high altar and discovered in 1986 during the re-ordering of the sanctuary.) Despite the obvious need for fund-raising Warmoll refused to introduce bench rents.

As we have seen, his persistence paid off, and not just in connection with the building of the church and associated fund-raising: his work for the education of the poor won general praise (see chapter 10 below) and he seems to have gradually become an accepted figure in the town, if perhaps a somewhat eccentric one. The following extracts are from a local non-sectarian monthly journal:

> Consistency and devotion to duty tell in the long run even with the intensely stupid and consequently bigoted partisan. The methods of the sects, whose devotees are trained to look solely at one point of the compass, to hug the little crotchet of their sect as the sole sublime truth of the universe, and to regard all outsiders as beyond the pale of hope and almost of social recognition, these methods may increase the numbers of the sects, but they diminish and often extinguish the charity which is, or should be, the brightest Christian virtue.

This is from *The Bedford Bee*, 13 August 1879. After this general attack on religious bigots, typical of the views of those who saw themselves as more 'enlightened', the writer continued by commenting on Warmoll and his work in the town:

> When first Canon Warmoll came to Bedford he was received with much the same sort of welcome as Bunyan received from his fellow Christians who put him in prison for preaching an unpopular gospel. Suspiciousness and the hate of ignorant Protestantism would probably have terminated in open hostility – as indeed we heard that it did on a few occasions – but for the leavening influence of calm superiority to the opposition of prejudice. Canon Warmoll came on a Quixotic mission, as might have been supposed, to the land of Bunyan, and under auspices which less brave men might have quailed under.

This was one of a series of articles entitled 'Our Public Men', with friendly cartoons; the piece could hardly have been more praiseworthy if it had appeared in the Catholic press. It also praises the church Warmoll was building, both physically and as a community, and speaks of his 'scientific attainments and broad sympathies'. The local Literary and Scientific Institute even elected him as its president and, according to the *Bee*, 'no scientific gathering is complete … unless the popular Canon is there to add his store of information'.[30]

30 *The Bedford Bee*, 13 August 1879.

Canon John Priestley Warmoll, *Bedford Bee* cartoon 13 August 1879. (courtesy of Bedford Central Library)

One needs to be cautious here; while the *Bee* probably reflected the views of some people in the town, its circulation was never large and it ceased publication altogether a year later, citing a lack of support. More in tune with popular opinion was *The Bedfordshire Times and Independent*, and its favourable description of Warmoll on the occasion of the opening of the new church is more balanced:

> Though a University man of high attainments and wide culture, the fact of his having been an Anglican clergyman added a fresh difficulty in the way of his social recognition; but though Mr. Warmoll found himself then and for some time afterwards a stranger, he is so no longer. Many people who … treated him with disrespect now acknowledge and appreciate his uniform good temper, his kindly disposition, and his unceasing exertions on behalf of the poor …[31]

It is of some interest that when he had been created a canon of the diocese in the previous year, the provost at his installation had made special mention of,

> his persevering labours and … conciliating conduct [that has] succeeded in putting away prejudice, securing the esteem and goodwill of Protestants.[32]

By the time of Warmoll's death in February 1885, the statistics show a steady growth in the number of Bedford's Catholics, compared with the early 1860s:

Annual Return 1885

Catholic population	290+
Baptisms	infants 15, converts 5

31 9 May 1874; Robbins, *John Priestley Warmoll*, p. 144.
32 Robbins, *John Priestley Warmoll*, p. 141.

Confirmations	20
Easter communicants	123
Average Mass attendance	155
Children of school age	64
Catholic children on rolls	35
Average school attendance	121
Marriages	2 (+ 1 elsewhere)
Burials	8 (+ 2 elsewhere)
Special collections	Peter's Pence 9/6[33]
	Bishop's income £1/0/0
	Poor missions 10/–
	Poor Schools Cttee 7/6
	St. Francis' Home £1/10s

It is noteworthy that while the average school attendance was 121, the number of Catholic children on the rolls was only thirty-five, not much more than a quarter of the total and certainly not enough to keep the schools going without the non-Catholic children; more will be said about this in chapter ten, on education.

We can get a clear picture of his pastoral success from his carefully maintained registers. Taking the baptismal ones (see pp. 189–99), we see that in his early years numbers were predictably low: in the period 1864–67 the annual totals were only five, two, four and four. They soon rose, however, so that for the ten years from 1870–79 the annual average was sixteen, with an outstanding peak of thirty-five in 1877. Twelve of these baptisms are marked 'conditional', meaning that they were of adults or older children where there was doubt whether they had been already baptised (perhaps in a different denomination), or there was some doubt about the validity of such a previous ceremony, or no reliable evidence to support a claim to have been baptised.

The marriage register (see p. 210), perhaps not surprisingly, gives a different picture: there were no Catholic weddings in the parish until 1872, when there were two; each of the next four years saw just one each year. The remainder of Warmoll's ministry saw between two and three each year, though this may be misleading: there were two years without any, and one year, 1883, with six. The sacrament of confirmation could only be administered by a bishop. The first visit for this is registered in January 1866; it must have been something of a notable celebration, with eight boys and fourteen girls confirmed. Episcopal visits followed at approximately five-year intervals; a peak year was 1877 when fifteen boys and twenty-five girls were confirmed.[34] The average annual number of deaths over the first ten years was three.[35]

Overall, the statistics give a picture of positive pastoral achievements in what remained a strongly Protestant town and its surrounding area. It must have seemed that Warmoll had established a strong enough hub for a Catholic community to

33 Peter's Pence: the annual worldwide collection for the personal upkeep of the pope.

34 The register lists the individual names, along with the names taken in confirmation; sponsors appear to act for groups of the children, not individually as became the practice.

35 See death registers, pp. 213–16.

coalesce around, with the provision of regular liturgical services backed up by seasonal celebrations, social events and, of course, the school. Certainly, local obituaries of him were highly praiseworthy, even allowing for some regret over his conversion to Catholicism in the first place. As one of them put it, he was 'an all round man':

> A man of the most varied intelligence, an ardent and accomplished naturalist, full of irrepressible genial humour, truly catholic in his sympathies, and ever ready to serve the public without respect of creed or class … a man whom to know was to love. [Leading Protestants attended his funeral] because he had proved himself so thoroughly a man of the broadest and most attractive character.

Later in the same paper there was a short account of 'what he did and what he was', ending as follows:

> His life and death have both given a fresh proof of the pleasant fact that a genuinely sympathetic and cultured human nature puts out of sight the differences that divide the majority of men.[36]

According to *The Bedfordshire Mercury* over 3,000 people lined the approach to the cemetery on the day of his funeral.[37]

As always, further extension on the foundations he had laid would depend on the quality of his successors in the town. And, of course, a deeply ingrained anti-Catholicism was still present, even though his achievements may have made it easier for a Catholic presence in the town to be accepted or at least ignored. For some, indeed, such success only heightened their fears of what the spread of Catholicism might imply. The point was made by a speaker in Bedford some years later (a Mr James Butcher of the Royal Institution) when he spoke of the Roman Catholic church in England showing a 'silken hand … but the iron was underneath', especially dangerous because England was 'asleep while the Roman religion was gradually crawling over the country'. Its influence, he claimed, led to 'superstition, misery and everything that was bad, while glorious Protestantism was marked by happiness and prosperity'. The talk included the usual accusation that Roman priests forbade their people to read the bible, but an unusual addition was the showing of over sixty lantern slides, including pictures of the English Protestant martyrs and some of the 'cathedrals and abbeys destroyed by the Roman Catholics'; not enough detail is included in the report to explain this very strange accusation. The talk, organised by the Prayer Book Revision Society in the Bedford Working Men's Institute, was entitled 'Why were our reformers burned?'[38] For her part, a middle-class Methodist lady even wondered in her diary whether the time had not come for a second Reformation, to sweep away the final traces of Romanism.[39]

Yet, perhaps for the majority of the town's citizens, what the Roman Catholics got up to became just another part of the religious scene, interesting perhaps

36 *The Bedfordshire Times and Independent*, 21 February 1885; other obituaries were equally praiseworthy.

37 *The Bedfordshire Mercury*, 21 February 1885.

38 *The Bedfordshire Standard*, 17 December 1887.

39 Richard Smart (ed.), *The Bousfield Diaries: A Middle-Class Family in Late Victorian Bedford*, BHRS, vol. 86 (Woodbridge, 2007), p. 118, for 21 July 1884; an enduring anti-Catholicism is evident throughout the diaries, which cover the years 1878–96.

because different, even a little exotic. In 1887, for example, the local press carried an announcement, without comment, of a coming Catholic talk with the title 'The English Catholic Martyrs: Who are they? Why did they suffer? What did they suffer?' The announcement was followed by an account of the national celebrations that had attended the beatification by the pope of fifty-four English Catholic martyrs who had died during the reigns of Henry VIII and Elizabeth: the celebrations included 'solemn Exposition of the Blessed Sacrament, singing of the *Te Deum* in thanksgiving, and sermons by bishops and reverend Fathers'. The piece quoted from a letter of the current English bishops 'glorifying our martyrs' and praising their fidelity and fervour, and ended by saying that the Catholic priest, Rev. Wrigglesworth of Midland Road, had celebrated the occasion and that the ceremonies were 'very joyous', with good congregations.[40] Times were indeed changing.

Elsewhere in the county Catholics were consolidating their position. At Shefford, Collis noted regularly in his diary the attendance at his Sunday services; for most weeks in 1869, for example, he comments on the number of Protestants attending in the afternoon: on 10 January he notes that 'not many Protestants' were there, but the following week 'the Church was full' and on 14 February 'many Protestants' were among the congregation. Unfortunately, we do not have any indication of the themes of his weekly sermons that clearly were attractive to his Protestant hearers. In his diary for Holy Week that year, however, he lists the sermons he preached each evening. On the Monday he used as his theme the Old Testament account of the people of Nineveh 'rising in judgement against this generation', while on Tuesday it was 'the justice and judgement of God as shown in the Fall of the Angels'. On Wednesday his theme was based rather enigmatically on the Book of Judges (chap. 2, vv. 4–5) 'on the place of weepers', and on Thursday 'The legacy (?) of Jesus'. He preached twice on Good Friday: in the morning he used a text from Psalm 27 on 'seeking the face of God', while in the evening his text was Luke 23, v. 48 when he stressed, according to his own account, the inability of the apostles 'even to watch one hour' with him. He ended this entry by reporting that on Easter Sunday a few Protestants attended Mass, while in the afternoon there were 'many Protestants' at the service.

One may speculate about possible reasons for his relative popularity with Shefford's Protestants. Perhaps the absence of a local Anglican church played a part, or was it, perhaps, his own Protestant past – though elsewhere conversion to Catholicism seemed to cause resentment and opposition rather than popularity. Whatever lay behind it, it continued for some time and could almost be described as the regular pattern: his diary reports 'a good number of Protestants' at the Sunday evening of 20 November 1870, for example. It was certainly not the architecture or general attractiveness of the old chapel, dating as we have seen from the 1790s. It had long been past its best and had suffered from a lack of basic maintenance and repair during the years of Shefford's decline as the county's Catholic centre. We have seen Collis' appeals in this regard (see pp. 82–5); while successful, he was not content with the results and continued to raise funds to replace it altogether.

An interesting account in *The Building News* for 28 May 1875 provides some information about his first plans to achieve this. It starts by saying how Shefford had

40 *The Bedfordshire Times and Independent*, 22 January 1887.

been a 'sheltered retreat', safe from the persecution usually experienced by Catholics in earlier times and able to have a hidden chapel. This, according to the article, had become far too small for the home attached to it and so a new one was planned. Designed by Mr S. J. Nicholl (of Kentish Town), the plans had been exhibited at the Royal Academy: it was to be of 'the plainest description' with the only ornamentation being around the altar, and with the former chapel serving as a sacristy. The writer finished by saying, rather enigmatically, that in order to fit in with the other buildings in the area the church would be 'in a late style of architecture'.

We can safely assume that these plans came to nothing because of a lack of funds. The foundation stone for the replacement was not laid until October 1882, with the church eventually being opened and consecrated on 5 July 1884.[41] The old church did become the sacristy, with part of it used for a time as a classroom for the orphanage (see Chapter 8 below). A modern note was struck in *The Tablet* advertising the solemn opening: the Great Northern Railway Company would run a special train for visitors on the day; this would leave King's Cross at 10 a.m., arriving in Shefford at 11.15 a.m.; it would return at 5.15 p.m., arriving at 6.35 p.m.[42] There is no indication of who these special visitors were.

The new building was dedicated to St Francis of Assisi. It had been designed by the architect S. J. Nicholl, and paid for by Mrs Yolande Marie Louise Lyne Stephens of Lynford Hall, Thetford, Norfolk, a noted and extremely wealthy supporter of Catholic causes. Of French origin, born in poverty in 1812, Yolande Duvernay became celebrated as a young ballerina in Paris and London, with a rather doubtful reputation, giving her first dramatic performance in Drury Lane, London in 1833 and, incidentally, becoming a firm favourite of the young Princess Victoria. After a very successful stage career in both cities, and a number of short-lived romantic attachments, in 1845 she married a very wealthy English entrepreneur, Mr Lyne Stephens, with properties in Paris and this country and a fortune based on the glass industry.[43] After his early death in 1861 she devoted her great wealth (she was reputed to be the richest lady in England) to Catholic good causes, especially building. As well as the church in Shefford and the orphanage, she paid for the bishop's new residence in Northampton (£12,000) and finally, among many other donations, paid for the erection of a new church and presbytery in Cambridge in 1890 at a cost of over £70,000! She died in 1894, at the age of eighty-one, leaving £5,000 to the bishop, £5,000 to repair the church in Cambridge and £2,000 to the orphanage in Shefford for the perpetual support of three boys: truly, an amazingly generous donor.[44]

The church, in a fourteenth-century Gothic style, was built of red brick, with ashlar dressings, and is still in use. The presbytery next door, dedicated to St George,

41 Full report in *The Catholic Times*, 13 October 1882.

42 *The Tablet*, 5 July 1884.

43 His family had lived for a time in the 1830s in Chicksands Priory in Bedfordshire; see Jenifer Roberts, *Glass: The Strange History of the Lyne Stephens Fortune* (Chippenham, 2003), pp. 235–6, 246–8.

44 She received a personal gift of agate rosary beads from the pope in recognition of her generosity. The fullest biography, rather critical and unsympathetic in its approach, is Jenifer Roberts, *The Beauty of Her Age: A Tale of Sex, Scandal and Money in Victorian England* (Stroud, 2016), p. 181. See also *The Tablet*, 8 September 1894, for a full obituary; a later account (13 October) gives her will as proved at over £645,000.

Mrs Yolande Marie Louise Lyne Stephens (1812–94), a key diocesan benefactor. Print from a portrait by Emile Auguste Carolus-Duran, 1890. (Photograph © The Fitzwilliam Museum, University of Cambridge)

was re-built at the same time; both it and the church (now Grade II listed buildings) were a striking public feature. Unlike the earlier chapel that it was replacing, there was nothing secluded about it: the brilliant red/pink of its front elevation was a clear statement of intent and an indication of how far Catholicism had developed over the years. No doubt because of the generosity of Mrs Lyne Stephens there was nothing temporary or unfinished about the building, unlike some of the other Catholic chapels being established at the time. It was not just Mrs Lyne Stephens: indeed, the names of those who were benefactors make up a truly remarkable list: Mrs Jane Dunn, the high altar; the Duchess of Buccleuch, a statue of Our Lady; Lord and Lady Kerr, the Lady altar; Anthony and Harriet Sefi, the pulpit; Lord and Lady Stafford, the font; Miss Amherst (sister of the former bishop), the shrine to St Francis; Major Lawson, a statue of the Sacred Heart; Sir Charles and Lady Clifford, the altar rails; John Eyston, altar plate and furniture; Giannetto Prince Doria Pamphili, cloth of gold vestments; the Rev. J. E. Crooke, altar vases; Mrs Isabella Bacchus, candlesticks for the Lady altar, and the Duchess of Norfolk, a thurible. There can have been very few, if any, other small-town churches with such a list of donors, some of whom no doubt were moved by the orphanage connection.[45]

It was planned to be the obvious Catholic presence in the town and surrounding area, with a decorated public entrance from the main street, while also serving as the chapel for the orphanage and the seminary. The boys from the latter had their own entrance above the porch, approached from the upper corridor of the home. It was only fitting that the principal benefactors of Catholicism in the area should be

45 The donors are listed in 'The Opening of St. Francis' Church. Abridged from a Local Paper', pp. 20–5, *Northampton Diocese Magazine*, 1884.

St Francis' Church, Shefford, north elevation, architect's drawing
(plan misnamed St George's Church), June 1882.
(courtesy of Bedfordshire Archives, X627/50/24)

commemorated in the new building: the west window carries a picture of Mrs Lyne Stephens, while the east window was a memorial to John Eyston, given by his widow. One of the smaller windows carried a memorial to Bishop Amherst.[46] A life-sized statue of St George, on the outer wall, was another public statement.[47]

Collis' diaries for the 1880s make no reference to Protestants attending his Sunday services in the new building; were they, perhaps, put off attending what was now a very public Catholic presence in one of the town's principal thoroughfares? Or did Collis just take their attendance for granted by this time?

It is clear from his own account written in 1885 that most of Collis' work was devoted to setting up an orphanage for boys; this seems to have been the bishop's principal aim in re-starting the Shefford mission and in appointing Collis there. It was opened in existing buildings in April 1870 as St Francis' Home. More will be said about this in a later chapter; suffice it to note here that while Collis complained of having to beg 'from door to door' for money for general purposes, a task he obviously hated, he received very generous support for the orphanage from several quarters (see pp. 115–16). On top of all that, he was for several years diocesan treasurer; in addition to the orphanage, he opened a diocesan seminary in the town in 1880 (see pp. 125–7). Clearly, a new role was developing for Shefford in the diocese.

46 For a full description of the furnishings and decoration see *The Tablet*, 5 July 1884.
47 The church registers are said to date from 1885, but those for the years to 1900 appear to be missing altogether.

Bishop Arthur Grange Riddell (1836–1907), bishop of Northampton, 1880–1907. (courtesy of the Diocese of Northampton)

Meanwhile, the diocese had a new bishop. Amherst's successor was Arthur Grange Riddell, appointed in 1880 and serving until he had to retire because of ill-health in 1907. Born in Paris in 1836 into what Philip Hughes described as 'one of those old Catholic families that were in earlier times the sole support of the Church', he was the third son of Edward Widdrington Riddell of York and the Hon. Catherine Stapleton, sister of the eighth Baronet Beaumont, and related to a number of noted gentry Catholic families such as the Throckmortons and the Gerards. Ordained in 1858, he had served in a number of missions, including Hull and Scarborough, before being consecrated bishop.[48]

Taking up Amherst's lament, the new bishop's 1880 Advent pastoral letter spoke of the poverty of resources in the diocese and of its having only 6,000 Catholics in all.[49] Later, in the 1890s, Manning unkindly referred to it as 'a dead diocese', and one can see why it might seem so to one as actively involved as the cardinal in every aspect of church life, from the infallibility debates of the 1870s to Leo XIII's ground-breaking social encyclical 'Rerum novarum' of 1891. There was, however, no lack of effort on the bishop's part to remedy matters, and his efforts were not fruitless: his aim was to open as many missions and Mass centres as possible, but he insisted that such ventures should not be started until at least some funding existed to support them long-term. During his years as bishop, twenty-five full missions were established (a couple of which eventually closed as non-viable), eighteen Mass

48 Philip Hughes, 'The Bishops of the Century', in Beck, *The English Catholics*, pp. 187–222, at p. 213; he wrongly gives York as his birthplace; see also pp. 309, 312. See L. R. Gregory, 'Saving Bishop Riddell', in *Catholic Archives*, The Journal of the Catholic Archive Society, vol. 41 (n.p., 2021), pp. 78–80.

49 NDA, Box 157, Bp Riddell's Assorted Papers.

centres set up, and fourteen chapels opened. Wealthy donors (including, of course, the Duke of Norfolk) played essential roles in this development (see, for example, some of the gifts and legacies listed below on pp. 115–16 for the Shefford orphanage). He was also dependent, obviously, on an increase in the number of clergy at his disposal. The diocesan synod in 1887 was attended by thirty-six priests, with a further thirteen 'legitimately excused'; in 1892 the number had increased to forty-eight, with six excused; by 1896 the total was sixty-one, serving a slowly growing Catholic population across the diocese which by that year had more than doubled to about 12,700. Basically, though, it was true that Riddell was very conservative in outlook; for example he remained throughout his episcopate totally opposed to Catholics attending Cambridge University and to the establishment of a Catholic house of studies there, even appealing, in vain as it turned out, to Rome to prevent it.[50]

One might ask, after surveying these years, whether a growing sense of community can be discerned among Catholics in the town or county. In absolute terms there was an increase in numbers, but it is very difficult to assess just what this growth might mean in different localities in terms of self-image, or of public acceptance or rejection; there is, perhaps, some danger of applying inappropriate modern societal analysis and terminology regarding 'community'. Was the pattern the usual one of a small core of ultra-committed Catholics, reasonably well known to each other, with a periphery of the less-committed though regularly church-going ones? It does not seem to be true in Bedfordshire, as perhaps it was in other parts of the country, that Irishness was a binding element, since, compared with some other counties at the time, Bedfordshire was relatively unaffected by Irish immigration.

The public image of Catholicism among the majority non-Catholic population is somewhat easier to assess. The build-up of Catholic social events, often well reported in the local press, is relevant here, as, of course, was the public image of the priest and the existence of Catholic schools, the latter frequently attended by non-Catholic children. We have seen positive developments in Bedford and an acceptance of Warmoll, but he was followed by, at best, a period of stagnation and the closure of Catholic schools which had played an important part in building up a positive image. As we have also seen, anti-Catholic gatherings could still draw in substantial audiences. Although, however, Catholic progress across the county was uneven, there were some promising signs: in Shefford, for example, there were some positive diocesan developments, as we will see in the next chapter.

50 See John Charmley, 'East Anglia in the Victorian Diocese of Northampton, 1850–1901' in Young, *Catholic East Anglia*, pp. 155–79. Also Lance, *The Returning Tide*, pp. 24–5 for detailed lists, and Brian Plumb, *Arundel to Zabi*.

Primary sources for Chapter 7

Letters of John Priestley Warmoll, 1864–66

A small number of Warmoll's voluminous collection of begging letters are re-produced here in full. Their outspoken tone is interesting, given his circumstances in a strongly Protestant town; he was, clearly, a successful fund-raiser and enjoyed support across a wide area of the country and beyond (see pp. 89–90). The letters appeared in the national Catholic weeklies, *The Table*t and/or *The Weekly Register* (see p. 88). They are reproduced here in chronological order; not all the lists of donations are included. There are also two news reports from the above papers, and an account by Canon Eccles, in charge of the neighbouring mission at Weston Underwood. The source and date are given at the head of each letter.

The Tablet, 13 August 1864

Dear Sir, For the last seven months I have been begging. My voice, without doubt, begins to sound hoarsely and unpleasantly, to be monotonous and even annoying. I may appear to be one of those unlucky beggars who never get into the trick of saying the right thing nor of seizing the happy moment. So much the worse for me. But, by your leave, I am not going to give up begging just yet. I will take voice lozenges, or anything that may be prescribed, but I am not going to give up begging because I am hoarse, for I have not obtained what I want.

The postage stamps and other little paper favours so kindly showered upon me from time to time are my meat and drink; they spread the necessary broadcloth upon my back, enclose my feet in decent boots, and in other ways save me from the gravedigger!

But this is not my object in becoming a mendicant. Bedford is a county town of 15,000 inhabitants, amongst whom are about 100 Catholics, and here, after the lapse of centuries, the Holy Sacrifice has now been offered daily for seven months past; the children have been as (*sic*) constantly instructed in their religion; the Faith has been preached, and the work of an infant Mission has been carried on. But what is this all to end in without some substantial aid?

For these months past, in order to save money for providing some more decent chapel than two small upstair rooms (*sic*), the Priest has lived without housekeeper or servant. And yet, here we are still. Holy Mass in an atmosphere unbearably close and suffocating. Fainting scenes, Sunday after Sunday. This has been cruel enough, but now the Irish harvest labourers are coming in, and generous as we know they are with what they have, it is not fresh air nor an increase of space they bring with them.

O dear readers of the TABLET (*sic*), (many of you have been very kind; and may God bless you for it,) don't throw this letter down without determining to send us something.

There is no Catholic family of wealth or influence in the neighbourhood to whom we can appeal, therefore we must look to you. Show this statement to your friends. Our position is not respectable in the sight of others, nor wholesome to ourselves.

I don't ask you any more for tables and chairs, for kettles or carpets. I have not got them, but I have given up all thoughts of such rubbish. Send me objects for a prize drawing (*sic*) if you please. But above all, I ask you for money that I may purchase a piece of ground whereon to erect an altar to God, upon which the Adorable Sacrifice will often be offered for you, around which I may assemble my poor people and speak to them freely of the Faith so dear to you, and where they may pray for their benefactors, who in helping them will have helped themselves on to the great gathering where we shall know each other, and where the self-denial *you* (*sic*) may have exercised and the hardship *we* have endured will be forgotten in mutual gratulations (*sic*).

Always yours in Christ, John Priestley Warmoll, Miss. Ap., Bedford[51]

The Weekly Register, 15 July 1865

Dear Sir, – It is a shame to trouble you again so soon, but may I remind such of your subscribers as take interest in this desolate Mission, that the Dag-days (*sic*) are down upon us! The Sundays of this powerful old season find one half of us still cooped up and crowded upon the altar in our small, stifling upper room, whilst the other half is out of sight, kneeling in uncomfortable draughts and dark corners, or uneasily balanced on the steep narrow stairs.

Imagine a poor Priest, bathed in perspiration, a perfect Kuhlborne[52] in point of moisture, attempting to preach to persons almost within reach of his arm, and whose tortures are but too plainly evinced by a constant use of the pocket handkerchief for detergent purposes, by eager gaspings toward the one window for breath, and by instinctive recourse to the smelling salts as a stimulus against fainting, while the rest of his flock are as completely out of sight as if at the antipodes.

Such, alas! is our state. But, *Deo gratias*! we have been doing better with regard to donations lately, chiefly owing to a plain printed statement of our circumstances which I have circulated amongst those persons with whose addresses I am acquainted. [*see next item*]

If any of your subscribers should desire copies they may apply to me for them, and their interest in the holy work entrusted to my unworthy care will not fail to be excited, or if already aroused, to be redoubled. – I am, dear Sir, your's (*sic*) very truly.

JOHN PRIESTLEY WARMOLL

Donations received:

Abundant and hearty thanks for the following anonymous contributions:–

Norwich, 2s.; J.H., 2s.; CMM of Erin, 1s.; one in affliction, 1s.; In memoriam, 2s. 6d.; collected by Mrs McCartin, 10s. 4d.; T.J.C., Manchester, 2s. 6d.; poor convert, 5s.; St. George's Southwark, 1s.; London, R.C. 2s. 6d. (these two are unwearied) Manchester 1s; G.Y. £1.5s; collected by a Child of Mary, 10s.; London E.C., 1s.

51 Note 'Miss. Ap.': 'missionary apostolic' instead of 'parish priest' or 'rector' as canonical parishes did not exist in England or Wales at this time.

52 Reference unknown.

The Weekly Register

printed statement of Warmoll's position and plans referred to above

Seventeen months have passed since I had the honour of being sent alone and a perfect stranger, to raise the standard of our Holy Religion in this intensely Protestant town.

There are in Bedford about 100 Catholics: there are militia barracks, a hospital, a large workhouse, large manufactories, and several lines of railway.

There was not, nor is there now in the town or county, a single Catholic family of any wealth or influence wherewith to forward the work.

Trusting entirely to Divine Providence for the rent, I hired a small house, the two bedrooms of which had to be thrown into one to form a chapel – a very temporary one, it was too fondly hoped. Miserably insufficient at first, it has become utterly so now, owing to stray sheep that have come to hand since. It is crowded to suffocation, actually and literally, on Sundays; and, while the sun beats without mercy upon the thin roof and walls of the room, a considerable proportion of the congregation have to hear Mass in the draught of a dark landing, and all down a steep narrow staircase.

As for myself, a tiny room over the wash-house has done admirably for me to sleep in, while it has served many other useful purposes as well. For all these months, servant or housekeeper would have been luxuries out of the question, even if I could have afforded the one or the other.

Having had no one to teach the children, I have instructed them daily myself since the Mission commenced. But I am not begging for a school-house, although of course I have none; nor for furniture, although my iron bedstead, the original cost of which was ten shillings, has broken down, and although the only table I possess is the broken three-legged deal one at which I am writing. No. I am begging for the very existence of the Mission, for ground whereupon to give it a footing, for a house and schoolroom-chapel wherein to shelter it.

Hitherto, it has been chiefly supported by charitable friends, who have seen my advertisements and appeals in the Catholic journals. A thousand thanks to them, and all honour for their liberality! But now owing, I daresay, to various other calls and attractions, almost all contributions of this kind have ceased; so that my receipts are really not covering the expense of advertising, and I know not whither to turn.

By dint of hard, and to me most painful begging, I have collected £480, which sum is safely in the London and County Bank. But what is that, when land has to be bought and buildings erected! Ground is becoming dearer here every day.

A multitude of Protestant sects, in this land of Cromwell, Bunyan, and Howard, flourish and build grandly. Besides this, I have a good reason, which I could not publicly mention, for believing that, with all the will in the world, I could not live another year like the last.

'Nothing succeeds like success' – so is nothing so disastrous to an undertaking as the want of it. Help us, I beg of you, to succeed once, and then I feel sure that a series of successes will have commenced.

I am yours, in Our Blessed Lord,

JOHN PRIESTLEY WARMOLL, Mis. Ap.
48, Offa Street, Bedford

The Tablet, 9 September 1865

BEDFORD MISSION

Dear Sir, – I know that you will have the kindness to insert the accompanying acknowledgements for the month of August. Pray allow me also, once more … to remind them and all your subscribers that ours is indeed an extreme case.

We have, it is true, *Deo gratias*! £620 towards purchasing ground and buildings expenses; but, then I have advertised weekly in three papers, have sent out nearly 1,500 printed circulars, and hundreds of written letters, and have begged from door to door. And during the period since the first Mass here after 300 years was said by me; what has been our state? I have never fully described it, because I have had reason to believe that even my understatements were by some considered to be exaggerated.

For twenty-two months our chapel has been a pair of small low bedrooms, making together an area of 22½ feet by 11 feet. The ante-chapel, a dark, draughty landing and a steep narrow staircase. Sunday, when all this is crowded to suffocation up to the altar, is a day to be dreaded. Devotion at Holy Mass has been next to impossible to all, and entirely so to some.

As to the common decency, to say nothing of the becoming dignity of our worship, the less said the better. We can admit no Protestant, however desirous of attending, and Sunday evening services are out of the question. …

The miserable lack of respectability in our poor little private house, brings down upon us the contempt and obloquy of our flourishing neighbours, while it does little towards raising the courage of those "who ought to be Catholics" (of which class, I am sorry to say, there are many here), and inducing them once more to kneel before the altar of their God among the children of their long-forsaken Mother. …

We are here all alone – a small garrison in a hostile land, cut off from the main army. Who will throw supplies into our little fortress?

A thousand thanks and blessings for those who have done so already.

I am, dear Sir, Yours in Christ,

JOHN PRIESTLEY WARMOLL.
48, Offa Street, Bedford.

Donations received:
Through M. Hall, Bath, £1; London, W.C. £5. (First half of note acknowledged before): Dublin, M.C., £5; through Mr. Mooney, £1 4s; An anxious Mother, Preston, £2; M.J., 10s; F.W., 5s; Langport, £1s; Harbourstown, 3s. 6d.; Preston, B.B., 3s. 10d.; York, 1s.; M.B.M. 5s.–5s. (*sic*); J.M.E, C.E., A.E., 1s. 11d; Clifton. 1s. 6d.

The Tablet, 4 November 1865

MISSION OF THE HOLY CHILD AND ST. JOSEPH, BEDFORD.

To the Editor of the Tablet.

Sir, – After sustaining a difficult part for a lengthened period, it is refreshing alike to one's audience and oneself to appear in a new character. My role today is fresh – that in fact of a landowner. Through the ever ready and generous charity of the Catholic public I have succeeded in purchasing a piece of ground, with the situation and price of which no one can find fault.

The success with which we are rewarded so far is the result of a struggle that can hardly be realised by persons not on the spot. But to be short (for I have told my sad tale so often that to repeat it would be worse than superfluous), the land cost £380 less expenses of conveyance, etc., (freehold). This leaves me nearly £300 in hand. My intention is this: Trusting to the good providence of God in a matter which is undertaken, I hope simply for His glory. I purpose, with the full permission and concurrence of his Lordship, the Bishop of Northampton, to build, at once, a priest's house and a schoolroom to serve as a chapel until it shall overflow. ... I am sure it will be evident to our friends, that while we avoid all extravagance and keep clear of all debt, it is highly desirable that our buildings should be substantial and dignified. The plans shall be drawn out forthwith, and, as soon as the estimate is suggested, it shall be made public.

Let it be something that will endure, something worthy of our holy cause, and that may be an earnest of brighter days to come when the sweet names of Jesus, Mary and Joseph shall be once more known and loved here as of old.

Yours in Christ,

JOHN PRIESTLEY WARMOLL, Miss Ap.

The Tablet, 25 November 1865

Sir, – It vexes me much to be compelled to trouble you again so soon; but here is a dead lock, and what's to be done?

This Mission has now been carried on for just two years in the wretched little house so often described. None but those who have been on the spot can conceive what difficulties and disadvantages we have had to encounter.

The congregation and its requirements have increased and will continue to do so. Our present quarters, too, have served us in an increasingly miserable manner as the period has advanced. But now I must seriously urge that it is physically impossible to go on thus through the summer. It would be rashness and folly to make the attempt. It is not my habit to stick at trifles, but that I see to be beyond my power, or the capability of tougher men than I.

Don't think that I am complaining. God forbid! I constantly marvel at the munificent generosity of Catholics, especially at the noble beneficence of nameless givers, and wonder how they can have sufficient left wherewith to enable them to appear in this world at all like other people.

Don't think me unthankful. My heart is full of gratitude for their alms, and runs over with appreciation of the beautiful spirit of charity that prompts them.

But to the point. I must have a place for a chapel in the summer or give up. Land has cost £380. About £300 clear remains in hand. Now I want to build a substantial school-room at once before the worst days of summer set in. It will cost £600. I am anxious, then, to get £300 as soon as possible that I may receive tenders. – Yours very truly.

JOHN PRIESTLEY WARMOLL, Bishop (*sic*).

The next two items are not by Warmoll: the first is a newspaper account, the second is by the priest at Weston Underwood, Canon Eccles.

The Tablet, 3 February 1866

THE BEDFORD MISSION,

Septuagesima Sunday was a bright day for the new Mission at Bedford, when it was cheered by the presence of his Lordship the Bishop of Northampton, who confirmed on that day 22 members of the congregation. It being the first time since that the holy sacrament of confirmation had been administered in that town for more than three centuries. This mission has now been struggling hard for more than two years in a most wretched little upper room, and there is every reason to feel confident that if a chapel or church were erected, there would soon be a large and flourishing colony of Catholics.

Never did the accommodation appear more miserable and absurdly inadequate than on this day of confirmation when those of the congregation who could enter the room were packed densely together, leaving barely space for his lordship between themselves and the altar.

We know that Father Warmoll has met with many generous friends who have enabled him to purchase the land required, and also to place some money in the bank towards building purposes. But it would be well if the exigencies of the case were better known, as they cannot be exaggerated, and if those who have not yet done so would come forward and take a share in aiding this promising but entirely isolated mission.

The Weekly Register, 26 May 1866

Seth Eccles (1800–84) was ordained in Rome, 1825. In his letter he claimed that he had served at Weston Underwood for forty years. He highlighted the need for a priest to serve in Bedford – and for contributions to support that work. Presumably he hoped that the former links between Weston Underwood and Bedfordshire would prove fruitful.

The Very Rev. Canon Eccles appeals on behalf of the Bedford Mission.

The following statement will, I have no doubt, touch the heart of more than one good Christian, and move them to stretch out a helping hand where help is so urgently wanted, and where it cannot fail to produce abundant fruits.

A few years ago, the inmates of a public-house were suddenly awakened and alarmed in the middle of the night by piercing cries of distress, "Send for a Priest! Send for a Priest! Oh, I see hell open before me! Oh, why did I not go to confession before? Send for a Priest, I see hell open before me!" And in the midst of these heart-rending cries and entreaties for a Priest an unfortunate Irish packman, after two or three hours of illness, expired in despair. Such is the dreadful fact. God knoweth that I lie not. This sad event occurred a short distance from Bedford; but then there was no Priest at Bedford.

Sometime after that, on a Sunday, immediately after Mass, I received a note from an Irish gentleman, requesting me to go to a village about three miles beyond Bedford, to administer the last rites of the Church to another Irish gentleman. They were going from London to the north on their way to Ireland. After a hurried breakfast I started at once, as the fly was ready for me. Bedford is thirteen miles from Weston, and I had to go nearly four miles beyond Bedford, and when I arrived at the village the gentleman was dead. Alas! there was then no priest at Bedford. But now there is a Priest at Bedford – a good, zealous, devoted Priest … in the midst of the severest privations, which at one time, as his doctor declared, threatened to undermine his constitution. And if he die there will be nothing left for the Catholics of Bedford and the neighbourhood but blank despair. For it required all the zeal, energy, and spirit of self-sacrifice of a converted Protestant clergyman to support all the hardships and submit to all the privations, which the Rev. J. P. Warmoll has endured in his persevering efforts to establish a permanent mission at Bedford. And his labours have not been without fruit. Many lost sheep have returned to the one fold; and he has administered the last rites of the Church to no less than six of his flock each year that he has been at Bedford. At that rate 240 Catholics have died at Bedford and in the neighbourhood during the forty years that I have been at Weston Underwood. Now, I am quite certain that at least 200 of these unhappy, forlorn Catholics died without the last sacraments. What a sad and deplorable death. How great is the spiritual desolation of this part of England. Between Cambridge and Banbury, or Hethe [presumably Heath?], nearly a hundred miles, there is only one Catholic chapel. If you, then, the more honourable members of Christ, will not assist us, the weaker members, would it not be unnatural, and contrary to the views and designs of the head? Remember the melancholy end of the Irish gentleman, and of others, who died before I could get to them, though I went immediately I was called. Little did these persons think that they should die at Bedford, or Wolverton, and die without the assistance of a Priest. And as little do you know where you shall die; but one thing is certain that if you are not insensible to the extreme spiritual necessities of the poor friendless, destitute Catholics of Bedford, God will take care of you in your last hour. A thought has just struck me – I was going to buy a new carpet, having used the other more than twenty years; but I will go without my carpet, and give £10 for Bedford Chapel, if some others will give the same sum.

Weston Underwood, Newport, Pagnele, (*sic*)

The Tablet, 8 September 1866

THE BEDFORD MISSION.

Sir, – At last our buildings – a chapel-schoolroom and presbytery – are in course of erection. For nearly three years we have experienced almost every difficulty and disadvantage that could attend the commencement in utter poverty of a solitary mission far advanced into a hostile land.

Our oft-mentioned bed-room chapel has long been a torture chamber after the plan of the Black Hole of Calcutta, although the congregation has been divided by my saying two Masses every Sunday. Our apology for accommodation is miserably unworthy and ridiculously insufficient, and our circumstances all along have furnished, naturally enough, the occasion of remarks more pointed than kind, and more entertaining to our neighbours than complimentary to ourselves.

Comparatively small as our number is, we have never been able to meet all together at once, whilst we had cruelly to exclude all Protestants however anxious to obtain admittance. Now, however, our walls begin to rise, and thanks to the untiring generosity of the Catholic public we are looking forward to start, fresh and fair, on our own ground.

The contract I have signed requires me to pay for the work which is to be completed about Christmas, more than £300 above what I have in hand, and I feel sure that our dear brethren in the Faith will not now, after all the difficulties of the past, suffer the work to fall to the ground. I have nothing whatsoever of my own, and the mission could not bear the burden of the slightest debt.

JOHN PRIESTLEY WARMOLL, Mis. Ap.
48, Offa Street, Bedford.

Chapter 8

Orphans and Ordinands

While it was too early in the 1870s to speak of the successful re-establishment of English Catholicism, there were some genuine signs of development. Even a diocese as bereft of resources as Northampton felt it should move from the provision of basic services towards developing what would be considered normal 'extras' in a Catholic diocese of the time. Such development would, of course, depend on the co-operation and leadership of the clergy; it would also depend equally on the financial support of the laity. In this chapter we will examine two particular areas where there was such fruitful co-operation in the last quarter or so of the nineteenth century.

A diocesan home for orphans

In March 1869 Bishop Amherst wrote to his clergy to announce the launch of a funding campaign to help the diocese establish a home and school for destitute and orphan children.[1] There had been considerable debate nationally in the 1850s about the need to set up residential facilities to deal with the 'Condition and Treatment of the Perishing and Dangerous Classes of Children and Juvenile Offenders', leading to an Act of Parliament in 1854, the first of a number of such Acts. This allowed the establishment of reformatories for junior delinquents: schools could be 'certificated' to receive young offenders below sixteen years of age who had first served a short prison sentence (of not less than ten days, however) and were then committed by the magistrates to the school for between two and five years. Costs would be covered by government grants, profits from the 'industrial' activities of the school, and, in theory, from any fees that could be extracted from the parents or relatives of the children. The Act also covered children found 'wandering' without any obvious means of support, even if they had not committed any crime. Attempts by Catholic MPs and others to include some provision for religious visitation and instruction of the Catholic inmates in such institutions failed, leading Cardinal Wiseman to declare in 1855, 'We must have Reformatory Schools of our own', and this became, in effect, official Catholic policy despite amendments to the national legislation that did allow specific religious provision. As the Catholic bishops explained in the same year, young delinquents had to be reformed without danger to their religious faith and this meant setting up suitable institutions across the whole of the country.[2]

1 King, *An Ancient Catholic Mission and its Modern Development*, pp. 50–1.

2 For Catholic appeals and reactions to the legislation of the 1850s, see John A. Stack, 'The Catholics, the Irish Delinquent and the Origins of Reformatory Schools in Nineteenth-Century England and Scotland', in *RH*, vol. 23, no. 3 (May, 1997), pp. 372–88; in the same

This was the background to Bishop Amherst's appeal of 1869: he referred to the Acts of Parliament of the 1860s that provided for orphans, destitute children and children of imprisoned parents to be sent to an industrial school, and an earlier Act that allowed poor law guardians to transfer Catholic children from public workhouses to certified Catholic industrial schools. The bishop had decided that it was time for the diocese to establish such an institution and that Shefford was the best place to locate it. Such children, he continued,

> need some place of shelter, where they may be cared for and educated in the principles of their religion … [there is no need to stress] the excellency of such work, the object of which is to provide for the helpless and destitute little ones of Christ's flock … urgently entrusted to our care by our Divine Lord himself. [Such institutions] have been the means of rescuing numbers of poor children from lives of wandering idleness, ignorance and crime.

As a result, in April 1869 the 'Catholic Industrial School for the Midlands' was opened, under the Rev. Collis' management in Shefford. The first annual report in 1870 was for the 'Northampton and Nottingham Diocesan School for Orphan and Destitute Boys', the two dioceses presumably combining to share the costs and to reach a wider group of benefactors. This arrangement remained in place until 1883, when the Diocese of Nottingham withdrew and set up its own institution; the previous year its title had changed to 'An Orphanage for Boys above the age of Seven Years', without any reference to 'the destitute'. Finally, in 1893 it was described in the annual report simply as 'An Orphanage for Boys'.[3]

It appears that the initial response to the school was not altogether positive, especially from the clergy, so much so that Collis was moved to write a long letter in its support.[4] He quoted at length from the bishop's initial letter. Then, in response to the argument that looking after orphans should be the responsibility of the mission in which they lived, he asked how could 'completely overtaxed' poor missions, such as Peterborough and Bedford, possibly do this? The Catholic orphans in poor places would inevitably end up in Protestant institutions and so lose their faith. In conclusion he pleaded for 'help for the helpless, help that will at once free these poor children from their present unhappy condition'. The whole was a moving appeal, together with a realistic analysis of the costs involved in setting up the institution and running it.

Whatever the response of the clergy to Amherst's appeal, there can be no doubting that of the laity. Only a month after Collis's article, the diocesan magazine could report that 'the munificence of the Duke and Duchess of Norfolk' had ensured that the orphanage was cleared of all its debt as far as the building fund was concerned.[5]

issue, Rev. David Lannon, 'Bishop Turner, the Salford Diocese and Reformatory Provision, 1854–1872', pp. 389–407. The latter is mistaken in listing Carlton, Bedfordshire, as a Catholic foundation (p. 390); the approved school there had no specifically Catholic connections; see Godber, *History of Bedfordshire*, p. 540.

3 BA, X627/33, Bound volume of St Francis' Home Reports containing Annual Reports, 1884–1904. See also King, *An Ancient Catholic Mission and its Modern Development*, pp. 9–13.

4 See *The Northampton Catholic Magazine*, vol. 1 (November, 1869), pp. 12–14.

5 *Ibid.*, December, p. 12.

St Francis' Home, Shefford, *Building News*, 6 October 1876. The building to the right of the church is the priest's house; to the left is part of the orphanage/boys' home. (content provided by THE BRITISH LIBRARY BOARD. ALL RIGHTS RESERVED. With thanks to The British Newspaper Archive, www.britishnewspaperarchive.co.uk)

Its upkeep, including substantial extensions and renovations, would not have been possible without a range of very generous donors and their continuing support. The 1877 report, for example, had referred to the condition of parts of the buildings:

> All engaged in the management of the Home, Director, Master, Matron, etc., are still lodged in buildings that are falling to pieces. Truth obliges us to say that the appearance of the front … can only be described by one word – disgraceful; but the managers … could not direct to its reconstruction means so urgently needed for the more important work of providing proper accommodation for the boys.[6]

By 1879 most of this had been rebuilt or repaired, replacing the 'tumble down old building' by 'an elegant frontage'.[7] An illustration in *The Building News* of July 1878 shows the plan for 'St Francis' Home: Shefford: School and Dormitory', drawn up by the architect Mr S. J. Nicholl. It was truly a magnificent proposal, witness to the ambition of Fr Collis and his belief that only the best would be good enough for the boys.

Benefactors included the Duke of Norfolk who gave no less than £2,000 over the next ten years, starting with £200 a few months after the opening (the Duchess gave a separate £50). Other donations included over £1,200 from a 'gentleman in Ireland'; £1,000 from a religious sister formerly a member of a gentry family (perhaps the Hon. Frances Verney-Cave, whose money helped to establish the lasting Adrian Foundation, while her mother, Baroness Braye, was described as a 'most generous benefactor'); £700 from another lady (used to buy the seminary property); £1,000 from a Mgr Davies of Costessey; a 'gentleman from Northampton' gave £300; another anonymous donor left a legacy of £200. The ever-dependable Mrs Lyne Stephens (see p. 100) was later to pay off the remaining debt on the boys' home with a gift of

6 BA, X627/32, Bound volume of St Francis' Home Reports containing Annual Reports, 1870–84.

7 King, *An Ancient Catholic Mission and its Modern Development*, p. 12.

£500 (and left £2,000 for its support in her will after her death in 1894). To judge from the special mention and thanks extended by Collis to the Eyston family from East Hendred in Berkshire (an old recusant family), they were very generous donors, mentioned alongside Mrs Lyne Stephens as one of 'two most noble benefactors'. John Eyston died in 1882, leaving £2,000 to the bishop and £500 to the Shefford orphanage. Collis's praise was fully merited when we learn from his report in 1884 that their joint funding enabled a large standing debt of £1,770 to be paid off.[8]

There were also a large number of local donations and legacies, for example, from Mr Henry Lewington, a local Catholic whose family features in the early Shefford registers.[9] Also, in 1892, a Mr John Fanning, described as being of 'View Mount, Waterford, Ireland, and Shefford', gave £100 to the home; two years later he gave £150, and finally in 1896 his wife, now a widow, gave £1,000 in line with his wishes, as the then manager put it,

> for the work of maintaining and educating orphan boys … and expressly to be a relief to me in the worry and anxiety necessarily resultant on the extreme difficulty (in these days) of collecting sufficient money to carry on the … work.[10]

Most of the donations were for the orphanage and the funding of boys there; there can be no doubting the appeal of such charitable work to a range of pious Victorian donors across the British Isles. Collis's terse 'begging all day' from time to time in his diaries shows his commitment to the work of fund-raising, and, it seems, his dislike of this essential task: in Norwich in September 1870 he added, 'hard work, little success', but overall he was undoubtedly successful as both the institution's founder and chief fund-raiser.

It was, of course, a diocesan enterprise and no doubt the bishop was responsible for enlisting a body of distinguished patrons and supporters from across the country, including, as we have seen, the Duke of Norfolk. The annual report for 1890, for example, gives the following list as a 'Management Committee' under the presidency of the Bishop of Northampton:

> His Grace the Duke of Norfolk EM
> Sir Henry Bedingfield, Bart.
> Earl of Denbigh
> Charles O. Eaton Esq.
> Earl of Ashburnham
> Lord Walter Kerr
> C. A. Scott-Murray Esq
> Rt. Rev. Monsignor Canon McKenna V.G.
> Rt. Rev. Monsignor Canon Scott D.D., V.G.
> Manager:
> Very Rev. Canon H. E. King

8 BA, X627/13, Financial Record Book St Francis' Home, Shefford, Bedfordshire 1875. On the Eyston family, see also p. 85, and Kirk, *Biographies of English Catholics in the Eighteenth Century*, pp. 75–6, for earlier clerical members of the family; Burton, *The Life and Times of Bishop Challoner*, vol. 1, pp. 182–4, gives a full account.

9 BA, X627/33, Bound volume of St Francis' Home Reports, see 16th Annual Report, 1885.

10 By this time the manager was the Rev. Henry King, a former student of the seminary, ordained in 1886; he promised an annual Mass in perpetuity for the Fannings; see BA, X627, King's summary, 'Notes on St Francis' Home'.

St Francis' Home, Shefford, *Building News*, 26 July 1878.

It is not clear what part, if any, this distinguished group played in the regular running of the home. No doubt they supported it financially, meeting once or twice a year perhaps to receive reports and so on.

The 1885 report lamented that 'it was a rare thing' for any of these benefactors to visit the home. Some apparently had given the excuse that it was remote and without rail connections, but the author of the report, presumably Collis, insisted that was untrue as there were links to both Hitchin and Bedford main-line stations.[11] Presumably these patrons supported a range of charities and institutions and could hardly have been expected to visit them all. They were listed in some of the annual reports as though they were a management committee, in others as a list of patrons; the latter seems a more reliable description.

The ethos of the home had changed in the early 1880s. Collis made his ideas about it clear in a letter he wrote to the bishop in July 1881 in which he argued that while obliged at the start to use the term 'Industrial School' in order to comply with the legislation, he now wanted to drop it in favour of 'a Boys' Orphanage'. His reasoning was that in the public's mind any reference to 'an industrial school' indicated 'a reformatory', with all the criminal connotations this had. He wanted to attract 'a better class of boy' and intended the 'home' to be supported by the boy's relatives and friends; in this way he hoped to avoid creating in people's minds 'any

11 BA, X627/33, Bound volume of St Francis' Home Reports, see 16th Annual Report 1885 and reports of 1890 and 1900; in the home's early days it had jointly served the Diocese of Nottingham and had the support of others with interests in that area, including the Earl of Gainsborough and Lord Stafford.

idea derogatory to the inmates of the School'.[12] He won his case and by the time of his death in 1893 his 'home' was being regularly referred to as 'an orphanage for Catholic boys of the Middle Class', with its prospectus stating it was 'intended principally for the reception of boys of the middle class who have lost one or both parents'.[13]

Moreover, it claimed, such boys were provided with a 'healthy and happy home' within a regime that included:

> Food, plain but plenty: daily Mass and careful religious instruction: an ordinary Elementary English Education by certified master and assistant: abundant outdoor exercise and games, cricket, bathing and drill.

This was not all that was on offer. In a passage marked by a surprising element of modernity, the prospectus claimed that the home was to be conducted on the principle of allowing the boys,

> as large an amount of liberty as is prudently possible, experience showing abundantly that the system of close restrictions and surveillance which obtains in some of our schools is often followed by lamentable results when restrictions and surveillance are removed, and the boys suddenly attain to a liberty which they do not know how to use.

In line with these principles, the boys were allowed a four-weeks holiday each summer, spent with family or friends, or, in some cases, at the home itself if the principal thought that was better for them. They could write to family or friends once a month. To be received into the home a boy had to have lost one or both parents, be 'respectable and of good character', be aged between seven and twelve and be in good health and 'sound mind and body'. A later prospectus claimed that the regime

> fitted the boys to attain a 'respectable and even a high' position once they had left the school, which was in itself 'picturesque, commodious, airy and comfortable'. At daily Mass they would join with the seminary students and be trained to sing the 'ancient and beautiful ecclesiastical chant'.[14]

Clearly, this was not just another run-of-the-mill Victorian industrial school and certainly not in any sense a Dickens look-alike. While a report in *The Tablet* in the late 1870s praised the extensive shoemaking department and spacious carpenter's shop, run by skilled staff who were there for many years,[15] a collection of letters from former inmates (perhaps pupils would be a better word) witness to the success of the home in its provision of worthwhile training and personal development, including service in the army and navy in South Africa and India.[16] Such letters, of course, have to be treated with care, but there seems to be no reason to not accept their generally positive air. The annual reports are a very useful source of detail here: the 1885 report, for example, claimed that 227 boys had been received into the home since it had opened; seven years later the number had risen to 327. Twelve had departed that year,

12 NDA, Box 161, F.iv.15, Collis to Bishop, July 1881.

13 See, for example, a report in *The Tablet*, 19 October 1889, that states that the school had been 'specially adapted' for orphans of the middle classes.

14 NDA, Box 157, Bp Riddell's Assorted Papers, Prospectus, January 1894.

15 *The Tablet*, 25 May 1878; and see below.

16 BA, X627/33, Bound volume of St Francis' Home Reports, 1899 and 1903.

of whom one had emigrated to Canada to join his sister, three had become apprentices, four were in the 'service of a gentleman', another four 'were being provided for by friends'; sadly, one eleven-year old had died of consumption.[17]

The Shefford home had something of a national reputation: a report in *The Catholic Times* in 1892 praised it for the success of the boys in the annual examinations, with the inspector reporting that he was 'greatly pleased' with the general tone of the place and the proficiency of the boys.[18] A major part of its success was due to the work of its lay staff and their long service: Mr Allen, headmaster for over sixteen years; Mr Mahoney, shoemaker for thirty years; a chief carpentry instructor who had been there 'for many years'; Mr Duggan, assistant master and 'prefect' out of school hours, himself a former pupil of the school.

The thirtieth report, in 1899, gave details of twenty boys who had left during the year.[19] Two had moved to an institution for deaf children; 'several' had gone into trades or service while the remainder were with relatives or friends. Interestingly, the report added that there were five boys currently studying for the priesthood (including one who later became principal of the home): one had been ordained a sub-deacon; one was in minor orders;[20] one had recently started his studies in the seminary; one had been professed as a member of a religious order (not identified), while another had been accepted into the Salesian Congregation.[21] An earlier report (1885) had celebrated the ordination to the priesthood of John Henry Ashmole who had done his whole course of studies in St Francis' Home and St Thomas' Seminary in Shefford – 'an Orphanage priest entirely' as the report boasted. He is listed in the 1900 report as 'Chaplain' to the patrons; it is not clear what such a post involved.

Whatever the precise nature of its intake, the orphanage continued to have a good number of boys on roll. Taking the annual total of boys over five-yearly periods, these go from 15 in 1870, to 66 in 1875, 78 in 1880, and 87 in 1885. This last number, however, proved to be too high for the accommodation and resources available, and the annual intake settled down to between 55 and 65 for the rest of the century and beyond.[22]

Despite this success in recruitment, however, it seems to have always run at a financial deficit, at least throughout the nineteenth century. When Collis died in

17 Canada was a common destination for young people from British homes and reformatories; a major Catholic scheme had been organised by Fr Nugent of Liverpool, 1822–1905; see J. Furnival, *Children of the Second Spring: Father James Nugent and the work of child care in Liverpool* (Leominster, 2005). In Bedfordshire, the Misses Trevor of Tingrith funded the emigration of local people to Canada, see Agar, *The Bedfordshire Farm Worker*, pp. 172–3: apparently they sent 'upwards of 100 men, women and children' to Canada at their own expense in the 1860s and 1870s.

18 *The Catholic Times*, 2 September 1892.

19 BA, X627/33, Bound volume of St Francis' Home Reports. These reports contain audited accounts for each year.

20 There were four 'minor orders' for candidates preparing for ordination to the priesthood: porter, lector, exorcist and acolyte. They had become purely transitory stages before ordination to the 'major orders' of sub-diaconate, diaconate and priesthood.

21 BA, X627, Records of St Francis' Boys Home, Shefford, introductory document.

22 Extensive lists of individual boys, giving personal details and other information, exist for the 1870s and beyond, under a generic heading of 'Boys Numerical Admission Registers' BA, X627.

April 1893 it was found that the orphanage had a total debt of about £900; within months this had been almost entirely paid off, with funds from the bishop and a £500 donation from Mrs Lyne Stephens. Collis was succeeded as manager by Rev. Henry King, a former student of the seminary; ordained in 1886, he had served on the staff from 1887 and saw it to be part of his new role to improve the buildings and ensure government grant aid.[23] It would appear, however, that the orphanage was not as popular as an object of charity as one might have expected. A long printed letter sent out in 1894 (anonymous, but probably from Lady Anabel Kerr), after listing some of the arguments people used for not supporting it financially, described the orphanage (more appropriately called a home 'in the truest sense', she alleged) in glowing language as similar in style to a Cambridge college and its gardens! On a recent visit, indeed, she found that,

> it seemed to breathe the real spirit of the old foundations; quiet, religion and learning formed the prevailing atmosphere of the place ... [It should be accepted] as the only Catholic School of its kind in England, where fatherless boys, who have been brought up in comfortable circumstances, may be properly educated without having to undergo any serious discomfort from the surroundings or the evil of bad companions.

The writer described how, back in 1875, she had founded the Boys' Association (properly known as the Association, or Foundation, of Young Gentlemen), with the express purpose of supporting the orphanage. The annual subscription was 2/6, which had first of all gone to the building fund, but later paid for the annual support of three of the boys. Subscribers had the satisfaction of knowing the three boys were well educated and 'in a happy home'.[24] The whole letter is so complimentary and praiseworthy, and indicative almost of a comfortable life-style, that it comes as no surprise that it failed to open the pockets of the charitably minded in a society that offered so many more worthy objects for charitable support.

By 1899 the annual deficit was £316, including £209 that had been carried forward from previous years. Looking at the accounts for that year in some detail, the principal sources of income were payments for the boys from relatives and friends (£250), the diocesan church collections (£76), annual subscriptions and donations (£365), income from invested foundation funds (£88), the trustees of the late Lady Stafford (£40) and the Association of Catholic Boys (£34). This provided an income of £853 for the year.[25]

On the expenditure side, the principal costs were for provisions and clothing (£426), salaries and wages (£130), repairs, rates and insurances (£127), what is described as 'washing, fuel and light' (£145), school 'net cost' (£64) and incidentals such as travel and postage (£65), all adding up to outgoings of approximately £960. These figures do not include any major building and repair works; these are covered in a separate building and furnishing account for each year. In 1870, for example, there had been a deficit on this account of £275; which by 1876 had risen to £749; by the 1890s it was regularly in the region of £300-£400. The appeal for additional

23 King, *An Ancient Catholic Mission and its Modern Development*, p. 18.

24 NDA, Coll. A. 6. 16, Assorted Papers concerning St Francis' Home, 26 January 1894.

25 Figures rounded up to the nearest pound.

subscribers to meet the ordinary running costs cannot have been that successful, but if nothing else, these accounts witness the undoubted commitment of a relatively poorly resourced diocese to the care and education of its orphan boys and to the generosity in the same cause of Catholic laity and clergy.

Annual reports incorporated annual appeals for funds, sometimes to meet ordinary running expenses, at other times to meet the costs of building and expansion. So, for example, *The Weekly Register* in June 1897 reported on the annual report for the previous year that had launched another appeal. There was an air almost of desperation in its account: the ordinary income of the home was insufficient to meet the everyday costs of maintenance and the managers must therefore increase their efforts to raise extra subscriptions. One way of doing this, they felt, was for each current subscriber to recruit an additional one: that, they believed, would solve the current problems. In this context it is noteworthy that the school did not qualify for a grant from the Education Department, although the managers stressed that they did everything to keep up to the standards of the agreed national code.

Despite this rather dire situation, the report announced a fresh building programme that would provide extra facilities such as new kitchens and dormitory (the old ones were described as 'ruinous and a source of anxiety'), and a new outside corridor to link the old and new parts of the building. In April 1897 the bishop had approved the spending of over £1,500, which included £1,300 on these new buildings and £150 on new kitchen equipment. The investment paid off and later that year the home was recognised for grant purposes by the Education Department. The writer in *The Weekly Register* had lamented the rather ad hoc and piecemeal appearance of the older buildings, due to their being built over the years with no overall plan in mind; the result had been a group of buildings 'exceedingly pretty and picturesque, but rambling and not altogether convenient'. The new building plan would, the writer was sure, keep the beauty and increase the usefulness of the whole.[26] There cannot have been many orphanages across the country claiming to provide 'pretty and picturesque' accommodation for their inmates and to which the word 'beauty' might be applied.

It is worth mentioning here a parallel development in the town of Bedford at this time. This was a home for orphan girls established and run by Anglican nuns in Bromham Road (St Etheldreda's). In addition, newly established Anglican deaconesses provided general assistance and nursing to the poor of the town; their work was especially noticeable in the small-pox epidemic of the early 1870s.[27]

A diocesan seminary

The English and Welsh bishops, at their fourth National Synod in 1873, faced the fundamental question of how their future priests should be trained. As we have seen earlier, the training of priests to serve in England had changed radically in the early nineteenth century and by the time of the restoration of the hierarchy in 1850 was carried out principally in three seminaries that provided secular clergy to serve

26 *The Weekly Register*, 19 June 1897.

27 Sr Hazel Smith, *The Annals of St Etheldreda's*, 2nd rev. ed. (Bedford, 2020); see especially the historical sections by Stuart Antrobus and Enid Desert.

the whole of England and Wales: Ushaw in County Durham in the North; Oscott, Birmingham, in the Midlands; and Ware in Hertfordshire, for the home counties.

One tradition remained strong, that of having 'mixed' colleges with clerical and lay students in the same institution. This went back to the days of the continental colleges: they had been the only places that young English Catholics could attend to get any secondary or higher education, since the penal laws prohibited Catholics from running educational establishments in England or Wales. Economically the colleges could not have survived without the fees of the lay students, but opposition had been growing to the mixed nature of the seminaries once they were re-established in England.[28] In the 1840s, Bishop Walsh of the Central District had wanted to separate lay and ecclesiastical students at his college at Oscott, arguing that the presence of lay students there created an atmosphere alien to the development of a truly priestly ethos among the clerical students. His successor, Bishop Ullathorne, agreed: greater seclusion from the world was required not only for the clerical students but also for the clerical staff teaching them, to prevent too great a worldly spirit from affecting both.

Surprisingly, there had been a seminary in Northampton as early as the 1840s, dedicated to St Felix, the apostle of the East Angles. The idea of having a separate seminary for the Eastern District had been launched by Bishop Wareing in 1842. It was located first of all at Giffard's Hall, in Suffolk, but had moved to Northampton by 1844.We know that one of the teachers there had been a Mgr Mark Oleron,[29] the administrator of the cathedral, who may later have been in overall charge of the college and who had taught divinity there at one time.[30] Collis referred to him as 'the late lamented VG'. The seminary enterprise was never successful, costing as it did too much in manpower and money, and attracting too few students. The bishop sent out a heartfelt appeal to his clergy in March 1850: after ten years in office he felt the district was 'in a more forlorn and helpless position than ever', especially with regard to the supply of priests. He launched a fresh appeal for the seminary, setting up a system whereby the wealthy in the district gave as much as they could from their surplus income, while those 'above the working class' gave 1d each week and the working class gave 1d a month. There would be a detailed accounting and reporting system to go alongside these collections, which Wareing was sure would solve the financial problems of the seminary and create the confidence required to attract new candidates.[31]

The scheme was not successful: the seminary ran until 1853, when it was decided that the number of students was too small to justify the costs in manpower and finance – it had always been 'an expensive white elephant', according to a recent account.[32] Wareing's diocesan report to Rome in 1854 contained no mention of it.

28 A number of English colleges abroad continued to supply priests to serve in England and Wales, principally those in Rome, Lisbon and Valladolid; there were also English seminaries in Douai and, briefly, Bruges. See Michael E. Williams, 'Seminaries and Priestly Formation', in V. A. McClelland and M. Hodgetts (eds), *From Without the Flaminian Gate* (1999), pp. 62–83.

29 Originally a French Capuchin (b.1807; ord. 1831; d.1880); later a priest in the Plymouth Diocese.

30 See Collins, 'An Ancient Catholic Mission', p. 48 and reference to Oleron's journal.

31 NDA, Coll. A. 3. 19, Pastoral Letters, Bishop Wareing.

32 A full account of it is in the diocesan archives, NDA, Coll. A. 3. 3, The Seminary of St Felix … latterly at Northampton; quotation from Young, *Catholic East Anglia*, pp. 143–7, 151.

Across the country as a whole, earlier episcopal synods had seen bitter battles over the ownership of the colleges, their funding and their day-to-day administration. An instruction from Rome in 1855 had recommended that the bishops follow the instructions of the sixteenth-century Council of Trent about the education and training of priests. This would mean each diocese having its own 'minor seminary', under the close supervision of the bishop and providing for junior (roughly equivalent to secondary) education, and a 'major seminary' (for a six-year training leading up to ordination); both sections should ideally recruit purely ecclesiastical students.[33] At the time, whatever the ideal, in reality most of the bishops had neither the funds nor the manpower to do this – and, in any case and despite the quarrels, the three inter-diocesan colleges, along with those abroad, were providing the required supply of clergy.

So, what was under discussion now in 1873 was, in a sense, fundamental: how far a seminary should adopt the sixteenth-century Tridentine ideal of as complete a separation as possible of their students from the world and be directly under the control of the local diocesan bishop. Bishop Ullathorne (now of Birmingham) gave the opening sermon to the assembled bishops at the synod: it was a moving and inspirational call, dwelling on the sacred role of the pastoral priest who above all else needed holiness to serve 'amid the miscellaneous hosts of daring unbelievers who scoff at the priesthood'. Even some priests, he claimed, had eyes with 'too secular a colour'; they must not think that perfection was 'an ivy that only grows on monastic walls'.[34]

The bishops followed his lead in their synodal decrees, stressing the need for seminary training to concentrate on developing holiness at every stage, for while all the faithful were called to be holy, priests must ascend to the very height of sanctity. They had to bear in mind that holiness in them was pre-supposed and must be nothing less than a resemblance to the High Priesthood of Christ. The priesthood, they argued, had been established to be a living reflection of the life of Jesus, labouring in lonely places, in poverty, and in the face of human opposition. The decrees stressed that the dignity of the priest rested on a double title: first, he was the companion of Jesus and had accepted a share in His mission; secondly, he had jurisdiction over the real and the mystical body of Christ. It was a very strong, positive and inspiring ideal, though perhaps rather daunting for would-be aspirants.

At the same time, however, the bishops were pessimistic when they viewed the world in which these future priests would be working. The disturbances and rebellions of human society, they were sure, arose from intemperate liberty and an unrestrained spirit of criticism. In particular, they condemned the *pestifer spiritus* (destructive spirit) of private judgement which was propagated everywhere by books, pamphlets and newspapers.[35] These, they believed, mixed up and confused sacred and profane matters and criticised both, leaving it to private judgement, as heretics did, to decide what was right and wrong. Young seminarians must be taught respect for authority and unquestioning obedience. In particular, the bishops laid down that only

33 *Decreta Quatuor Conciliorum Provincialium Westmonasteriensium 1852–73*, 2nd. ed. (London, no date), pp. 160–1.

34 W. B. Ullathorne, *Ecclesiastical Discourses Delivered on Special Occasions* (London, 1876), pp. 115–46, at p. 135.

35 *Decreta*, pp. 162–6, 219.

those books approved by themselves should be read in seminaries, and that students studying philosophy and theology must be separated from lay students; moreover, young boys (under eighteen) who hoped to be priests should ideally also be educated apart from other children. Manning, no doubt influenced by his Anglican background, did not accept this separation of young clerical and lay students, and thought a 'mixed education' would be good for both; at his college of St Edmund's, Ware, however, the young would-be clerical students wore cassocks. In the new Southwark seminary, under Fr. (later Cardinal) Bourne, boys from the age of fourteen or fifteen wore both cassock and biretta. Moreover, the decrees ordered that, as part of their commitment to the Lord, seminarians should not visit their parents even in the holidays without the permission of their bishop.

Given this context it is not surprising that the bishops were concerned about the curriculum taught in the seminaries, especially that for the senior students. What is surprising to modern minds, however, is their insistence on the use of Latin in the teaching of theology and scripture. They admitted that this might create problems for several of their students but insisted that the advantages of using Latin for both teaching and examining far outweighed the drawbacks. It enabled dogmatic definitions to be remembered and discussed accurately and was, indeed, 'the bond of orthodoxy and the trumpet of universal truth'. A few Catholic writers at the time questioned the wisdom of such an approach, believing that it would lead to 'current formulae being substituted for real thought' and would make it difficult for priests to engage in discussion with an increasingly well-educated laity.[36] The bishops, however, stuck to their point and Latin was used in the seminaries for the teaching of theology and scripture well into the twentieth century.

In a joint pastoral letter,[37] the bishops expanded on the negative aspects of some of these decrees. A basic assumption was that the times were more dangerous than those their forefathers had lived through: active persecution might have killed the body but had not harmed the soul, whereas the present 'days of subtil (*sic*) errors and poisonous refinement' were more perilous than ever and the whole atmosphere of the nineteenth century was hostile to God and the Church, to divine revelation and even to the 'truths of the natural order'. What made all this worse, they were sure, was that the 'unprecedented activity of the press' was spreading this spirit through every class, 'reaching even to the skilled and unskilled' parts of the population: 'From the highest to the lowest class', unbelief had its literature and its apostles.

It is strange that after the synodal decrees about separate seminary education being necessary at all ages, the pastoral letter praised the traditional English practice of mixing lay and clerical students in junior colleges: the bishops argued that the 'early friendships formed in boyhood bind together the Laity and the Clergy through life'. They accepted that rising intellectual standards, among both Catholics and non-Catholics, demanded a higher intellectual culture in the clergy, while the more numerous and developing Catholic middle-class demanded a suitable, and separate, education for its eighteen-to-twenty-two year olds: as a result, the English church must work towards establishing a Catholic university. But there was also a warning

36 Peter Doyle, 'The Education and Training of Roman Catholic Priests in Nineteenth-Century England', in *JEH*, vol. 35, no. 2 (April, 1984), pp. 208–19. See also *Decreta*, p. 169, n. VII.
37 *Ibid.*, pp. 208–19.

for these emerging middle-class Catholics: they needed to be careful about which books they should allow in their homes and exclude 'recent books of fiction ... and works professing to be history and philosophy'.

This pessimistic, anti-world outlook dominated episcopal thinking, despite progress in several areas and a steady growth in numbers of the Catholic laity and clergy. It was the background to what Bishop Amherst of Northampton might hope to achieve for his ecclesiastical students, who up to then had generally completed their theological training at Oscott or one of the English colleges abroad. It appears that it was his idea initially to use the buildings of the orphanage, or Boys' Home, in Shefford (under the care of Fr Collis, who, perhaps, had attended the earlier diocesan seminary of St Felix), to house a small number of young students who might combine their studies with looking after the boys in the home. We know from the annual report of the home for 1881 that the bishop (now Arthur Riddell, 1880–1907) visited there in that year and conferred Minor Orders on two students,[38] while later that year a student left Shefford to complete his studies in Lisbon. Not surprisingly, the sharing of the orphanage buildings and grounds soon proved unsatisfactory. Fortunately, donations and legacies enabled the bishop to purchase an adjacent site in 1883 which became the diocesan seminary, dedicated to St Thomas Aquinas. The annual report spoke in glowing terms of the new arrangements, with their ample gardens and grounds providing 'an abundance of room to breathe in', and with ample space for further expansion.[39]

Whatever the physical setting of the seminary, it was only to be expected that a diocese like Northampton, with an ongoing shortage of priests, would find it difficult to staff it; strangely, this issue seems not to have played a part in the hierarchy's preliminary discussions about the establishment of diocesan seminaries.[40] It is difficult to find precise details of who taught what in the seminary in Shefford, but we know that in the mid-1880s two priests were on its staff, in addition, perhaps, to Collis himself: John Freeland and John Henry Ashmole (both ordained only in 1885). Collis reported that there was opposition from some of the clergy to having the new priests on the staff; the opposition was surely understandable given the state of the diocese and its shortage of clergy. In January 1887 he sent an anguished appeal to the bishop not to move Freeland to a parish: despite all the problems, he had argued a few months earlier, the work of establishing a seminary in the diocese 'had been blessed' and the five priests ordained from it were rendering good service. Moreover, having the seminary next door to the orphanage had led to a number of the boys developing a vocation to the priesthood. To move Freeland would, he claimed, set the whole scheme back ten years.[41] It is clear that the seminary, despite the problems involved in running it, was close to his heart.

38 See note on p. 119.

39 See King, *An Ancient Catholic Mission and its Modern Development*; BA, X627/32, Bound volume of St Francis' Home Reports.

40 It was not just in Northampton; for similar difficulties elsewhere, where Catholics and clergy were more numerous, see George T. Bradley, 'The Leeds Seminary – An Experiment in Clerical Education', in R. Finnegan and G. Bradley, *Catholicism in Leeds, 1794–1994* (Leeds, 1994), pp. 57–70. See also, on Liverpool, Peter Doyle, *Upholland College: One Hundred and Fifty Years of Priestly Training* (Wigan, 2018).

41 He added that Ashmole 'was not very strong in health'; he lived until 1938.

Among the relatively few documents relating to the running of the seminary we have the catalogue of its library, drawn up by John Freeland in 1884.[42] For such a small institution it is extensive, with 354 separate titles; a large number of the works are multi-volume (e.g. Thomas Aquinas' *Summa* in ten volumes, Butler's *Lives of the Saints* in twelve, the works of Bossuet also in twelve, in French), but nothing comes remotely close to its run of the quarterly, *The Dublin Review*, in no fewer than ninety-three volumes; founded in 1836 it was conservative in outlook, a strong advocate of papal infallibility and opposed to all forms of theological liberalism.[43] A note in the catalogue adds that this was donated by Bishop Amherst's sister; a very small number of other works are recorded as donations from current or recently deceased clergy.

The whole collection is listed alphabetically, not catalogued by subject. It is by no means only a theological collection, although, of course, all the traditional Catholic theological and spiritual works are included. Most of the accepted classical authors are represented: from Caesar and Cicero through to Virgil and Xenophon (in Greek and Latin) by way of among others Homer and Ovid, reflecting no doubt the dominance of these authors in contemporary schools and universities. There were a small number of scientific titles, and some representing contemporary controversies, for example Cardinal Wiseman's *Lectures on Science and Religion* and St George Mivart's *The Genesis of Species*. Another contemporary issue is represented by Estcourt's work on the validity of Anglican Orders.

The collection has a considerable number of Latin and French titles and a range of French, Portuguese and Dutch dictionaries, no doubt reflecting the location of the principal English seminaries abroad before the nineteenth century. There are several collections of sermons, including the fifteen volumes of Massillon's complete works. (Jean-Baptiste Massillon (1663–1742) was among the most famous of eighteenth-century preachers, whose sermons were 'marked by unsurpassed brilliance … he was unrivalled as a preacher of moral seriousness'.)[44] Church history is principally represented by Bede's *Ecclesiastical History* and John Lingard's *The Antiquities of the Anglo-Saxon Church*; there are also the four volumes of Döllinger's early *History of the Church*. Finally, literature is represented by Milton's *Paradise Lost and Regained*, the complete works of Shakespeare (as well as Theobald's five-volume edition of the plays), and Arnold's *Manual of English Literature*, Boswell's *Life of Johnson*, and Rousseau's *La Nouvelle Heloise*.

Overall, the collection represents a solid, if rather eclectic, Catholic library of the day, with a scholarly range of both secular and theological works. More than likely it had been originally the library of a priest (or priests) such as Collis himself. The collection would not seem systematic enough for the library of an institution where students were coming to the study of philosophy and theology for the first time, though it does contain what appear to be five volumes of introductory studies on logic, first principles, moral philosophy, psychology and general metaphysics. It would have suited a 'gentleman scholar' (lay or ordained) with a general, learned interest in religion and theology.

42 BA, X627/42, St Thomas Seminary, Shefford, February 1884. Catalogue of Books.

43 See entry in *ODCC*, under 'Dublin Review'.

44 *ODCC*, under 'Jean-Baptiste Massillon'. The library had two sets of this work.

Amongst the other seminary papers in the archives is the 'Ledger for 1893' (in fact it covers 1893 and 1894):[45] this gives running costs in 1894 of £422, with a total debt of £155. A note says this equates to £60 per student (seven at this time, reducing to six the following year). The annual debt varies between £95 and £155. Unfortunately, we have no information about other aspects of the institution including its staffing, day-to-day curriculum and the pastoral training provided. Presumably the bishop thought it was adequate and rejoiced at having even a minute supply of clergy to meet the expanding needs of his diocese.[46]

The first students from the seminary to be ordained priests, in July 1884, were Patrick Grogan and James Collins; at the same time John Henry Ashmole was ordained deacon – he was ordained to the priesthood the following year. A few days later the Rev. Grogan was appointed as an assistant priest to Shefford, while the Rev. Collins went to St John's, Norwich.[47] It appears that there were no further ordinations to the priesthood at the seminary until 1892, though some of the students had transferred to other seminaries for the completion of their studies. In 1892 two students were ordained priests in Shefford, the Revv. G. Page and J. Drake. The following year the Rev. Henry P. Connor, who had been ordained in Spain at Valladolid, moved to Shefford as a member of staff; also that year, the Rev. A. O'Sullivan was ordained priest there, while a year later in 1894 John Lickert began his studies there, going on to be ordained in Rome in 1903. Finally in our period, there were two ordinations in 1896 at Northampton Cathedral of students who had spent at least part of their studies there, the Revv. Thomas Scott and Henry Long.

It was always going to be a struggle to keep the seminary going, and that not just financially: finding adequately qualified staff, and being able to appoint them to non-parochial work, was a problem faced not just by the Diocese of Northampton. By the early 1890s there were nine diocesan seminaries across the country in addition to four abroad, and it is not surprising that given these difficulties there was a major move to replace them with a much smaller number of institutions, each serving a number of dioceses and providing a richer curriculum from a better qualified staff.

When Archbishop Vaughan took over in Westminster in 1892 he chose Oscott, in Birmingham, to be a central seminary for the Midland dioceses and encouraged the bishops to close their small colleges and transfer their students there – on condition, of course, that they shared in the considerable costs of enlarging and running the new college. This was what lay behind Bishop Riddell's appeal in a pastoral letter of 1897: his diocesan share in these costs was to be £2,000 and he simply did not have the funds to enable him to provide such an amount. Without substantial extra donations it would be impossible to have anything like the required funds available for the enlarged Oscott. He pointed out that the annual collection for the diocesan seminary had, in fact, declined from just over £100 per year when it started to only £67 in the previous year. He praised the work of that small institution which, he

45 BA, X627/43, Seminary of St Thomas Aquinas, Shefford. Ledger 1893.

46 One would expect there to be some records at Oscott College, to which the Bedfordshire students were transferred in 1907, but its archives are silent on the matter.

47 NDA, Box 157, Bp Riddell's Assorted Papers. Collins served abroad in his later years; see Fitzgerald-Lombard, *English and Welsh Priests 1801–1914*, pp. 65–70 for Northampton clergy.

claimed, had produced over the years 'a goodly number of pious, zealous and self-sacrificing priests'; it had to be kept going for the good of the church in the east of England. At the same time he urged all, rich and not-so-rich, to contribute to the setting up of what he called the 'Oscott Professorial Fund'; those with lesser means might be able to adopt a student there and pay the whole or part of his pension.[48] The fate of the new central seminary lies outside this account; suffice it to say that when Archbishop Bourne succeeded Vaughan in 1903 he reversed the decision and withdrew his students; the central seminary did not survive. In practice, the college in Shefford continued for a few more years, eventually closing in 1908. Unfortunately the diocesan directories do not name its teaching staff.

Wherever they were trained, in their missionary lives the secular clergy were heavily involved in fundraising and church building. Their key role, however, was of course a pastoral one, providing for their people's spiritual needs by offering them an easily accessible sacramental life and the opportunity to develop regular devotional practices.[49]

48 NDA, Box 157, Bp Riddell's Assorted Papers, Bishop's Pastoral Letters, 6 March 1897.
49 See Judith Champ, *The Secular Priesthood in England and Wales*, esp. chapter 9.

Chapter 9

Elsewhere in Bedfordshire

Luton

Looking at the development of a Catholic presence in the county we have seen how Shefford was first, and alone, for about a century. That presence began to weaken by the mid-nineteenth century, when it was overtaken by the county town of Bedford under the inspirational leadership of Fr Warmoll. What is noticeable by its absence at this time is any such development in Luton, soon to become the leading town in the county.[1] According to the 1851 religious census there was no Roman Catholic presence in the town where one might surely have been expected, and this even though in a pastoral letter of December 1844, Bishop William Wareing of the Eastern District had claimed that there was 'good hope' of establishing a Catholic mission in what was 'a rising and improving town'. He was very positive about the possibility and in 1845 oversaw the setting up of a joint mission based in St Albans, with the Rev. Stephen Ward as the priest serving both towns.[2]

The development of this twin mission would, as elsewhere, depend on attracting outside financial assistance and Ward wrote the by now customary begging letters from newly established missions. A long letter of his in *The Tablet* (9 August 1845), mainly dealing with the situation in St Albans, explained his position with relation to Luton:

> I have, besides attending the Catholics of St. Alban's, to attend the Catholics of Luton, a very rising, prosperous town, about ten miles distant, where I am obliged to say Mass in a very small room at a private house, having nothing for an altar but a common table. Yet the Catholics of Luton, though few in number, are indeed very zealous, and would go beyond their means in contributing to the erection of a chapel, where the performance of the sacred rites of religion could, with more decorum, propriety, and solemnity, be performed. On the 1st of June I celebrated the first Sunday Mass that Luton had known for centuries …

All he needed, he continued, was a small chapel that would act as 'the grain of mustard seed', helping to bring in and provide shelter to the many 'wandering Catholics' that were in that part of the country, 'for the most part Irish … strayed sheep without a shepherd'. At the end of the letter he stressed that he had the approval of both the 'Right Reverend Dr. Griffiths, Vicar Apostolic of the London District (re St Albans) and of the Right Reverend Dr. Wareing, Vicar Apostolic of the Eastern District (re Luton).'

1 See population figures, p. 86.
2 NDA, Coll. B. 5. 12, Luton Churches.

In the November of the same year he wrote an even longer letter on the same lines. One might conclude after reading it that he was feeling a little sorry for himself; or perhaps he just knew what would appeal to the charity of the his better-off readers:

> I officiate alternate Sundays in these two towns, which are ten miles apart, and there is not either a Catholic priest or chapel within fifteen or twenty miles ... Here, then, is a circumference of district, containing from thirty to forty miles in diameter, without chapel or priest but myself. Hence the public may clearly see, as I have two chapels to attend in this vast tract of country without any priest to substitute in my place in case of my absence, that it must be exceedingly inconvenient to me to be obliged to leave these missions in order to make personal claims on the public, whereas this general claim ... will save me the great burden of making individual claims ... [otherwise] what am I to do, or to whom shall I apply for aid?[3]

A few months later he repeated his dislike of approaching individuals for donations: they could, after all, easily use the 'money-order Office'. It is not clear whether his objection was based on a personal dislike of begging in person, or the impracticability of doing so effectively in both St Albans and Luton: despite some geographical exaggeration on his part, and his reference to a 'vast tract of country', the two towns did not constitute an obvious twinning, though there were some compensations. In an aside in a letter of April 1846 he paid tribute to the Protestants among whom he was working: he had met with 'nothing short of respect' from them and had found them,

> an orderly, tranquil people ... prayer is more successful than argument in subduing obstinacy and in effecting reconciliation.

The situation was eased somewhat when some months later he moved from St Albans to Luton permanently, and so could now dedicate his undivided attention just to that mission.[4] As part of that effort he had taken a large hall, '50 feet in length by 20 feet in breadth', and installed an altar, thus providing for the devotional needs of his small congregation. His next plan was to collect enough money to erect a proper chapel. Meanwhile he was distributing tracts, received 'with respect by the hitherto ignorant people'. He was, the paper claimed, surrounded by error 'in all its various phases', with only a few labouring Irish to help him with their 'morsels'. But, the writer concluded, the prospects for the mission in Luton were excellent as long as the new pastor received proper support from the general Catholic body.

What happened next is not at all clear. According to the *Laity's Directory* for 1847 the mission at Luton was without a priest ('vacant') and the Rev. S. Ward was at Barton upon Humber, in Lincolnshire. Certainly the Luton mission closed sometime in 1847 and there appear to have been no definite plans to develop a separate mission there for the next thirty years or so. It lost what connection it had originally had with St Albans after 1850 with the restoration of a full hierarchy: St Albans became part of Westminster Archdiocese and Luton returned to Shefford's care, in the Diocese of Northampton, while Barton upon Humber was in the Nottingham Diocese. The *Catholic Directory* in the 1870s regularly stated 'Luton. Served from Bedford', but on a number of occasions a note was added: 'No room at present where Mass can be said'. What had happened to

3 *The Tablet*, 8 November 1845.

4 *The Tablet*, 26 April, 1846, and 29 March, 1847; copied in NDA, Coll. B. 5. 12, Luton Churches.

Ward's 'large hall'? What, indeed, happened to Stephen Ward himself? In Fitzgerald-Lombard's extensive lists there are a number of priests named Ward, but none with the Christian name Stephen and none in the pre-1850 Northampton or the Nottingham diocesan listings with the right dates. He remains a shadowy figure.

Between 1851 and 1861 Luton overtook Bedford as the largest township in the county.[5] It had for some years been growing away from the rest of the county both socially and economically. It had already lost its aristocratic figurehead when the Marquis of Bute left Luton Hoo for good and the estate was sold in 1847. The aristocratic Bute influence had been strong from the 1760s, perhaps more important in the arts and architecture than in politics, though Bunker talks of things in this regard being 'tantalisingly obscure' as the Bute archive was inaccessible.[6] What we do know is that they had been patrons of the town's Anglican living and decidedly Protestant in outlook. Overall it is difficult to assess the family's role in the town and surrounding areas; it was not that the Marquis played no part in local affairs, but as Bunker shows in his study of the town in the mid-nineteenth century, that involvement was chiefly in the routine roles expected of the local noble family, rather than a serious commitment on its part; as a result it appears that the Marquis was a somewhat remote figure.

The town had Bute Street named after them; they owned the patronage of the town's Anglican church, appointing family relatives to be its (largely non-resident) vicars. The relative weakness of the Church of England was due largely to its absentee vicars and the refusal of its Bute patrons to allow any change; this was also, perhaps, the reason for a general refusal to pay church rates in the 1830s, so that what had been a fine medieval parish church was sadly neglected and in need of a full restoration. Whether Bunker's harsh judgement that the established church 'lay in a state of utter torpor' for the first fifty years of the nineteenth century is totally justified or not, it appears to be not too far off the mark – it was certainly no counter to the strong Non-conformist presence.[7] There was, certainly, an independence of outlook that had been nurtured by the absence of gentry control; as Bunker says, Luton had no examples of powerful individuals who had gained positions in business or politics; rather it was a town with a 'small number of medium-sized manufacturers' and a very large number of 'independent small scale units producing goods and services'. A sense of individualism was far more potent than any sense of collective identity arising from social class, religion or politics. Not surprisingly in such a setting, the 1851 religious census shows the strength of Non-conformity in the town. It was not only a matter of providing religious services: the churches did a great deal to make up for a general lack of recreational facilities and served as a social forum, providing 'a focal point for discussion, agitation, and mobilisation on particular issues'.[8] By the 1870s Luton was a 'thriving industrial centre', with a population in excess of 20,000,

5 See p. 86 for population figures.

6 See quotation from *Travellers Companion* in 1785: generally anti-aristocratic, but on the local Marquis of Bute: '(his) great erudition and noble endowments meliorate even the name of Stewart; and verify the assertion, that, from evil good may arise'. Stephen Bunker, *Strawopolis: Luton Transformed 1840–1876*, BHRS, vol. 78 (Bedford, 1999), p. 28; and see p. 133.

7 Bunker, *Strawopolis*, p. 133. See Chris Pickford, *Bedfordshire Churches in the Nineteenth Century*, BHRS, vol. 77, pp. 437–60, for a full description of the church and its complete refurbishment in the second half of the century.

8 Bunker, *Strawopolis*, p. 138.

and had overtaken Bedford in size.[9] It was flourishing more than its neighbours through being the centre of the straw hat trade, earning for itself the name of 'Strawopolis' (Sir Robert Peel had quipped that all its houses were 'built on straw'). As a result, its women, in particular, had a considerable amount of independence, economic prosperity and self-reliance: according to the returns of 1851 adult women in south Bedfordshire had the highest rate of 'economic activity' in the whole of the country. Rodell has argued that this relatively strong position of female workers was especially important for the growth of Methodism, allowing women to take on the financial commitments of membership.[10] Moreover, as the town lacked a dominant gentry or leisured class it became noted for its general political independence.[11]

After the departure of Ward and the failure to replace him, the Catholic presence lost any position it might have been gaining. Meanwhile the Butes, in the person of the third Marquis (1847–1900), were reputed to be the wealthiest family in Britain: he was the owner of Cardiff docks, Welsh coal mines and extensive Scottish lands and business interests. He was also a noted scholar and linguist. Then, in 1868, he abandoned the family's Protestantism to become a Roman Catholic, and spent the rest of his life using his vast wealth to support mainly Catholic causes. These included building Catholic churches and schools and supporting a range of charitable institutions, in addition to being involved in a number of universities, including a period as rector of St Andrew's, and educational commissions, and writing and translating liturgical and scholarly works.[12]

At long last, one might think, in 1881 the new bishop of Northampton, Arthur Grange Riddell (1880–1907), and his vicar general visited the town to look into the founding of an independent mission. In his Advent Pastoral he announced, 'During the coming year we purpose establishing, if possible, a mission at Luton, where there are about 150 Catholics at a distance of eight miles from the nearest chapel'. No doubt it was the family's former connection with the town that lay behind the bishop's appeal in 1881 to the Marquis of Bute, by now the leading supporter of Catholic charities and projects, to enquire about obtaining a suitable plot of land.

Two years later, in 1883, the bishop described the town as the 'capital of the straw plaiting district', with a general population of 23,000 (the census of 1881 gave 23,959). Again he adverted to the fact that the 150 Catholics were too far from the nearest chapel for most of them to be able to practise their religion – it was obvious, he claimed, that a 'speedy effort' to remedy this situation was needed. *The Tablet* adds to one of its reports, 'No place in England is in more need of a priest than Luton', but does not elaborate. What we do know is that a house at 21 Rothesay Road was taken on a lease of three years, to serve as both presbytery and chapel, and in January 1884 the Rev. Joseph Aloysius O'Connor took up residence (born in Ireland in 1859, he had been ordained in Italy only in 1883; he left the diocese in 1895; his date of death is not listed).[13] An account in *The Catholic Times* of the opening of the chapel in Rothesay Road reads:

9 Allsopp, *The Education and Employment of Girls in Luton*, p. 3.
10 Bunker, *Strawopolis*, pp. 2–3; 138. Rodell, *The Rise of Methodism*, p. 226.
11 Allsopp, *The Education and Employment of Girls in Luton*, pp. 3, 5.
12 For Luton Hoo and the Butes, see Anne Allsopp, *A History of Luton: From Conquerors to Carnival*, 2nd ed. (Andover, 2018), pp. 57–63; also Bunker, *Strawopolis*, esp. pp. 28–38.
13 Kelly dates his arrival in Luton wrongly as having happened in 1893; perhaps that was the date of his appointment – *The Catholic Times* and *The Tablet* both date his arrival in the town

> The little Catholic flock in Luton have the happiness at last of seeing a mission established in their town. The temporary little chapel of the presbytery at no. 21 Rothesay Road was blessed on Sunday last by Rev. Father O'Connor, assisted by Rev. J. Freeland, from the Seminary, Shefford, and Holy Mass was celebrated at 11 o'clock in the presence of forty Catholics, who had received notice beforehand, and were admitted by ticket as a measure of precaution adopted by the priest on this first occasion. The arrangements for admission were carried out by Mr. Bachini; and Mr. Sills presided at the little harmonium which had been engaged for the services. The small choir, trained by Mr. Sills, entered heartedly into the work, and the congregation assisted in the most edifying manner. After Mass Father O'Connor addressed a few eloquent words of encouragement to the congregation. The mission is much in need of assistance from the charitably disposed.[14]

A few weeks later the paper gave an account of an evening service on 1 February 1884, and concluded: 'Great things will be accomplished at Luton, if the charitably disposed Catholics of England send assistance which is much needed for this poor mission'. Interestingly, in the light of this and other similar comments about the mission's poverty, the bishop's log book recorded the purchase of a piece of land in Castle Street in July 1884 for £1,850; could this have been the result of the appeal to the Marquis? No doubt spurred on by this and the appointment of a resident priest, between 1884 and 1886 there were regular appeals in the Catholic press, especially *The Universe* and *The Catholic Times*, for funds to build a proper chapel.

Eventually, in December 1886 an iron chapel was opened by Fr O'Connor in Castle Street, and in January 1887 the bishop set up a convent of Ursuline nuns (a renowned teaching order; referred to by Bell as the Sisters of the Congregation of St Mary) in Rothesay Road where they were to open a boarding and day school. Another unusual development was the arrival in the town of some French emigrés, members of the Third Order of St Dominic de Langres. They bought a house in the town and paid £25 per year to the diocese; some years later, in 1904, the bishop granted them leave to reserve the Blessed Sacrament in their chapel (it seems the house closed in 1907). 1887 also saw an official visitation by the bishop and the conferring of the sacrament of confirmation. Despite these signs of early success, the bishop in 1891 was still listing Luton as one of the missions across the diocese that needed 'special assistance' financially to keep going; he added that while 'the Lord loved cheerful givers he just wished there were more of them.'[15]

The Rev. O'Connor left Luton in 1892 and was replaced later that year by the Rev. Ashmole (1853–1938; ordained in 1885), who served there until leaving to be cathedral administrator in 1898. The Rev. Stanley was there for a few months before the Rev. Dudley Cary-Elwes took over for the next four years, being replaced in 1902 by Fr Henry O'Connor. Cary-Elwes' family came from Great Billing, Northamptonshire; he was already known in Bedford as a public speaker and commentator and went on to become bishop of Northampton in 1921.[16]

to January 1884. There were two priests named O'Connor at this time in the diocese; the other was Fr Henry O'Connor (1867–1952) ordained priest in 1893.

14 *The Catholic Times*, 25 January 1884.

15 Young (ed.), *Catholic East Anglia*, p. 173; see also *The Tablet*, 5 December 1891.

16 See Robbins, *John Priestley Warmoll*, pp. 147, 182. There is a small photograph of him, taken some years later, in Lance, *The Returning Tide*, p. 33.

Further episcopal visits and confirmation took place in 1895 and 1899. According to a much later report from the bishop, the plot of land mentioned as being worth £1,850 was still 'lying idle' in 1905, and it was not until 1910 that a new chapel in Castle Street was opened. Unfortunately, the early registers for Luton are missing; the first available ones date from 1915.

Leighton Buzzard

Leighton Buzzard is a market town in the south-west of the county, close to the Buckinghamshire border and on the Grand Union canal, about ten miles from Luton. It experienced population growth through the nineteenth century, but not on the scale of either Bedford or Luton: in 1841 it was in the region of 4,000 (including Linslade), in 1871, 7,000, and in 1901, 8,400. It had some industry in the form of straw basket making, plaiting, and, importantly, sand extraction, but it was essentially a market town, with a key rail link to London from 1838; its poor law union workhouse served fifteen surrounding parishes. Along with its close neighbour, Linslade, it had a reputation as something of a wealthy playground, particularly for the hunting fraternity – indeed, a recent study has called it 'the most fashionable hunting scene in Britain' by the end of the century, with prosperous hotels, and nearby hunting lodges and country houses, no doubt all helped by its links to the capital.[17]

There was also a strong historic Non-conformist presence in the town, with an attendance level of the Wesleyans in 1851 approaching 40%, compared with about 16% for the Church of England. Also strongly represented there were the Quakers, who were to play a key part in the commercial development of the area and, later, in opposing the establishment of a non-religious School Board for the town in the 1890s.[18]

Roman Catholics were as good as non-existent in the town, at least as far as any public presence was concerned. Long-standing opposition to them had been increased some years before when the local vicar, Joseph Stevenson, and his wife had become Catholics in 1862. Ten years later he was ordained as a Catholic priest for the Birmingham Diocese, and afterwards became a Jesuit.[19] While he did not serve as a priest in Leighton Buzzard, he did visit the mission there and gave occasional talks, as reported in the Catholic press; one of his talks, for example, had been on 'The Early History of Leighton'. According to a report in the Catholic press, he had said Mass for the first time in the town since the Reformation, in 'the little Oratory not far from the old Vicarage which he had built in his Protestant days'. His daughter (also a convert) attended, with another former lady of his congregation who had also become a Catholic and had helped to establish the Catholic mission there.[20] The lady in question was probably Mrs White, whose role we will examine later.

17 Paul Brown and Delia Gleave, *Sand, Planes and Submarines: Leighton Buzzard and the First World War* (Stroud, 2017), pp. 11–12.

18 Rodell, *The Rise of Methodism*, p. 160; on the Quakers, Bell, *Belief in Bedfordshire*, pp. 123–6, and Allsopp, *The Education and Employment of Girls in Luton*, p. 65; on its general development, Paul Brown, *Leighton Buzzard and Linslade: A History* (Chichester, 2008). It was to play a surprising key role in the 1914 war; see Brown and Gleave, *Sand, Planes and Submarines*.

19 Fitzgerald-Lombard, *English and Welsh Priests*, pp. 28, 222.

20 See *The Tablet*, 5 November 1892.

It seems that from 1881 a priest from Wolverton said Mass regularly in nearby Linslade and we know that from May 1892 Mass was said monthly in Leighton Buzzard itself by the Rev. Henry Parkes of Wolverton, temporarily in charge of the mission, in a room over a general shop in North Street. According to the report in *The Tablet* this development was met, not surprisingly in the circumstances, by 'much opposition' in the town.[21] The Rev. Parkes' persistence, however, paid off and a report in October 1893 claimed that the number of Catholics in the town had increased by then from an 'initial three', so that a church was now needed to accommodate them.[22] The same report also stated, rather oddly in the circumstances, that a 'statue of the Blessed Virgin Mary and Child' had been set up in 'the Catholic Church' there. Presumably this was in the room used by Parkes as a temporary chapel. There is a brief notice in the bishop's records that he conferred confirmation in Leighton Buzzard on 28 August 1894.

While no indication of numbers is given, obviously some progress was being made.[23] An appeal for funds 'to put the Mission on a firm footing' had appeared in the press early in 1894.[24] Interestingly, subscriptions could be sent either to Parkes in Wolverton, or to John Orlebar Payne MA, 'a quondam Anglican curate near Leighton Buzzard' now living in Highgate, London.[25]

Developments had been facilitated by financial assistance from a Mrs White, the convert widow of a local wine merchant, who lived in Coyle House. In a letter to Bishop Riddell in September of that year she explained,

> I gave yesterday to Father Parkes my 'Midland Railway' papers which he suggested forwarding on at once by post, but I advised him to wait and take them to you himself. It is with great happiness to me that at last the commencement of a mission is made here & [I] trust it will bring a Blessing to the Town. Yours very sincerely, Mrs E. White.[26]

The 'papers' in question were shares in the railway, worth £436 and bringing in an annual income of about £25. The bishop had decided that the money should be used solely for the 'Leighton Buzzard mission where Mass is now said once a month'. The gift, and an additional one-off one of £25 from her, allowed the room in North Street to be used regularly by Rev. Parkes.

Two years later the bishop appointed the first resident priest in the town, the Rev. Charles E. Reilly (1864–1916), who took up residence late in October 1895 and set about raising funds for a permanent chapel.[27] As was usual at the time, he launched a nationwide appeal through the columns of the Catholic press. *The Universe* in May and June 1896, for example, headlined a column about Leighton Buzzard rather strangely as 'The Hub of Anti-Catholic Influence', going on to describe the mission there as 'tiny and pinchingly-poor' in a district 'long dominated by Protestantism and

21 *The Tablet*, 28 May 1892.
22 *The Catholic Times*, 6 October 1893.
23 NDA, Coll. A. 6. 20, Diocesan Synod, Visitation of Bedford.
24 *The Tablet*, 10 March 1894.
25 See p. 9, fn 5.
26 https://www.sacredheartlb.org.uk/parish-history/early-days/, Sacred Heart Catholic Church – Leighton Buzzard; accessed online September 2021.
27 He had been ordained in 1894; later he served in the Diocese of Southwark from 1908.

where anti-Catholic influences are still strong'.[28] The appeal continued the following week when contributors to the building fund were urged to leave 'the dead sea of Protestantism' and join 'the barque of Peter – the ark of the one true Church'. It was unusual at the time for such appeals to say anything openly derogatory about any of the Protestant churches, but Reilly was not pulling any punches: he urged his readers to be as generous as their means would allow and even be willing to make sacrifices in the cause of building a church,

> in a district where the old faith is reviving, where at last the dark night of heresy is departing, and souls delivered from doubt and the long agony of uncertain years find in the Catholic communion the 'serene regions of truth' and the Catholic Church to be the 'shadow of a great rock in a weary land'.[29]

His metaphors may have been mixed but his meaning was quite clear.

As we have seen, the first confirmations in the town had already been conferred by the bishop and in August 1896 he was in the town again to repeat the ceremony. By Christmas that year there were enough Catholics in the neighbourhood to put on a special concert in the town's Victoria Hall. It is reported that the Catholic children of the town put on a 'capital programme' of songs, recitations and musical drill, with tea provided. Further appeals followed in 1897 (this time in *The Tablet* and *The Weekly Register*). Reilly spoke, rather ambitiously it may seem, about what great things the French Catholics had achieved in erecting a magnificent church dedicated to the Sacred Heart in Montmartre, Paris; could not English Catholics help him to build a church, also dedicated to the Sacred Heart though in a more humble style, in Leighton Buzzard?[30] His appeals were successful in the end and by December 1897 he had built a tin church on a plot of land that he had bought, with the bishop's approval, for £250 – it measured 60 ft. × 138 ft. He was also appealing for funds to build a presbytery and lift some of the 'pecuniary cares' that were troubling him. In another of his odd claims he stated that the people's contributions would be 'a lever to lift the Protestant community into the regions of Truth and Light'.[31] By this time there seem to have been about forty Catholics in the town and surrounding area.

The new church was in the Beaudesert part of town. A report in the local press about the new church was mainly positive:

> The Roman Catholics appear to have concluded that they now have established themselves in Leighton, and the erection of a church as a separate building has been commenced on a site on the south-west side of the Beaudesert Road, near to the junction with the Vandyke and Hockliffe Roads. The structure is said to be but a temporary one, of iron, until circumstances and expected requirements shall justify the erection of a more substantial and permanent building. The church will be an iron one, of rather handsome design, consisting of a nave, with front porch, sanctuary and sacristy, with pointed bell turret over the nave.[32]

28 *The Universe*, 30 May 1896.
29 *The Universe*, 6 June 1896.
30 *The Tablet* and *The Weekly Register*, May 1897.
31 *The Tablet*, 11 December 1897.
32 *The Leighton Buzzard Observer*, 14 September 1897. The reference to a 'temporary' building is interesting; it remained in use until 1953!

The report added that the cost of the church, in addition to the site costs, would be £150; the contractor was Mr Humphreys of Knightsbridge, with a local builder, Mr Tutt, providing the brickwork foundations. Apart from the low overall cost, the advantages of the pre-fabricated building methods were the speed of construction – a mere six weeks.

While the local press had said there would be no special opening, just a visiting preacher (perhaps aware of local Protestant opposition, evidenced in the breaking of Reilly's windows by 'a mob'), in practice there were special services on consecutive Sundays, with a formal 'Opening Service' at which the Rev. Fr. Dunstan OSF, superior of the Franciscan house in Buckingham, preached. The notice in the local press advertised 'all seats free' and that 'the non-Catholic public is specially invited'.[33] To mark the opening, Mrs White donated various items for its furnishing – statues of Our Lady and St Joseph, six large candlesticks and an 'American organ' – while another, anonymous, donor gave a monstrance and pyx, vestments and other ceremonial items; finally, Fr Reilly's parents donated a silver chalice (valued at £18).

An appeal in *The Tablet* in December, however, stressed how short Reilly was of funds: in particular, he needed a proper presbytery. A later letter of February 1898 explained that he needed £400 to complete matters: thirty ten-pound notes 'would end his misery'. Interestingly, later that year a letter from Lady Herbert of Belgrave Square, London, in *The Tablet*, appealed on his behalf for £60 to 'complete church and presbytery'; the priest was also looking after Dunstable, she claimed, and devoting his life to evangelizing 'this spiritually destitute part of England'. The appeal was clearly successful as the priest's house was completed in 1898, designed by an architect, Mr M. S. Reilly, of Croydon, Surrey (a relative, perhaps?).[34] Mass had been said in Dunstable for the first time in October 1894, with a regular monthly Mass there starting about a year later,[35] but it was not until the 1920s that it had a resident priest and purpose-built chapel. Reilly, however, was not content: in February, 1899, he was writing to the papers again to beg money to build a 'proper church' to replace the iron one; he promised 'prizes' for the most successful fund raisers – he had been given a silver watch, pieces of jewellery and two musical instruments for the purpose. Nothing came of this final venture.[36]

Clearly, Reilly was not one to keep his head down, especially if he felt he was being unfairly treated because of his Catholicism. In a rather bizarre incident in late 1898 he publicly accused the local burial board of refusing to allow him to put a Catholic inscription on his mother's tombstone in the form of a quotation from St Ambrose: 'We have loved her in life, let us not forget her after death', and then of making him wait much longer for permission than local Protestants had to wait. It is clear that there was no truth in his accusation, but he wrote some very angry letters to the *Leighton Buzzard Observer* to press his case.[37]

33 *The Leighton Buzzard Observer*, 14 December 1897.

34 *The Tablet*, 11 December, 1897; 5 February 1898; 12 November 1898; NDA, Box 157, Bp Riddell's Assorted Papers, Bishop's Logbook (unpaginated) under Leighton Buzzard.

35 *The Tablet*, 26 October 1895.

36 *The Weekly Register*, 4 February 1899. The new church had to wait until 1953.

37 NDA, Coll. A. 6. 20, Diocesan Synod, Visitation of Bedford.

In 1900 he retired because of ill-health and was replaced by Canon George Frederick Stokes (1846–1928), formerly the priest in Wolverton who had said Mass occasionally in Leighton Buzzard in the early 1880s.[38] The early mission registers 1895–1900 exist (see pp. 220–2).

Elsewhere in the county there were two or three Mass centres in operation by the end of this period, but none of them had been formally established as missions. In Ampthill, for example, permission had been granted by the bishop in 1897 to the Rev. Middleton of Bedford to say Mass in the town 'now and then'; this did not result in the establishment of a mission. It was not until 1905 that a chapel was established in Biggleswade (a town of virtually no growth, with a population of 4,460 in 1851 and only 4,943 forty years later), with Mass said monthly by a priest from Shefford or Hitchin, who also provided a Sunday evening service every week; some years later this became a mission/parish in its own right. Finally, Mass was said in Dunstable in temporary accommodation from 1895; this also developed later into a mission in its own right.[39]

Biggleswade Chapel (at the far end of the cul-de-sac), c. 1905.
The contrast with the churches built in Bedford and Shefford, both built with money from wealthy patrons, is striking.
(courtesy of Biggleswade Historical Society)

[38] NDA, Box 157, Bp Riddell's Assorted Papers, Bishop's Minute Book 1900. The bishop decided that Mrs White's donation, however it had been used, belonged to the diocese. The incumbent, however, was allowed £20 per year from the interest as part of his stipend. See Bishop Riddell's Mission Book, p. 8.

[39] Bernard Kelly, *Historical Notes on English Catholic Missions* (London, 1907, repr. 1995). See also *Northampton Diocesan Directory* (Northampton, 2017), p. 65.

Chapter 10
Education and schools

> We clearly see and deeply lament the very general and most pressing want of a religious education for the children of the Poor in our respective Districts; and with our united voice, we now proclaim to you with all the earnestness of our souls, that on the success of this our common effort in behalf of the children of the Poor, not only our religious progress and prosperity, but also the eternal salvation of thousands does depend.[1]

This was the first statement of the English and Welsh vicars apostolic as a body on education, in 1847, when they agreed to set up the Catholic Poor School Committee as the body to negotiate with the government for financial assistance for Catholic schools.[2] Although, as we have seen, the Relief Acts of 1778 and 1791 had removed the ban on Catholic teachers working in England and Wales as well as the ban on the establishment of Catholic schools, it was not until after the Emancipation Act of 1829 that the provision of education had become a major interest and concern. It is worth noting the stress on 'eternal salvation' in the above appeal: this was to be the constant rationale behind appeals by the bishops for financial help.

When the new hierarchy met for their first synod in 1852 the education of the poor was again one of their priorities and they laid down what a priest's priority should be when opening a new mission:

> Wherever there may seem to be an opening for a new mission, we should prefer the erection of a school, so arranged as to serve temporarily as a chapel, to that of a church without one. For the building raised of living and chosen stones … is of far greater importance than the temple made with hands. And it is the good school that secures the virtuous and edifying congregation.[3]

A 'good school' in this context was clearly to be judged by the quality of its religious instruction. There was to be a system of Catholic school inspectors to ensure this, and it was to be a key duty of the local clergy to give catechetical instruction to the children on Sundays and in the schools. This became a regular theme, with the bishops castigating wealthy Catholics (the gentry and professional classes in particular) for not doing more financially to help such provision: they were accused of having only a 'feeble interest in the great work of educating the poor'.[4] It is clear from

1 *The Tablet*, 26 February 1848.
2 Maurice Whitehead et al, 'Education and Schooling', in *The Oxford History of British and Irish Catholicism*, vol. 4, *Building Identity, 1830–1913*, pp. 94–118, at pp. 95–6.
3 Synodical Letter, 17 July 1852, quoted in Maurice Whitehead, 'A View from the Bridge: The Catholic School', in McClelland and Hodgetts (eds), *From Without the Flaminian Gate*, pp. 217–44, at p. 219.
4 *Ibid.*, from the 1854 Report of the Catholic Poor School Committee.

the language used that the overwhelming concern of the bishops was the religious education that the poor would receive in such schools and the fear that attendance at non-Catholic establishments would gravely endanger their faith. There were, indeed, a few die-hards not convinced of the supposed value of universal education: its effects on the poor were not always beneficial, they claimed, and it often seemed to make them 'both saucy and indifferent'.[5]

The 1860s were the decade that saw an explosion in the provision of Anglican and Non-conformist elementary schools across Bedfordshire, with an additional almost thirty established by 1869, giving a total of seventy-three on the government's grant-aided list. Some of these schools replaced established older ones (for example at Cranfield), others were entirely new (for example at Willington). All were open to government inspection as a condition of their application for funding according to the new payment-by-results system. Not all the school managers and teachers welcomed this, claiming it set artificial limitations on the curriculum and put too much stress on the 'three Rs'. There is no doubt, however, of the advances it produced in the provision of elementary education before 1870, so much so that Bushby claims that by then every parish in the county had some means of providing its children with a basic education. Those involved in organising and running this county-wide provision were very largely the Anglican clergy, supported financially by the gentry or charities, with a small number of additional Wesleyan institutions.[6] It was the same clergy who in the main were to oppose the provisions of the 1870 Act, seeing in them a threat of secularisation through the establishment of Board Schools to replace their parochial establishments.

Education in Bedford

Given this context, it is interesting that in Bedford town none of the churches had established specifically church schools before the 1860s, leaving such provision to the Harpur Trust charity and a few individuals. The first church to do so had been the Roman Catholics under the Rev. Warmoll, who was keen to provide education especially for the younger children of the poor in his congregation. His biographer says that he had had some experience of teaching while serving as an Anglican curate at Hurstpierpoint, and probably also in Pimlico. There is some uncertainty about the exact dates of the schools' erection (and, in some instances of their closure), but it seems to be accurate to say that in 1867 the first school building was opened in Brereton Road under, from at least 1869, a Miss Parkes; this replaced an informal school that Rev. Warmoll had run in his house.[7]

With the move towards universal schooling in 1870, however, it was clear that efforts would have to be made to establish a national Catholic system, and financial support to set up a Catholic National Fund was forthcoming on an unprecedented

5 See Bishop Goss, in Peter Doyle, *Mitres and Missions in Lancashire: A History of the Roman Catholic Diocese of Liverpool 1850–2000* (Liverpool, 2005), p. 153.

6 D. W. Bushby (ed.), *The Bedfordshire Schoolchild: Elementary Education before 1902*, BHRS, vol. 67 (Bedford, 1988), pp. 6–7.

7 Robbins, *John Priestly Warmoll*, p. 153.

scale: the Duke of Norfolk and the Marquis of Bute each pledged £10,000, Lord Howard of Glossop £5,000, and seven others £1,000 each.[8] Moreover, Catholics nationally felt confident enough to attack the spread of Board Schools after 1870, on the grounds that they were irreligious and so a danger to Catholic children who might have to attend them. In 1875 the bishops went as far as forbidding Catholic teachers to work in such schools, while Bishop Bagshaw of Nottingham published a pamphlet, 'The Danger to Christianity of the School Board System'.

Not surprisingly, such developments (and the growth of so-called 'Roman tendencies' within the national church) re-aroused the more extreme anti-Catholicism latent in sections of English society. Recent work on opposition to Catholic schools in Victorian times, for example, quotes a late-nineteenth century Anglican clergyman declaring that Catholic schools were a threat similar to the Spanish Armada, only now the enemy was already within the walls! Earlier perceptions had seen Catholic schools not as places of education but as 'outposts of a prospective, papal empire'.[9]

Part of this opposition may have arisen from the large number of religious sisters (and some brothers) who were teaching in Catholic schools, among whom were a considerable percentage of 'foreigners'. Between 1840 and 1880 the number of convents in England and Wales grew amazingly from twenty to over 300 (representing sixty-two active congregations or orders), with the large majority of the nuns being non-English: just over half of them were French, half a dozen were Belgian and most of the rest were Irish. While by no means all of these nuns were dedicated to teaching (nursing and various forms of social work were other priorities), the Catholic elementary school system could not have developed as it did without their input. Only one of these congregations (the Ursulines) was active in Bedfordshire before 1900, but the Sisters of Notre Dame (a Belgian Congregation) had opened a convent in Northampton in 1852 (taking over from an earlier congregation of two Belgian sisters that had been set up there in 1847). Their brief, as laid out by Bishop Wareing (vicar apostolic of the Eastern District, from 1850 bishop of the Diocese of Northampton) was to open a day school to teach 'reading, writing, catechism and plain needlework', a night school for young women, and a workroom where girls could earn a living from needle work without 'being exposed to the contaminating influence of shops and factories'.[10]

The Education Act of 1870 changed the whole scene in the town of Bedford and the Roman Catholics were no longer alone among the churches in providing elementary schools. The Harpur Trust continued to be the largest provider, and a

8 *Ibid.*, p. 155. It was Bishop Goss, in fact, who organised the meeting where these pledges were made. For a detailed account of the development of the Catholic elementary school system, see A. C. F. Beales, 'The Struggle for the Schools', in Beck (ed.), *The English Catholics 1850–1950*, pp. 365–409, esp. pp. 365–85 for the period covered in this book.

9 See Aidan Cottrell-Boyce, 'Scandal in Somerstown: Conspiracism and Catholic Schools in Early Victorian England', in *BCH*, vol. 35, no. 4 (October, 2021), pp. 415–39.

10 For the work of the Sisters of Notre Dame, Jennifer Worrall SND (ed.), *Jubilee: Sisters of Notre Dame de Namur Celebrate 150 Years in Britain, 1845–1995* (privately published, 1995), pp. 1–89. See also Susan O'Brien, 'French Nuns in Nineteenth Century England', in *Past and Present*, vol. 154 (February, 1997), pp. 142–80, and her chapter 'Religious Life for Women', in McClelland and Hodgetts (eds), *From Without the Flaminian Gate*, pp. 108–41.

return in 1876 to the Education Department includes churches and private individuals, and lists the official numbers that each school could accommodate:

Harpur Trust:		
Mr Bates' School	490	
Miss Mitchell's School	546	
Hawes Street	139	
Ampthill Road	692	
Tower School	165	
Total	2,032	
Churches:		
Holy Trinity	195	
Roman Catholic	134	
Primitive Methodist	40	
St Peter's Mission School	156	
Total	525	
Schools to be opened shortly:		
Roman Catholic	277	
St Paul's	260	
St Cuthbert's	120	
Total	657	
If the school in Horne Lane[11] now occupied by Mr Porter and built for the elementary school be allotted it will accommodate	350	
	350	
Children attending schools belonging to the Harpur Trust not elementary between 5 and 13		
Grammar	126	
Modern	89	
Lower	195	
	410	
Total		3,974

As the Education Department had calculated that there was a need for 2,520 places, the figures showed that the schools were actually (or could be) providing an excess of 1,454. The report claimed that a total of 3,131 children were, in practice, attending these schools out of the census count of 3,226, so, officially, only 95 were not attending at all.[12]

One must be careful, however, in how one uses these statistics, especially the number of pupils listed: these were the numbers that the schools were registered for; actual regular attendances appear to have fallen short of these, sometimes markedly so. Furthermore, these statistics had been drawn up with a very particular aim in mind: to show the authorities in the Education Department that, in line with the Education Act of 1876, there was enough provision available in the town to negate

11 It was used as an infants' school from 1880.

12 From D.W. Bushby, 'Elementary Education in Bedford 1868–1903', in BHRS, vol. 54 (Luton, 1975), pp. 29–31, 103–4.

the need for a Board School (often referred to as 'God-less' institutions) and may well overstate the provision of places (so, for example, some of the schools were 'shortly to be opened', and the Hawes Street school very shortly closed). The move to avoid the setting up of a school board was successful, and from 1877 the town had two bodies responsible for elementary education: the Harpur Trust Elementary Schools' Committee and the School Attendance Committee. The former actually ran elementary schools, the latter ran no schools but made the bye-laws that all the schools had to follow; membership of these two bodies often overlapped.[13]

As far as the Roman Catholics of the area were concerned, as we have seen, the Rev. Warmoll had made a start – in his dining room – in May 1867. He employed a schoolmistress for the infants – a Miss Matilda Parkes (from Oxburgh), and soon added a Miss Catherine O'Keefe. Bushby states this was the first attempt by any church in Bedford to open a school. After about a year he had two 'schools' running: a mixed school for older children and one for infants, each with sixty pupils. There were not, of course, anything like that number of Catholic children in the area: of the 120 attendees, about 100 had Protestant parents. Warmoll wrote, 'In spite of surrounding prejudices, and of many inducements to go elsewhere, they came to us'.[14] The Brereton Street school moved to Church Street in 1874, probably earlier, providing places for 150 children. This was officially visited by HMI in the same year,[15] and a grant of £43. 8s. 4d. was awarded in 1876, the rest of its funding coming from voluntary contributions and school pence.[16] In 1877 a new, larger school was opened in Priory Street at a cost of £1,700, providing 200 places; Church Street remained as the infants school.[17]

When HMI had visited in 1874 they had reported: 'Both schools are orderly; but as they are filled with children who have recently come to them, there is little in the way of instruction to judge of'. Warmoll commented in his Christmas letter of that year that no government grant could be expected for a year at least and so he asked for donations to improve conditions in the existing buildings and also to build a new school altogether. By August the following year he could report:

> Our ship is built and safely launched, but her difficulty lies in tiding over the harbour-bar. Upon this she has slightly grounded. A little aid will liberate her.

The language was unusually metaphorical and perhaps not altogether clear to his readers, but the usual tug-boats appeared, provided the 'little aid' and the ship was safely afloat. No doubt it was helped by having as its crew two teachers, both of whom were noted as having passed the official teachers' examination and so could claim provisional certificates.[18]

13 *Ibid.*, p. 31.
14 Robbins, *John Priestley Warmoll*, p. 153.
15 Her Majesty's Inspectorate for Schools had begun operating in 1840 and was the government's official grant-awarding body.
16 'School pence': commonly used to refer to the pennies children were expected to pay for their schooling.
17 Robbins, *John Priestley Warmoll*, pp. 153ff.
18 NDA, Coll. B. 5. 1, Church of the Holy Child and St Joseph, Bedford; also Bushby, 'Elementary Education in Bedford 1868–1903', pp. 154–5.

Getting children to attend school regularly was a consistent problem for all elementary schools at that time; it did not become a legal requirement until 1880 and even then could be patchy, especially in rural areas where children were expected to help with seasonal work. Some indication of attendances and attitudes may be gained from the official logbook kept by Miss O'Keefe:

> Attendances for August 1875:
>
> 9th: school re-opened. Attendance very good.
> 10th: school excursion by train to Weston (Underwood).
> 11th: attendance low; timetable not followed faithfully. Children tired after yesterday's happy holiday.
> 16th: numbers low this afternoon because circus in town.
> 20th: average low this month. A few of the children are gleaning.

There was a note of alarm in her entry for 29 October 1875: she had received from the Education Department,

> the somewhat startling news that the Second Standard would be required to practise their work on paper (*sic*) in future. This has compelled me to depart from the timetable for the present to let classes 3 and 4 have their sums at one time.

By November that year Canon Warmoll could note that there were signs of slow improvement, even though the children were generally 'of a low class'; any hope of future grants would depend on improved results in the following year.[19] In 1876 the schools did receive a grant of £43. 8. 4; the rest of the money needed came from voluntary donations of £36 and school pence of £33. 10. 8. The log book noted that the school room was too small for the numbers attending – children were 'overflowing into the sacristies quite up to the church door'; perhaps this was at least part cause of the poor results.

Things were about to change quite radically. Warmoll's appeals were, as usual, very successful. In May 1876 he announced that the Duke of Norfolk had donated £300 towards a new school (plus a 'generous sum' for the church); an anonymous donor had given £200 (plus £400 for the church); another, £100, with even more than the others towards the church. As a result, he could announce in December 1876 that on a site in Priory Street 'extensive schoolrooms, substantial and plain' were being roofed, thus averting the threat of a school board, but there was still a debt of £1,000.[20] The builders were Samuel French of Kempston. The site was part of the grounds of the pre-Reformation Franciscan Friary in Priory Street. The school opened officially on 7 August 1877, apparently without any mention in the local press.

The schoolmistress of the new school was Catherine O'Keefe. The infant school continued in Church Street under Matilda Parkes, later assisted by a Miss O'Neill. At times there were over 200 children in attendance in Priory Street, though fewer than fifty of them seem to have been Catholics.

One might have thought that Warmoll would have been a happy man or at least a contented one, but not quite everything was going well. He reported only a month after

19 *Ibid.*, p. 156.
20 *The Weekly Register*, 2 December 1876.

the opening of the school that he had not been able to meet the deadline for repaying the last instalment of the debt on the building and his old fears were recurring: if, as seemed likely, he had to close the new school,

> (the buildings) and the site would fall into Protestant hands, a School Board formed and all the money we have collected would be returned to the donors.[21]

Since this did not happen, we can only conclude that one or more of his donors came to its rescue.

A piece in *The Architect* in June the following year gave a brief mention:

> These schools were recently erected for the accommodation of 300 children of both sexes. The walls are faced with red brick relieved with blue brick patterns and bonds. The windows and other dressings are stained and varnished, and covered with local tiles relieved by crest and filials [finials?].[22]

A listing from 1878 provides the building costs:

	£	
Lands for schools & playground	472	
Building new schools	1,670	
Architect's commission	75	2,217

The debts were paid off remarkably quickly, so that in late 1879 Warmoll could report that only £100 remained; at the same time he reported the withdrawal of the Catholic Poor Schools Committee's grant, the downside, no doubt, of his success as a fund-raiser. If we take into account the other building debts he listed at that time, not to mention his day-to-day expenses, his success was quite amazing:

Land for church and presbytery	380	
Building presbytery and large room	1,450	
Architect's commission	74	
Building church	3,572	
Architect's commission	185	
Clerk of Works salary	200	
Roads and pavement	59	5,920

Clearly there could be no doubting his commitment to the schools and the education of the poor and his determination that that education should be firmly religion-based. He continued to fear that a school board would be set up, as he wrote later:

> By prompt action alone could the catastrophe be averted. A remarkably felicitous purchase secured a large site, than which nothing better could be desired. It seemed better to me that the schoolroom erected upon it should be large with a view to future needs, and decidedly cheaper and more satisfactory in the long run that, like the church and house, they should be substantial.[23]

All was not well, however, and in 1880 the HMI report (in the school logbook) declared that the school was only

21 *The Weekly Register*, 15 September 1877.

22 30 June 1878.

23 Robbins, *John Priestley Warmoll*, p. 157.

> in moderately fair shape. The numbers have increased, but the attainments generally are not very perfect. The issue of a certificate to the teacher of the Mixed School must be deferred until better results are obtained in Writing and Arithmetic.[24] [a note indicated that four children entered for the exam were not qualified to be entered]

This raises one of the major problems of the day, how to recruit and keep good teachers. Bushby shows that the Catholic school in Priory Street employed nine different teachers in the years between its opening in 1877 and its closure in 1889; of these, only one stayed for three years, the remainder lasted only one or two years. This, clearly, was not a pattern that enabled the development of a consistent regime in the school or helped immature teachers to learn from their elders.

Despite the HMI's less than fulsome report in 1880, Warmoll continued to be reasonably optimistic, reporting in the log book for September 1883:

> Examined Standards VII, VI, V and IV. Was generally much gratified at the progress they have made, with three or four anticipated exceptions. A few children in Standard V hardly did justice to their ability ... through a lack of the full attention required.[25]

His interest, and practical involvement, obviously continued to the end. Sadly, as we will see, his Catholic schools legacy did not last (see pp. 149–52).

Education in Luton

In general, there is no doubt about the contribution of the Harpur Trust to elementary education in the town of Bedford; indeed, the Report of the Endowed Schools Commission in 1868 claimed that it had few if any equals in the whole of the country, so much so that by 1883 the town was being talked of as 'the metropolis of education in England'.[26] In this context comparison with Luton is telling: whereas the Trust provided a good education to both boys and girls, Luton did not see the provision of schools for either group as having any particular importance, and when they had to be established after 1870 their contribution was reported as being 'utilitarian and thin'. From the numbers point of view, however, the percentage of children in attendance was relatively comparable to those elsewhere: an unofficial census in 1874 showed that of the 2,868 children registered as being of school age, the average attendance was 1,861.[27] When it came to religious education in the town, to begin with there was considerable disagreement and strong opposition between the supporters of the various religious schools and the school board (pp. 140–1), even though the latter offered a religious syllabus that to modern eyes seems quite thorough, though of course strictly non-denominational:

> The Bible and the fundamental principles of Religion and Morality shall be taught by the Teachers ... no attempt shall be made to direct attention to attach children

24 *Ibid.*, pp. 160–1.

25 *Ibid.*, p. 161.

26 Bushby, 'Elementary Education in Bedford 1868–1903', p. 13; Allsopp, *The Education and Employment of Girls in Luton*, pp. 12–13.

27 Allsopp, *The Education and Employment of Girls in Luton*, pp. 13, 69.

> to any particular denomination, and that subject thereto the following course of Religious Instructions shall be adopted and carried out.[28]

There followed a description of some of the courses to be followed in the different years: parts of the bible, with certain sections to be learned by heart; the hymn book to be used in assemblies, along with set prayers; an assembly, with prayers and singing was to take up fifteen minutes, followed by half-an-hour of 'Religious Instruction' from 9.15 to 9.45 each day. Finally, from 1874, the board agreed to pay the fees of children attending the church schools in cases where severe poverty prevented parents from being able to afford them.[29] If followed, all this would be far from producing the 'God-less regime' feared by the proponents of the church schools.

In Luton the new priest, Fr O'Connor (see pp. 132–3) shared the common concern of the Catholic clergy to provide at least elementary schooling for Catholic children under their care, to avoid what were seen as the dangers of non-religious Board Schools or openly Anglican ones. He appealed for help in opening a small school, asking for schoolbooks, and adding to the end of his appeal in *The Universe*, almost as an afterthought, 'Can anyone suggest an energetic certificated schoolmistress?' This was in 1884. A few years later, in 1887, the bishop persuaded the Ursuline nuns to open a convent in the town. They were justly renowned across Europe for their work in education since their original foundation three centuries earlier, and had been running schools in England since 1851, mainly working in London.[30] Presumably they helped to solve Fr O'Connor's staffing problems.

Education in Leighton Buzzard

Leighton Buzzard did not have a school board until late in the century because of the generous private endowments that the town could call on. When one was established in 1893, it ran into strong religious opposition, especially from the Quakers in the area. It seems there was no Catholic day school, though there was an active Sunday school, to judge by the number of children who performed in a Catholic Christmas concert.[31]

Impact and legacy

Overall, it is difficult to get a clear picture of the children in all this. An experienced HMI, in 1889, did what he could to describe what he saw as the typical Bedfordshire child – an impossible task, but perhaps his views are worth quoting to fill out the context for the above. The description is not in any sense a Catholic one, but there

28 *Ibid.*, p. 73.
29 *Ibid.*, p. 74.
30 The Ursulines had been founded in 1535 specifically to provide education for girls; the *ODCC* describes them as 'the oldest and most considerable teaching order of women in the RC Church'. See also Beck (ed.), *English Catholics 1850–1950*, p. 346. They had been working in London, and amongst the very poor in Swansea since 1860.
31 See p. 136.

is no reason to think the Catholic child was different from his neighbours in this regard. He stated,

> When I first came into this county … people were at some pains to inform me that Bedfordshire children were stupid. I do not think so. The truth seems to be rather that they require a great deal of teaching, and teaching of a lively and stimulating character. There is no lack of brains, but, as a mistress once expressed it, you must dig deep to find it. The children have no appetite for knowledge … (but) when properly taught, Bedfordshire schools and children can hold their own.

The one subject in which the HMI thought there was considerable room for improvement was reading: in itself 'by far the most important of all subjects', in the Bedfordshire schools it was the weakest, but even here, given time, there was hope of improvement: the HMI added, rather enigmatically, 'When he can be induced to open his mouth he will learn to read'.[32]

Warmoll, and others, had worked hard to provide Catholic children with schools that would ensure they had a fair knowledge of their faith and, no doubt, could 'hold their own' in secular subjects as well. In other parts of the country, especially in the bigger urban centres, the input of various religious orders was key to the development of an effective Catholic educational system, but with the exception of the Ursuline nuns in Luton none were active in the county in these years – after all, numbers would hardly have justified investment by bodies such as the Irish Christian Brothers. They concentrated their considerable efforts on educating the largely urban (and often Irish) Catholic poor, refusing to accept government grants so that they were free to develop their own curriculum – an approach for obvious reasons not always popular with bishops or parish clergy, but one that met with undoubted success.[33]

An important element in the educational field throughout the whole county, and especially outside Bedford, was that of the Sunday schools movement. It is difficult, however, to assess its contribution in individual places: whether to see it in terms of the teaching of basic literacy and numeracy, or to concentrate on its moral and strictly religious legacy, or to concentrate on those that offered a mixture of both approaches. Some interesting work has been done on the average numbers attending these schools, in which by mid-century Bedfordshire led the whole country: the percentage of the population in attendance rose from 6.1% in 1818 to 15.7% in 1833 and to an impressive 19.7% in 1851. The religious census of 1851 included the figures for Sunday school attendance. As with the rest of the census, interpretation of the returns is not straightforward, especially where people attended more than once, but some of the numbers of Sunday school scholars are remarkable: in Luton, for example, the parish church of St Mary listed a morning attendance of 400, an afternoon one of 420, and 130 in the evening, while the Union Chapel in Castle Street led the Non-conformist challenge, claiming 450 attendees in the morning and 400 in the afternoon. Several other Non-conformist places of worship had 150–300 attending their Sunday schools.[34] At the same time the county was one of the lowest in the

32 Bushby, *The Bedfordshire Schoolchild*, pp. 247–8.

33 See Coldrey's chapter in Patrick O'Sullivan (ed.), *Religion and Identity*, vol. 5 of *The Irish Worldwide: History, Heritage, Identity* (London, 1996).

34 Full figures in Bushby, 'The Ecclesiastical Census, Bedfordshire, March 1851', pp. 109–200; figures for Luton, pp. 182–6.

country when it came to providing day school places, coming in at fortieth out of a total of forty-two units.[35] The Sunday schools remained an accepted and important part of life, especially in Luton, until well into the twentieth century.[36] Despite this, however, levels of literacy remained low in the town compared with other areas, and it may be that the supporters of the schools would have been more satisfied with the verdict of the Union Chapel leaders there that the schools were successful because they prevented 'Infidelity and Popery (from) gaining over the youth in our provincial town', rather than for the skills they imparted. Allsopp has no doubt that the main aim of the Sunday schools in Luton was 'to produce a generation of children steeped in the Christian way of life and with values of cleanliness, punctuality, obedience and industriousness'.[37] The people of the town appear to have been satisfied with the system and in addition to have welcomed the social life that the schools provided. It has not been possible to find details of what was provided in the Catholic Sunday schools where they existed, but one may assume that the stress here would also have been on religious teaching and practice.

For the years after Warmoll it is important to strike a note of caution, for it is clear that by no means all his efforts to establish a Catholic education system in Bedford flourished, or, indeed, even survived. As early as November 1885 the bishop sent out a pessimistic pastoral letter, stressing the sad state of the Catholic schools across his diocese. He complained that certain politicians (the occasion of the letter was a forthcoming election) were advocating 'universal, secular, compulsory and free' schools controlled by the state through local school boards, and that Catholics would lose out under such a scheme. Already their schools were disadvantaged compared with the Board Schools, less attractive in appearance and only being able to pay lower salaries, and so employing the less able teachers; moreover they had to rely on donations from their people who were also paying local school rates but not benefiting from them. He quoted the case of Shefford, where Catholics paid the general high rates for the schools but gained nothing. Under the new proposals, he argued, the Church and Catholic parents would lose all input and control: he condemned this wholeheartedly:

> Here we detect the cloven foot of the enemy of God and of man, and therefore we reject the proposal of free education.[38]

He recommended a Royal Commission to look into the whole question of the education of the poor.

The problem in Bedfordshire, however, was more immediate and practical. As more free schooling became available, fewer non-Catholic parents were willing to pay the fees the Catholic schools needed, and there were not enough Catholic children available to keep them going. As one writer to *The Tablet* put it,

> The school (in Bedford) is a source of great anxiety, owing chiefly to the want of voluntary subscriptions and the consequent crippling of the Government grant.[39]

35 Allsopp, *The Education and Employment of Girls in Luton*, p. 14.
36 *Ibid.*, pp. 47, 59.
37 *Ibid.*, pp. 53, 60.
38 *The Tablet*, 19 December 1885.
39 M. J. Shanasy, 19 December 1885. See p. 151, fn 2 for the writer's background.

The Bedford Catholic schools had a chequered career. It seems that the Church Street infants school had closed sometime before 1889, with its classes transferring to Priory Street. This had had its best year in 1880, with an average attendance of 189; by 1889 attendance had declined to just over 100 (only thirty-six of whom were Catholics) and in December of that year it too had closed, with the Catholic children being re-housed in the former Church Street premises. This school was not open to government inspection and so could not apply for grant aid. Numbers declined and it may well be that for some of the years between 1891 and 1900 it operated only as a Sunday school.[40]

There is no doubt that Warmoll had been over-ambitious, a fact recognised by the bishop in 1890 when he wrote to Canon Collis in April to say that he was willing to sell or let out the Catholic school buildings in Bedford for other uses. As there were 'three competitors' for them, he felt assured of getting 'a good price'; he had an agent in the town assessing the offers. By July he was able to report that the school would be let out for three years at a rental of £100 a year, with an option to buy at the end of the lease for £2,000. The money was to go towards the upkeep of the Bedford mission, especially for the maintenance of the remaining school next to the priest's house, which he claimed was sufficient for all the Catholic children in the town.[41] It was a very successful business transaction, but marked the end of Warmoll's hopes.

In 1898 the English and Welsh bishops issued a pastoral letter about the Catholic school system. This had grown from an intake of 8,400 children in eighty-nine schools in 1849, to over 295,000 children in 1,006 schools in 1896. These schools, they argued, should be funded on the same basis as the Board Schools, for the destruction of denominational schools would mean the destruction of Christian England; there must be 'no slumbering, no supineness, no relaxation' in the efforts of churches, parishes or parents in this regard.[42] The so-called 'fight for the schools' became the dominant issue for Catholics throughout the country; it was a rallying cry for the next fifty years, keeping alive for some a residual sense of persecution and generally providing a battleground against what was seen as an increasingly secular world. It was, however, to take several years (and the work of the Daughters of the Holy Ghost sisters)[43] to establish even the beginnings of a limited Catholic educational presence in the principal towns of Bedfordshire.

40 Bushby 'Elementary Education in Bedford 1868–1903', p. 37.

41 NDA, Coll. A. 6. 17(c), Bishop Riddell's Correspondence.

42 AAW, 'A Joint Pastoral Letter of the Cardinal Archbishop and the Bishops on the Catholic School Committee', 5 June 1898, p. 9; see also *The Tablet*, 12 June, for extracts from the letter. On the general issue of government support for Catholic schools in these years, see A. C. F. Beales, 'The Struggle for the Schools', in Beck (ed.), *The English Catholics*, pp. 365–409, esp. pp. 379–85.

43 In Bedford from 1904, in Lansdowne Road.

Chapter 11
The end of a beginning

Looking at the final years covered in this study, we get a mixed impression of the state of Catholicism across the county. In Bedford, Warmoll's immediate successor was the Rev. George Wrigglesworth (1851–1900). He had done his priestly training in Rome and had been ordained in 1883, moving to Bedford in 1885, where, however, he remained for only two years. For whatever reason, he failed to be accepted by the people of the town; following someone like Warmoll was not going to be easy, and a lack of tact and sense of rejection on his part did not help, although he was described as a 'pious and devout' priest and a 'great organizer'.[1] There is, however, another side to the picture that does not reflect too well on Warmoll's legacy, as revealed in correspondence to *The Tablet*. According to this, the new priest immediately faced 'serious financial difficulties'; the presbytery was unfurnished and had not been renovated for some years – 'considerable expenditure' would be needed to make it 'at all habitable', apart from necessary structural repairs. This meant that the new priest faced an immediate bill of £70 or £80, which the congregation could not meet without help from friends elsewhere. As a result, the writer earnestly appealed to

> old friends of the Bedford mission to think of it this Christmas, and to come to the aid of a struggling and most devoted priest, who is already loved by his flock, the members of which are straining every nerve to find him even the barest necessities of life ... Although many cries for help come from many country missions, none is more genuine and more pressing than that which now reaches them from Bedford.[2]

This would imply that the picture we have of Warmoll's ministry and legacy is perhaps too rosy. In the New Year Wrigglesworth himself took to the press: he was grateful, he said, for the Christmas offerings of the poor, but they had only amounted to £2. 5s. 5d! The wealthy parishioners needed to do more to enable him to raise the £75 he needed for immediate repairs:

> the rich should give of their gold during the octave of the Epiphany – you did it for Fr Warmoll – Friends of the late Provost to the rescue![3]

For whatever reason, and despite his initial popularity, Wrigglesworth seems to have fallen out with his new parishioners fairly soon: Robbins suggests he received little sympathy or support from them as they compared him unfavourably

1 Robbins, *John Priestley Warmoll*, p. 236.

2 *The Tablet*, 19 December, 1885. The writer was one M. J. Shanasy, who described himself as 'one of the very few surviving members' of Warmoll's congregation that first Christmas in Little Grove Place (see p. 87).

3 NDA, Coll. A. 6. 7, Wrigglesworth's Appeal, January 1886.

with Warmoll and were put off by a certain tactlessness on his part. In 1887 he was appointed to King's Lynn, where he was to be successful as the pastor.[4] His replacement in Bedford was the Rev. George Osman: born in 1847, he was a convert to Catholicism, and was ordained in 1871 for the Westminster Archdiocese, though on his own 'patrimony' (i.e. supporting himself financially, independently of a diocesan bishop). He served much of his priestly ministry in the Diocese of Northampton, into which he was incardinated in 1882 and of which he became a canon later that year. He took up residence in Bedford in December 1887 and was very happy with the appointment; his friend, Canon Collis, reported that he had never seen him look better and that he was sure he would get on very well with the people who seemed to their new pastor to be 'very cheerful'.[5]

What happened after this is not clear. According to Robbins the next three years in Bedford were 'disastrous';[6] the schools closed and the congregation declined. Collis reported in 1890 that Osman was having a major row with the bishop and was thinking of taking him to court; in the end he resigned and left the town. In a very friendly letter to Collis he 'rejoiced' in doing so and admitted that he 'should have done it a long time since'. He later retired altogether from the diocese.[7]

He was succeeded by the Rev. Robert Christopher Middleton (1853–1906), also a convert from Anglicanism. He served in Bedford from 1890 and seems to have restored the reputation of Catholics in the town fairly quickly. In October 1891, for example, he organised a Harvest Thanksgiving in the church which was reported as being 'fully decorated' with flowers and vegetables, and 'very crowded … even densely packed' with Catholics and non-Catholics, especially on the Sunday evening, all apparently 'highly gratified with the whole of the superb decorations'; it was reported that the services were 'characterised by every sign of joy'. The occasion included an appeal for Bedford Infirmary, with local children bringing toys for the children in the hospital.[8]

A few years later, in October 1896, Middleton took on the duties of Catholic chaplain to Bedford prison. Then, in 1897, he arranged with the bishop to say Mass 'now and then' in Ampthill, but this failed to develop into a self-contained mission. A second priest, the Rev. W. Cooper (recently ordained at the English College, Rome) was appointed as curate in July 1898, a clear indication that Middleton's missionary endeavours were bearing fruit in the town; a few years later the congregation was reputed to be regularly around an amazing 700 strong.[9]

Similar interest was reported elsewhere in the 1890s, with local Protestants attending occasional Catholic services. So in Luton, in October 1892, the church

4 Robbins, *John Priestley Warmoll*, p. 236. A note in *The Bedfordshire Standard* for 21 January 1888 reported that he had been invited to Sandringham to meet the Prince of Wales on 6 January.

5 NDA, Coll. A. 6. 17 (d), Canon Collis' correspondence with the Bishop, November 1885 – December 1887.

6 Robbins, *John Priestley Warmoll*, p. 236.

7 The date of death is not noted; he may have left the priesthood. See NDA, Coll. A. 6. 17(c), Bishop Ridell's Correspondence, January 1881–92 (unpaginated): letters 3 April, 8 & 9 July, 1890.

8 *The Catholic Times*, 23 October 1891.

9 *The Weekly Register*, 23 July 1898. Middleton died suddenly in October 1906, at the early age of fifty-three; see *The Catholic Times*, 26 October 1906. Rev. William Cooper (1869–1927, ord. 1897).

was packed with a 'very large' congregation, most of them non-Catholics, to hear Fr Ambrose, a Passionist priest from Highgate in London, preaching 'very eloquently' on 'Salvation, a Personal Matter'; the report announced that he would be preaching morning and evening on the following Sunday as well.[10] Also in Luton, we find Rev. Wrigglesworth, formerly of Bedford, giving a lecture on the Roman catacombs to a substantial 'mixed congregation'; the lecture was illustrated by almost 100 'limelight views' and was in aid of church funds.[11] These were, of course, occasional events, but at least they offered something of a balance to the active anti-Catholicism still to be found in the county.

We can also get some picture of the state of Catholicism in these years from the formal visitation reports of the bishop; apart from the detailed reports of each visitation, the whole visit is sure evidence of the acceptance of episcopal authority. In June 1891, for example, the bishop was in Bedford, shortly after Middleton took over as priest in charge. Taking into account that these reports tended to list what was wrong or lacking, presumably so that they could be checked at the next visitation, a principal area of concern was what might be called proper record-keeping: the need for a census of the Catholic population (names and addresses), the proper recording of Mass offerings and intentions, a complete listing of mission property and the keeping of a 'mission book' listing such things as basic history, trustees, insurance and statistics. (A concern shared by the modern historian.) In addition to these fairly run-of-the-mill items (hardly surprising after the unsatisfactory incumbencies of Wrigglesworth and Osman), there were two injunctions concerning children: the first decreed that all children over the age of seven who had not made their first Holy Communion were to be 'brought or sent' to confession on or about 'each Ember week'; no explanation for this is given.[12] Secondly, what were called 'the rights of children to be trained in a Catholic school' were to be announced regularly from the pulpit 'for fear of their losing the precious inheritance of the faith'. There would appear to be a reference here to the decline in the Catholic schools since Warmoll's day. Finally, the priest himself was ordered to undertake a 'spiritual retreat' within the year.[13] The report of the bishop's next visitation of the town mission, in May 1894, was shorter. There was, again, a stress on the proper keeping of mission records and inventories, and on getting young Catholic children to attend the mission school. There was, additionally, the very unusual proposal that the altar boys should be taught to sing Vespers on Sundays and feast days, so that they and the choir could sing alternate verses of the psalms. Unfortunately there is no account of the response

10 *The Catholic Times*, 28 October 1892.

11 *Ibid.*, 22 February 1894.

12 Ember weeks: there were four sets of Ember Days each liturgical year (with three days in each), marked by fasting and abstinence; their very early history and development are somewhat obscure; see entry in *ODCC*.

13 NDA, Box 157, Bp Riddell's Assorted Papers, 'Visitation Regulations'. This box contains a number of similar items, all relating to various activities of Bp Riddell; for example, 'Missions of the Diocese of Northampton from the Year 1880 to (blank)', giving basic information about all the missions; 'Log Book of the Diocese of Northampton' – a very brief but carefully kept diary of the bishop's activities, including his visits to Rome, the opening of schools and missions, the recruiting of students for the priesthood, sale of the schools in Bedford, confirmation visits across the diocese, correspondence, etc.

to this suggestion.[14] In 1898 there was another episcopal visitation of the mission, with the customary conferral of confirmation. Unusually, however, the bishop also visited the prison, to inspect the chapel there; presumably it was being used by a Catholic chaplain for the saying of Mass for the Catholic inmates; this was possibly one reason why Bedford needed a second priest.[15]

As the century drew to its close, matters seemed to be settling into something of a pattern for Bedfordshire's Catholics. There were regular visitations by the bishop, a small number of ordinations most years at the seminary in Shefford, appeals from hard-pressed clergy for the building of chapels and presbyteries, and a steady increase in the number of Catholics across the county. In addition to his regular visitations around the diocese, the bishop organised a number of diocesan bodies or committees in an attempt to ensure its more effective administration. One of these was the Diocesan Board of Finance, established in 1881, which met annually to decide what financial help could be given to struggling missions out of the funds raised by the annual Diocesan Mission Fund appeal.[16] From the minutes we can see, for example, that in March 1896 the priest at Leighton Buzzard successfully requested a grant of £30. The following year, Luton was granted the same amount, though no request had been made by its priest; two years previously he had been granted £50. It is of some interest that neither Shefford nor Bedford featured at all in these lists, either as requesting or being granted financial help from the diocese; presumably by this stage both were stable enough and had sufficient income on a regular basis to survive and even expand.

While progress was slow, and some developments failed to become permanent altogether (at Ampthill, for example), or for several years (as at Dunstable), the idea of Catholicism being a 'missionary church' was strong. This was partly to 'win back' existing Catholics to a regular practice of their faith, but was also motivated by a desire to enrol new members. A pastoral letter of the bishop in December 1897 urged all Catholics to play their part in helping this work of conversion, 'to receive back our brethren in the embrace of perfect charity', while at the same time the priest at Leighton Buzzard spoke much more bluntly in his appeal for funds 'to lift a Protestant community into the region of Truth and Light'.[17]

The following year saw the ordination of two priests at Shefford (Frs. Reed and Garnett) and the holding of a diocesan synod that was attended by fifty-two diocesan clergy; its principal business concerned the maintenance of sick and retired clergy.[18] Then, in April 1899, the bishop was in Luton to confer confirmation and carry out a formal visitation of the mission before moving on to Leighton Buzzard to inspect the new iron chapel and priest's house.[19]

Across the diocese as a whole a number of religious orders, male and female, were assisting in the work of establishing Catholic services: Benedictine priests were active running missions in the east of the diocese, and ten congregations of nuns worked in

14 *Ibid.*
15 NDA, Coll. A. 6. 20, Diocesan Synod; Visitation of Bedford, 1898.
16 Its minute book is one of the items in Box 157.
17 NDA, Coll. A. 6. 19, Pastoral Letters, Bishop Riddell.
18 NDA, Coll. A. 6. 20, Diocesan Synod; Visitation of Bedford, 1898.
19 NDA, Coll. A. 6. 21, Confirmations in Luton, Visitation of Leighton Buzzard.

various towns across it, but none in Bedfordshire until the early years of the twentieth century. The *Catholic Directory* listed just three charitable institutions: the orphanage for boys in Shefford, one for girls in Ipswich, and an 'Asylum for the Aged Poor and Destitute Children' in Northampton. Finally there were three official diocesan funds, for which the bishop made appeals each year and published annual accounts: the Ecclesiastical Education Fund (for the training of students for the priesthood), the Diocesan Mission Fund (to help the establishment and running of new missions) and the Clergy Fund (for the maintenance of sick or retired priests).[20]

The sixty years or so after 1840 were marked by church building, restoration and re-ordering across all denominations on a scale not witnessed before, not just in the towns but across the county. A few examples will show the extent of this activity which cannot have gone unnoticed by the general public. New Church of England parish churches were built in Souldrop (1860–61), Steppingley (1860) and Woburn (1865–68); St Lawrence's, Willington, was restored in 1877, and Meppershall in 1875–77; St Cuthbert's, Bedford, was built 1845–47, St Martin's, Bedford, in 1889 (replacing a tin church of only two years earlier); Queen's Park, Bedford, got an iron church in 1895, while in Bedford town centre St Paul's underwent repairs and rebuilding almost continuously from the 1830s to 1908. The list could go on and on.[21] The very small number of Roman Catholic churches, built in the general style of the day, were more likely to pass with much less notice in the last quarter of the nineteenth century than would have been the case in the first. Various causes, social as well as theological, affected both buildings and furnishings: pew rents and box pews were gradually being replaced, altars and pulpits were being re-designed, while fittings, furnishings and vestments were being replaced or introduced.[22]

To mark the end of the nineteenth century and the start of the new, the English and Welsh Catholic bishops published a pastoral letter to their people: 'The Church and Liberal Catholicism'. It was the occasion, one might have thought, at the start of a new millennium, for some expression of hope and encouragement and even of joy and satisfaction at what had been achieved in the previous fifty years. From the outset of their letter, however, the bishops expressed themselves in terms of apprehension and even fear at the way English society was developing, with, they thought, far too much attention being given to the individual and his so-called rights; there was a lack of 'filial docility and reverence' even among Catholics. It is interesting that in its fully supportive report on the letter, *The Tablet* spoke of the need for English Catholics to develop 'unfaltering faith and unswerving loyalty' to their bishops and to Rome.[23] We do not know the impact of the bishops' rather doom-laden message on the Catholics

20 *The Catholic Directory*, 1901, pp. 218–20.

21 This is no more than a very small selection. See Chris Pickford's outstanding volumes for Church of England developments: *Bedfordshire Churches in the Nineteenth Century*, Parts I–IV.

22 See, for example, Gordon Vowles, *Henry Clutton. Victorian Architect of Gothic Revival Churches and Country Houses* (Willington, 2022); Clutton was instrumental in both the Church of England and the Roman Catholic building programmes.

23 Peter Doyle, '"To Whom Should We Turn?" Aspects of the Relationship between the English and Welsh Hierarchy and Rome, 1880s–1920s', in *RH*, vol. 29, no. 4 (October, 2009), pp. 523–39. The letter was a warning of the dangers of modernists, in practice a very small group in the country.

of Bedfordshire and their priests, working hard with few resources to establish the Church there and overcome the latent but widespread anti-Catholicism, but one may imagine a certain disappointment with the lack of praise and positive message.

In practice, across England and Wales as a whole these years were in many ways the start of a decade of imaginative and positive Catholic development, especially of lay initiative and involvement. These developments lie outside the range of this study, but grew out of late nineteenth-century ideas and initiatives, emerging slowly from the papal social encyclical *Rerum Novarum* (1891) and the social commitments of Cardinal Henry Edward Manning (b. 1808; archbishop 1865; d. 1892). Among leading lay groups and organisations were the Catholic Social Guild, the Catholic Evidence Guild, the Catholic Women's League and the Catholic Federation, all an indication of a greater confidence and growing involvement in social issues, beyond the traditional involvement in care homes and orphanages.[24]

To conclude, one might claim that while almost all eighteenth-century Church of England clergymen would have looked in horror at most of the nineteenth-century developments in their own churches, and even more at the general acceptance of Roman Catholicism in English society, their eighteenth-century Roman Catholic counterparts, as they passed from persecution to full citizenship, would have been struck with wonder at their own modest yet significant growth across the county.

The growth is best illustrated by the mission registers that make up the remaining part of this account. The provision of properly laid out, printed registers seems not to have been adopted by the Catholic authorities throughout the country until the second half of the nineteenth century; certainly those for Shefford continued to be informal, some rather untidily and carelessly written, down to the 1850s. Latin was commonly but not universally used from the 1820s. The newly established bishops in their national synods after 1850 paid little detailed attention to the keeping of registers, but were clear that they must be kept 'sedulously and carefully' and in 'the approved format', while the responsibility for looking after them fell to the rector of the mission. By the time of their fourth meeting in 1873 they were rather more detailed in their regulations; each mission was to have a secure archive or safe for its registers and documents, including the bishop's pastoral letters and synodal decrees; the responsibility for safeguarding the contents of the archive lay on the senior priest or rector.[25] We are particularly fortunate in having a full set of those relating to the mission centred on Shefford, covering about eighty years from the 1770s.[26] Unfortunately, its registers covering the second half of the nineteenth century appear not to have survived; also lost are those covering the early years of the mission in Luton. What we do have, however, is a full set of those covering baptisms, marriages and deaths in the new mission of Bedford from the 1860s to 1900, along with those from the new mission in Leighton Buzzard, in the south of the county, beginning in the last months of 1895.

24 See Peter Doyle, 'Charles Plater S.J. and the Origins of the Catholic Social Guild', in *RH*, vol. 21, no. 3 (May, 1993), pp. 401–17, at pp. 403–4.

25 *Decreta*, pp. 15, 32, 228.

26 For comparison, see Hadland, *From Country House Catholicism to City Church*, on the early Catholic registers of the area centered on Oxford.

The Registers

Shefford
Early mission registers, 1770s–1859

Introduction

The first regularly-kept registers for any mission in Bedfordshire were those compiled by Christopher Taylor, resident priest in Shefford from 1786 to 1812; his entries run from April 1787 to March 1811. No doubt a relic of the recusant past, when evidence of a person's Catholic faith was better kept secret, there was no agreed format for the registers: Taylor just used an ordinary hard-cover notebook, with plain, unlined paper, measuring 4 × 6.5 ins.[1] As can be seen, some of his entries are very short, and there are very few from his last years.

The lack of formality in the keeping of the registers meant that the priests had some freedom to add comments; this is especially noticeable in the death notices, allowing what in some cases were mini-tributes of the deceased (see e.g. p. 163). Despite the above synodal reference to an 'approved format', in Shefford in the 1850s the entries still have a very informal, indeed at times scribbled, appearance.

Shefford became the main Roman Catholic centre in the county, a position it held for almost a century. With regard to burials, the town was not itself a Church of England parish and did not have its own cemetery. As a dependent chapelry of nearby Campton it was there that its citizens were buried, including some Catholics (see p. 42). A range of local cemeteries appears in the Shefford Catholic registers, including Biggleswade, Blunham (sometimes appearing as Blomham), Luton, Bromham, Southill and Hitchin, giving some idea of how widespread its Catholic reach was.

The Shefford registers reproduced here have been transcribed from the originals into three typed sets or 'volumes'. The first volume is inscribed on the outside cover of the original:

> A Register of Christenings, Marriages and Burials kept by the Rev. Chris. Taylor during his mission at Sutton Place in Surrey, at Thorndon in Essex, and at Shefford in Bedfordshire.

Some early pages have been torn out, presumably dealing with the earlier missions that the Rev. Taylor had served.[2] The remaining entries run from 15 April 1787 to 15 August 1824, with a single later one from 8 July 1832. After Taylor's death in 1812 the entries were continued by his successor, the Rev. John Potier (1812–23), and

1 NDA, Box 144, Early Registers, including three Shefford sets, 1787–1858.

2 See *Essex Recusant*, Essex Recusant Society: a journal of research and study in Post-Reformation Catholic history in Essex, vol. 1, p. 37.

then by the Rev. Thomas Griffiths (with just a few entries for 1823–24). Something is said about these three incumbents in the relevant part of the main text.

A word is required here about the almost complete absence of marriages in these early registers. Before Hardwicke's Marriage Act of 1753 (operative from 1754), there was no legal obligation to have a formal ceremony or any public notice about a marriage or any witnesses to it. In an attempt to prevent clandestine and perhaps bigamous unions, the Act laid down that all marriages had to be announced by banns and performed in the local Anglican church, with witnesses; the only exceptions allowed were Jewish and Quaker marriages. This Act remained in force until 1837. It was possible, of course, for Catholics to have a Catholic wedding after (or even before) the official ceremony, but this seems to have been very rare in the early registers; indeed, Christopher Taylor may have officiated at only one in his twenty-five years in Shefford (and that a mixed marriage in September 1804).

Editorial procedures

The entries have been transcribed largely as originally written, with some editorial standardisation. There are occasional gaps in the original text, usually marked by a —, to indicate where a name (e.g. of a sponsor or witness) was not known or only partially known, or even forgotten. Where parents were named, the mother's maiden name was usually given in brackets, introduced by 'née'; this has been omitted in these transcripts. The original spellings have been retained throughout, with the principal surname in each entry in capital letters. Some birth dates are given in shortened form.

Treatment of names

In the Latin entries it is unclear whether the name 'Maria' should be translated as Mary, Maria, Marie, or May; in the absence of other information, Mary has been generally used here. Similar difficulties arise with some other names, for example, 'Anna' may indicate Anne, Ann, or Anna; Anne is used here throughout; 'Catherina' may be Catherine or Kathleen; 'Helena', Helen or Ellen; 'Joanna', Joan or Jane.

The names 'Elizabeth' and 'Fitzpatrick' are generally spelt with an 's'; occasionally Fitspatrick is given as two words.

Irish surnames are frequently mis-spelt, though they usually appear correctly the second or third time round. Prime examples are 'Mc a nally', 'Gagogan', 'Mack Cormack'.

List of clergy in charge at Shefford

These notes are based on those by Fr Collins (see p. xi) and extended by the editor.

Rev. Christopher Taylor

Rev. Christopher Taylor was responsible for recording: baptisms, 12; deaths, 11; marriages, 1; converts, 1; confirmed, 10.

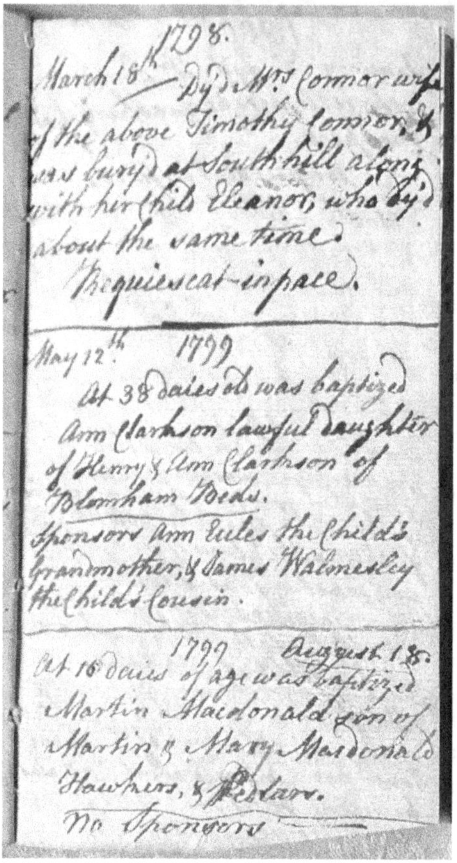
1798.
March 18th Dy'd Mrs Connor wife of the above Timothy Connor, & was bury'd at Southhill along with her Child Eleanor, who dy'd about the same time.
Requiescat in pace.

May 12th 1799
At 38 daies old was baptized Ann Clarkson lawful daughter of Henry & Ann Clarkson of Blunham Beds.
Sponsors Ann Eeles the Child's Grandmother, & James Walmesley the Child's Cousin.

1799 August 18.
At 16 daies of age was baptized Martin Macdonald son of Martin & Mary Macdonald Hawkers, & Pedlars.
No Sponsors

Page from Shefford Mission Register, 1798–99. (courtesy of Diocese of Northampton)

Of the baptisms, one was of a child at Warmington, east Northamptonshire, a village well within the 'riding district' of Buckden when there was no resident missioner there; the child was only one day old. One baptism was of a child in Shefford whose non-Catholic parents had requested it in danger of death. The only other child from Shefford was a child of the only marriage performed by Taylor.

Taylor seems to have been responsible for a single adult convert, who died a few days later.

The confirmations listed were all from one family, the Clarksons in Blunham; Taylor mentioned this family in his letter of 1809 to the Lancashire priest Barrow (see p. 81 above).

Taylor did not use Latin in his entries except for the routine 'requiescat in pace' and, once, for his brother, 'Requiem aeternam dona ei Domine, Et lux perpetua luceat ei' ('Eternal rest grant unto him, Lord, and let perpetual light shine on him'). None of Taylor's entries are signed. Occasional entries are used to give obituaries or comments by Taylor.

Rev. John Potier

Rev. John Potier arrived in Shefford on the 17 November 1812. His first entry in the register was for 14 February 1813, the last, 10 October 1819; one is unsigned but is probably in his handwriting. He died on 31 March 1822. He was responsible for: baptisms, 16; marriages, 0; deaths, 0; confirmed, 0.

Rev. Thomas Griffiths

There are three entries by Rev. Thomas Griffiths: 14 December 1823 – 15 August 1824; one unsigned on 4 January 1824; one in his writing but performed by Rev. Chabot 18 April 1824, which is also noted in volume 2. Also there is one unsigned, dated 8 July 1832.

Volume 1 (1787–1824)

A single, loose page found inside the second volume of the Roman Catholic registers, in an unknown hand, may be included here: it is headed 'Extract from Campton Parish Register' and contains these names and dates:[3]

1776 John NODDINGS, bur. 21 Aug.
1781 Bur. Stephen ROBINSON 12 Feb. A Roman Catholic Priest
1781 Elizabeth NODDINGS, 6 June.
1783 Mary NODDINGS, 14 Oct.
Edward DIXIE, from St. John's St. London, Innholder (Gravestone may still be seen, with "May he rest in peace" upon it).
1812 Bur. Rev. C. TAYLOR, 8th June.

Year	Date	Event
1787	15 April	bapt. Mary DOWLING, at Shefford; d. of John & Jane, of Hitchen (*sic*); one month old. Sponsor – Susan Bowyer.
	—	bapt. Michael LITTLE lawful son of Mich. Little & — Little of Blunham Beds. Sponsors Mr & Mrs Pugh the Child's Uncle & Aunt.
[1788/ 89?]	11 March	bapt. John DOWLING at 7 daies old, lawful son of Jn & Jane of Hitchin Herts. Sponsors Michl. Little & Susan Bowyer.
1790	27 Septr.	Dy'd Mrs Eliz. DOVE aged 72 & was bury'd at Biggleswade, Bedfordshire. Requ. in pace (*sic*).
1791	—	bapt. Matthew DOWLING at 3 weeks old, lawful son of John & Jane, of Hitchin, Herts. Sponsors Mr Clarkson of Blunham Beds & —
	21 August	Dy'd Mr. Jn. FRENCH, aged 53; & was bury'd at Biggleswade, Beds. Requiescat in pace.
	—	At 13 daies old was baptized Seth CLARKSON, lawful son of Hen. & Ann of Blunham in Bedfordshire. Sponsors Wm. Walmesley the Child's relation in Lancashire & Mrs Coleman of Shefford, Bedfordshire.[4]

3 See also start of vol. 3 below, p. 178.

4 The Clarkson family feature in the early history of the Mission. They were originally from Lancashire; see for example p. 81 above. The Walmesleys were also a well-known Lancashire Catholic family; one of whom was vicar apostolic; see Kirk, *Biographies of English Catholics*

Year	Date	Event
1793	17 Jany.	Was baptized Daniel DOWLING son of Jn & Jane of Hitchin Herts. Child 6 weeks old. Sponsor Miss Mary Dixie. *[see p. 45 above]*
	23 Septr.	At one day old was baptized Thos. MEADOWS, son of Wm. & Mary, of Warmington, Northamptonshire. Sponsors Thos. & Eliz. Wood of Bennefield *[Northamptonshire]*, the Child's Grandfather & Grandmother.
	1 Octr.	At 2 weeks old was baptized Michael CLARKSON, son of Henry & Ann of Blunham Beds. Sponsors Mich. Mason of Crandon parish, Essex, & Mary Dixy (*sic*) of Shefford Beds.
1794	13 Novr	Was baptized at 10 daies of age, Wm. CLARKSON, son of Henry & Ann, of Blunham, Beds. Sponsor, Wm. Walmesley the Child's Uncle in law, & —.
1795	8 April	At 4 daies old, was baptized Michael DOWLING, lawful son of Jn & Jane of Hitchin (Herts). Sponsor Mary Dixie.
1796	27 Jany.	Dy'd Mr. Thos. BOWER, Tanner of Shefford, aged 63, & was bury'd at Campton. Requiescat in pace.[5]
1797	19 Feb.	At 5 weeks of age, was baptized Eleanor CONNOR, daughter of Timothy & — Connor when working at South hill house.[6] Sponsors John Dowling & Mary Dixie.
	6 May	At 3 weeks of age, was baptized Jane DOWLING daughter of John & Jane of Hitchin Herts. Sponsor Mary Dixie.
1798	18 March	Dy'd Mrs CONNOR wife of the above Timothy Connor, & was bury'd at South hill along with her child Eleanor, who dy'd about the same time. Requiescat (*sic*) in pace.
1799	12 May	At 38 daies old was baptized Ann CLARKSON daughter of Henry & Ann of Blomham (*sic*) Beds. Sponsors Ann Eccles the Child's Grandmother, & James Walmesley the Child's Cousin.[7]
	18 August	At 18 daies of age was baptized Martin MACDONALD son of Martin & Mary Macdonald, Hawkers & Pedlars. No Sponsors.
1800	23 January	dy'd Mr. Lewis COCHERELLE, aged 54, & was bury'd at Campton. Requiescat in pace.
	19 October	dy'd the Revd. Wm. GREGSON O.S.B. at Weston Underwood Bucks. aged 68, & was bury'd in the Chancel of said Weston-Church. Requiescat in pace.[8]
1801	—	Dy'd Daniel DOWLING a child of 7 years of age, & was bury'd at Hitchin.
	12 Febry	dy'd John DOWLING father to the above Child, & was bury'd at Hitchin. Requiescat in pace. NB. Child & father dy'd within a fortnight of each other.
	31 March	Dy'd Robert DOWLING eldest son of the above John Dowling aged about 20, & was bury'd at Hitchin. Requiescat in pace.
	19 April	The ceremonies of Baptism were perform'd on Edmund DOWLING son of the above said John Dowling when 18 months of age. The Sacrament having been administer'd soon after his birth. Sponsors John Clarkson of Blomham (*sic*), & Lucy Dixie of Shefford.

in the Eighteenth Century, pp. 242–3 and Bossy, *The English Catholic Community 1570–1850*, pp. 327, 351, 374.

5 He left his property to Mary Dixie.

6 Southill House was, and still is, the home of the wealthy Whitbread family. Child and mother died 1798.

7 A number of early entries have Blomham instead of Blunham.

8 His dates were 1728–1800, making him seventy-two; his name in religion was Gregory.

Year	Date	Event
1802	*[30 May]*	On the 30 May being Sunday within the Octave of the Ascension were confirmed by the Rt. Revd. Bishop Douglass ten Children of Henry & Ann Clarkson of Blomham Beds:– Namely John, George, Thomas, Edmund, James, Seth, Michael, William, Henry & Ann CLARKSON.[9]
	26 Aug	dy'd Mr. Charles CLARK of Buckden (Hunts.) aged 63 & was there bury'd. Requiescat in pace.
1804	3 Septr.	were married John GODFREY, & Mary DOBBS. She a Catholic, He a Protestant.
1805	14 June	was born & baptized Lucy lawful daughter of John & Mary GODFREY. Sponsors — NB This Child was rebaptized by the Rector of Campton Edmund Williamson. Such is the bigotry & ignorance of Protestants as to profane the institute of … which they denigrate … … belittle sacraments *[final lines very unclear because crowded at end of page and partly crossed out]*
1806	5 March	Dy'd the Revd. James TAYLOR (of Rome, & Doüay (*sic*) Colleges) at Hales-place near Canterbury, leaving me, Chris. Taylor his affectionate Uncle to regret his loss with flowing tears. His age was but 44; & this amiable young man's earthly remains are deposited in the South Vault within St. Stephen's Church near Canterbury, & lie upon those of Sir Roger Manwood 'Requiem æternam dona ei Dmne, Et lux perpetua luceat ei.' *['Eternal rest grant to him O Lord, and may perpetual light shine on him']*
1807	11 March	Dy'd Mrs Ann CLARKSON of Blomham Beds. Aged 53, & was bury'd at s*[ai]*d. Blomham. Requiescat in pace!
1808	22 May	Dy'd Mrs Mary WARE aged 27 years & was buried at Biggleswade, Beds. Requiescat in pace!
1809	23 May	Was baptized Wm. PRICE lawful son of Sam. & Ann Price of Shefford (Protestants). The Child being dying, as they thought *[this added later]*, the Rector of the Parish (being) from home the Parents (religiously) beg'd me to baptize it. *[then three lines beginning 'This infant', heavily scored out and illegible]*
1811	18 March	Dy'd Geo. BRIGGS, & was buried at Southill in Bedfordshire. His age was about 25, & he became a Convert in his last illness, & received all the rites of the Church. Requiescat in pace.
1812	4 June	Dy'd at Shefford, Beds Revd. C. TAYLOR in his 85th year, Minister of St. George's Catholic Church, provided with all the Rites of the Church he was Interred at Campton in a Vault with the Founders of the sd. Chapel. When young, he travelled in France & Italy; spoke the Italian & French languages, and was perfect master of the Latin and Greek. He received his education at Rome, when he was chosen by the Fellows of the English College to preach before the Pope, Cardinals etc a Latin Sermon, which, at that time, used to be be delivered every year, on St. Stephen's day, by an English Student. Having perfected his Education, he returned to his native Country; his profound and universal Education secured him the esteem of Persons of the highest Distinction. *He was a benevolent Man, who loved his Country, and was a kind Friend to suffering Humanity, taking great pleasure to instruct the humble and illiterate; his numerous Friends and acquaintances, with those who have profited by his pious and exalted Labours, bear testimony to the amiable Virtues which even always (*sic*) he exercised for the Glory of God and the Welfare of his Fellow-Creatures! Requiescat in pace. Amen.*[10]

9 Bishop John Douglass (1743–1812); vicar apostolic London District, from 1790.

10 Extract between asterisks printed in *Bedfordshire Notes & Queries*, vol. 1, p. 13. Bellenger gives his dates as 1730–1812. It is unclear who was responsible for the next three entries.

Year	Date	Event
	7 or 8 June	Dy'd at Bedford and buried there Samuel BOYD – about 33 years of age. He received only the Extreme unction being speechless more than a week when a Clergyman was called for. Requiescat in pace. Amen.
	2 August	at 5 weeks old was baptized Joseph CURTIS son of William & Ann Curtis of Portman in the Parish of Everton. Sponsors Joseph Firby, Mary Curtis.
	25 Octr	Were Married James GOODMAN and Sarah CLARK. She is a Catholic, he a prodestant (*sic*).[11]
		Came to Shefford 17 Nov 1812 – J. POTIER.[12]
1813	14 Feb	At 11 months ½ Old (*sic*) was baptiz'd Eliz lawful daughter of Jn & Mary GODFREY. Sponsor Ann Aylett.
	21 Feb	At six weeks old was baptiz'd James Wm. CURRY, lawful son of Richard & Jane Curry. Sponsors James Keef and Eliz. Keef.
	10 April	At 2 Weeks old was baptiz'd William MORIN the son of Patrick & Lucy Morin. Sponsor Thomas Quinn.[13]
1814	27 Mar	was baptiz'd Chas. Isac. son of Jn & Mary GODFREY. Sponsors Hen: Clarkson, Ann Aylett.
	3 April	was baptiz'd Peter CURTIS lawful Son of William & Ann Curtis. Sponsors Michael Clarkson & Ann Clarkson.
	22 May	was baptiz'd Joseph lawful son of Anthony & Ann SCACHI. Sponsors Hen: Clarkson Ann Aylett.
	16 Aug	was baptiz'd conditionally Ric: HUGHES son of Rich: & Ann Hughes travellers Sponsor Cath. Townley.
	18 Sep	was baptiz'd Raymond son of Thomas & Ann QUINN. Sponsors Hen: Clarkson & Ann Aylett.
	24 Oct	was baptiz'd conditionally Helen daughter of Augustin & Ann NARY. travellers. Sponsor Ann Aylett.
1815	2 July	was baptiz'd Ann lawful daughter of Richard & Catherine CHARLES. Sponsors Pat: Marnin Ann Aylett.
	31 Decr.	was baptiz'd Sarah lawful daughter of John & Mary GODFREY. Sponsors Hen: Clarkson Mary Jinks.
1816	27 Octr	was baptiz'd Peter MORYN, the son of Peter & Lucy. Sponsor Hen: Clarkson.
	27 Octr	was baptiz'd Ann QUINN the daughter of Thos. & Ann. Sponsor Ann Aylett.
	31 Dec	Was baptiz'd Sarah the Daughter of John & Mary GODFREY Sponsors Hen: Clarkson Mary Jinks *[a repeat of this entry for the same date in 1815 – a copying error, perhaps, with no comment in the register]*
1817		*[The only entry is in Latin, in a different hand, but see next but one entry. There is confusion about the dates, with perhaps no entries for 1818 and a gap until 1823/24.]*
	2 July	Was baptized Anne, d. of Richard and Catherine CHARLES. Godmother Ann Aylett.
1819	10 Oct.	Thomas ROLPH was baptised conditionally on his conversion to the Catholic Faith.

11 It is unusual to have a marriage entry in this register; perhaps due to the visiting priest.
12 There is a noticeable increase in baptismal activity compared with Taylor.
13 The name appears elsewhere as Moryn.

Year	Date	Event
1817/18	14 Sept.	*[in Latin]* was baptized Mary d. of Thomas & Mary CAVENY (Hunt). Godmother Esther Wood *[same hand as 2 July above]*
		[There are five entries in Latin: the first three on a separate page with the two following on another separate page. Rev. T. A. Griffiths later became co-adjutor bishop in the London District in 1833 and succeeded as vicar apostolic in 1836; he died in 1847.[14] *Presumably he was not appointed permanently to Shefford at any time.]*
[1823]	14 Dec	was born and baptized Honor DEMPSEY, d. of Michael & Margaret (Lovel), married. Godfather John Caherty Godmother Louisa Anna Caherty. T.A.Griffiths Miss. Apos.
[1824]	4 Jan	was baptized Mary CHARLES (b. 28.12.1823) d. of Richard & Catherine Married. Godfather Michael Dempsey.
	[18 April]	Testimonies of the Parents: born 9 January 1824 & baptized 18 April 1824 John William, s. of Thomas & Anne CLARKSON (Aylett) married. Godfather Henry Clarkson, godmother Esther Chiesa. By Rev. — Chabot; given to me, T. A. Griffiths Miss: Apos. [*Chabot followed Potier but only stayed for four months – see below]*
	8 Aug	was baptized Isabella, (b. 29.6.1824), d. of Edmund & Sarah CLARKSON (—) married. Godfather Thomas Clarkson. Godmother Alice Clarkson.
	3 Nov.	was baptised Mary Susan MURPHY, (b. 15.8.1824 in St. Neots), d. of Patrick & Susan (Fuller) married. Godmother Mary Riley. T. A. Griffiths Miss. Apos.
[1823]	*[31 March]*	On the 31 of March 1823 died the Revd. Jn POTIER, Priest of Shefford. He had been parish Priest a considerable number of years at Old Hall Green. And had established a school there for the education of 8 scholars. Being sent by the Bishop to the town of Shefford, he continued his school, and was acknowledged by every one to be a man of upright principles, of eminent sanctity, and of an unbounded charity. He died regretted by all, but in particular by his faithful congregation. He was succeeded by the Revd. Mr. Chabot, who continued his residence at Shefford for about 4 months only, and afterwards returned to his own congregation at Carshalton. To him succeeded the Revd. G. Rolfe on the 13 of Novr. /24 from O.H. Green *[Old Hall Green: see p. 62]*
1831/32	*[8 July]*	*[in Latin]* 8 July was baptised William HANOVER b. 28.12.1831, s. of Edward & Sarah (Andrew), married. (Godmother) Margaret Riley. *[This is the only entry on the page after the end of the Potier obituary]*
		[End of volume 1]

14 See Fitzgerald-Lombard, *English and Welsh Priests 1801–1914*, pp. 147, 151.

Volume 2 (1824–1844)

The register is a plain paper, hard backed book; it measures 6½ × 7¾ ins. Almost all the entries are in Latin and are given here in translation They are laid out somewhat more formally than in the first volume: surnames are in large writing in the left-hand margin and most entries have the place name written faintly also in that margin; this has been incorporated into the text. Most of the pages are divided by ruled lines in ink indicating the different entries and most are signed, though sometimes only with 'by me, etc' without the name of the priest. Entries for the different events are kept together in separate parts of the register, covering these dates:

Baptisms	*18 April 1824 – 18 August 1844*
Confirmation	*25 October 1835*
Marriages	*2 December 1825 – 3 September 1842*
Deaths	*11 October 1827 – July 1844*

A list of the clergy involved and their dates in Shefford has been added, presumably by Fr Collins:

Claude Sebastien Chabot	*18.4.1824*
George Rolfe	*13.11.1824–18.2.1838*
Charles Threlfall	*4.3.1838–16.1.1839*
Peter Coop	*14.4.1839–8.4.1844*

In addition, four priests are named, with just one entry each: William Hayes, 7.6.1828; James Doyle, 13.5.1832; John Maguire, 8.7.1832, and James Whelan, 24.9.1837.[15]

Baptisms

Each entry starts with the date of baptism, followed by the date of birth in brackets. The mother's maiden name is in brackets after her first name. Unless otherwise noted, all the entries down to 1838 are signed by the Rev. George Rolfe in the form 'A me, Geo Rolfe, Miss. Apos.' (or some minor variant of this), that is 'By me, George Rolfe, Missionary Apostolic.' As neither parishes nor dioceses existed canonically at this time in England and Wales, priests were in charge of missions technically directly under papal authority; whatever its official implication, if any, the term denotes a certain standing.

Year	Date	Event
1824	18 April:	(b. 9.1.1824): baptized, William John CLARKSON, s. of Thomas & Anne Clarkson, married. Godfather Henry Clarkson, godmother Esther Chiesa. By me E.S. Chabot, Miss. Apos. *[Note on first page proper, at the bottom, marked to go in here:]* "This register was given to me (Geo Rolfe) by the Revd. S. Chabot after he had been absent from the Chapel several months. G.R."[16]

[15] It is interesting to see the use of Irish clergy here after Challoner's and other eighteenth-century constant condemnation of them as missioners.

[16] An odd comment – perhaps there had been a problem with getting the records. See above, p. 63.

Year	Date	Event
1825	19 January	(b. 12.1.1825):[17] Mary Elizabeth CLARKSON, d. of Henry & Esther (Dunton), married. Godfather William Clarkson, godmother Alice Clarkson. Blunham.
	26 January	(b. 28.11.1824): John CAMPBELL, s. of Charles & Mary (Pursar), married. Godfather Peter Kenny. Huntington.
	26 January	(b. 12.7.1823): (condit. bapt.) Frances GIFFORD, d. of Alexander & Anne (Nugent), married. Godmother Elisabeth Ellington. Huntingdon.
	25 April	(b. 8.4.1825): Thomas CLARKSON son of Thomas & Anne (Aylett), married. Godmother Esther Clarkson, godfather Henry Clarkson. Blunham.
	27 April	(b. 21.2.1825): Patrick SWEENY s. of Michael & Mary (McGinty), married. Godfather John Mines. *[no place; presumably Irish]*
	24 April	(b. 20.4.1825): John STEEL son of Mary Steel. Godfather Michael Dempsey, godmother Catharine Stewart. Shefford. *[this entry is out of order; presumably the child was illegitimate]*
	16 June	(b. 15.4.1825): Mary GURNERIO d. of Peter & Mary (Southworth), married. Godfather Charles Campbell. Huntingdon.
	25 Sept.	(b. 8.9.1825): Honor (Honeria) HALLIGAN, d. of Mary & Daniel, married. Godmother Margaret Dempsey, godfather Wm. Stewart. Biggleswade.
1826	8 June	(b. 29.4.1826): Anne CLARKSON, d. of Thomas & Anne (Aylett), married. Godmother Esther Clarkson, godfather Henry Clarkson. Blunham.
	1 Oct.	(b. 28.9.1826): Margaret DEMPSEY, daughter of Michael & Margaret (Lovell), married. Godmother Margaret Sharp, godfather James Matthews. Shefford.
	20 Oct.	(b. 26.9.1826): Mary GAGOGEN *[presumably* Geoghegan*]*, d. of Mary & Francis (Henright), married. Godfather Michael Dempsey. Shefford.
1827	20 Feb.	(b. 13.2.1827): Margaret CLARKSON, d. of Henry & Esther (Dunton), married. Godfather William Clarkson, godmother Alice Clarkson. Blunham.
	7 June	(b. 7.3.1821): condit. Denis *[?]* BUTTERFIELD, s. of George & Mary. Hitchin.
	7 June	(b. 8. 1822): condit. Ellen BUTTERFIELD, d. of George & Mary. Hitchin.
	10 June	(b. 15.2.1825): condit. George BUTTERFIELD, s. of George & Mary. Hitchin.[18]
	9 Aug.	(b. 5.8.1827): Henry CUNDALL, s. of John & Anne (Batt.), married. (ceremonies carried out 2 Sept). Godfather John Wilson, godmother Jane Wilson. Hitchin.
	1 Sept.	(b. 10.8.1827): William LINNIHAN *[Lennihan?]*, son of Thomas & Margaret (Shelley), married. Godmother Mary Owens. Shefford.
	17 Sept.	(b. 3.9.1827): Anne BUTTERFIELD, d. of George & Mary (Sullivan). Godmother Joanna Wilson, godfather John Wilson. Hitchin.

17 In the original registers the birth dates are given in full, in Latin, e.g. Die 28 Novembris 1824. They have been transcribed here, and in following entries, in this shortened form.

18 See also Anne Butterfield, 17 September, and the note from King regarding the whole family: he claims Rolfe 'ferreted them all out' in Hitchin and baptised 'the lot' conditionally.

Year	Date	Event
1828	27 Feb.	(b. 7.2.1828): Elisabeth CLARKSON, d. of Thomas & Anne (Aylett), married. Godmother Alice Clarkson, godfather (by proxy H. Clarkson) George Clarkson. Blunham.
	3 April	(b. 21.3.1828): Isaac VINE, s. of — & Anne (Hughes), married. Godmother Margaret Dempsey. Shefford.
	11 May	(b. 30.4.1828): James WARBURTON, s. of James & Joanna (Driscol), married. Godmother Julia Sheen. Hawker. Shefford.
	13 July	(b. 27.6.1828): Charlotte DONALLY (*sic*) d. of James & Elisabeth (McKay), married. Godfather Edward Riley, godmother Catherine Riley.
	7 June	(b. 13.5.1828): Dennis RILEY, s. of Edward & Catherine (Murray), married. *[Rev.]* W. Hayes. *[in margin]* See the 1st page. 13 July 1828 ceremonies and prayers were added. Godfather James Donally, Godmother Elisabeth Donally. By me Geo. Rolfe, Miss. Apos.[19]
	3 August	(b. 4.4.1828): Mary Anne MURPHY, d. of Patrick & Susan (Fuller), married. Godfather Owen Riley, godmother Mary Riley. St. Neots.
	2 December	(b. 21.11.1828): Mary WHITE, d. of Thomas & Biddy (Esther), Godmother Margaret Dempsey, godfather Michael Dempsey. Hitchin.
1829	30 May	(b. 8.10.1828): Mary McHUGH, d. of Michael & Elisabeth (McCawley), married. Godmother Margaret Schanal, godfather David Schanal. Irish.
	7 June	(b. 7.6.1829): John DEMPSEY, s. of Michael & Margaret (Lovell), married. Ceremonies & prayers performed 21 June, Godfather — Sharp, Godmother Eliza Elvey. Shefford.
	16 August	(b. 30.7.1829): Charles BUTTERFIELD, s. of George & Mary (Sullivan), married. Godfather John Boyle, godmother Margaret Dempsey. Hitchin.
	21 December	(b. 26.11.1829): Elisabeth WILSON, d. of John & Brigid (Kinty (*sic*)), married. Godmother Mary Owens. Tramp. Shefford.
1830	14 March	(b. 5.2.1830): Henry HANOVER, s. of Edward and Sarah (Andrew), married. Godfather Michael Dempsey, godmother Elisa Elvey. St. Neots.
	26 April	(b. 11.3.1830): John VINE, s. of Mathew & Ann (Hughes), married, (with ceremonies & prayers added 28 same month). Godmother Bridget Glover. Biggleswade.
	28 April	(b. 11.1.1830): James GLOVER, s. of Edward & Bridget (Canning), married. Godmother (by proxy) — Sharp. Biggleswade.
	11 July	(b. 30.6.1830): William BANKS *[STEWART?]*, s. of Catherine (Banks) & John Stewart, married. Godfather James Banks, godmother Mary Banks. Hawkers at Hitchin. *[the name in the margin is STEWART – no doubt Banks is a mistake]*
	31 October	(b. 18.9.1830): condit. Ellen SULLIVAN, d. of John & Mary (McGuire), married. Godmother Mary Matthews. Travelling paupers.
	5 December	(b. 23.11.1830): Elisabeth WALKER, d. of James & Elisabeth (Kelly), (Protestant) married. Godmother Ellen Kelly, godfather Michael Dempsey. Of Poor house. *[presumably 'Protestant' applies to the father]*
	26 December	(b. 1.11.1828): condit. Mary Anne WILSON, d. of — & — Wilson (Riley). Godmother Margaret Dempsey, godfather Michael Dempsey. St. Neots.

19 William Hayes (1775–1855, ord. 1779); student at Valladolid; priest of the Midland District, at King's Cliffe, Northamptonshire; see Anstruther, *Seminary Priests*, vol. 4, p. 135.

Year	Date	Event
1831	18 Feb.	(b. 27.12.1830): Martha ODELL, d. of William & Elisabeth (Grummet), married. Protestant parents. 'Because of the danger of death, without ceremonies. Mr Williamson being ill'.[20]
	9 April	(b. 23.3.1831): Robert JOHNSON, s. of Lacey – & William Johnson, married. Protestant parents. 'Because of the danger of death, without ceremonies. Mr Williamson being ill'. *['William' as the father's name is crossed out]*
	21 April	(b. 27.3.1831): Henry CLARKSON, s. of Henry & Esther (Dunton), married. Godmother Alice Clarkson, godfather Seth Clarkson. Blunham.
	15 August	born & bapt: Michael DEMPSEY, s. of Michael & Margaret (Lovell), married. Godmother Eliza Delaney, godfather Michael Delaney. Shefford.
	27 August	(b. 25.8.1831): Seth Henry CLARKSON, s. of Seth & Elisabeth (Kay), married. Godfather Henry Clarkson, godmother Esther Clarkson. Blunham. Other ceremonies performed 28 Sept 1831.
	27 Sept.	(b. 12.8.1831): Eliza BARRY, d. of George & Pamela (Paddon), married. Godfather Edw. Mo*[rgan?]*. Stevenage.
	6 Nov.	(b. 8.10.1831): James BUTTERFIELD, s. of George & Mary (Sullivan), married. Godmother Mary Mathews, godfather J. Mathews. Hitchin.
	18 Dec.	(b. 11.12.1831): William CHIESA, s. of Andrew & Esther (Wood), married. Godmother Mary Owens, godfather Thomas Samford *[?]*. Shefford.
1832	20 January	(b. 9.1.1832): Mary QUINLON (*sic*), d. James & Elisa (Banks). Godmother Margaret McCarthy.
	24 June	(b. 2.2.1832): condit. Peter Augustin (*sic*) KEATH, s. of John & Frances (Fagan), married. Godfather Neale McShane. Luton.
	13 May (*sic*)	(b. 22.4.1832): Helen DILLON, d. of Patrick & Helen (Cummins), married. Godfather Michael Dempsey, godmother Margaret Dempsey. Luton.
	8 July	(b. 28.12. 1831): William HANOVER, s. of Edward & Sara (Andrew), married. Godmother Margaret Riley. John Maguire.[21]
	22 August	(b. 13.8.1832): Elisabeth CLARKSON, d. of Thomas & Anne (Aylett), married. Godfather Henry Clarkson, godmother Esther Clarkson. Blunham.
1833	19 April	(b. 24.9.1826): condit. and without ceremonies: William RICHARDS, s. of James & Anne (Macknally (*sic*)), married. St. Neots.
	19 April	(b. 29.5.1829): condit. & without ceremonies: James RICHARDS, s. of James & Anne (Macknally), married. St. Neots.
	19 April	(b. 8.2.1832): condit. & without ceremonies: Sara Anne RICHARDS, d. of James & Anne (Macknally), married. St. Neots. *[the Richards family, according to King, were 'a nice little nest of three']*
	2 June	(b. 9.4.1833): Margaret REGAN, d. of John & Phoebe (Coleman), married. Godmother Margaret Sharp, godfather Thomas Dempsey. Maulden.
	2 June	(b. 15.3.1828): condit. & without ceremonies: Richard REGAN, s. of John & Phebe (*sic*) (Coleman), married. Maulden.

20 Rev. Edmond Williamson was the Anglican rector at Campton, responsible for its restoration in the 1820s–30s; see Pickford, *Bedfordshire Churches in the Nineteenth Century*, vol. 73, pp. 156, 158.

21 Rev. John Maguire (1801–65, ord. 1825) later of the Westminster diocese.

Year	Date	Event
	16 Sept.	(b. 3.4.1833): Elisa SHEEHY, d. of Patrick & Catherine (Falvey), married. Godfather Jos. Fitsgerald (*sic*), godmother Mary Fleming. St. Albans.
	16 Sept.	(b. 12.8.1831): condit. Sara WOODBINE, d. of Charles & Elisa (Roach), married. Godfather Patrick Sheehy, godmother Mary Sullivan. St. Albans.
	2 October	(b. 21.9.1833): Anne WHITE, d. of Thomas & Bridget *['Biddy' crossed out]* (Esther), married. Godmother Emily Rose —, godfather Peter Deigham. Hitchin.
	2 October	(b. – 9.1833): Mary Anne BUTTERFIELD, d. of George & Mary (Sullivan), married. Hitchin.
	23 October	(b. 27.9.1833): (without ceremonies) Eliza CHIESA, d. of Andrew & Esther (Wood), married. St Albans.
	3 November	(b. 12.4.1829): condit. John WESTON, s. of Edward & Emily. Grenfield.
	3 November	(b. 23.9.1833): Joseph WESTON, s. of Edward & Emily (Arnold), married. Godfather John Ryan, godmother Honor Dempsey. Grenfield.
	22 November	(b. 21.11.1833): David DEMPSEY, s. of Michael & Margaret (Lovel), married. Godmother Bridget Young, godfather Patrick Murphy. Shefford.
1834	2 March	(b. 27.2.1834): bapt. (validly by her father), Mary DOOLEY, d. of Anthony & Winifred (Price), married. The ceremonies were performed 19 March. Godfather Michael Dempsey, godmother Margaret Dempsey. Hawker from Buckden.
	30 March	(b. 16.3.1834): Mary Anne DILLON, d. of Patrick & Ellen (Cummins), married. Godfather Thomas Dempsey, godmother Mary Owens. Market Street *[presumably Shefford]*
	6 April	(b. 22.3.1834): without ceremonies Mary O'BRIAN (*sic*), d. of James & Katherine (Connor?), married. Vagrant.
	5 May	(b. 2.4.1833): Elisabeth VINE, d. of Mathew & Anne (Hughes), married. Godmother Margaret Sharp. Bedford – from Biggleswade.
	3 June	(b. 11.5.1832): William STOCKER, s. of John & Margaret (Riley), married. Godfather Owen Riley, godmother Elisabeth Smith. St Neots.
	14 April (*sic*)	(b. 23.3.1832): John CASEY, s. of John & Mary (Fay) – without ceremonies. St Albans.
		On 9 June, ceremonies performed; godmother Mary Dockray.
	9 June	(b. 24.4.1834): Anne FITSPATRICK, d. of Bartholomew & Anne (—), married. Godmother Catherine Stewart, godfather Richard Stewart. St Albans.
	17 July	(b. 23.6.1834): Margaret MOORE, d. Patrick & Mary (Cullen), married. Godmother Honor Dempsey. Tramp.
	3 August	(b. 6.7.1832): Charlotte WALLER, d. of Charles & Anne (Hunter), married. Godfather Michael Dempsey, godmother Honor Dempsey. Hitchin.
	16 Sept.	(b. 31.8.1834): Anne-Esther CLARKSON, d. of Henry & Esther (Dunton), married. Godmother Anne T. Clarkson, godfather Thomas Clarkson. Blunham.
	21 Sept.	(b. 15.2.1832): condit. Hugh McCLOSKY, s. of Daniel & Henrietta (Reagan). Godmother Ellen Palmer, godfather Michael Dempsey. Poor Travellers. Shefford.
	21 Sept.	(b. 23.11.1833): condit. Daniel McCLOSKY, s. of Daniel & Henrietta (Reagan). Godmother Ellen Palmer, godfather Michael Dempsey. Travellers from Lodging house.

Year	Date	Event
1835	3 February	(b. 24.1.1835): Thomas Felix CORR, s. of Felix & Emma (Hancock), married. Godfather Owen Riley, godmother Mary Anne Riley. St Neots.
	3 February	(b. 21.1.1835): Elisabeth RICHARDS, d. of James & Anne (Macanally), married. Godfather Felix Corr, godmother Emma Corr. St Neots.
	1 March	(b. 27.12.1834): Francis REGAN, s. of John & Phoebe (Coleman), married. Godmother Margaret Dempsey, godfather Michael Dempsey. Maulden.
	10 March	(b. 25.12.1834): Hannah MURPHY, d. of William & Sarah (Burch (*sic*)), married. Hitchin. Ceremonies performed 29 March – Godfather James Mathews, godmother Mary Mathews.
	19 April	(b. 16.11.1834): Ellen O'HARE, d. John & Charlotte (Elson). Godfather Thomas Lawford, godmother Phillis Owens.
	9 March (*sic*)	born & …. 1835 (*sic*): baptised by Revd. Boland (of Reading, Berks) – as her mother testifies to me – Margaret CONOLLY, d. of John & Catherine (King), married. And the ceremonies supplied 3 June 1835. Godfather Thos. Lawford, godmother Phillis Owens.[22]
	21 June	(b. —1835): received the ceremonies of baptism (the sacrament having been given in danger by William Atchison, Hitchin),[23] Margaret BUTTERFIELD, d. of George & Mary (Sullivan), married. Godmother Mrs. Close, godfather Mic. Dempsey. Hitchin.
	30 August	(b. 4.8.1835): Ellen HUGHES, d. of Michael & Margaret (Pawley), married. Godfather Patrick Dillon, godmother Mary Dillon. Hemel Hempstead.
	24 September	(b. 28.8.1835): John Owen STOCKEN, s. of John & Margaret (Riley), married. Godfather Peter McShane, godmother Mary Riley. St Neots.
	7 October	(b. 2.7.1835): without ceremonies, Anne BOLTON, d. of – & Bridget (Dillon). Hawker.
	17 December	(b. 23.10.1835): condit. Mary McCLOSKY, d. of Daniel & Harriet (Read). Sponsors Mary King & Michael Dempsey. Hawker: Shefford.
1836	24 January	(b. 3.1.1836): Helen DILLON, d. of Patrick & Helen (Cummins), married. Godmother Ellen Hughes, godfather John Ryan (by proxy Barnabas Dempsey). Luton.
	7 March	(b. 31.8.1835): without ceremonies, Mary WOODBINE, d. of Charles & Elisabeth (Roach), married. St Albans. Ceremonies supplied 25 May 1836. Sponsors were Joseph Fitsgerald & Mary Fitsgerald.

[Inserted here is a page of names of those 'Confirmed by Illus(trious) & Most Revd. B(isho)p Griffiths, Sunday 25 October 1835'. The page has been ruled to provide columns: Names, Names in Confirmation, Place of Residence. Twenty-one candidates are listed, eleven from Shefford, five from Hitchin, two each from Luton and St Neots, and one from Maulden. See p. 64 above for the detailed list and comments. A copy of the bishop's list from AAW is noted there.]

Year	Date	Event
1836 cont.	7 March	(b. 6.4.1830): condit. without ceremonies: Mary FITSPATRICK, d. Anne & Cornelius (—) Bartholomew (*sic*), *[see next entry]* (—) married. St Albans. Ceremonies supplied *[no date]*
	7 March	(b. 30.1.1836): condit. and without ceremonies: Teresa CHIESA, d. of Andrew & Esther (Wood), married. St Albans. Ceremonies supplied 25 May 1836 – Sponsors Elisabeth Woodbine & Bartholomew Fitspatrick.

22 Presumably John Francis Bowland (1770–1857, ord. 1795) of the London District; at Reading 1821–37; see Anstruther, *Seminary Priests*, vol. 4, p. 44.
23 William Atchison not found in clergy lists; probably a layman.

Year	Date	Event
	20 March	(b. 10.3.1836): Mary DEMPSEY, d. of Michael & Margaret (Lovell), married. Godfather John Boyle, godmother Mary Lines. Shefford.
	25 April	(b. 15.3.1836): Charles CASEY, s. of John & Mary (Fox). Godfather John Murray (by proxy Stewart), godmother Esther Chiesa. St Albans.
	7 May	(b. 11.4.1830): condit. Emma LILLE, d. of John & Anne (Madden), married. Beggar *[*doubtful, (*sic*) *in margin].*[24]
	25 June	(b. 2.11.1828): condit. Robert TAILOR, s. of William & Elisabeth (Allcock) married. Godmother Mary Allcock. Baldock. *[in margin:* a cripple & idiot*]*
	25 June	(b. 7.11.1835): Catharine TAILOR, d. of William & Elisabeth (Allcock), married. Godmother Mary Allcock. Baldock.
	26 June	(b. 8.10.1835): Michael BOYLE, s. of John & Anne (Leane). Godfather Peter Deagan, godmother Margaret Dempsey. Hitchin.
	26 July	(b. 31.5.1836): without ceremonies, Maurice DUGGAN, s. of Elisabeth & Maurice (Doland), married. St Albans.
	20 August	(b. 4.11.1835): Anne WESTON, d. of Edward & Emily (Arnold), married. Godfather Patrick Regan, godmother Mary Lawless. Grenfield.
	6 Sept.	(b. 13.5.1836): Henry WALLER, s. of Charles & Anne (Hunter), married. Godmother Mary Mathews. Hitchin.
1837	1 Jan.	(b. —.11.1836): Cecilia REGAN, d. of John & Phoebe (Coleman), married. Godfather Edw. Weston, godmother Margaret Dempsey. Maulden.
	6 Feb.	(b. 31.10.1836): James FITSPATRICK, s. of Bartholomew & Anne (Mc a nally (*sic*)), married. Godmother (by proxy) Ellen Steel. St Albans. *[obvious difficulties with Irish names;see 7 Sept below for correct form]*
	28 June	(b. 30.4.1837): Elisabeth RUSH, d. of Isaac & Mary (Mullen), married. Godfather Robert Rush, godmother Bridget Rush. Travellors (*sic*).
	2 July	(b. 6.6.1837): Henry BUTTERFIELD, s. of George & Mary (Sullivan), married. Sponsors Peter Deighan & Margaret Sharp. Hitchin.
	2 July	(b. 5.6.1837): June Elisabeth STOCKEN, d. of John & Margaret (Riley), married. Sponsors Peter McShane & Honor Dempsey. St Neots.
	27 August	(b. 25.4.1837): John LILLEY, s. of Sarah & James (Nichols), married. Godfather John Gatherne, godmother Phillis Owen.
	7 Sept.	(b. 20.8.1837): Ellen RICHARDS, d. of James & Anne (Macanally), married. Ceremonies supplied 9 November 1837. Sponsors Mary Delaney & John McLaughlan. St Neots.
	24 Sept.	(b. 23.8.1837): born & bapt. John MURPHY, s. of Patrick & Hannah (Bryan), married. Godfather Patrick Dillon, godmother Phillis Owen. Luton. By me, J. Whelan.[25]
	5 October	(b. 17.9.1837): Thomas George CLARKSON, s. of Henry & Esther (Dunton), married. Godmother Ann Clarkson, godfather Thomas Clarkson. Blunham.
	8 October	(b. 21.9.1837): Timothy CALLAGHAN, s. of William & Mary (McCloskey), married. Godmother Phillis Owens. Hawker, St Albans.

24 Presumably name is LILLEY – see later entries; not clear what ‘doubtful’ refers to – perhaps status as beggar.

25 Rev. James Whelan (1801–45, ord. 1833), London District.

Year	Date	Event
	9 November	(b. 26.10.1837): Hugh BURNS, s. of Hugh & Elisabeth (Delaney), married. Godmother Mary Ann Delaney, godfather John Burns. Hawkers. Shefford.
1838	18 Feby.	(b. 11.1.1838): Thomas WESTON, s. of Edward & Emily (Arnold), married. Godfather Patrick Regan, godmother Margaret Dempsey. Grenfield.

[Last regular entry by George Rolfe; one later entry, 19 May below. Replaced by Rev. Charles Threlfall (1802–39, ord. 1828 for the London District). The format of the register remained the same.]

Year	Date	Event
	4 March	(b. 9.12.1837): Hannah FEIRON, d. of James & Cecilia (Quinn), married. Godfather Peter Deighan, godmother Ellen Dillon. Luton. By me Charles Threlfall. M.A.
	13 May	(b. 17.4.1838): John HEDITCH, s. of Joseph & Lucy (Godfrey), married. Godfather John Godfrey, godmother Sarah Godfrey. Shefford.
	2 Sept.	(b. 1.8.1838): Ellen BOYLE, d. of John & Anne (Lane), married. Godfather Samuel McDonnell, godmother Ellen Dillon. Hitchin.
	14 October	(b. 14.9.1838): Thomas REGAN, s. of John & Phoebe (Coleman), married. Godfather Edward Weston, godmother Margaret Dempsey. Maulden.
	1 November	bapt. Joan COLLINS, an adult, godmother Frances Houchin. Shefford.
1839	6 January	(b. 15.12.1838): James HUGHES, s. of Michael & Margaret (Gantly), married. *[in very faint writing in margin:]* without ceremonies. Supplied the ceremonies, Peter Coop 5 May 1839.

[Fr Threlfall died 3 March 1839. The registers kept by Fr Coop, his successor, are more untidy with horizontal lines less regular, etc; but information still on the whole full, though chronological order is incorrect at times. Peter Coop was born 1809, ordained 1837, and died as a priest of the Southwark diocese in 1868.]

Year	Date	Event
	14 April	(b. 1.4.1839): Andrew DILLON, s. of Patrick & Helen (Cummins), married. Godfather Peter Dieghan (*sic*) *[see entry below for 19 May]*, godmother Honor Dempsey. Luton.
	8 May	(b. —): Ellen WALLER, d. of Charles & Anne (Hunter), married. Godfather John Dempsey, godmother Mary Burns. Hitchin.
	19 May	(b. —): Sarah Anne FERON, d. of James & Cecilia (Quinn), married. Godfather Peter Deighan, godmother Bridget Cummins. Luton. *[see earlier Feiron 1838 – same couple]*
	9 November	bapt: Joseph WALLER, s. of Joseph & Elisabeth (Godfrey), married. Shefford. On the same day the child died. *[in margin:* Without ceremonies*]*
1840		*[Entries for the year are out of order]*
	9 August	(b. 10.7.1840): Condit. James HARRINGTON, s. of John & Mary (Davis), married. Godfather Michael Horson, godmother Sarah Lilley. Bedford.
	28 June	(b. 2.6.1840): Sarah REGAN, d. of John & Foebe (*sic*) (Coleman), married. Godfather Edmund Weston, godmother Margaret Dempsey. Maulden.
	6 Sept.	(b. 3.8.1840): Eleonor HEDITCH *[also spelt* HEDDICH *in same entry]*, d. of Joseph & Lucy (Godfrey), married. Godfather Henry Lewinton, godmother Elisabeth Waller. Shefford.
	17 May	(b. 13.4.1840): Mary CATAN, d. of James & Mary (Murphy), married. Godfather Peter Coop (*sic*), godmother Margaret Dempsey. Biggleswade. *[it is very unusual to have the celebrant as godfather]*

Year	Date	Event
1841	28 November	(b. 21.11.1841): Helen MARKEY, d. of Francis Helen (Kitchener), married. Daniel Markey Godfather, Catherine Kearney. Luton. *[a confused entry: presumably Kearney is the godmother. Strangely, this is the only baptism recorded for the year]*
1842	13 March	(b. 26.2.1842): Condit. Martin McHUGH, s. of John & Joan (Geraghty), married. Godfather Henry Gambol, godmother Margaret Dempsey. Apsley Guise. *[the name is spelt* Machugh *in the margin, while Henry Gambol appears later as Henry Gamble – 5 November 1843]*
[Unusual note at end of page:] 16 June ceremonies supplied for Eliza DELLORSO, d. of Antony (Antonio) Dellorso & Elisabeth (Ley) married. Born 31 March 1832. By me Peter Coop Mis. Ap. Godmother C. Coop *[presumably a relative; perhaps mother or sister, acting as housekeeper?]*		
[See misplaced entry for 15 January under 1843 below]		
	17 July	(b. —): William DAVIS, s. of George & Joan Davis (married). Godmother Marg Dempsey. On the same day the ceremonies were supplied on — Davis their son. Godmother Margaret Dempsey.
	19 August	was baptized and on the 4th day of the same month was born (*sic*), Catherine CAULFIELD, d. of William & Sarah (Mc oughan (*sic*)), married. Godfather Michael Dempsey, godmother Margaret Dempsey. *[in margin in large letters:* SONDON*]*
	18 December	*[added in small writing at bottom of the page; obviously missed out earlier]* 1840 born & 31 January 1841 bapt. Mary Anne HUGHES, d. of Michael & Margaret Hughes. Married. Godfather Michael Dempsey, godmother Catherine Cain *[or Carr]*
	9 Sept.	(b. 5.8.1842): Charles HEDITCH, s. of Joseph & Lucy (Godfrey), married. Godmother Elizabeth Godfrey.
1843	13 February	(b. 30.8.1842): Condit. Joseph MACLUSKY, s. of Daniel & Harriet (Rudd), married. Godfather P. Coop M.A., Godmother Margaret Cherry. Biggleswade. *[note Coop as godfather]*
	2 July	(b. 2.6.1843): Caroline SAMWAY, d. of William & Sara (Aylett), married. Godfather Thos. Clarkson, godmother Anne Clarkson. Tempsford. *[where given, place names are written vertically alongside entries]*
	1 October	(b. 3.8.1843): Peter MARKEY, s. of Francis & Ellen (Kitchener), married. Godfather Peter Markey, godmother Ellen Dillon. Luton.
	8 October	(b. 29.1843): Lucy WESTON, d. of Edward & Emily (Arnold), married. Godfather Michael Dempsey, godmother Margaret Dempsey. Greenfield *[followed by illegible word, could be* 'Illiterate'*]*
	5 November	(b. 1.10.1843): Catherine Anne BOYLE, d. of John & Anne (Lane), married. Godfather Henry Gamble, godmother Sara Gamble.
	10 December	(b. 10.11.1843): Anne REAGAN, d. of Thomas & Foebe (*sic*) (Coleman), married. Godfather Richard Reagan, godmother Margaret Dempsey.
[Two entries out of place follow; one of them (15 January 1842) has Fr Coop as godfather and celebrant, and a relative of his as godmother, as in later entry for 3 April 1844.]		
1842	23 August	(b. 13.8.1842): Emma Louisa CLARKSON, d. of Thomas & Anna (Dunton), married.
1842	15 January	(b. 21.12.1841): Mary Magdalene WILLIAMS, d. of John & Juliana. Married. Godfather Peter Coop Priest, godmother Cecily Mary Coop.
1844	24 March	(b. 22.2.1844): Joan WALLER, d. of Charles & Anne (Hunter) married. Godfather Henry Gamble, godmother Margaret Dempsey.
	3 April	(b. 3.2.1844): Anna FARRELL and Mother Farrell, married. Godmother Cecily Mary Coop. *[unclear entry]*

Year	Date	Event
	7 April	(b. 3.3.1843): Condit. Anne WARRINGTON. John Makown Bridget Makown *[No signature by priest but in Coop's hand. Name could be McKeown; Bridget's signature her own, perhaps]*
	18 August	*[At the very end of this volume, after the marriages and deaths, is a single baptism entry by Fr Coop that fits in here:]* (b. 8.4.1844): Sarah TURNER, d. of John & Anne (Stacey), married. Godfather Peter Deighan, godmother Mary Deighan. *[illegible word in the margin:* Ippellots*]*

Marriages

Starting in 1837, marriages could take place legally in Catholic places of worship. This list by George Rolfe almost certainly indicates that before that date a number of Catholic couples had their marriages celebrated or blessed in the church, no doubt in addition to having a legal ceremony in the Anglican church – hence the lack of witnesses and other family information. Since Catholic priests were not licensed as registrars, one had to be present to fill out the civil register even after 1837 (see note on p. 159 above). Irish names predominate, perhaps because of current practice in Ireland.

Year	Date	Event
1825	Dec. 2	Rich. Charles — to Eliza Lawford. Witnesses were Sara Jaspar & Betsy Godfrey. G. Rolfe.
1827	May 5	Mary Sullivan to Geo. Butterfield G. Rolfe.
1830	Jan 3	Biddy Esther to Thomas White G. Rolfe.
1831	May 29	Mary Riley to Michael Boyle G. Rolfe.
1832	Jan 20	Elisa Banks to James Quinlon G. Rolfe.
1835	April 19	Charlotte Elson to John o Hara (*sic*) Shefford by me G. Rolfe.
1835	May 31	Sara Pankers to Wm Murphy Hawkers Hitchin by me G. Rolfe.
1837	May 22	Maria Dillon to Michael Larkins before the witnesses Michael Dempsey & Margaret Hughes by me G. Rolfe.

[The page is clearly divided into two by this line; the lower half has the first of two lengthy entries in Latin by Fr Threlfall and marks the proper start of the marriage register, though the very detailed entries do not last. Editor's translation.]

In the year 1838 on the 19th day of May, no lawful impediment having been found, I Charles Threlfall, Missionary Apostolic at Shefford, Bedfordshire, interrogated Brian LARNEY, son of Thomas and Joan *[?]* Larney of Cabbinteely Co Dublin, and Elizabeth Mary CLARKE, daughter of Charles and Elizabeth Clarke *[line smudged here]* and having verbally received their mutual and solemn consent to the present marriage, I married them in the presence of known witnesses Elizabeth Wood and Robert Oliver. 19th May 1838 Charles Threlfall Missionary Apostolic

In the year 1839 on the 10th November, no lawful impediment having been found, I Peter Coop, Missionary Apostolic at Shefford, Beds., interrogated Samuel McDONALD of St Paul's Walden Herts, and Mary JETMANS, and having received their mutual consent, solemnly spoken, to the present marriage, I married them before known witnesses Peter Deighan and *[the entry ends thus, with a line across the page; this is followed by four extremely short unsigned marriage entries in English:]*

1840	9 December	Married Peter DEIGHAN to Mary LAKE. Witnesses John & Ann Boyle.
1841	7 February	Married John GREEN to Bridget GLOVER. Witness Michael & Margaret Dempsey.

Year	Date	Event
1842	3 June	Married Neil McSHANE to Catherine KEARNEY .Witness Peter McShane John MaCowan (*sic*).
1842	3 Sept.	John SMITH to Honor DEMPSEY. Witnesses Mich. Dempsey Thos. Co *[rest hidden by repair to page]*

Deaths

There are five pages of entries, some very detailed with comments about the deceased. All are in English. They throw a fresh light on Fr Rolfe and his pastoral concerns – see pp. 63–5.

Year	Date	Event
1827	11 Oct.	Died at Blunham 11th of Oct 1827 Wm CLARKSON aged 32.
	26 Nov.	The Rt Revd Dr. Poynter, V. Apostolic of the London District.[26]
1828	6 Sept.	Mrs. M. HALLIGAN at Shefford after a long illness which she bore with the most exemplary patience. Aged 37.
1829	31 January	Anna Maria HUGHES at Shefford. Aged 76. This beneficent Lady employed her fortune almost wholly in the charitable exercises of Religion. To the poor Catholics of Shefford, she was a most kind benefactress. To the improvement of the chapel here, and to the support of its pastor she contributed very abundantly, and the future improved condition of the Shefford Mission will be mainly indebted to her legacies (provided certain people be just & honest? (*sic*)) *[see p. 65 above]*
1834	8 November	Mrs Miyston *[very unclear]* – at Shefford, in the 82nd year of her age.
1835	March.	Mr. HALLIGAN (husband of above) at Biggleswade suddenly without sacraments. *[perhaps in the Union Workhouse, established in 1834]*
	April.	John O'HARE, who left Bedford Infirmary, came & lived here for 3 weeks, then returned to Bedford, and tho' in the last stage of consumption went lately to Northampton, where he died two days after his arrival. He was attended by the Revd Wm Foley of said place.[27]
	4 *[?11]* June.	Seth CLARKSON, of Biggleswade, brother to the Clarksons of Blunham. From no fault of his own, he failed in his business, and gave up his all to his creditors whilst able to pay 20% in the pound. This misfortune so preyed upon his mind that it brought on a fatal illness of mind as well as body. The 3 last days of his life he had but few moments of reason. He was attended by Myself and received the last sacraments. God only knows what will become of his wife & children.
1836	3 January	Clifton: Helen JENKS, d. of the Jenkes' (*sic*) of Oundle, aged 24 of a consumption … (*sic*) She was fully aware of her end and had well provided for it, by the reception of the sacraments. The perfect happiness afforded to her a day or two before her death was to see her parents reconciled to each other. She prayed that she might live to see this reconciliation ratified by their receiving the sacraments. Both parents, her brother & sisters communicated at Clifton at about 9 in the morning, and she herself was a corpse at ¼ past 10. May this reconciliation of all parties be lasting, and may the lessons taught them & me in her death bed produce their fruit in our souls.

26 See above re Poynter, pp. 47–9.

27 Presumably of the Midland district (ordained 1820, died 1843); there was another William Foley, of the London District (ordained 1832), date of death not known.

Year	Date	Event
	11 June	Patrick DOGHERTY aged 20, an Irishman travelling up the country for hay & harvest work. He was first taken ill at Potton, and was removed to Biggleswade, where he died rather suddenly, having received none of the sacraments. This account I had after his death. *[Biggleswade had a workhouse after 1834]*
	2 November	Mrs O'HARA, travelling hawker, at Hitchin after an illness of 4 or 5 weeks, leaving a husband and 4 children. She received the last sacraments of the church.
1837	30 April	Mrs GODFREY, formerly housekeeper of the Revd C. Tailor (*sic*) and long a resident of this Place. She has left behind her 4 daughters grown up, and one son, and a husband a Protestant *[added above the line]* (afterwards became a Catholic in 1838 in his last illness). Her complaint which was first dropsy, deprived her for about 2 months of her reason, and ended in a Decline. She received the last sacraments previous to her mental malady and again the day before her death.
	13 May	Mr FITS PATRICK (*sic*) of St Albans, a poor hawker, leaves a wife & one child. He received the last sacraments.

[There is a new page here; entries are generally shorter and signed by the priest. No dates of the month are given.]

Year	Date	Event
1838	February.	Mr GODFREY after a long and painful illness during which he became a Catholic, and prepared for his end as a fervent Christian. Chas. Threlfall. *[see 3 March, below]*
	May.	– BUTTERFIELD of Hitchin, of consumption, after being taken into the Church, and living two months as a Catholic, and preparing himself for the sacraments he had the consolation of receiving them all. C. Threlfall.
	August.	Mrs SHARP who lived in the Polehanger way *[a farm in Meppershall, on the Shefford road]* and there died after a full and fervent preparation, and was buried at Campton. Chas. Threlfall.
	September.	A woman of the name of BYGRAVE who kept a lodging house just by Stevenage though I believe in the parish of Gravely, fully attended. Chas. Threlfall.
	September.	Antony LYONS who died in the Union at Luton before attention could be given him. Chas Threlfall.
1839	3 March.	Revd. Charles THRELFALL Parish Priest of this Mission of Shefford in his 36th year, of Consumption. He had been on this Mission 1 year all but a day. He had been Parish Priest of Old Hall Green where he had been educated Well prepared: With all the rites.[28] P. Coop.
	24 March.	Mary RILEY (Convert) wife of Mr Riley received all the rites of the Church in a Providential manner: died and buried at St Neots. P. Coop.
	9 July.	Mrs Elisabeth LARNEY (Clark) aged 67 of mortification in the bowels caused by stricture of the same: was in extreme suffering more than a week: received all the rites of the Church: buried at Campton. P. Coop.
	9 October.	Mr RILEY aged 41 at St Neots of Lockjaw caused by his nose striking against the edge of a table whilst he was dozing in his chair: received all the rites of the church: buried at St Neots. P. Coop.
	2 December.	Mr John CAHERTY at Shefford Landlord of the Black Swan aged 51 of liver complaint brought on by a long habit of drinking spirituous liquors. Received all the rites of the church: buried at Campton. P. Coop.

28 This was the site of the seminary, St Edmund's College, in Hertfordshire, see p. 62 above.

Year	Date	Event
	–	Sawford at Shefford. (*sic*) John SAWFORD Aged 59 nine (*sic*) received all the rites buried at Campton. P.C *[this is a scribble at end of the page; no date is given; the remaining entries have surnames as mini-headings]*
1841	June	HANOVER of St Neots (Hunts) John Hanover aged 60 received all the rites is buried at St Neots June 1841.
1842	Sept.	HUNTER Hitchin (Herts) George Hunter aged 70 dyed at Hitchin receiving all the rites of the Church burried (*sic*) at Hitchin.
1843	–	DAVIS Shefford Mary Ann Davis aged 42 received the last Sacraments burried (*sic*) at Campton.
	October	RILEY St Neots Sarah Riley received all the rites of the Church buried (*sic*) at St Neots.
1844	June	DONLEY Bedford. George Donley Age 49 received the last sacraments buried (*sic*) at Bedford.
	July	O'BRIAN Biggleswade Union Samuel O'Brian received the rites of the Church buried *(sic*) at Biggleswade.

Volume 3 (1844–59)

A hard cover, plain paper note book, the same size and appearance as volume 2. Some pages are missing from the back of the book. A loose page is inserted at the front of the book, with some historical entries in a different hand and unsigned. For Noddings entries see p. 161 above.

Year	Date	Event
1728	–	Bapt. Mary, the child of a travelling woman.
	–	Bur. of travelling boy who died 1728.
1784	–	Bur. of poor Irish *[*'lab' *crossed out]* harvestman.
1753	Feb. 17	Bur. St John Willowes of Shefford.
1754	May 7	Wheatley *[both February 1753 and May 1754 entries are as written but crossed out]*
1754	*[Aug. 14.]*	Edward Cupis of Shefford (Bur.) Aug. 14.
1776	*[Aug. 21.]*	John Noddings bur. Aug. 21.
1781	*[Feb. 12.]*	Bur. Stephen Robinson, a Roman Catholic Priest. Feb 12.
	[June 6th]	Elizabeth Noddings June 6th.
1783	*[Oct 14]*	Mary Noddings Oct 14.
1786	*[Jan 20]*	Edward Dixie from St John's St London, Innholder. Jan 20 (stone still to be seen, "May he rest in peace").
1730	*[April 15]*	Susannah wife of Willm. Noddings Butcher April 15. *[it looks as though this entry was entered later since it is squeezed in above what follows]*

Year	Date	Event
1743	*[Oct 5]*	Willm. Noddings of Campton. Oct 5. Bur. Grave stones still visible – + Here lieth the body of William Noddings, who Departed this life 3rd October 1743 in the 75th year of his age. Give him O Lord eternal rest And let perpetual light shine unto him May he rest in peace. Amen *[Similar inscription on Susannah Noddings; the two stones are side by side]*

[End of inserted loose page. The transcription of volume 3 starts with a summary by Fr Collins of events and clergy.]

Baptisms 25. 12. 1844 – 20. 12. 1858
Marriages 31. 7. 1848 – 7. 9. 1857
Deaths 14. 7. 1849 – 1. 1. 1859
Confirmation 27. 8. 1854

Clergy:
John Taylor December 1844 – October 1849
Patrick J. Quinlivan May 1850 – March 1854
William J. Poole June 1854 – May 1855
Charles F. Cuddon September 1855
Henry J. Thrower (canon) September 1856 – September 1857
John Rigby S.J. September 1858
William Hammond January 1859

[First page proper of volume 3 headed:]

Births, Marriages, & deaths at Shefford.

[Rev. John Taylor's baptism entries, all in English, are carefully laid out, with the principal surname and place entered in a left-hand margin, as in George Rolfe's earlier entries, and signed. His first entry is given here in full; after that they have been abbreviated. In some cases he acts as the sponsor of the child; there is an unusual use of 'sponsor' instead of 'godparent'.]

Year	Date	Event
1844	Dec 25th	I baptised Sarah, born Nov 19th 1844, daughter of James & Mary KEYTON. Sponsors Michael Mic Kaowna & Bridget Mic Kaowna (*sic*) Biggleswade. J. Taylor. *[from later entries, it is clear that the sponsors' name was McKeown]*
	Dec 26th	William, born — 1844, s. of William & Sarah SAMWAY. Sponsor J. Taylor. Blunham. *[no signature]*
1845	Jan 5th	Mary Magdalen, b. Dec 7th 1844, d. of John & Juliana WILLIAMS. Sponsors Rev. P. Coop & Miss Coop. Elstow.[29]
	Jan 6th	Emma, b. Feb 26th 1844, d. of John & Elizabeth HIGGINS. Sponsor J. Taylor. Shefford. *[no signature]*
	March 23rd	William b. Feb 17th 1845, s. of Edward & Emma WESTON. Sponsors Richard & Margaret Regan. Greenfield.
	March 27th	Francis Lewis, b. Feb 25th 1845, s. of Lewis & Victoria HENRY. Sponsors Lewis Henry & Francine Briand. Silsoe. *[presumably a different member of the family as sponsor, or an error?]*
	May 12th	John, b. Jan 7th 1844, s. of Robert & Ann DEAR. Sponsor John Taylor. Shefford.

29 Presumably Miss Coop was his sister, perhaps acting as his housekeeper, as was not unknown at the time.

Year	Date	Event
	Oct. 19th	Lucy, b. Nov 15th 1844, d. of John & Emma SMITH. Sponsor Mrs Collens. Shefford.
	Oct. 22nd	Mary Anne, b. Oct 22nd 1845, d. of Joseph & Lucy HEDDITCH. Sponsor Mrs Waller. Shefford.
	Nov. 9th	Anne, b. Sept 12th 1845, d. of John & Ann TURNER. Sponsors Peter Deighan & Jenetta Lewinton. Gosmore.
1846	May 17th	Agnes, b. April 14th 1846, d. of John & Phoebe REGAN. Sponsors Francis Megan Margaret Regan. Maulden.
	May 21st	Mary, b. May 5th 1846, d. of Michael & Mary MURPHY. Sponsor Sarah Conlon. Travellors (*sic*).
	Sept. 20th	Amelia, b. Aug 22nd 1846, d. of Charles & Ann WALLER. Sponsor Mrs Mic.Kaowna (*sic – see above for McKeown.*) Hitchin.
	Oct. 4th	Cornelius, b. Sept 3rd 1846, s. of John Shreves & Emma SMITH. Sponsor J. Taylor. Shefford. *[no signature]*
1847	Jan 31st	Mary Agnes, b. Jan 3rd 1847, d. of John & Juliana WILLIAMS. Sponsors Thomas Phillipson & Matilda Mac-Donnell (*sic*). Elstow.
	Feb. 14th	Bernard Charles, b. Jan 3rd 1847, s. of John & Elizabeth HIGGINS. Sponsor J. Taylor. Shefford.
	March 21st	Edward, b. Jan 27th 1847, s. of Edward & Emma WESTON. Sponsors Francis & Margaret Regan. Greenfield.
1848	Feb. 6th	Jane, b. Jan 7th 1848, d. of John & Phoebe REGAN. Sponsors Michael & Jane Dunn. Maulden. *[unsigned]*
	July 9th	Agnes, b. June 12th 1848, d. of William & Sarah SAMWAY. Sponsors Thomas Heditch Ann Clarkson. Blunham. *[unsigned]*
	July 24th	Isabella Mary, b. July 24th, d. of Hon. William & Mary Teresa PETRE. Sponsors James Alexander Douglas, Louisa Clifford. Ampthill.[30]
	Aug. 13th	Helen, b. July 16th 1848, d. of Justin & Catharine RYAN. Sponsor Revd. John Taylor. Bedford.
	Sept. 24th	Joseph John, b. July 9th 1848, s. of John & Mary SCULY *[Scully? very unclear and name not in the margin]*. Sponsors McGrath John, McAfry Maryann *[no place]*
	Dec 24th	Michael, b. Nov 27th 1848, s. of James & Mary O'BRIEN. Sponsor Jane Dunn. Hitchin.
1849	Jan 4th	John, b. Feb 16th 1848, s. of William & Catherine HUCKEL. *[usually spelt Huckle]* Sponsor John Taylor. Colmworth.
	Feb 11th	Rose Ellen, b. Dec 14th 1848, Son (*sic*) of William George & Mary Ann HARRISON. Sponsors Michael McKowen, Mrs McKowen. Ampthill *[see note under 24 December 1844]*
	March 4th	Mary, b. Feb 17th 1849, d. of Thomas & Bridget MADIGAN. Sponsors Margaret Regan, John Logan. Traveller.
	April 22nd	Anstice *[?]* b. Jan 28th 1849, s. of William John & Mary CASHMERE. Sponsor Catherine O'Brien. Langford. *[in margin:* From Railway*]*

30 The Petre family of Ingatestone Hall, Essex, were a renowned Catholic noble family; ten members of the family feature in Kirk's *Biographies*. Isabella Mary married Frederick Stapleton-Bretherton of Rainhill, Lancashire, another recusant Catholic family. She died in July 1919. It was unusual to have the baptism on the day of birth; presumably there was a danger of her dying.

Year	Date	Event
	July 6th	George, b. May 14th 1849, s. of Charles & Ann WALLER. Sponsor John Taylor. Hitchin.
	Sept 2nd	John, b. June 16th 1849, s. of David BLAKE & Esther Blake. Sponsors William Langley, Eleanor Swanson. Stevenage.
	Sept 19th	William, b. Aug 24th 1849 *['Aug' crossed out]*, s. of William MORAN & Bridget Meegan. Sponsor John Taylor. Maulden.
	Oct. 17th	Thomas b. Feb 22nd 1849, s. of William & Catherine HUCKELL. Sponsor Eliz. Magourty. Colmworth.
	Oct. 19th	Margaret, b. May 15th 1849, d. of Thomas & Susanna FRANEY. Sponsor Elizabeth Thompson. Traveller.

[Entries from here on are in Latin again, by Fr P. J. Quinlivan, in his untidy, sprawling writing and so difficult to read. Usually there are no lines between the entries, which are unsigned unless noted otherwise. No mention is given of marital status and often the wife is given with maiden name. The first of his entries is given here in full in English; editor's translation.]

Year	Date	Event
1850	May 19th:	was baptized by me in the church of Saint George in Shefford in Bedford Mary, d. of Richard GRACE & Margaret Dillon (*sic*), sponsors John Gainer & Mary Gainer. *[no place]* P. J. Q.
	10th March	William HIGGINS was baptized on the tenth day of March one thousand eight hundred and fifty (*sic*) in the church of St George. Sponsors H. Lewington & Joanna Higgins.
	–	Ellen FOULDRAIN, d. of John McCORMACK & Apollonia Rosalia Fouldrain *[unclear; no place]*
	[August 4.]	Same day, John DELANY, s. of John Delany & Judith his wife. *[no place]*
	Sept. 8	Susanna, d. of William HICKLEY & Catherine his wife. *[no place]*

[There is no mention of the change of status from Eastern District to Diocese of Northampton]

Year	Date	Event
	Dec. 6	Mary Frances *[on the line above; could relate to previous entry]* d. of John HOWARD & Mary (Hornik) his wife. Sponsors were Elizabeth Hornik *[just a scribble]* and Charles Belsea *[?]*. Biggleswade.
	Dec 8	Joseph REAGAN, s. of John Regan (*sic*) & his wife. Sponsors were Mr Dunn & Mrs Dunn. Maulden.
	Dec 29	Joan TRAINER, d. of John & Joan Trainer his wife. Sponsors were James Whelan & Mary Lestrange. Arlesey.
1851	–	Mary Elizabeth, legitimate d. of John SCOTT. Baldock.
	Feb 7th	William, legitimate s. of Charles WALLER. Sponsor Mrs Collins. Hitchen.
	Feb 8th	Catharine COLLINS, d. of Cornelius Collins at Biggleswade.
		[There follow two entries without a month; probably February]
	10th	Mary BEAUX *[?]*, d. of J. Beau & his wife. *[no place]*
	16th	William MURRAY, legitimate s. of Peter Murray & Mary his wife. Sponsors were Patrick Galorn *[?]* & Elizabeth Thorndon. Sandy.
	14th April	Samuel WILLIAMS, legitimate s. of Samuel Williams & Margaret his wife. Sponsors were Michael Sullivan & Martha Bates. Biggleswade.
	22 April	John & Martha STONEHAM, s. & d. of Timothy Stoneham. Sponsors J. Whelan & E. Kennedy. Hitchin.
		[A number of minimalist entries follow]
	2 May	Bridgewater Mary, son of John & Mary HALLIFAX.
	5 *[May]*	William & Caroline LYONS, children of Robert Lyons & Mary Hickey.

Year	Date	Event
	8 Sep	Margaret McLOUGHLIN, d. of Peter McLoughlin & Mary his wife. Sponsors were Mrs Collins & Philip McKeown.
	10th	Baptized in the little chapel (*sacello*) of St George in Shefford Sarah SAWFORD.
	23	Edmund QUILTY, s. of John Quilty & Mary his wife. By me, PDQ, Priest (*sic*)
1852	Feb 3rd	baptized by me Richard ARMSTRONG.
	[Feb] 6th	baptized by me William HUCKLE.
	May 10th	Michael John GALLIVAN (*sic*); s. of Patrick Gallivan & Annie (?Linehan) (*sic*). Sponsor Mrs McKeown.
	May 10th	Margaret FLYNNT, d. of James Flynnt & Mary Gale. Sponsor Catherine Flynnt.
	May 16th	Charles WALLER, s. of Charles Waller & Catherine (? Hunter) (*sic*) his wife. Sponsor Mrs Collins.
	–	Luton Ellen FERNET (*sic*), legitimate d. of James Fernet & Ellen his wife. Sponsor Ellen Fernet.
	July 5th	James, illegitimate son of William MORAN & Briget Reagan. Sponsor P. Clikery P. J. Quinlivan.
	August 19th	Sara Anne HIGGINS, legitimate d. of James & Elizabeth Higgins by me P. J. Quinlivan.
1853	Feb 20th	Michael BEAU, legitimate s. of Patrick Beau & Anne (Doly). Sponsors were Dennis Kelly & Joan Dunne, by me.
	Feb 21st	Elizabeth McGRATH, d. of Michael McGrath & Bridget Manly.
	March 4th	Mary HARRINGTON, d. of John Harrington & Margaret Carney. Sponsor M. McKeown by P J Q.
	April 4th	Elizabeth HUCKLE d. of William & Elizabeth Huckle, married. Godfather John McKeown by me P. J. Q Miss. Apos.
	July 16th	John s. of John CASTLE & Bridget Burke, by me P. J. Q.
1854	13 March	(b. 2.2.1854) Febiana *[?]* MORAN & Bridget Moran *[maiden name illegible]* not married. *[line perhaps omitted, the 'not' added in later]* Godfather John Higgins, godmother Delia Murphy. Biggleswade. By me P. J. O'Quinlivan (*sic*) Miss. Apos.

[Fr Quinlivan left the diocese of Northampton in 1854 and may have returned to his native Ireland. He was succeeded at Shefford by Fr W. J. Poole (1828?–67, ord. 1854), who signed the next seven entries – and wrote them very clearly in English. He revived the practice of using margins for surnames and place names.]

Baptisms

[Each page carries a similar heading]

1854	9th June	Helen, b. 14.4.1854, d. of William & Helen WELCH (Resden). Sponsor Mrs John Higgins. Bedford.
	23rd July	Jane, b. 28.12.1853, d. of William & Anne CHIPPERFIELD, (O'Flaherty). Sponsor Elizabeth Davis. Hitchin.
	17th Sepr.	William, b. 20.4.1854, s. of William & Anastasia BREWER (O'Neill). Sponsor Elizabeth Evans. Luton.
1855	4th Feb.	Margaret, b. 19.1.1855, d. of John & Bridget McGUINESS (Pyne). Sponsor Eliz. Evans. Shefford.

Year	Date	Event
	20th Feb.	Margaret, b. 26.1.1855 d. of William John JOY & Anne Joy (Wilson). Sponsor Catharine Riley. Hawnes *[Haynes?]*
	25th March	Sarah, b. 3.3.1855 d. of Michael & Mary RINN (O'Donnell). Sponsor Elizabeth Dorrell. Warden.
	6th May	Catharine, b. 6.12.1854, d. of Daniel & Dorothy GIBLIN (Lennon). Sponsor Jane McFarren. Cotton End.

[This is the last Poole entry; he was replaced by Rev. Charles Francis Cuddon (1824–80, ord. 1854), who left Northampton for Westminster in 1856. Note after Cuddon's two entries: 'I came to this Mission on 14th Aug 1856 succeeding the Revd. C.F. Cuddon. H.J.Thrower'. Thrower (1824–91, ord. 1849) did not stay long: in 1858 he left Northampton for Liverpool; he died 1891.]

Year	Date	Event
	20 Sept.	1855 baptized (conditionally) an old man named John ATKINSON in a dying state at the Infirmary, Bedford. C. F. Cuddon.
	29 Sept.	I baptized John, born 22 May last, s. of John & Mary WALSH (McCloskey). Godmother Elizabeth Sheen. Cambridge. C. F. Cuddon.
1856	15 Sept.	Daniel s. of Daniel & Eliza BUCKLEY (Donovan), married, b. 1.9.1856. Sponsor — Dunn. Travelling. H.J. Thrower Canon. *[his usual signature]*
	15 Sept.	Thomas, s. of Thomas & Anastasia BREWER (O'Neill), married, b. 24.7.1856. Sponsor Delia Murphy. Luton.
	12 Oct.	Thomas, s. of Thomas & Mary Ann EGAN (Santry), married, b. Sept 24.9.1856. Sponsors Patrick, Mary Horner. Bedford.
1857	23 March	privately at the Father's House, Henrietta, d. of John & Ellen CARTER (Butterfield). The Mother was dying. Hitchin. NB The Father is a Protestant, but promised the wife to let the Grandmother bring up the child a Catholic. *[see entry below for mother's death on 24 March; the child was three weeks old]*
	6 May	I baptized (simple rite) & signed with holy chrism, there being no Sponsors to be had, Edward McDRISCOLL, s. of John & Ellen (Collins) married, b. 24.4.1857 at Etlesley (*sic; presumably Eltisley*), Cambs. Tramp.
	19 July	William HUCKLE, s. of Wm. Huckle & Catharine (McGorty) married, b. 7.6.1857. Sponsors Dominick (*sic*) Phillip & Ann Thewly. Bedford.
	16 August	David FARRELL, s. of James & Elizabeth Farrell (Murray) married, b. 8.4.1857. Sponsor Susan Sullivan. Bedford.
	30 August	Elizabeth Ann MADDEN, d. of Bartholomew & Catherine Madden (Donigan), married, b. 24.7.1857. Bedford. Sponsors John Williams, Julia Williams.
1858	17 September	James MORING, s. of William & Bridget Moring (Magan) married, b. 8.8.1858, Luton. Sponsor Delia Murphy. John Rigby S.J.

[This is the only entry for a baptism in 1858. John Rigby was a Jesuit (1809–89, ord. 1834). This and the next entry (in Latin) by William Hammond (1828–1900, ord. 1855), of Northampton diocese, are the only ones on this last page of baptisms.]

Year	Date	Event
1859	23 January	Emma, b. 20.12.1858, d. of John & Eliza HOLOMON (Hardy) married. Godfather Michael McKeowne, godmother Ellen Welsh. Bedford. By me William Hammond.

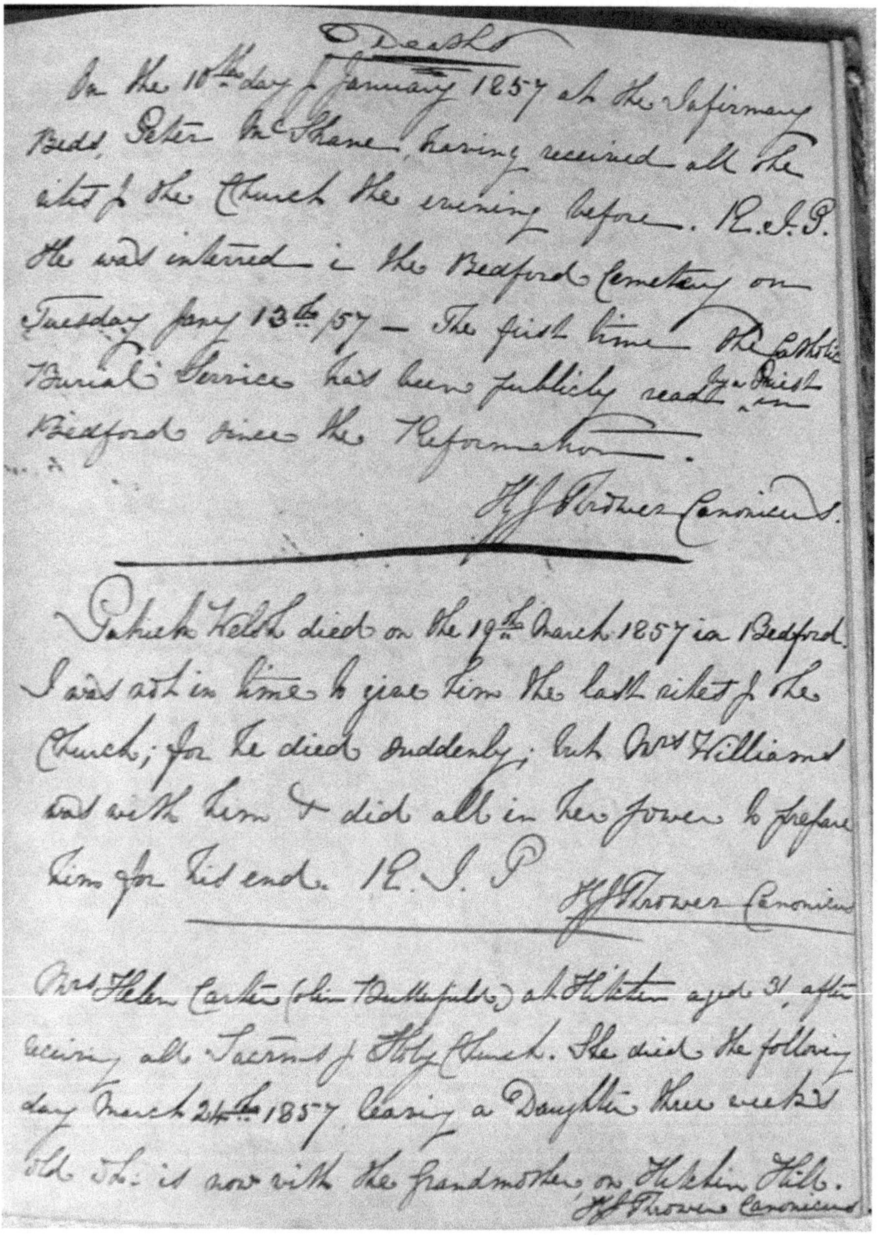

Deaths

On the 10th day of January 1857 at the Infirmary Bedford, Peter McShane, having received all the rites of the Church the evening before. R.I.P. He was interred in the Bedford Cemetery on Tuesday Jany 13th /57 – The first time the Catholic Burial Service has been publicly read by a Priest in Bedford since the Reformation.

H J Thrower Canonicus.

Patrick Welsh died on the 19th March 1857 in Bedford. I was not in time to give him the last rites of the Church; for he died suddenly; but Mrs Williams was with him & did all in her power to prepare him for his end. R.I.P.

H J Thrower Canonicus

Mrs Helen Carter (olim Butterfield) at Hitchin aged 31, after receiving all Sacraments of Holy Church. She died the following day March 24th 1857, leaving a Daughter three weeks old. She is now with the grandmother on Hitchin Hill.

H J Thrower Canonicus

Page from Shefford Mission Register, deaths 1857.
(courtesy of Diocese of Northampton)

Year	Date	Event
[Starts a new page]		

Deaths

[This register is unusual for its comments. Entries have not been abbreviated.]

Year	Date	Event
1849	14 July	Mr Henry CLARKE of Shefford died at Shillington 14th July 1849.
1850	March	Died at Shefford after having received the rites of the Catholic Church, Jno Collins (*sic*)
1855	4 Jany.	Died at Campton, Mrs Lucy CLARKE aged 88. A most devout Catholic, I attended her & gave her the rites of the Church excepting the H. Viaticum wh. I thought prudent to keep from her. W. J. Poole.
	13 Jany.	Died at Shefford Sarah Anne HIGGINS aged 2 years & 8 months.
1857	10 Jan	On the 10th day of January 1857 at the Infirmary Beds, Peter McSHANE, having received all the rites of the Church the evening before. R.I.P. He was interred in the Bedford Cemetery on Tuesday July 13th/57 – The first time the Catholic Burial Service has been publicly read by a Priest in Bedford since the Reformation. HJThrower Canonicus.[31]
	19th March	Patrick WELSH died on the 19th March 1857 in Bedford. I was not in time to give him the last rites of the Church; for he died suddenly; but Mrs Williams was with him & did all in her power to prepare him for his end. R.I.P. HJThrower Canonicus.
	March 24th	Mrs Helen CARTER (formerly Butterfield) at Hitchen aged 31, after receiving all Sacr(a)m(ent)s. of Holy Church (*sic*). She died the following day March 24th 1857, leaving a Daughter 3 weeks old who is now with the Grandmother, on Hitchin Hill. HJThrower Canonicus. *[see entry above for 23 March 1857 in the list of baptisms; the father was a Protestant]*
	April 19th	On April 19th (Low Sunday) 1857, in the 77th year of her age, Mrs Frances Teresa LEWINTON, after receiving with great faith & devotion all the Sacram(ent)s of Holy Church. She was a Convert & for many years before her death was in the daily habit of reciting the Rosary, Penit(ential) Psalms, & Litanies of S(acred) H(ear)t, Holy Name & B(lessed) V(irgin) M(ary) – in fact nearly the whole Garden of the Soul. She was sensible to the last & was able to receive Holy Comm (union) although quite unable for many days to retain the least food or drink on her stomach. Buried at Campton. R.I.P. *[for* 'The Garden of the Soul' *see pp. 19–20]*
1859	Jany. 1st	Jane PLUNKETT died Jany. 1st 1859 in the Union at Hitchin, and was buried Jany. 3rd at Hitchin, (*sic*) *[rest of page left free, as though for more]*

[On a new page is a list of those confirmed by Bishop Wareing on 27 August 1854: see above p. 73]

[New page]

Marriages

[All the marriage entries begin with 'I married']

Year	Date	Event
1848	July 31st	Jonathan TYLER to Mary Ann Healey. Witnesses Edward Murrell & Sarah Wright. John Taylor Minister *[see p. 68 above on Taylor]*
1849	Sept. 9th	John MACK CORMACK (*sic*) to Apollonia Rosalia Foldrain. Witnesses were Larah Conlon & Henry Lewinton. John Taylor Minister *[see earlier Foldrain, p. 181]*

31 This is an interesting entry in the light of Fr Warmoll's experience of opposition when he led a burial service there in 1865, which he claimed was the first post-Reformation Catholic burial there – see pp. 90–1 above.

Year	Date	Event
	Nov. 12th	James DIXON, to Elizabeth Lambe(r)th. Witnesses were Mr F. Smith & Miss Smith. John Taylor.
1852	July 5th	Patrick GALLIVAN (*or*, GALLINAN) to Anne Lincon (*sic*) Witnesses Philip McKeown & E. Thomson. P. J. Quinlivan.
	July 12th	Patrick MEARS to Anne O'Toole. Witnesses William Foth *[?Hoth]* and Mary Donaghue P. J. Quinlivan Minister.
	Aug 17	William FOTH *[?]* to Mary Donaghue. Witnesses Patrick Mears & Anne O'Toole *[no signature]*
1853	Feb 5	John BENSON to Ellen Denny *[nothing else on the page; PJQ's hand-writing]*
1855	15th January	James McFARLANE and Mary Anne Darcy. Witnesses Michael McKeowne and Delia Murphy. Minister William Poole.
1856	27th February	Patrick MURPHY & Honora Hagety (*sic*). Witnesses Michael McKeowne (*sic*) and Elizabeth Sheen. Charles Francis Cuddon Minister.

[These last two entries take up one page, starting at the top of the page; the rest of the page is empty]

Year	Date	Event
1857	7th Sept.	William MOORING & Bridget Magan from Luton. Witnesses Mary New, Emma Higgins. HJ Thrower Canon.

[There follow two pages, in Quinlivian's writing, that bring the registers to an end with a list of regular churchgoers; the names are in two columns; the comments were obviously added later, but it is not clear when. See earlier text, pp. 72–3.]

Bedford
The Church of the Holy Child and St Joseph registers, 1864–1900

Introduction

Current location of registers
Most of the mission records are in the diocesan archives in Northampton; Bedford Record Office has some of the registers on microfilm.

Civil registration
Births and deaths were also registered civilly, though not baptisms.

Ministering priest
Where the priest is the resident priest, as is the case in almost all the entries, no name is given; where a visiting priest is noted, for whatever reason, his name is attached to the entry. The resident priests for the period covered in these registers were:
1863–85: John Priestley Warmoll (1830–85)
1885–87: George Wrigglesworth (1851–1900)
1887–90: George Osman (1847–?)
1890–1906: Robert Christopher Middleton (1853–1906)

Format
A major difference from the earlier Shefford registers is that there was a standardised format for use throughout the diocese after 1850; the registers were properly printed and bound as official records and were kept in Latin. Sponsors (in Latin 'patrinus' and 'matrina') are indicated by 'gf' and 'gm', for 'godfather' and 'godmother'. 'b' and 'bp' stand for 'born' and 'baptised', 's' and 'd' for 'son' and 'daughter'.

Upper case 'C'
An upper case 'C' in the margin of the register would seem to indicate an adult convert to Catholicism.

Female Christian names
'Maria': this is used throughout the Latin registers, with no indication whether the English version would be Mary, Marie, or even May; Mary has been used throughout in these transcriptions. Similarly, 'Anna' – Anne, Ann, Anna; Anne is used here throughout; also 'Caterina' – Catherine, Kathleen, Kate; Catherine is used throughout.

Irish and Italian names

Obviously Irish names occur regularly but do not dominate. Italian names occur occasionally here, but do not become frequent until after 1900.

Baptismal registers, 1864–1900

Notes

Format of entries

After 1850, official registers were kept in Latin (occasionally the English format of Christian names was used). Surnames were usually printed separately in the margin. The following is an example of a complete entry from the Bedford register of baptisms for 1864:

> Walton Die 24 Januarii 1865 natus et die 19 Februarii 1865 baptizatus est Bernardus Josephus Walton filius Henrici et Susannae Walton (olim Lowe) conjugum:
> a me Joanne Priestley Warmoll Mis. Ap.
> Patrinus fuit Franciscus Tandy Matrina fuit Anna Walton.

This may be translated:

> Walton Born on the 24th January 1865 and baptized on the 19th February, Bernard Joseph Walton, son of Henry and Susanna Walton (formerly Lowe) married,
> by me John Priestley Warmoll Miss. Apos.
> Godfather was Francis Tandy, Godmother was Anne Walton

A shortened version is used here:

> 1865 Walton Bernard Joseph, b. 24 Jan, bp. 19 Feb; s. Henry & Susanna (Lowe).
> Gf: Francis Tandy; gm: Anne Walton.

The recording priest used a ? when unsure of information.

'Condit.'

Indicates a conditional baptism, that is where there was doubt whether the person had already been baptised, or doubt whether the earlier baptism was valid in the eyes of the Church. This, and other notes, such as 'in danger of death', often appear in the left-hand margin below the surname; in this transcription such notes are given after or as part of the main text. The age of the person is generally not given.

Godparents

As noted above, these are indicated by 'gf' and 'gm'. In several cases only one godparent is named; where a name is not decipherable, this is indicated by '*[unclear]*'. Usually in the case of emergency baptisms administered in imminent danger of death no godparent names are given; this is also usually the case where an older person is baptised conditionally. In some cases ceremonies omitted in danger of death were noted as having been performed later.

Maiden name

This was indicated in brackets after the wife's name, introduced by 'olim' ('formerly'); in these transcriptions the name is just in brackets.

Year	Surname	
1864	Walton	Caroline Elizabeth, b. 19 May 1863, bp. 31 Jan; d. Henry & Susanna (Lowe). Gm: Lucy Westhorn.
	McGourty	Mary Anne, b. 9 Jan, bp. 18 Jan; d. Mary Anne McGourty (outside marriage). Gm: Bridget McKewen (*sic*).
	Hills	William James, b. 8 May 1863, bp. 1 April; s. Thomas & Rebecca (Jones). Gm: Catherine Huckle. *[note added]* Died Oct 1866.
	Lightfoot	Alfred Joseph, b. 19 May, bp. 3 June; s. William & Catherine (Doyle). Gf: Michael McKeown; gm: Ellen Welsh.
	Richards	Charles Robert, b. 3 July 1821, bp. 18 August (condit.)
1865	Walton	Bernard Joseph, b. 24 Jan, bp. 19 Feb; s. Henry & Susanna (Lowe). Gf: Francis Tandy; gm: Anne Walton.
	Whittle	William John Ignatius, bp. 7 Sept (condit.)
1866	Cole	Mary Teresa, b. 29 May ?, bp. 14 Jan; d. William (deceased) & Susanna (former Lowe, now Walton) (condit.)
	King	Anne Joan, b. 16 Mar 1865, bp. 13 Mar; d. Margaret King (outside marriage). Gm: Mary Kelly. Imminent danger of death; no ceremonies.
	Stafford	Mary Helen, b. 26 July 1865, bp. 3 July; d. Helen (outside marriage). Gm: Mary Stafford.
1867	Byewater	Joseph, b. 23 Sept 1797, bp. 23 Sept (condit.)
	Wilson	William James, b. ? 1867, bp. 6 Oct; s. William Nassau & Caroline (Woodward). Gf: William Lightfoot; gm: Helen Lynch.
	King	John William, b. 21 April 1867, bp. 1 Nov; s. Margaret King (outside marriage). Gm: Mary Kelly.
	Jones	Mary Elizabeth, b. 28 Nov, bp. 19 Dec; d. Henry & Mary (? Windmill) (*sic*). Gm: Mary Anne Harpur.
1868	Purser	George Thomas, b. ?, bp. 7 March; s. George *[unclear]*. Gf: Francis Tandy; gm: Mary Murphy.
	Bye	George, b. ?, bp. 8 March; s. William & Mary Anne (ceremonies omitted).
	Bye	Frederick, b. ?, bp. 13 April; s. William & Mary Anne (ceremonies omitted).
	Sullivan	Mary Helen, b. 31 March 1863, bp. 1 June; d. George Eaton & Mary Anne (Goulding). Gm: Matilda Parkes.
	Bye	Mary Anne, bp. 10 Sept (condit.)
	Tildesley	Michael Augustine, b. 28 Sept, bp. 16 Sept; *[sic; presumably these dates should be reversed]*; s. William & Elizabeth Mary (Costloe). Gf: Augustine Costloe; gm: Katherine Brady *[perhaps Kathleen?]*
	Cronin	Florence Kate, b. 13 Aug 1868, bp. 23 Oct; d. Daniel & Rose (Moore). Gf: John Brady; gm: Mary Anne Brady.
1869	Maley	Charles, b. 13 Nov 1868, bp. 31 Jan; s. Antony & Mary (Dempsey). Gf: Richard Welsh; gm: Ellen Welsh.
	Nisbet	Rose Aloysia, bp. 19 June (condit.)
	Rabbitt	Elizabeth Mary, bp. 27 June (condit.)
	Simkin	Isaac Augustine, bp. 6 August (condit.)
	Dobson	Henry Edward, b. 24 July 1869, bp. 15 Aug; s. Robert & Emily (Connor). Gf: William Dobson; gm: Ellen Welsh.

Year	Surname	
	Polton	Richard Polton, b. 12 Sept 1869, bp. 15 Oct; s. Thomas & Sarah (Cronin). Vagrants. In danger of death? (*sic*). Ceremonies omitted.
	Basil	Frances Mary, b. 1 May 1869, bp. 27 Oct; d. Elizabeth Basil (outside marriage). Gm: Alma Mary Bye.
	Carter	Wilfred Joseph, b. 24 Oct 1869, bp. 21 Nov; s. Joseph Fabioni & Frances Agnes (Conrey). Gm: Elizabeth Conrey.
	Basil	Ada Anabella Mary, 18 Nov 1869, bp. 30 Nov; d. John Crediford & Anne —. Danger of death; ceremonies omitted.
	Dillon	Mary Elizabeth, bp. 10 Dec; d. Michael & Mary — (condit.)
	Basil	Mary Anne, bp. 26 Dec (condit.)
1870	Sugden	Henry Joseph, bp. 27 Jan; s. Sugden (deceased) (condit.) popularly known as Simkin.
	Dillon	Robert, bp. 27 Jan; s. Michael & Mary — (condit.)
	Basil	John (Junior), bp. 28 Jan (condit.)
	Brinckworth	Catherine, b. 14 Feb 1870, bp. 1 Mar; d. Daniel & Helen (Leahey). Luton. (Urgent necessity)
	Simkin	Helen Elizabeth, bp. 1 Mar (condit.)
	Shanessey	Mary Josephine, b. 3 Mar 1870, bp. same day; d. Michael Joseph & Anne Elizabeth (Wardill). Father in imminent danger of death.
	Spencer	John, b. 26 May 1849, bp. 6 April (condit.)
	Shaedelin	Aloysius Paul, b. 26 Aug 1869, bp. 6 April; s. Francis Xavier & Anne Maria (Bruxer). Gf: Joseph Bruxer; gm: Maria A. Eugenie Bruxer (condit. without ceremonies; baptised by the Father in imminent danger of death).
	Rose	Benjamin James, b. June 1870, bp. 11 July; baptised by the maid Lucy Eyre in danger of death.
	Grainger	Charles, b. 2 July 1870, bp. 21 July; s. George & Sarah (Stettard). Gm: Matilda Parkes.
	Simkin	Anne Eliza, bp. 7 Sept; d. Isaac Augustine (condit.)
	Simkin	Elizabeth Helen, bp. 7 Sept; d. Isaac Augustine (condit.)
	Dillon	Mary Anne, bp. 7 Sept; d. Michael Dillon (condit.)
	Horsewood	Joan, bp. 23 Sept (condit.)
	Corthing	Catherine, b. 2 Sept 1870, bp. 2 Oct; d. Thomas & Charlotte (Camm?) (*sic*). Gf: John McKeown; gm: Ellen Welsh.
1871	Tildesley	Francis John, b. 2 Jan 1870, bp. 26 Jan; s. William & Elizabeth Mary (Costloe). Gf: John Brady; gm: Mary Anne Brady.
	Dobson	Mary Vincentia, b. 31 Jan 1871, bp. 5 Feb; d. Robert & Emily (Connor); Gf: Henry Frederick Dobson; gm: Matilda Parkes.
	Horsewood	Helen Mary, b. 17 Sept 1863, bp. 13 Mar; d. John & — (condit.)
	Dillon	Richard, b. 4 Dec 1856, bp. 20 Mar; s. Michael Dillon (condit.)
	Basil	John Henry, bp. 10 April; John Crediford & Anne — (condit.)
	Hacker	Arthur, bp. 15 April (condit.)
	Hacker	Alice Elizabeth, bp. 15 April (condit.)
	Rainbird	Joan Mary, bp. 22 May (condit.)
	Carter	Monica *[unclear]*, b. 21 June 1871, bp. 9 July; d. Joseph Fabian & Frances Agnes (Conrey). Gf: John ?; gm: Matilda Parkes.

Year	Surname	
	Shanady	Frances Anne, b. 11 July 1871, bp. 8 Aug; d. Michael Joseph & Anne Elizabeth (Smith Wardill); Gf: Edward ?; gm: Frances Smith Wardill.
	Wardill	Frances Anne, bp. 30 Dec (condit.)
1872	Crowther	Joan Martha, bp. 29 Jan (condit.)
	Church	Mary Anne, bp. 7 Feb (condit.)
	Blake	Francis, b. 27 April 1866, bp. 2 April; s. James & Sarah (Nobbs). Gf: Thomas Caton *[Calon?]*; gm: Matilda Parkes.
	Cogan	Elizabeth, b. 21 March 1872, bp. 9 June; d. Richard & Sarah Julie (Griggs). Gf: Edward de V. Corcoran; gm: Anastasia Topp.
	Schaedelin	Mary Laura, b. 16 June 1872, bp. 7 July; d. Francis Xavier & Mary Anne (Bruxer). Gf: Alphonse Bruxer; gm: Amandina *[?]* Bruxer.
	Brinkworth	William, b. 25 May 1872, bp. 11 July; s. Daniel & Helen (Leahy). Gm: Matilda Parkes. Celebrant: William Blackman, Miss. Apos.[1]
	Haynes	Alice Gertrude Mary, bp. 13 Sept (condit.)
	Wilson	Adelaide Margaret Mary, bp. 1 Nov (condit.)
	Barton	Thomas Alexander John, b. 18 Nov 1872, bp. 1 Dec; s. William Thomas Nicholas & Mary Anne (Church). Gf: William Huckle; gm: Rebecca Wittrick.
	Tatman	Helen Mary, bp. 9 Dec; d. John & Sarah (Milner) (condit.)
	Topp	Arthur Edward McKay, bp. 23 Dec; s. William Edward & Anastasia Agnes (Cole) (condit.)
	Topp	William Bertram, bp. 23 Dec; s. William Edward & Anastasia Agnes (Cole) (condit.)
	Topp	Albert Frederick, bp. 23 Dec; s. William Edward & Anastasia Agnes (Cole) (condit.)
	Topp	John Henry Cole, bp. 23 Dec; s. William Edward &Anastasia Agnes (Cole) (condit.)
1873	Carter	Etheldreda Mary, b. 25 Dec 1872, bp. 26 Jan; d. Joseph Fabian & Frances Agnes (Conrey). Gm: Mary Aloysia Lion.
	Dobson	Arthur Robert, b. 25 Jan 1873, bp. 2 Feb; s. Robert & Emily (Connor). Gf: William Huckle; gm: Anne Huckle.
	Westropp	Agnes Ellen, bp. 27 Feb; d. John & Agnes (Williams). Gf: William Higgins; gm: Matilda de Wackenheim *[?]*. Ceremonies omitted in urgent danger of death.
	Gnâpp	George Cecil, b. 23 Feb 1873, bp. 6 April; s. Mischka & Augusta Elizabeth (Harding).
	Wyatt	Aloysia Joan Agnes Mary, b. 6 June 1865, bp. 11 May; d. Thomas & Esther (Lunn… ?) (*sic*) (condit.)
	Tildesley	Thomas George, b. 8 May 1873, bp. 1 June, Pentecost; s. William & Elizabeth Mary (Costloe). Gf: Joseph Tildesley; gm: Matilda Parkes.
	Farmer	Gertrude, bp. 31 Aug; d. Harrington & Sara (Chambers). Gf: Michael McKeowne (*sic*); gm: Joan Crowther.
	Carter	Ellen Mary, b. 12 Sept 1854, bp. 15 Oct (condit.)
	Webb	George William, b. 28 Oct 1872, bp. 15 Oct; s. George & Alice (Coleman). Ceremonies omitted in urgent danger of death.

1 Rev. William Blackman of the Northampton diocese (1840–1911, ord. 1864).

Year	Surname	
	De Brenni	Emma Mary, bp. 16 Oct (condit.)
	Chapman	Emma Mary, b. 22 April 1851, bp. 18 Oct (condit.)
	Gurney	Elizabeth Martha Mary, bp. 8 Dec (condit.)
	Taylor	Elizabeth, bp. 18 Dec (condit.)
	McKay	Catherine Mary, bp. 19 Dec (condit.)
1874	Hopper	Benjamin, b. 22 Jan 1874, bp. 22 Feb; s. Benjamin & Isabell (Parkins). Gf: John Lightfoot; gm: Mary Anne Blake.
	Ketterer	George Conrad, b. 2 April 1874, bp. 3 May; s. Conrad & Florence (Stolz). Gf: Columba Stolz; gm: Joan Brady.
	De Brenni	George Joseph, bp. 8 May; s. Charles & Emma (Crook). Gf: Michael McKeown; gm: Ellen Elizabeth Cundale.
	De Brenni	Rose Mary, bp. 8 May; d. Charles & Emma (Crook). Gf: Michael McKeown; gm: Ellen Elizabeth Cundale.
	Westropp	John Edwin, bp. 11 May; s. John & Agnes (Williams) (condit. ceremonies omitted in danger of death, baptised by the Mother.)
	Prigmore	Charlotte Mary, b. 13 June 1870, bp. 14 May; d. John William & Mary Anne (Wells). Gf: Joseph Prigmore; gm: Matilda Parkes. *[note added:* The first Baptism in the new church *see pp. 91–6 above]*
	Prigmore	Anne Mary, b. 12 July 1862, bp. 12 July; d. John William & Mary Anne (Wells) (condit.)[2]
	Arthur	Mary Anne, bp. 22 July (condit.)
	Barnard	Mary Anne, bp. 26 July (condit.)
	Schaedelin	George Julius, b. 29 July 1874, bp. 16 Aug; s. Francis Xavier & Mary Anne (Bruxer). Gf: Michael Joseph Shanady; gm: Elizabeth Ellen Cundale.
	O'Grady	Mary Anne Margaret, b. 14 Aug 1874, bp. 6 Sept; d. Edward & Martha (Sears). Gf: William Lightfoot; gm: Mary Anne O'Grady.
	Bennett	Flora Elizabeth, b. 25 Aug 1874, bp. 11 Oct; d. Joseph & Flora (Trolly).
	Schaeffler	Elizabeth Margaret Mary, bp. 16 Oct (condit.)
	Cogan	Joseph Savill, b. 26 Nov 1874, bp. 18 Dec; s. Richard & Sarah Julia (Griggs). Gf: John Tracey; gm: Joan Rainbird.
	Conlin	Mary Anne, bp. — Dec (condit.)
	Senteline (?)	Anne Sophia, bp. 24 Dec (condit.)
1875	Dillon	Winefrid Mary, bp. 6 Jan (condit.)
	Dillon	Michael Daniel (? Desmond) (*sic*), bp. 6 Jan (condit.)
	Hollins	Joseph William, b. 12 Feb 1875, bp. 7 March; s. Thomas & Mary (Tildesley). Gf: Joseph Tildesley; gm: Elizabeth Tildesley. William Blackman Miss. Apos.
	Prigmore	Emily Joan Mary, b. 3 Aug 1872, bp. 20 March; d. John William & Mary Anne (Wells). Gf: William Lightfoot; gm: Kathleen O'Keefe.
	Gnâpp	Michael, b. 5 April 1875, bp. 23 April; s. Michael & Augusta Elizabeth (Harding). Gf: Joseph Brien; gm: Alice Haynes.
	Wells	George Alban, bp. 1 July (condit.)

2 The frequency of 'Mary Anne' or 'Anne Mary' as Christian names is noteworthy in these entries.

Year	Surname	
	Westrop	John Charles, b. 29 May 1875, bp. 18 July; s. John & Agnes (Williams). Gf: William Tildesley; gm: Elizabeth Tildesley.
	Wells	Alban Vesey, b. 12 July 1875, bp. 24 July; s. George Alban & Felicity Katherine (Harding). Gf: ? Hardy; gm: Irene Hardy.
	Thoms	Emma, bp. 18 Aug (condit.)
	Durrant	Mary Anne, bp. 20 Sept (condit.)
	Carter	Lucy Agnes, b. 18 Sept 1875, bp. 17 Oct; d. Joseph Fabian & Frances Agnes (Conrey). Gm: Mary Aloysia Lion.
	Hatley	Francis Ludovic, b. 29 Aug 1874, bp. 26 Oct; s. John & Henrietta (Scrivener). Gm: Sylvia Anne Scrivener.
	Farmer	Arthur William, b. June 1875, bp. 30 Oct; s. Harrington & Sarah (Chambers) (condit.)
	Hearn	Wilfrid John, b. 12 Oct 1875, bp. 30 Oct; s. David & Catherine (Brady). Gf: John Brady, gf: Mary Anne Brady.
	Sykes	Henry, bp. (?) Nov (condit.)
	Turner	Charles, b. 13 Dec 1875, bp. 24 Dec; s. William Henry & Clare. (ceremonies omitted, imminent danger of death).
1876	Back	Minnie Mary, b. 16 Dec 1875, bp. 16 Jan 1876; d. Henry & Sarah Jane (Rose). Gf: Michael Joseph Shanessy.
	Lunnon	John Thomas, b. 30 Dec 1875, bp. 23 Jan; s. William John & Margaret (Fair?) (*sic*). Gm: Matilda Parkes.
	Lee	Thomas Joseph, bp. 24 March (condit.)
	Jackson	Emily Matilda, b. 26 Feb 1876, bp. 2 April; d. William & Emma (Thoms). Gm: Matilda Parkes.
	Shanasy	Eveline Lucy, b. 5 April 1876, bp. 30 April; d. Michael Joseph & Anne Elizabeth (Wardill). Gf: Edmund Quillinan; gm: Matilda Parkes.
	Brady	John William, b. 31 March 1876, bp. 11 June; s. James & Mary (Bookey?) (*sic*). Gf: Joseph Tildesley; gm: Joan Brady.
	Browne	Sophie, b. 24 Nov 1874, bp. 11 June; d. William & Elizabeth (Bradshaw). Gm: Joan Rainbird.
	Browne	Robert, 25 June 1876, bp. 26 June; s. William & Elizabeth (Bradshaw). In danger of death; ceremonies omitted.
	Tildesley	Sarah, bp. 4 Sept (condit.)
	De Brenni	Lucy, bp. 27 Sept; d. Charles & Emma (Crook). (In danger of death, ceremonies omitted.)
	Thoms	William Henry, b. 15 May 1873, bp. 19 Nov; s. Emma Thoms (Jackson). Gf: Michael McKeown. (Outside marriage)
	O'Grady	Edward George William, b. 28 Nov 1876, bp. 3 Dec; s. Edward & Martha (Sears). Gf: William Lightfoot; gm: Mary Anne O'Grady.
1877	Wells	Hurlestone Vesey, 31 Jan 1877, bp. 5 Feb; s. George Alban & Felicity Catherine (Hardy). (In danger of death, ceremonies omitted.)
	Wells	Hardy Vesey, 31 Jan 1877, bp. 5 Feb; s. George Alban & Felicity Catherine (Hardy). (In danger of death, ceremonies omitted. condit.)
	Sills	Frederick Bernard, b. 28 July 1873, bp. 11 Feb; s. William & Elizabeth (Wildman). Gf: ? Hambling.
	Sills	Horatio *[unclear]* Francis, b. 18 Oct 1875, bp. 11 Feb; s. William & Elizabeth (Wildman). Gf: Benj. Geo. Hambling (*sic*).

Year	Surname	
	Hawkes	Albert Edward, b. 17 Jan 1877, bp. 11 Feb; s. James & Teresa (Chambers). Gf: Joseph Chambers; gm: Sarah Chambers.
	Hamilton	Catherine Sylvia Seymour, b. 30 Dec 1876, bp. 15 Feb; d. Benj. George & Sylvia (Seymour). Gf: John Fr. Bateman; gm: Anne Worsley.
	Hollins	Frederick, b. 18 (?10) Jan 1877, bp. 18 Feb; s. Thomas & Mary (Tildesley). Gf: William Tildesley; gm: Joan Brady.
	Darrington	Leonard Thomas, b. 24 Dec 1858, bp. 29 March; s. Samuel & Sarah (Frost) (condit.)
	Wildman	Henry James, bp. 30 March (condit.)
	Wildman	Henrietta, bp. 30 March (condit.)
	Wildman	Henry John James, bp. 30 March (condit.)
	Spencer	Ellen, bp. 30 March (condit.)
	Wildman	Henrietta Maria, bp. 23 April; d. Henry James & Henrietta (condit.)
	McCaffery	Hugh William, b. 4 March 1877, bp. 20 May; s. Hugh & Sarah (Jordan). Gf: James Lester; gm: Rosanna Toole. *[additional note]* married Helen Wilson in church of BVM, Clapham, 3 August 1918.
	Back	Laura Alice, b. 24 April 1877, bp. 20 May; d. Henry & Joan (Rose). Gf: Elkenah (?) Sellers; gm: Bridget Breen.
	Tildesley	John Joseph, b. 8 Mar 1876, bp. 23 May; s. John & Sarah. (ceremonies omitted in danger of death.)
	Schaedelin	Francis John, b. 16 May, bp. 25 May; s. Francis Xavier & Mary Anne (Bruxer) (condit. ceremonies omitted in danger of death; ceremonies added August.)
	Naish	Henry John, b. 8 May 1877, bp. 10 June; s. William Henry & Ellen (Flood). Gf: Joseph Tildesley; gm: Catherine O'Keefe.
	Carter	Bernard Pius, b. 3 Jan 1877, bp. 1 July; s. Joseph Fabian & Frances Alice (Conrey). Gm: Matilda Parkes. *[additional note]* He was married to Bertha Joan Bateman in the church of the Holy Annunciation *[unclear]* Peterborough, 16 Feb 1909. John Freeland.
	Hearn	Francis David, b. 16 July 1877, bp. 5 Aug; s. Daniel *[unclear]* & Catherine (Brady). Gf: Joseph Tildesley; gm: Joan Brady.
	Wildman	George Roland, bp. 18 Aug; s. Henry James & Henrietta (condit.)
	Prigmore	Elizabeth Ellen Mary, bp. 18 Aug; d. John William & Mary Anne (Wells) (condit.)
	Gnâp	Beni Joseph, b. 1 July 1877, bp. 19 Aug; s. Michael & Augusta (Harding). Gm: Alice Haynes.[3]
	Dooley	John James, b. 20 June 1877, bp. 19 Aug; s. Matthew & Henrietta (McCormic ?) (*sic*). Gf: Philip Flanagan; gm: Ellen Flanagan.
	Griggs	Edward, b. 9 Aug 1877, bp. 21 Aug; s. Thomas & Mary Anne (Blake). Ceremonies omitted in danger of death. *[additional note]* 15 Jan 1923 married Kathleen Mary Wynn here in the church of the Holy Child Jesus and St Joseph, Bedford.
	Hinson	Florence, b. 4 Sept 1877, bp. 13 Sept; d. — Hinson & Emily (Scutchins). Ceremonies omitted in danger of death.
	Russell	John, b. 27 Aug 1877, bp. 23 Sept; s. Joseph & Mary (Robinson). Gf: Francis Woods; gm: Bridget Woods.

3 The surname appears earlier ending in 'pp' – see April 1875.

Year	Surname	
	Tildesley	Mary Elizabeth, b. 28 Aug 1877, bp. 23 Sept; d. William & Elizabeth (Costloe). Gf: James Tildesley; gm: Mary Hollins.
	Sills	Margaret 'Marie' Elizabeth, b. 26 Aug 1877, bp. 27 Sept; d. William & Elizabeth (Wildman). Gm: Joan Rainbird.
	Sills	Elizabeth, bp. 27 Sept (condit.)
	Sheahan	Ellen Frances, b. 5 Sept 1877, bp. 5 Oct; d. Ellen Sheahan. Gf: Daniel Sheahan; gm: Norah Sheahan. Born outside wedlock.
	Lunnon	Sarah Mary, b. 1 Oct 1877, bp. 28 Oct; d. William John & Margaret (Fain/Tain?) (*sic*). Gf: Michael Montaggue (*sic*); gm: Florence Ketterer.
	Oakfield	Henry, b. 17 March 1876, bp. 19 Oct; s. William Moore & Charlotte (Baker/?Barker) (*sic*). Ceremonies omitted.
	Shanasey	Gertrude Mary, b. 20 Sept 1877, bp. 4 Nov; d. Michael Joseph & Anne Elizabeth (Wardill). Gf: Edmund Quillinan; gm: Catherine O'Keefe.
	Sennitt	Elizabeth Anne, bp. 12 Dec (condit.)
1878	Jackson	John William, b. 11 Dec 1877, bp. 9 March; s. William & Emma (Thoms). Gf: William Lightfoot; gm: Joan Rainbird.
	Read	George Augustine, b. 7 April 1878, bp. 31 (*sic*) April; s. James Joseph & Mary Anne (Clifford). Gf: George Read; gm: Susanna Read.
	Tracey	Gertrude Alice, b. 7 April 1878, bp. 28 April; d. John & Anne (Quin). Gf: Charles Francis Pemberton; gm: Rosanne Roole.
	Burns	Lily Magdalen Weals (?), b. 23 March 1878, bp. 6 May; d. William & Faith (Cook). Gf: James Aloysius Burns; gm: Frances Julia Burns.
	Tully	Ellen, b. 29 May 1878, bp. 9 June; d. James & Margaret (Shea). Gf: Francis Wood; gm: Bridget Woodman *[unclear]*.
	McCaffery	William Henry, b. 20 June 1878, bp. 14 July; s. Hugh & Sarah (Jordan). Gf: Jeremy Carew; gm: Frances Carew.
	Back	Henry (John), bp. 23 Aug (condit.)
	Schaedelin	Aloysius Joseph, b. 6 Aug 1878, bp. 26 Aug; s. Francis Xavier & Mary Anne (Bruxer). Gf: Emile Schaedelin; gm: Bertha Schaedelin.
	Wreford	Mary (Daisy), bp. 9 Oct (condit.)
	Sims	William Thomas, b. 8 Sept 1878, bp. 10 Nov; s. *[unclear]* & Mary Anne (Ashmole). Gf: William Sims.
	Wildman	Agnes Catherine, b. 18 Oct 1878, bp. 23 Nov; d. Henry & Henrietta (Sinfield). Gf: William Lightfoot; gm: Mary Matilda Parkes.
1879	Setchell	Benjamin James Thomas, b. 16 Jan 1879, bp. 17 Feb; s. James Thomas & Elizabeth Margaret Mary (Schaeffler). Gf: Henry Wildman; gm: Eliza Delaney.
	Carter	Winefrid Mary, b. 24 Feb 1879, bp. 23 March; d. Joseph Fabian & Frances Agnes (Conroy). Gm: Mary Matilda Parkes.
	Tildesley	Catherine Mary, b. 21 Feb 1879, bp. 27 Mar; d. Joseph & Joan (Brady). Gf: William Tildesley; gm: Mary Anne Brady.
	King	John, bp. 8 April (condit.)
	Dooley	Edward James, b. 26 Feb 1879, bp. 27 April; s. Matthew & Henrietta (McCormick?) (*sic*). Gf: James Sweeney.
	Woods	Mary Anne, b. 21 April, bp. 11 May; d. Francis & Bridget (Morissey). Gf: Thomas Heeney; gm: Teresa Brian.
	O'Brian (*sic*)	Margaret Elizabeth Beatrice Anne, b. 3 May 1879, bp. 23 May; d. John & Anne (Arthur). Gf: T —; gm: Margaret Phillips.

Year	Surname	
	Naish	Emily Helen, b. 25 April 1879, bp. 25 May; d. William Henry & Helen (Flood). Gf: Patrick Bannon; gm: Mary Bannon *['Bannon' unclear]*
	De Brenni	Frederick Ludovic, b. —, bp. 29 May; s. Charles & Emma (Crook). Gm: Joan Rainbird.
	De Brenni	Reuben Lucas, b. 8 April 1879, bp. 29 May; s. Charles & Emma (Crook). Gm: Joan Rainbird.
	Franklin	Augustus M —, bp. 6 June (condit.)
	Wells	Irene Mary Vesey, b. 22 May 1879, bp. 8 June; d. George Alban & Felicity Katherine (Hardy). Gm: Irene Hardy.
	Griggs	Henry Thomas, b. 13 June 1879, bp. 22 June; s. Thomas & Mary Anne (Blake). (Ceremonies omitted, in danger of death.)
	Shanesy	Bernard Joseph, b. 20 June 1879, bp. 27 July; s. Michael Joseph & Anne Elizabeth (Wardill). Gf: Edward De Vere Corcoran; gm: Florence Ketterer.
	Okefield	Florence, b. 11 Aug 1879, bp. 25 Aug; d. William Moore & Florence (Baker). Ceremonies omitted in danger of death.
	O'Grady	Sarah Helen, b. 15 June 1879, bp. 31 Aug; d. Edward & Martha (Sears). Gf: William Lightfoot; gm: Mary Anne O'Grady.
	Harris	Mary Anne, b. 17 June 1878, bp. 3 Sept; d. William & Mary (Miller). Vagrant. Ceremonies omitted in danger of death.
	Bryant	Frederick, 26 Sept (condit.) Morgan Albert, b. 6 Sept 1879, bp. 19 Oct; s. Albert & Margaret (Foley). Gm: Elizabeth Setchell.
	Tracey	John Edward, b. 2 Oct 1879, bp. 20 Oct; s. John & Anne (Quinn). Gf: Richard Quinn; gm: Mary Anne Toole. Ceremonies omitted; supplied 17 Feb 1881.
1880	Fynn	Margaret Catherine, 8 Jan 1880, bp. 17 March; d. John & Ellen (Carter). Gf: Edward Wilfrid Fynn; gm: Mary Catherine Fynn.
	King	Mary King, bp. 26 March (Maiden name Griffiths) (condit.)
	King	Gertrude, bp. 27 March; d. John & Mary (Griffiths) (condit.)
	King	Charles John, bp. 27 March; s. John & Mary (Griffiths) (condit.)
	King	Mary Ives, bp. 27 March; d. John & Mary (Griffiths). Gm: Matilda Parkes.
	Scutchings	Esther Matilda, b. 14 April 1868, bp. 27 March (condit.)
	Smith	Rose Laura, b. 5 April 1868, bp. 27 March; d. Thomas —; Gm: Matilda Parkes (condit.)
	Smith	Ada Mary, b. 15 April 1869, bp. 27 March; d. Thomas —; Gm: Matilda Parkes (condit.)
	Bannister	William Henry, bp. 28 March (condit.)
	Setchell	George Louis, b. 4 April 1880, b. 9 May; s. James Thomas & Elizabeth Margaret Mary (Schoeppler). Gm: Matilda Parkes.
	Cole	Elizabeth, bp. 22 May (condit.)
	Bricknen	Catherine, b. 6 April 1880, bp. 13 June; d. John & Anne (Simpson). Gf: John Brahany; gm: Joan Rainbird.
	Suter	Otto Xavier, b. 11 June 1880, bp. 16 June; s. Otto & Julia (Hagenbach). Gf: Xavier Suter; gm: Teresa Hagenbach.
	Bannister	Frederick Peter, bp. 3 Aug; s. William Henry (condit.)

Year	Surname	
	Griggs	Florence Emily, b. 5 Aug 1880, bp. 20 August; d. Thomas & Mary Anne (Blake) (no ceremonies, danger of death)
	Brahany	Francis Joseph, b. 12 Aug 1880, bp. 5 Sept; s. James & Sarah Jane (Lowe). Gf: John Ward; gm: Ellen Brahany.
	Carter	Raymund Philip, b. 21 Sept 1880, bp. 16 Oct; s. Joseph Fabian & Frances Agnes (Conroy). Gm: Matilda Parkes.
	Dillon	Daniel, bp. 23 Dec (condit.)
	Bannister	William Frederick, bp. 25 Dec; s. John & Amelia Anne (urgent danger of death)
	O'Brien	John, b. 28 Dec 1880, bp. 28 Dec; s. John & Anne (Arthur). Gf: William O'Brien; gm: Mary Anne Toole. (urgent danger of death; ceremonies supplied 6 Feb 1881)
1881	Tildesley	Florence Agnes, b. 10 Jan 1881, bp. 13 Feb; d. Joseph & Joan (Brady). Gf: John Henry Wootton; gm: Elizabeth Tildesley.
	Wells	Denis George Vesey, b. 21 Jan 1881, bp. 3 March; s. George & Felicity Katherine (Hardy). Gf: Henry Hardy.
	Fletcher	Suzanna (Suzie) Mary Teresa, bp. 7 March (condit.)
	Donaghmore	John, b. 29 Jan 1881, bp. 12 March; s. James & Anne (Bolton). Gm: Matilda Parkes. Bapt. by William Blackman.
	Sims	Hannah Mary, bp. 27 April; d. Samuel & Mary Anne (condit.)
	Prigmore	Catherine Mary, bp. 28 April; d. John William & Mary Anne (Wells) (condit.)
	Whittle	William, bp. 30 April; s. William John (condit.)
	King	Florence, b. 28 April 1878, bp. 7 June; d. John & Mary (Griffiths). Gm: Mary Anne Read.
	Smith	Thomas Crosby, bp. 15 June (condit.)
	Cole	William Henry, b. 29 July 1881, bp. 21 Aug; s. Mary Elizabeth Cole, unmarried. Gf: Francis Ryan; gm: Elizabeth Lightfoot.
	Clarke	Mary Joan, bp. 2 Sept; d. Thomas Robert & Mary Anne (condit.)
	Naish	Francis Ford, b. 15 March 1881, bp. 3 Sept; s. William Henry & Ellen (Flood). Gm: Matilda Parkes.
1882	Childs	Mary Anne, b. 15 Dec 1881, bp. 15 Jan; d. William & Clare Elizabeth (Marsh). Gf: Thomas Rose; gm: Mary Anne Rose.
	Short	Etheldred Mary (Ethel May), b. 1 Jan 1882, bp. 22 Jan; d. Charles Alfred & Agnes Anne (Kilger). Gf: James Toole; gm: Mary Lemon.
	Blake	Florence, b. 1 Feb 1881, bp. 8 Feb; d. Sarah Blake (outside wedlock). Gm: Mary Anne Griggs (condit.) *[there is an illegible note in the margin]*
	Simms	Henrietta Mechtilde *[Maud/Matilda]* Maryann, b. 28 Sept 1880, bp. 22 Feb; d. Samuel & Mary Anne (Ashwell). Gm: Anne Huckle.
	Berrington	Mary Anne, b. 12 Nov 1860, bp. 24 March (condit.)

[The next five entries are misplaced in the register; the order given here is correct according to the dates of the baptisms.]

Year	Surname	
	Hyde	Elisabeth Mary, bp. 3 June (condit.)
	Street	Edward James Francis, b. 20 May 1882, bp. 18 June; s. Charles & Rosanne (Kilger). Gf: James Pemberton; gm: Rose Toole.
	Sinfield	Edward George, b. 8 June 1864, bp. 7 July (Of Haynes; condit.)

Year	Surname	
	Lightfoot	Sarah Catherine, b. 7 Sept 1882, bp. 22 Oct; d. William & Mary Elisabeth (Cole). Gf: Henry Sykes; gm: Lucy Anne Sykes.
	Hayward	Laura, bp. 27 Oct (condit.)
	O'Brian (*sic*)	Francis Percy, b. 20 Oct 1882, bp. 19 Nov; s. John & Anne (Arthur). Gf: Richard Young; gm: Joan Young. *[added note]* he married Martha Mary Rowley, 21 Sept 1946, Holy Cross Church, Watford.
	Howe	Julia (Mary), bp. 22 Dec (condit.)
	Smith	Wilhelmina Mary, b. 12 Feb 1876, bp. 24 Dec; d. Thomas Crosby & Elizabeth (King). Gm: Matilda Parkes.
1883	Hunt	Mary Anne, b. 18 March 1879, bp. 26 March 1883; d. Alured & Frances (Daniels). Gf: Thomas Hunt; gm: Mary Anne Hunt.
	Hunt	John, b. 30 Jan 1881, bp. 26 March; s. Alured & Frances (Daniels). Gf: Thomas Hunt; gm: Mary Anne Hunt.
	Dillon	Thomas Francis, b. 2 March 1883, bp. 1 April; s. Edward & Bridget Teresa (Regan). Gf: Thomas Wallace; gm: Mary Wallace.
	Tanner	Emma Gertrude Mary, bp. 18 April (condit.)
	King	Hilda Ursula, b. 13 March 1883, bp. 22 April; d. Joan & Mary (Griffiths). Gm: Joan Rainbird.
	Emery	Sarah Charlotte, b. 1 April 1883, bp. 13 May; d. Francis & Elizabeth (White). Gm: Julia White.
	Brady	Catherine Elizabeth, b. 17 July 1880, bp. 22 May; d. James & Mary (Boothey). Gf: Joseph Tildesley; gm: Catherine Tildesley (condit.)
	O'Neill	John Eustace, b. 8 July 1883, bp. 30 July; s. John & Ada Frances (Baker). Gm: Felicity Wells. *[added note]* Sept 1914 married in Sacred Heart Church, Hampton Wick, Dorothy Irene Southgate. By J. Freeland.
	Short	Percy James, b. 21 July 1883, bp. 5 Aug; s. Charles Alfred & Mary Anne (Kilger). Gf: James Toole; gm: Rosanne Street.
	Stratton	Lilian Mabel Anne, b. 6 Oct 1882, bp. 20 Aug; d. Emily Stratton (out of wedlock). Gm: Sarah Parrott.
	Shearcroft	Mary Emily, b. 4 Aug 1883, bp. 26 Aug; d. Leonard & Lucy (Barnaby). Gf: James Henry Waldron; gm: Miriam Sargent.
	Tildesley	Alice Mechtild *[Maud]*, b. 10 Aug 1883, bp. 26 Aug; d. Joseph & Joan (Brady). Gf: David Hearn; gm: Catherine Hearn. *[added note]* 19 Sept 1918 in Holy Child and St Joseph's, Bedford, married Percy Duke Dyke.
	Brahany	Ellen Mary, b. 21 Aug 1883, bp. 16 Sept; d. James & Sarah Joan (Lowe). Gf: James Read; gm: Mary Anne Read.
	Ryan	Lawrence, b. 7 Aug 1883, bp. 7 Sept; s. Lawrence & Laura (Haywood). Gm: Joan Rainbird.
	Lehmann	Oswald Joseph, b. 18 Sept 1883, bp. 28 Oct; s. Joseph & Augusta Teresa (Isele). Gf: Joseph Tildesley; gm: Cecily Isele.
	Phinn	Augusta Gertrude, b. 11 Sept 1883, bp. 28 Oct; d. John & Elaine (Carter). Gf: James Blanchford; gm: Mary Anne Dillon.
	Stratton	Emily Elizabeth, bp. 17 Nov; d. Samuel & Anne (condit.)
	Ahearn	Mary Ellen, b. 9 Nov 1883, bp. 9 Dec; d. James Joseph & Emma (Bishopp). Gf: Michael Murphy; gm: Mary Eliza Lightfoot.
1884	Blades	Sophie Maria (widow), bp. 9 Feb; d. Joseph Foster (condit.)
	Burbridge	Frances Mary, b. 22 Jan 1869, bp. 15 Feb; d. William & Elizabeth Wheatley (Bloodworth). Gm: Joan Rainbird.

Year	Surname	
	Longland	Elizabeth Mary, bp. 25 March (condit.)
	Lightfoot	Alfred Ernest, b. 2 March 1884, bp. 13 April; s. William & Mary Elizabeth (Cole). Gf: Henry Sykes; gm: Anne Sykes.
	Read	Joseph Gabriel Dominic, b. 19 March 1884, bp. 13 April; s. James & Mary Anne (Clifford). Gf: James Brabury; gm: Anne Berrington.
	Carter	William Bede, b. 14 May 1884, bp. 7 June; s. Joseph Fabian & Frances Agnes (Conroy) *[no godparents are named]* *[added note]* married 24 May 1923 Anne (Nancy) Frances Freeman, in church of St Joseph & the English Martyrs, Bishop Stortford (Herts). G. Wainright.[4]
	Wright	Elizabeth, b. 6 April 1884, bp. 8 June; d. William & Catherine (Ahearne) *[no godparents named]*
	Huckle	George, b. 30 May 1884, bp. 27 June; s. William & Sarah Anne (Billson). Gm: Joan Rainbird.
	Street	Lydia, b. 29 July 1884, bp. 24 Aug; d. Charles & Rose Anne (Kilger). Gf: James Toole; gm: Lydia Frances Street. *[added note]* married Albert Victor Basson, in Sacred Heart Church, Kilburn, London, 3 Jan 1915. J. Freeland.
	Cross	Carlton Leopold George, b. 14 Aug 1884, bp. 27 Aug; s. Alfred & Anne (Crawley). Gf: Charles Edmund Cross; gm: Gertrude Cross.
	Short	Charles Reginald, b. 26 Oct 1884, bp. 10 Nov; s. Charles & Mary Anne (Kilger); Gf: Charles Francis Pemberton; gm: Teresa Toole.
	Greham (*sic*)	Daniel, b. 15 Oct 1884, bp. 14 Dec; s. Joseph & Amelia (Stratton). Gf: Daniel Greham; gm: Margaret Anne Greham.
1885	Daniels	Thomas Ebenezer, bp. 13 Feb 1885 (condit.)
[Death of Rev. J. P. Warmoll in February 1885]		
	Parrott	Olivia Agnes Durn, b. 1 Nov 1884, bp. 23 Feb; d. John Gamby & Jane Elizabeth (Trueman – *sic*). Gm: Mary Elizabeth Longland Bedford (*sic*) by me, John William McShane.[5] *[illegible note in margin]*
	Wells	Eric Francis Veysey, b. 5 Feb 1885, bp. 1 March; s. George & Alice Catherine (Hardy). Gf: Francis Xavier Schaedelin. Bedford by me, John William McShane *[illegible note in margin]*
	Wells	Alice Catherine Veysey, b. 5 Feb 1885, bp. 1 March; s. George & Alice Elizabeth (Hardy). Gf: Francis Xavier Schaedelin. Bedford. by me, John William McShane.
[The Rev. George Wrigglesworth in charge now until 1887. He tends to add an address to each entry, usually in the margin.]		
	Maxwell-Heron	Charlotte Margaret, b. 17 Jan 1885, bp. 28 March; d. Frederick William & Anne (Harrison). Gf: Montague Lamb; gm: Hannah Simpson. by me, George Wrigglesworth, Miss. Ap. *[note partially illegible]* She married Charles Albert Carey in St Edmund's … 25 January 1911 … Albany St, Bedford.
	Bannister	Mary, b. 20 Jan 1858, bp. 29 June; d. William Henry & Sarah (Hywell?) (*sic*) Commercial Rd.

4 Presumably the priest listed as William Wainwright (1886–1983, ord. 1913).

5 John William McShane (b. in Antrim 1849, ord. 1878) had a chequered career, serving in Westminster, Northampton 1879–85, Salford and Nottingham dioceses; no date of death is given.

Year	Surname	
	Bannister	Frances, b. 19 Jan 1860, bp. 29 June; d. William Henry & Sarah (Hywell?) (*sic*) Commercial Rd.
1886	Brown	Isabelle Edith Guise, b. 11 June 1886, bp. 5 July; d. John Francis & Pauline Caroline (Cooke). Gf: William Brown; gm: Isabelle Nicholls. *[later note]* Married in Johannesburg to Jordan Grant, 25 May 1911.
	Huckle	Florence Anne Huckle, b. 16 June 1886, bp. 11 July; d. William & Sarah Anne (Billson). Gm: Mary Anne Richardson. 15 Cavendish St.
	Wootton	Thomas Spicer, b. 16 July 1886, bp. 22 Aug; s. John Henry & Mary Anne (Hunt). Gm: Joan Margaret Clifton. 27 Goldington Rd.
	Short	Frederic Gordon, b. 2 Aug 1886, bp. 22 Aug; s. Charles Alfred & Mary Anne (Kilgar). Gf: James Toole; gm: Mary Toole. Barracks.
	Shearcroft	Elliott John George, b. 28 July 1886, 22 Aug; s. Leonard & Lucy (Barnaby). Gf: James Elliott; gm: Anne Forsythe. *[address unclear]*
	Chater	Mary Sophie Paula, b. 8 May 1848, bp. 15 Sept; d. Thomas & Martha (Wilson) (condit.) By me: Christopher Scott, Vic. Gen.[6] *[address unclear]*
	Lightfoot	Beatrice Ellen, b. 28 Aug 1886, bp. 26 Sept; d. William & Mary Elizabeth (Cole). Gf: Francis Spencer; gm: Ellen Spencer. Pattishall St (?)
1887	Lightfoot	William, b. 1818, bp. 28 Jan 1887 (condit.)
	Magrino	Angelo, b. 30 Jan 1887, bp. 6 Feb; s. Raymond & Caroline (Tremarca) Gm: Maryanne Maher. *[in margin]* La Senerchia in Italy.[7]
	Ardin	Gertrude Mary, b. 24 June 1867, bp. 27 Feb 1887; d. William James & Mary Agnes (Troy). Gm: Maryanne Maher. *[in margin]* St. John's St.
	Barnes	Albert James, 20 Jan 1887, bp. 14 April; s. James & Martha. Gm: Eliza Higgins (condit. already baptised by non-Catholic). Barracks.
	Lehmann	Frederick Rudolph, b. 7 May 1887, bp. 5 June; s. Joseph & Agnes Teresa. Gf: Joseph Tildesley; gm: Joan Rose Tildesley.
[The next three entries are described as 'vaga'; this has been taken as 'vagrant']		
	Healey	David Patrick, b. 19 May 1887, bp. 13 June; s. James & Elizabeth (? Minnis) (*sic*). Gm: Catherine Healey. vagrant.
	Healey	Catherine, b. 8 April 1873, bp. 13 June; d. Thomas & Esther (Horton). vagrant.
	Baker	Louisa, bp. 16 Aug; d. John & Anne (Daly). Gm: Catherine Reed. vagrant.
	Hayes	Alfred Adolphus Aloysius, b. 11 Sept 1860, bp. 19 Nov; s. the Honourable Edmund Bradshaw Hayes & Mary (Banchell?) (*sic*) (condit.)
[From December 1887, the priest in charge was Canon Osman]		
	Fennell	Henry, b. 1 Nov 1887, bp. 27 Dec (*sic*); s. James & Frances (Coleman). Gf: Edward Lawlor.
	George	Mary Blanch, b. 7 Oct 1887, bp. 11 Dec; d. Joseph & Lavinia (Harman).

6 Rev. C. Scott (1838–1922, ord. 1862) Northampton diocese.

7 Senerchia is a small village in Campania, southern Italy. Was this one of the earliest Italian immigrants in Bedford? No home address is given.

Year	Surname	
	Tildesley	Frederick Joseph, b. 11 Nov 1887, bp. 11 Dec; s. Joseph & Joan (?) (Brady). Gf: John Brady; gm: Mary Hollins. *[added note]* married with dispensation 7 Oct 1920, to Annabel Florence Thompson in this church. Canon Freeland.
	Carter	Thomas Moore, b. 10 May 1824, bp. 18 Dec; s. Thomas and Sarah (Pick) (condit.)
1888	Shearcroft	Lucy Agnes, b. 11 Dec 1887, bp. 7 Jan; d. Leonard and Lucy (Barnaby). Gf: James Elliott; gm: Mary Anne Elliott.
	Dillon	Henry Herbert, b. 13 Dec 1887, bp. 29 Jan; s. Richard and Joan (Hunt). Gf: Edward Lawlor; gm: Elizabeth Morgan.
	Lightfoot	Alfred Ernest, b. 20 Feb 1888, bp. 25 March; s. William and Mary Elizabeth (Cole). Gf: Daniel O'Mahoney; gm: Anne Berrington. Baptised by Joseph Postley, OSB.
	Brown	Ethel Adeline, b. 14 Feb 1888, bp. 1 April; d. John Francis & Pauline Caroline (Cooke). Gf: William Brown; gm: Isabella Barrett. Minister: Rev. Bertrand Wilberforce O.P.[8] *[faint note]* See entry on next page – baptism 28 July 1889. Kathleen says marriage entry is for her sister.
	Holden	Patrick James, b. 9 April 1888, bp. 7 May; s. James & Eliza (Cleary). Gf: David Joseph Breen; gm: Annie Berrington.
	Wall	Mary Elizabeth Igtler (?), b. 26 Sept 1842, bp. 11 May; d. Joseph & Mary Anne (Craig) (condit.)
	Demery	Louis Felix, b. 13 April 1888, bp. 14 May; s. William & Mary Matilda (Parkes). Gf: Felix Parkes; gm: Rebecca Mary Wittrick.
	Gray	Ethel Bertha, b. 1 May 1888, bp. 30 May; d. Charles & Helen (McGrath). Gm: Catherine McGrath.
	Higgins	Anne Mary, b. 1 Aug 1888, bp. 15 Aug; d. Francis & Mary (Fitzgerald). Gm: Mary Anne Faulkner.
	Magrino	Angelo, b. 28 Aug 1888, bp. 29 Aug; s. Raymund & Caroline (Trimarco). Gf: Edward Lawlor.
	Bryant	Marion Frances Anne, b. 2 Oct 1888, bp. 14 Oct; d. Frederick & Eliza (Wittrick). Gm: Rebecca Wittrick *[added note]* married John Mulroy, in Holy Cross church, St Helens, 25 (?23) Sept 1916.
	Lehmann	Leonard, b. 5 Nov 1888, bp. 30 Nov; s. Joseph & Cecilia (Isele). Gf: Frederick Leopold Lehmann.
1889	Kennedy	Agnes Mary, b. 10 Feb 1889, bp. 24 Feb; d. Michael & Joan (Bromley). Gf: John Bromley; gm: Mary Kennedy.
	Short	Florence, b. 3 Feb 1889, bp. 1 March; d. Charles Edward & Mary (Kilger). Gm: Cecily Toole.
	Burr	Elizabeth, b. 1 Jan 1870, bp. 1 March; d. John & Hester (Smith) (condit.) *[repeat entry below]*
	Brown	Mary Kathleen Guise, b. 9 June 1889, bp. 28 July; d. John Henry & Pauline Caroline (Cooke). Gf: Peter Sabela; gm: Irene Sabela. Married Laurence Gilbert Roy in church of the Immac. Conception, Jo'burg, South Africa, 1 Feb 1918. J. Freeland. *[faint note across top of entry]* her sister's husband, see baptismal register 1886
	Burr	Elizabeth, b. 1 Jan 1870, bp. 1 March 1889 (*sic*); d. John & Hester (Smith) *[repeat of entry above, though without the conditional note]*

8 A. B. Wilberforce (1839–1904) grandson of William Wilberforce; related to Cardinal Manning.

Year	Surname	
	Reilly	Patrick, b. 10 Sept 1889, bp. 18 Sept; s. Charles & Bridget (Costelloe). Gf: Edward Lawlor.
	Berrington	Teresa Winefride, b. 18 Nov 1869, bp. 31 Nov; d. Thomas & Sophie (Simms) (condit.)
	Dillon	Henrietta Joan, b. 21 Sept 1889, bp. 18 Nov; d. Richard & Helen (Hunt). Gf: Denmark (*sic*) Dillon; gm: Teresa Bryan.
1890	Pillow	Constance Mary, b. 2 Jan 1890, bp. 2 Feb; d. Frederick & Alice (Costello). Gm: Alice Partridge.
	Bonugli	*[partial entry here at the end of the page]* Helen Bonugli, b. 31 Dec 1885, bp. 1 Jan 1896 (condit.) *[unsigned and lightly crossed through]*
	Ryan	Kathleen Margaret Helen, b. 9 Nov 1889, bp. 3 April; d. Lawrence Joseph & Teresa (Heyward). Gm: Helen Masterman.
	Lehmann	Rosina Agnes, b. 20 Feb 1890, bp. 11 April; d. Joseph & Agnes (?). Gm: Ada Marianne Smith.
	Hewett	Teresa May, 22 Feb 1890, bp. 22 Feb; d. ? & Teresa (Toole). Gf: James Toole; gm: Rose Toole.
	Lightfoot	John Francis, b. 29 April 1890, bp. 29 June; s. William & Mary (Cole). Gf: John Mower; gm: Nora Mower.
	Maybury	Michael Albert, b. 1 June 1890, bp. 13 July; s. Michael & Elizabeth (Longland). Gf: William Lightfoot; gm: Mary Lightfoot.
	Craigen	Maude Belle, b. 1 July 1890, bp. 9 Aug; d. James & Mary Anne (Murch). Gf: George F. Evans; gm: Ellen Evans.
	Brown	Philip Harold Guise, b. 3 Aug 1890, bp. 24 Aug; s. John Francis & Pauline Caroline (Cooke). Gf: William Brown; gm: Mary Fuller.
	Tildesley	Francis James, b. 3 Sept 1890, bp. 28 Sept; s. Joseph & Joan Rose (Brady). Gf: William J. Tildesley; gm: Helen B. Tildesley. *[added note]* he married 15 Aug 1959 Eliza M. Tindal (a widow, nee Dickens) in Bedford.
1891	Peacock	Catherine Mary, b. 12 April 1891, bp. 20 April; d. Julian Edward Oliver Woodfuffe & Sarah Catherine (Kirby). Gm: Mary Fraser. *[added note]* Westminster. British Colombia.
	Bonugli	Francis Xavier, b. 9 Dec 1890, bp. 6 July; s. John & Emma (Corrington). Gf: Nicholas Bonugli.
	Develin	Edgar Alfred, b. 3 June 1891, bp. 19 July; s. James & Clare (Reed). Gf: Edgar Develin.
	Riley	Frances Hillyer, b. 27 July 1891, bp. 28 Aug; d. Charles & Bridget (Costello). Gf: William Costello.
	Bryant	Aidan George Swinburne, b. 21 Aug 1891, bp. 30 Aug; s. Frederick George & Eliza Mary (Whittrick). Gf: James Joseph Read; gm: Mary Anne Read.
	Smith	Sarah Elizabeth, b. 3 July 1891, bp. 16 Sept; d. Thomas & Minnie (Fox). *[added note]* at home in danger of death.
	Ryan	Beatrice Mabel, b. 25 Aug 1891, bp. 17 Sept; d. Lawrence J. & Laura (Hayward). Gf: William Connolly.
1892	Berrington	Winefrid Frances, b. 20 Nov 1891, bp. 2 Jan 1892; d. Thomas William & Frances (Wills). Gm: Mary Berrington.
	Dillon	Joseph Denmark, b. 14 Dec 1891, bp. 14 Feb; s. Richard & Jane (Hunt). Gf: Daniel Dillon; gm: Winefrid Dillon.

Year	Surname	
	Greham (*sic*)	Agnes Josephine, b. 29 April 1892, bp. 12 June; d. Joseph & Emily (Stratton). Gf: Frederick Bryant; gm: Amelia Mower.
	Brown	Pauline Monica Guise, b. 16 May 1892, bp. 12 June; d. John Francis & Pauline Caroline (Cooke). Gf: Arthur B. Cooke; gm: Emma Strickland. *[additional note]* Married in Johannesburg, S. Africa, 15 June 1918, to Oxhome Richard Jeppe (?). J. Freeland.
	Lennon	Margaret, b. 27 May 1892, bp. 15 June; d. Edward & Louisa (McGrath). Gf: Matthew Lynce (*sic*); gm: Ellen Gray.
	Gray	Edith Mabel, b. 5 April 1891, bp. 15 June; d. Charles & Ellen (McGrath). Gf: Edward Lennon; gm: Louisa Lennon.
	Gadd	Frances Eliza, b. 16 Sept 1876, bp. 30 April (condit.) *[in margin]* Contessa.
	Magrino	Adam Raymund, b. 14 Oct 1892, bp. 23 Oct; s. Raymund & Caroline (Trimarco). Gf: John Bonugli.
	Green C	Amelia Mary, bp. 19 Nov (condit.)
	Ryan	Francis Patrick, b. 28 Oct 1892, bp. 26 Nov; s. Laurence J. & Laura (Haywood). Gf: Edward Griggs; gm: Ada M. Page.

[There are no entries for either 1891 or 1892. Numbers in the following years show a marked increase. The priest in charge is now Rev. Robert C. Middleton, until after 1900.]

1893

[Christian names frequently in English]

Year	Surname	
	Short	Alice Rose, b. 11 Dec 1892, bp. 9 March; d. Charles Alfred & Mary Anne (Toole). Gf: James Toole; gm: Rose Toole.
	Coughlan	Lilian Mary Etheldreda, b. 9 Feb 1893, bp. 15 March; d. Denis & Lavinia Mary (Ebbs). Gf: Frederick West; gm: Florence Inskip. Priest: J. H. Ashmole.[9]
	Holden	Daisy Elizabeth, b. 1 Feb 1893, bp. 16 March; d. James & Elizabeth (Cleary). Gm: Emma M. de la Morronnais.
	Youngs	Winefrid Anne, b. 14 Dec 1892, bp. 20 March; d. Herbert J. & Elizabeth (Berrington). Gm: Anne Berrington.
	Grey	George Evelyn, b. 23 March 1893, bp. 24 April; s. Charles & Ellen (McGrath). Gf: Thomas McGrath; gm: Mary Harrington.
	Baldwin	Albert John, b. 23 April 1893, bp. 10 May; s. William James & Margaret (Donnelly). Gf: James Charleton; gm: Alice Charleton.
	Munt	Cecily Elizabeth, b. 16 April 1893, bp. 10 May; d. Frederick & Cecily May (Toole). Gm: Eliza Crichley.
	Wakenell	Agnes Mary, b. 28 July 1870, bp. 27 May (condit.)
	Wright	Margaret, b. 4 Feb 1892, bp. 14 June; d. George & Catherine (Power). Gf: John Power; gm: Margaret Power p.p.
	Wright	Agnes, 16 April 1893, bp. 14 June; d. George & Catherine (Power). Gf: George Power; gm: Agnes Power p.p.
	Watkinson	Mabel Emma, b. 27 Feb 1893, bp. 16 July; d. Charles Joseph & Ernestine (Sage). *[in margin]* In danger of death. *[later]* Died.
	Hammond Hewett	Kathleen Minnie Mary, b. 19 May 1893, bp. 28 July; d. John & Teresa (Toole). Gm: Minnie Hewett.

9 Rev. John Henry Ashmole (1853–1938, ord. 1885); see p. 119.

Year	Surname	
	Curtis	James Walter, b. 29 June 1893, bp. 30 July; s. Henry & Frances (Sabatino). Gm: Anne Sabatino.
	Lightfoot	Ludovic (Louis) (*sic*) Gilbert, b. 25 Aug 1893, bp. 3 Sept; s. William & Elizabeth (Cole). Gf: Michael D. Dillon; gm: Mary Anne Read.
	Course	Joseph William, b. 15 Aug 1893, bp. 9 Sept; s. Joseph & Mary (Barry). Gm: Ellen Kearns (?)
	Fraser	Catherine Elizabeth, b. 16 April 1893, bp. 10 Sept; d. Loudown (?) & Catherine (Dillon). Gf: Michael D. Dillon; gm: Elizabeth M. Dillon (condit.)
	Stratton	Arthur Edward, b. 31 March 1893, bp. 10 Sept; s. William & Rose (Kelly). Gf: William Lightfoot.
	Lennon	Arthur Victor, b. 21 Oct 1893, bp. 11 Nov; s. Edward & Louise (McGrath). Gf: John Maddon; gm: Margaret Lynch.
	Cummins	Philip James, b. 27 Dec 1892, bp. 15 Nov; s. Patrick & Sarah (Whelan). Gm: Elizabeth Lane *[Lake?]*
	Ryan	Agnes Cecily, b. 5 Nov 1893, bp. 16 Nov; d. Laurence J. & Laura (Hayward). *[in margin]* At home 'in extremis'.
	Freer	Mary (May Minnie) (*sic*), b. 8 Dec 1893, bp. 23 Dec; d. Robert & Mary (Kent). Gf: Robert Kent; gm: Jane Kent.
	Ibbett	Clare Nora Mary, b. 16 Dec 1893, bp. 24 Dec; d. George & Bridget (O'Malley). Gm: Ada M. Page.
1894	Tildesley	William Thomas, b. 30 Dec 1893, bp. 21 Jan; s. Joseph & Jane Rose (Brady). Gf: Wilfred J. Hearn; gm: Elizabeth Huckle. *[in margin]* married Pauline Shaver at St Joseph's, Bedford, 23 May 1919.
	Friar	Frederick Henry, b. 22 Jan 1894, bp. 11 Feb; s. John & Phoebe (Nesman?) (*sic*). Gm: Ernest Parrott. *[in margin]* Tramp.
	Matthews	Michael Richard, b. 15 Feb 1894, bp. 23 Feb; s. James & Mary Agnes (Smith). Gf: Frederick G. Bryant; gm: Elizabeth Bryant.
	Ibett	Gertrude Stella, b. 2 Jan 1894, bp. 25 Feb; d. Thomas & Anne (McCardle). Gf: Francis Ibett (?); gm: Elizabeth McCardle.
	Hibbett C	Emily Aloysia (*sic*), b. 21 Dec 1877, bp. 15 March; d. George & Mercy (Wilmer?) (*sic*). Gm: Sophie Wording. *[added note]* name was Ibbett.
	Randall	Ada Mary, b. 1 April 1894, bp. 5 May; d. illegitimate, of Rose Florence Randall. Gm: Ellen Kerns. Potton.
	Dawson C	Benjamin, b. 9 Jan 1867, bp. 9 May; s. Daniel *[rest is blank]* (condit.)
	Marchant	Sydney Ernest, b. 8 May 1894, bp. 27 May; s. George & Elizabeth (Jackson). Gf: T. Francis Parrott.
	O'Brien	? Kathleen Emma, b. 6 May 1894, bp. 30 June; d. William Charles & Mary Elizabeth (White). Gm: Ellen Kerns.
	Dillon	Florence May, b. 27 May 1894, bp. 2 July; d. Richard & Jane (Hunt). Gm: Mary Maher.
	Bowen	Denmark James, b. 8 May 1894, bp. 22 July; s. Edwin & Winifred (Dillon). Gf: Michael D. Dillon; gm: Elizabeth Dillon.
	Brown	Frances Veronica Guise, b. 21 Aug 1894, bp. 9 Sept; d. John Francis & Pauline Caroline (Cooke). Gm: Isabel Brown.
	Wright	George William, b. 20 Aug 1894, bp. 16 Oct; s. George & Catherine (Power). Gf: Patrick Crowley; gm: Ellen Power *[both godparents are marked 'p.p.' – presumably by proxy]*

Year	Surname	
	Hewett Hammond/ Hammond Hewett[10]	Eillene (*sic*) Rose, b. 1 Oct 1894, bp. 28 Oct; d. John & Theresa (Toole). Gm: Rose Toole. *[added note]* Married David Mclaren (?) in Sacred Heart Church, Kilburn, 29 Oct 1913.
	McDermott	Ada Dorothy Alice Fuller, b. 6 Dec 1894, bp. 25 Dec; illegitimate d. of Margaret Hastings McDermott. Gm: Alice McDermott.
1895	Wringe	Lucy, b. 11 Jan 1895, bp. 6 Feb; d. Richard & Jane (Mead). Gf: Richard Wringe; gm: Sarah Wringe.
	Witherow	Catherine Elizabeth, b. 14 Dec 1894, bp. 14 Feb; d. Stephen & Kate (Young). Gf: Edward Lennon; gm: Louisa Lennon.
	Bryant	Frederick Joseph, b. 6 Feb 1895, bp. 10 March; s. Fredk. (*sic*) & Eliza (Wittrick). Gf: George Read; gm: Rebecca Wittrick.
	Moloney	Joan, b. 7 March 1895, bp. 25 March; d. illegitimate of Margaret, vagrant. Gf: Truman Francis Parrott. *[note: 'Patrick' was initially entered as the father, but crossed out and replaced by 'illegitima'; 'vaga' is entered for mother's maiden name]*
	Wilcox	Philip Augustine, b. 19 May 1895, bp. 9 June; s. Augustine & Agnes (Wilcox (*sic*)). Gf: Edward J. Wilcox; gm: Winefride Wilcox. Woburn.
	Bell C	Mary, bp. 27 July (condit.)
	Kenealy	Nora Blanche, b. 28 Feb 1891, bp. 7 Sept; d. Edward Michael & Harriet (Dennis). Gm: Ellen Kerns. Pertenhall.
	Fitzgerald	Agnes, b. 5 Feb 1860, bp. 7 Sept (condit.)
	Short	Margaret Muriel, b. 6 Aug 1895, bp. 3 Oct; d. Charles Alfred & Mary (Kilger). Gm: Rose Street.
	Blaydes	Frederick Charles, b. 10 Feb 1895, bp. 3 Oct; d.(*sic*) Amelia Blaydes. Gm: Sophie Allen *[an odd entry: given as 'd', with no father named; presumably illegitimate, though this usually mentioned]*
	Lennon	Kathleen Elizabeth, b. 12 Sept 1895, bp. 10 Oct; d. Edward & Louise (McGrath). Gf: Richard Grady; gm: Elizabeth Hammett.
	Kenealy	Margery Vivian, b. 24 April 1893, bp. 12 Oct; d. Edward Michael & Harriet (Dennis). Gm: Ellen Kerns. Pertenhall.
	Clifford	William Thomas, b. 11 Oct 1895, bp. 20 Oct; s. William Henry & Lucy Anne (Daniel). Gf: John Hearne; gm: Ellen Tildesley.
	Cummins	Alfred George, b. 21 Jan 1895, bp. 9 Nov; s. Patrick & Sarah (Whelan). Gf: Patrick Cummins; gm: Elizabeth Baines. Renhold.
	Munt	Florence May, b. 4 Nov 1895, bp. 2 Dec; d. Frederick & May (Toole). Gm: Rose Toole.
	Bell C	Esther Frances (Mary), b. 15 March 1841, bp. 21 Dec (condit.)
1896	Bonugli	Helen, b. 31 Dec 1895, bp. 1 Jan (condit.) *[added note]* Married Thomas Ernest Franke, 21 Aug 1913, in Holy Child & St Joseph's, Bedford, by John Freeland.
	Billson	Edward Gordon Penryn, b. 20 Aug 1895, bp. 4 Jan; s. Anstruther Harte Penryn & Emily Booker (Parker). *[no godparents named. Latin note in margin:]* 'Privately out of necessity'.

10 The name appears in both forms in the same entry. See entry below for 10 May 1896.

Year	Surname	
	Goffer	Olive Lucy, b. 23 Nov 1895, bp. 16 Feb; d. Frederick & Alice (Ganner). Gm: Catherine M. Tildesley.
	McDonald	Francis Bernard, b. 27 March 1896, bp. 26 April; s. George Edward & Lilian (Flint). Gf: H. Lightfoot.
	Hammond Hewett	Bertram Roy, b. 21 April 1896, bp. 10 May; s. John & Theresa (Toole). Gf: Charles Pemberton; gm: May Munt. *[see entry for 28 October 1894]*
	Bonugli	Violet Louisa, b. 25 Jan 1896, bp. 10 May; d. John & Emma (Covington). Gf: Leo Pierrotti; gm: Helena Bonugli. *[see earlier partial entry on p. 205 above]*
	Source C	Alice Magdalen ?Sara, bp. 16 May (condit.)
	Dillon	Joseph Daniel, b. 26 May 1896, bp. 5 July; s. Richard & Jane (Hunt). Gf: Daniel Dillon; gm: Anne Flynn.
	Critchley	Leo Reginald, b. 29 June 1896, bp. 21 July; s. Daniel & Eliza (Gibson). Gf: Thomas Noble; gm: E. T. M. Noble.
	Dawson	Mary Frances Olive, b. 25 June 1896, bp. 26 July; d. Benjamin & Frances Mary (Bazzill). Gf: James Read.
	Dawson C	Benjamin, bp. 26 July; s. Benjamin & Frances M (condit.)
	Dawson C	??, bp. 26 July; s. Benjamin & Frances M. (condit.)
	Munt	Frederic, b. 3 Sept 1896, bp. 3 Sept; s. Frederic & Olive (Toole). *[added note]* At home because 'in extremis'. Died 3 Sept.
	Kenealy	Michael, b. 28 April 1896, bp. 26 Sept; s. Edward Michael & Harriet (Dennis). Gm: Teresa ?Lavelle *[in margin]* Pertenhall. By J. H. Ashmole.
	Wringe	William, b. 10 Oct 1896, bp. 4 Nov; s. Richard & Jane (Meade). Gf: Edward Wringe; gm: Sarah Wringe.
	Pettitt	Alfred Bernard, bp. 13 Nov; s. Alfred & Anne Louise (Rose). Gf: J. W. Tebbs; gm: Alice N. Man? At home out of necessity. Ceremonies supplied 6 Sept 1897.
1897	Granville	Mary, b. 26 Feb 1897, bp. 12 March; d. Charles Dashwood & Louise Mary (Stephenson). Privately in danger of death. Eaton Socon.
	Mathews	Joseph Henry, b. 6 March 1897, bp. 28 March; s. James & Mary Agnes (Smith). Gf: Alfred Lees; gm: Ellen Mathews.
	Maguire	Edward, b. 23 March 1897, bp. 8 April; s. Adam Raymund & Caroline (Tremarco). Gf: Edward Greggs.
	Watkinson	Catherine Edith, b. 18 Jan 1897, bp. 11 April; d. Charles Joseph & Ernestine (Sage). Gf: Joseph Tildesley; gm: Louise Lagny. *[added note]* married Richard Williams in this church, 8.2.54, with dispensation from MR *[mixed religion]* with convalidation *[dispensation granted after marriage]*.
	Hamblet	Ellen, b. 8 March 1897, bp. 11 April; d. William & Ellen (Bess) *[blotted in original]* Gf: William Richards; gm: Maud Parrott.
	Goffer	Maud Grace, b. 3 June 1897, bp. 16 July; d. Frederick & Alice (Gannon). Gm: Florence?
	O'Brien	Frances May, 28 May 1897, bp. 14 July; d. William Cornelius & Mary Elizabeth (White). Gf: Daniel O'Brien.
	Le Caron C	Arthur Balfour, b. 3 March 1880, bp. 4 Aug; s. Henry & Nana (*sic*) (Melvin).

Year	Surname	
	Lennon	Edith Maud, b. 18 July 1897, bp. 6 Aug; d. Edward & Louise (McGrath). Gm: Mary Harrington. *[added note]* Married Harold Vincent Wood on 26 Feb 1973 (*sic*) at St Edward's, Garden Rd, Nottingham.
	Munt	Theresa, b. 8 Aug 1897, bp. 15 Aug; d. Frederic & May (Toole). *[in margin]* at home 'in extremis'.
	Tebbs C	Frederick William, b. 13 May 1874, bp. 29 Aug; s. G. Tebbs.
	Source	Alice, b. 26 June 1897, bp. 4 Sept; d. Frank & Alice (Inskip). Gm: E. McGowan.
	Wright	Helen, b. 8 Dec 1896, bp. 17 Sept; d. George & Catherine (Power). Gf: Thomas Maguire; gm: Bridget Power.
	Darlow	Ellen Beatrix, b. 26 July 1897, bp. 10 Oct; d. Alfred James & Mary Theresa (O'Connor). Gm: Rose A. Grehan. *[in margin]* 5 Lansdowne Cottages, Kempston.
	Stevens	Gertrude Alice, b. 23 Sept 1897, bp. 24 October; d. George & Elizabeth (Mann). Gm: Elizabeth McGowan. Ickwell Green.
	De Notke/Nolke C	Elizabeth Esther, bp. 20 Dec (condit.)
	De Notke/Nolke C	Louise Anne, bp. 20 Dec (condit.)
	Wildman C	William, bp. 24 Dec (condit.)
1898	Fraser	Margaret Winefrid, b. 6 June 1897, bp. 2 Jan; d. Sondoun (?) & Catherine (Dillon). Gf: Daniel Dillon; gm: Elizabeth Dillon.
	Hanrahan	James, b. 22 Dec 1897, bp. 13 Feb; s. James & Rose Helen (Watts). Gf: William Hanrahan, p.p.(?)
	Hamson	Mary, b. 3 May 1898, bp. 4 May; d. James & Margaret (Clifford). *[in margin]* 'in extremis'.
	Bonugli	Frederick John, b. 1 March 1898, bp. 8 May; s. John & Emma (Covington). Gf: John Ravello *[Ruello?]*; gm: Ellena Bonugli.
	Huckle	William Christopher, b. 8 Oct 1897, bp. 12 May; s. John & Marion Elizabeth (Mitchell). Gm: Alice Wells.
	Hamblett	Dorothy, b. 20 April 1898, bp. 6 June; d. William & Helen (Biss). Gf: Richard Hamblett; gm: Catherine Hamblett.
	Holden	Wilfrid Alfred, bp. 9 June. *[in margin]* at home 'in extremis'.
	Hewett	Maureen, b. 7 July 1898, bp. 10 Aug; d. John Hammond & Teresa (Tool *sic*). Gm: Mary Munt. *[priest]* William Cooper[11] *[added note]* Married 24 July 1919 John Thomas Coltman, at St Joseph's, Bedford.
	Ross	Mary Petica (?) Caroline, b. 2 May 1898, bp. 1 Sept; d. John L. & Gertrude Mary (Pollok). Gf: William H. Ross p.p.; gm: Mary T. Ross.
	Mace	Alice May, b.— May 1898, bp. 3 Nov; d. Henry John & Elizabeth (Herbert). *[added note]* at home, in danger of death.
	Eardley	Ella, b. 10 May 1888, bp. 22 Nov *[no parents or godparents noted]* (condit.)
	Eardley C	Ada, bp. 22 Nov *[no other details]* (condit.)

11 Rev. William Cooper (1869–1927, ord. 1897) Northampton diocese.

Year	Surname	
1899	West C	Mary Elizabeth Tredwell, b. 19 Feb 1899, bp. 19 March; d. William Charles & Annie M. M. (*sic*) (Roberts). Gf: Thomas Roberts, p.p.; gm: Wilhelmina Roberts. *[added note]* Married William Ivor Marks, Cardiff, at Holy Child Jesus & St Joseph's, Bedford, 27 Sept 1932. (AGW) (*sic*)[12] Hinde George, bp. 25 March (condit.) Prison.
	Harvey	Helen, b. 24 Sept 1892, bp. 13 April; d. Joseph S. & Mary (Halloran). Gm: Catherine Harvey.
	Harvey	Charles William, b. 23 April 1895, bp. 15 April; s. Joseph S. & Mary (Halloran). Gm: Catherine Harvey. *[note in margin]* Married 19 Sept 1940 Jean McGregor at Bedford. A.G. Whyatt.
	McDermott	Kathleen, b. 14 March 1899, bp. 22 April; d. Bridget McDermott (unmarried). Gf: T. Griggs. William Cooper M.C.
	Stratton	James Wilfrid, b. 1(10?) March, 1899, bp. 3 May; s. William & Rose (Kelly). Gm: Roselea Dines.
	Stevens	Leonard George, b. 3 June 1899, bp. 8 June; s. George & Elizabeth (Mason). Gf: Thomas McGrath; gm: Catherine McGrath. Ickwell Green.
	Lennon	Bernard, b. 16 Aug 1899, bp. 28 Sept; s. Edward & Louise (McGrath). Gf: Thomas McGrath; gm: Catherine McGrath.
	Munt	Reginald William, b. 24 Sept 1899, bp. 28 Oct; s. Frederick & Cecily May (Toole). Gm: Theresa Hewett.
	Jackson	Eileen Barry, b. 7 Oct 1899, bp. 19 Oct; d. Edgar Michael & Mary Florence (?Gordson) (*sic*). Gf: Edgar Francis Jackson, p.p.; gm: Mary Fitzpatrick, p.p. *[added note:* 'p.p.' *added after gf and gm.]*
	Connolly	John William, b. 22 Sept 1899, bp. 3 Dec; s. William & Mary Anne (Day). Gf: George Read; gm: Ellen T. Noble.
1900	Dickenson	Winefrid, b. 27 Jan 1900, bp. 6 Feb; d. Thomas & Bessie (Evans). Gm: Agnes W. Stokes.
	O'Brien	Thomas, b. 25 Dec 1899, bp. 20 March; s. Ellen O'Brien unmarried. Gf: Alfred Lightfoot.
	Harvey	Frederick George, b. 19 Nov 1899, bp. 21 April; s. Joseph Mary (Halloran). Gm: Catherine Harvey.
	Watkinson	Maude Ilene (*sic*), b. 4 Jan 1900, bp. 29 April; d. Charles Joseph & Ernestine (Page). Gf: F. J. Tildesley; gm: Florence Tildesley.
	Darlow	Thomas Walter, b. 23 May 1899, bp. 8 May; s. Alfred James & Mary Theresa (O'Connor). Gm: Esther M. Russell ? Kempston.
	Goffer	Malcolm Frederick, b. 5 April 1900, bp. 13 May; s. Frederick & Alice (Ganner). Gm: Alice M. Tildesley.
	Cameron	Constance Victoria Violet, b. 23 May 1900, bp. 2 Aug; d. William Alexander & Sarah (Griggs). Gf: Thomas H. Griggs; gm: Margt. (*sic*) Collins.
	Burrows C	Minnie, b. 10 Dec 1868, bp. 29 Dec; d. James & Harriet (Gee).

[The early months of 1901 saw a greater number of Italian names in the baptismal register, such as Sciarazza, Scettrini, and Vaccaro.]

12 Presumably the A. G. Whyatt of two entries down; untraced.

Marriage registers, 1872–1900

Notes

Format

As with the other registers, the marriage ones were completed in Latin, for example:

> Anno 1874 die 29 mensis Januarii Ego Joannes Priestley Warmoll in Matrimonio conjunxi David Hearne Sheffordiae filium David Hearne, et Catherinam Brady, filiam Patricii Brady. Praesentibus testibus Joanne Brady et Maria Anna Brady.
> Joannes Priestley Warmoll.

This may be translated:

> In the year 1874 on the 29th January, I John Priestley Warmoll joined in matrimony David Hearne of Shefford, the son of David Hearne, and Catherine Brady, daughter of Patrick Brady. In the presence of the witnesses John Brady and Mary Anne Brady.
> John Priestley Warmoll.

A shortened version is used here:

1874	Hearne/Brady	David (Shefford) & Catherine, 29 Jan.

Civil registration

Because Catholic clergy were not official registrars, marriages had to be celebrated in the presence of the civil registrar who attended the church for the ceremony and had the civil register signed by the two parties and the witnesses (of whom there had to be two legally recognised, one male and one female, no matter how many 'bridesmaids' might be in attendance). So the parish registers were not a unique record. The names of the two official witnesses have been omitted here.

Dispensations

Some of the entries say 'with dispensation'. There were two impediments recognised by the Catholic Church at the time as affecting the validity of a marriage; one was entitled 'mixed religion' where a non-Catholic partner had been baptised but not as a Catholic; the other was entitled 'disparity of cult', where the non-Catholic partner had not been baptised at all. In both cases, the Catholic partner needed a dispensation (normally granted by the local bishop) for the marriage to be valid in the eyes of the Catholic authorities. The entries here do not specify which impediment had been removed.[13] The granting of dispensations increases notably in the 1890s.

Surnames

The name of the male partner comes first in each pairing.

[13] T. Bouscaren, S.J., & A. Ellis, S.J., *Canon Law. A Text and Commentary* 3rd ed. (Milwaukee, US, 1957), pp. 505–9.

Place names

If no place is named after either partner it may be assumed that they are from Bedford. There are some years when no Catholic marriages took place.

Year	Surnames	
1872	Burton/Church	William Thomas Nicholls & Mary Anne, both of Bedford, 11 Feb.
	Westropp/Williams	John & Mary Agatha, both of Bedford, 17 April.
1873	Rabeder/Clarke	Joseph John *[place of residence not clear]* & Rachel (Bedford), 11 Dec.
1874	Hearne/Brady	David (Shefford) & Catherine, 29 Jan.
1875	Back/O'Toole	Henry (Luton) & Sarah Joan Rose (Bedford), 2 Feb.
	Jackson/Thoms	William (Bedford) & Emma (Bedford), 8 Aug.
1876	Madden/Wardill	Joseph (Bridlington) & Francesca (Bedford), 3 Feb.
1877	Griggs/Blake	Thomas (Bedford) & Mary Anne (Bedford), 1 April.
	Burns/Case	William (Bedford) & Faith (Bedford), 19 Aug.
	Burke/McGlynn	David (Bedford) & Ellen, 3 Dec.
1878	Tildesley/Brady	Joseph (Bedford) & Joan, 1 May.
	Schaeffler/Wilson	Louis (Ludovic) Edmund (Liep?, Alsace) & Adelaide Margaret (Bedford), 29 Aug.
1879	Braheny/Lowe	James (Bedford) & Sarah Joan (Bedford), 4 June. With dispensation.
1881	Short/Kilger	Charles Alfred & Anne Mary (Toole) Kilger (*sic*), 18 Feb. With dispensation. *[one witness is named Toole, the other Kilger; see next entry]*
	Street/Kilger	Charles & Rosanne, 8 July. With dispensation.
	Lightfoot/Cole	William & Mary Elizabeth, 21 Aug.
	Brown/Haynes	James William (London) & Isabelle, 30 Aug.
1883	Ryan/Hayward	Laurence Joseph (Bedford) & Laura, 3 Jan.
	Demery/Parker	William Thomas (Bedford) & Matilda Mary, 25 Jan. Priest: Canon William Blackman. *[bride's name could be Parkes]*
	Tynan/Dean	William (Bedford) & Constance, 19 July.
	Plum/Wildman	William (Bedford) & Henrietta Marian, 23 Sept.
	Wootton/Hunt	John Henry (Bedford) & Mary Anne (Sandy), 18 Nov.
	Grehan/Stratton	Joseph (Bedford) & Emily (Bedford), 18 Nov. Dispensation from the reading of the banns.
1884	Allen/Blades	John (Bedford) & Sophie (widow; maiden name Foster), 19 Feb.
	Bryant/Wittrick	Frederick George (Bedford) & Eliza Mary, 16 July.
1885	Daniels/Nugent	Thomas Ebenezer (Beeston. Sandy) & Anne Nugent, 16 Feb. Priest: John William McShane.
	Dillon/Hunt	Richard (Bedford) & Joan, 5 Aug. Priest: George Wrigglesworth.[14]
1886	Griggs/Blake	Thomas (Bedford) & Sarah, 4 Jan. With dispensation.

14 The new parish priest. Rev. John William McShane, in the previous entry, was currently of the Nottingham diocese, having served in Northampton diocese until 1885; see earlier entry, p. 199.

Year	Surnames	
	Mooney*[?]*/ Jackman	Edward (Kempston) & Emma (Kempston), 23 Sept. With apostolic dispensation.
1888	Peacock/Kirby	Julian Edward Oliver Woodruffe (Bedford) & Sarah Catherine (Bedford), 4 April. Priest: Robert Middleton.
1889	Tobin/Tobin[15]	James (Bedford) & Julia (Rossberry, Cork), 28 Oct.[16]
	Munt/Toole	Frederick & Cecily May (or Meg), 23 Dec.
1890	Maybery/*[blank]*[17]	Michael & Elizabeth, 26 March. *[added note]* This copied faithfully from a paper found: Robert C. Middleton. *[in a different hand]* The marriage was that of a soldier.
1891	Hill/Widgery	John (Kentish Town, London) & Emily Jane (Bedford), 10 Feb.
[The priest from now on was Robert C. Middleton]		
	Higgins/Featon	Francis (Kempston) & Hannah (formerly Cahill; Kempston), 3 Oct.
	Payne/Pickett	Charles Smith (Kempston) & Jane (Kempston), 17 Nov.
	Youngs/Berrington	Herbert John & Elizabeth (Bedford), 26 Dec.
1892	Mower/Pestell	John & Ruth, 29 Aug. With dispensation.
	Dean/Darby	Daniel Darby (*sic*) & Florence Lydia, 31 Aug.[18]
	Course/Hancock	Joseph & Mary (formerly Barry), 4 Sept. With dispensation.
1893	Bower/Dillon	Edwin (Derby) & Winefrid (Bedford), 3 April. With dispensation.
	Bulbeck/Ennis	George & Elizabeth, 25 Oct. Priest: William Kay SJ. *[ord. 1863; d. 1908]*
	O'Brien/White	William Cornelius (Portsea) & Mary Elizabeth (Stagsden), 31 Dec. With dispensation. *[Immediately before this entry is a partially completed one for the same couple, dated 28 Dec, but all crossed out, with the explanation* 'Civil impediment discovered at the last moment, "sea ?"*]*
[There are no entries for 1894; henceforward Christian names are mostly not in Latin]		
1895	Fuller/McDermott	Henry Foster & Margaret Hastings, 5 Feb.
	Lawrence/Wooding	Benjamin & Sophie Clifton, 15 April. With dispensation.
	Blunton/Boylan	Alfred & Susan, 5 July. With dispensation.
	Collins/Smith	Bartholomew (Warmingford, Essex) & Ellen Mary Smith (Bedford), 31 Oct. With dispensation.
1896	Fegan/Stapleton	John & Annie, 10 March. With dispensation.
	Harcourt/Kay	Henry Merritt & Marianne Josephine, 22 April.
	Dillon/Flynn	Michael Denmark & Hannah, 23 Sept.
	Stevens/Mann	George (Ickwell) & Elizabeth, 25 Nov. With dispensation.
1897	Oliver/Grehan	Charles Bertram & Rose Anna, 18 Oct.
	Hanson/Gibbs	George Edward & Clara, 18 Oct. With dispensation.
	Ryan/Wakenell	Edward Bernard Aloysius (alias Edmund) & Agnes Mary, 24 Oct.
	Connolly/Day	William & Mary Ann, 17 Nov. With dispensation.

15 Possibly an error?

16 One of the witnesses, Ellen Perkins, signs with an X 'her mark', countersigned by the priest G. Osman.

17 Uses only married name.

18 His name was Daniel Darby Dean; hers Florence Lydia Darby.

Year	Surnames	
1898	Schofield/Carter	Ernest & Winefrid Mary, 8 Jan.
1899	Cambers/Page	Benjamin George Collins & Ada Marie, 7 Aug. With dispensation.
	Brogan/Sherwood	Michael Joseph (Castlepollard, Ireland) & Elizabeth, 24 Sept.
	Barradale/Read	Thomas & Susanna, 30 Dec. With dispensation from the Reverend Bishop of Nottingham.
1900	Swingler/Sharpe	Raymond Vincent Thomas & Alice, 7 May.
	Conway/Oram	William Edwin (Sheerness) & Annie (Eaton Socon), 19 June.
	Trimarco/Congo	Constantino & Martha Ann, 20 Aug. With dispensation.[19]
	Malone/Sullivan	Alfred & Maura Anne, 25 Dec. With dispensation. *['Malone' is very unclear]*

Burial registers, 1864–1900

Notes

Format of entries

The burial registers after 1850 were completed in Latin. In the following example italics indicate the parts left blank for the priest to complete:

> Anno *1864* die *8* mensis *Septembris Elena Monica Tandy* ex *hoc oppido* aetatis *28*, in communione S. Matris Ecclesiae animam Deo reddidit Sacramentis munit*a*, cujus corpus die *12* mensis *Septembris* sepultum est in *Coemeterio.*
>
> *Joannes Priestley Warmoll Mis. Ap.*

This may be translated as:

> In the year 1864 on the 8th day of the month of September, Ellen Monica Tandy of this town, aged 28, in communion with Holy Mother Church returned her soul to God fortified by the sacraments; her body was buried on the 12th day of September in the Cemetery.
>
> John Priestley Warmoll Miss[ionary] Ap[ostolic]

A shortened version is used here: year heading, surname followed by Christian name, place of residence at time of death, age, reception of last rites or not, date of death (d.) and date of burial (b.). So the above entry would read,

> **1864** Tandy Ellen Monica, of Bedford, aged 28, with last rites, d. 8 Sept, b. 12 Sept.

The recording priest used a ? when unsure of information. Not all entries are complete.

Last rites

These usually included the Sacraments of Penance (Confession) and Extreme Unction (Last Anointing); if the dying person were conscious, they might also receive Holy Communion ('viaticum'). To report this the register carried the Latin statement as

19 The Italian names are not clear; the witnesses were Vincenzo and Carolina Sciaraffa; was this the first fully Italian marriage in Bedford?

above. The phrase about the reception of the sacraments was often altered: the person might have died suddenly, or received only baptism or penance on their deathbed. In the entries recorded here, this is indicated by the inclusion of 'last rites' or the name of the rite received. Where infants were concerned, their age was not always recorded; instead of last rites, the entry sometimes indicated whether the baby had been baptised or not. 'Sudden death': this indicated that no last rites had been performed.

Place of burial

This was usually Bedford. 'Cemetery' in the text indicates Bedford, sometimes called the 'Common cemetery'; a small number of burials are noted as having taken place in the cemetery in Kempston.

The 'New Burial Ground' in Bedford was opened in Foster Hill Road by Statutory Instrument in June 1855, replacing all the old, over-full and unhealthy churchyards in the town, except for those belonging to Trinity Church and the Moravian Chapel. The new cemetery consisted of two sections: the Anglican section, where burials were conducted by the relevant Anglican clergyman, and an 'Unconsecrated Portion, set apart for Burials solemnized by other Religious Bodies, at which the relatives or friends of the deceased may select their own Minister'. Matters were not always as simple as that, of course: see pp. 90–1 above for reactions to Warmoll when he took a funeral there. (Originally known as 'Bedford Cemetery', it was re-named 'Foster Hill Road Cemetery' after the opening of a new cemetery in Norse Road in 1987.)[20]

Where an Anglican churchyard was the only local burial ground it remained possible for the incumbent to forbid the burial of non-Anglicans there or to forbid a non-Anglican clergyman to say prayers over a grave. How often and where this right was exercised varied widely. The Burial Laws Amendment Act of 1880 gave the right of burial in the local churchyard to any parishioner whatever their religion (or none).

Signature of the officiating priest

Where the resident priest officiated, his name is not given for each entry.

Gap in register entries

There is a gap in the register between March 1887 and July 1890, with no entries for 1888 or 1889. One may presume there were deaths between those dates but for some reason no formal entry was made in the register; any loose sheets used have apparently not survived.

Year	Surname	
1864	Walton	Catherine, of Bedford, infant, d. ? March, b. 28 March.
	McGourty	Mary Anne, of Bedford, infant, d. 1 June, b. 4 June.
	Stewart	Elizabeth, of Bedford, infant (? 16 weeks), d. 19 Aug, b. 22 Aug.

20 A copy of the original Statutory Instrument is printed in Linda Ayres, 'How it all Began – James Wyatt', in Adrian Bean (ed.), *Bedford's Victorian Cemetery* (Bedford, n.d., but 2022?), pp. 10–13. The document gives details of opening times, fees, notices of interments, etc., and is dated June 1855. See also J. A. Hilton, 'The Rise and Fall of the Catholic Mortuary Chapel', in *NWCH*, vol. L (Wigan, 2023), pp. 5–10. The relevant Acts of Parliament are 15 & 16 Vict. cap. 85 and 16 & 17 Vict. cap. 134.

Year	Surname	
	Tandy	Ellen Monica, of Bedford, aged 28, last rites, d. 8 Sept, b. 12 Sept.
1865	Walton	Lucia A., infant aged 6 months; d. 7 Jan, b. 7 Jan.
	Huckle	Catherine, of Bedford, aged 46, last rites, d. 25 March, b. 27 March.
	Tandy	Eleanor Mary, of Bedford, aged 61, last rites, d. 29 Oct, b. 2 Nov.[21]
1866	King	Anne Joan, of Cambridge, infant (1), d. 18 Mar, b. 20 Mar.
	Richards	Charles Robert, of Bedford, aged 41 *[? but see baptisms, p. 189]*, last rites, d. 16 April, b. 21 April. Priest: William Blackman.[22]
	Lightfoot	Alfred[23] Joseph, of Bedford, infant (3), d. 23 June, b. 26 June.
1867	Caton	Patrick, of Bedford, aged 25, last rites, d. 4 May, b. 8 May.
	Shanassy	Mary Agnes, infant (11 weeks), d. 30 May, b. 30 May.
[There are no entries for 1868]		
1869	Dobson	Mary Alice, infant (2), d. 18 Feb, b. 22 Feb.
	Murray	Mary, of Bedford, aged 88, last rites, d. 9 April, b. 12 April.
	Basil	Ada Amabelle (*sic*) Mary, of Bedford, infant, d. ? Dec, b. 7 Dec.
1870	Fieren	Peter (Luton), aged 67, last rites, d. 26 Feb, b. 1 March.
	Conroy	John, of Bedford, aged 29, last rites, d. 19 March, b. 23 March.
	Williams	Julian, of Bedford, d. 25 June, b. 28 June.
	Rose	Benjamin, of Bedford, 3 weeks old, d. 15 July, b. 18 July.
1871	Horsewood	John, of Bedford, aged 31, last rites, d. 25 Jan, b. 28 Jan.
	Borman	Mary, of Bedford, aged 58, last rites d. 25 April, b. 28 April.
	Haynes	Emma Elizabeth, aged 20, d. 28 Sept, b. 3 Oct.
	Shanasey	Frances Anne Mary, aged 3 months, d. 6 Nov, b. 8 Nov.
	Brady	Patrick, of Bedford, aged 68, last rites, d. 23 Dec, b. 28 Dec.
1872	Shanassey	William Joseph, of Bedford, aged 3 days, d. 10 Dec, b. same day.
1873	Dobson	Robert Ambrose, of Bedford, aged 33, last rites, d. 28 July, b. 31 July.
	Taylor	Elizabeth, of Bedford, having received sac*[rament]* of penance, d. 22 Dec, b. same day.
1874	Cundall	Paul Dominic, of Bedford, infant, *[no dates, but apparently pre-April]*
	Kellerer	Conrad, of Bedford, last rites, d. ? April, b. 30 April.
	Westropp	Edwin John, of Bedford, one week old, d. 13 May, b. 15 May.
	Holmes	Thomas, of Bedford, aged 22, died a Catholic, d. 18 July, b. 22 July.
1875	McKearns	Bridget, of Bedford, aged 95, last rites, d. 30 Dec 1874, b. 2 Jan 1875.
	Mitchell	Christopher, of Bedford, aged 58, last rites, d. 14 April, b. 20 April.
	Williams	John, of Bedford, aged 75, last rites, d. 2 May, b. same day.
[Out of place in the register]		
	Caton	Bridget, of Bedford, aged 65, died a Catholic, d. 16 Feb, b. 21 Feb.

21 The two Tandy women were hosts to Fr Warmoll when he first arrived in Bedford; see p. 87.

22 William Blackman (1840–1911, ord. 1864) Northampton diocese.

23 Aluredus, this name is variously translated as Alfred and Avery.

Year	Surname	
1876	Corrigan	John, from Castlerea, Ireland, a Catholic, killed on the railway 1 July 1876, b. 12 July in Bedford cemetery.[24]
	Shanassey	Eveline Lucy, of Bedford, aged 4 months, d. 13 Aug, b. 16 Aug.
	Tildesley	Sarah, of Bedford, aged 33, baptised, d. 20 Sept, b. 23 Sept.
	De Brenni	Lucy, of Bedford, infant, d. 4 Nov, b. 9 Nov.
1877	Tildesley	Joan, of Bedford, infant, d. 30 April, b. 4 May.
	Lalley	John, of Bedford, aged 58, with last rites, d. 3 Sept, b. 8 Sept.
	Phipps	Anne, of Bedford, aged 24, anointed with Extreme Unction, d. 9 Dec, b. 13 Dec.
1878	Antcliffe (?)	Mary, from London, aged 60, received Eucharist, d. 13 May, b. 16 May.
	Degacher	Matilda (Mechtilde), of Bedford, aged 67, last rites, d. 19 May, b. 23 May.
	Tracey	Anne, of Kempston, aged 3 years 10 months, d. 31 May, b. 3 June.
[Note in margin in different hand: 'For Hugh McCaffrey see note at end of book'*]*		
	McCaffrey	Hugh, died in June 1878 and was buried by Rev. Francis Warmoll. Aged 35, he belonged to the barracks in Kempston. *[this note is on the rear fly-leaf of the register, where it was entered by the 'Cemetery Registrar']*
	Woods	Mary, of Kempston, infant, d. 17 Nov, b. 19 Nov in Kempston.
	Flannagan	Christopher, of Kempston, infant, d. 17 Dec, b. 19 Dec in Kempston.
1879	Russell	*[no name or dates given]* of Kempston, infant, b. in Kempston.
	Lalley	Susan, of Bedford, aged 54, last rites, d. 16 March, b. 20 March.
	Griggs	Thomas Henry, of Bedford, infant, 6 months, d. 13 July, b. 16 July.
	O'Grady	Edward, of Bedford, aged 26, last rites, d. 6 Aug, b. 11 Aug.
	Corcoran	James, of Bedford, aged 78, last rites, d. 21 Aug, b. 26 Aug.
	Bryan	Edward, of Bedford, aged 50, last rites, d. 25 Sept, b. 29 Sept.
	Harrington	Thomas, of Bedford, aged 55, last rites, d. 28 Oct, b. 1 Nov.
1880	Barrie	Patrick, of Bedford, aged 35, died suddenly, a Catholic but no last rites, d. 17 Jan, b. 24 Jan. *[added note unclear, but could be 'South street']*
	Murphy	Patrick, of Kempston, aged 21, last rites, d. 21 Jan, b. 24 Jan, Kempston Cemetery.
	Harris	infant, 5 months, d. 1880.
	Griggs	Florence, of Bedford, 39 days old, d. 13 Sept, b. 15 Sept.
	Bannister	William Frederick, of Bedford, aged 18 months, d. 25 Dec, b. 28 Dec.
1881	Sullivan	James, a soldier, aged 23, died suddenly in prison with last rites, d. 16 Jan, b. 19 Jan.
	O'Halloran	Thomas, of Kempston, aged 46, (last rites) (*sic*), d. 3 July, b. (?) July.
1882	Donelley	Bridget, of Bedford, aged 85, with last rites, d. 6 Jan, b. 10 Jan.
	Brady	James, of Bedford, aged 30, with last rites, d. 25 Aug, b. 29 Aug.
	Griggs	Mary Anne, of Bedford, aged 25, with last rites, d. 26/27 Sept, b. 2 Oct.
	Simms	Henrietta Matilda/Maud (Mechtildis), infant, d. 1 Dec, b. 9 Dec.

24 He was a labourer, killed when he jumped from a train at Bletchley; press reports of the inquest, under such headings as 'Fatal jump from a Train', said no one, even the police, knew his name. See *Bedfordshire Times and Independent*, 8 & 22 July 1876.

Year	Surname	
1883	Egan	John, of Bedford, aged 87, last rites, d. 12 March, b. 16 March.
	Huckle	Hannah, of Bedford, aged 55, last rites, d. 4 April, b. 7 April.
	Caton	Thomas, of Bedford, aged 63, last rites, d. 17 May, b. 19 May.
	Sims	Hannah Mary, of Bedford, aged 13, last rites, d. 9 July, b. 14 July.
	Sullivan	James, of Luton, aged 45, in good standing, d. 31 Aug, b. 4 Sept in Luton Parish Cemetery.
	Young	Mary Anne, of Kempston, aged 17, last rites, d. 26 Sept, b. 28 Sept in Kempston cemetery.
	Bazzill	John Credford, of Bedford, aged 83, last rites, d. 24 Nov, b. 29 Nov.
1884	Lightfoot	Alured Ernest, aged 3 months, d. 23 June, b. 27 June.
	Smith	Rose Laura, of Bedford, aged 16, last rites, d. 18 Aug, b. 21 Aug.
1885	Warmoll	Rev. Jo. (*sic*) Priestley, Provost of the Cathedral Church, aged 55, d. 14 Feb, b. 19 Feb. By William Canon Blackman.

[Rev. George Wrigglesworth was now the resident priest, replacing Rev. Warmoll: see pp. 151–2 above. He seems to have had some problem with spelling names. His handwriting is neat but very small and sometimes difficult to decipher.]

Year	Surname	
	Sterling	Louise, from Brighton, aged 35, last rites not administered because of ignorance of the circumstances, d. 6 April, b. 10 April.
	Gostellow (*sic*)	William, suddenly in the street (and so no last rites); d. 1 May, b. 4 May.
	Bazzell	John Henry, of Bedford, aged 23, last rites, d. 22 June, b. 25 June.
	McCushen (*sic*)	Francis Aaron Cass, of Biggleswade, aged 19, conditional last rites, d. 27 June, b. 30 June.
	Grehan	Daniel, of this town, aged 22, d. 18 Aug, b.— in St Mary's Cemetery, Maltam (*sic*).
	Fisher	Eleanor, from Sheffield, aged 78, with conditional absolution, d. 21 Sept, b. 24 Sept in the cemetery in Sheffield.
	Lemon	Mary, from Kempston, d. 27 Sept, b. 30 Sept in Kempston cemetery.
	Huckle	George, of Bedford, aged 17 months, d. 18 Oct, b. 23 Oct.
	Hearne	Catherine, of Bedford, aged 36, last rites, d. 10 Dec, b. 14 Dec.
1886	Steer	Sophie, of Bedford, aged 89, last rites conditionally administered, d. 19 Feb, b. 23 Feb.
	Magher	Michael, of Bedford, aged 84, last rites, d. 14 April, b. 16 April.
	Hunt	Thomas, of Sandy, aged 63, with penance and Eucharist, d. 3 May, b. 6 May in church cemetery, Sandy.
	Martyn	Ellen Louise, of Pertenhall, aged 68; Penance and Holy Eucharist a little while before, d. 9 May, b. 13 May by non-Catholic minister in Pertenhall Cemetery. *[very unusual, even unique]*
	Taylor	Samuel, aged 38, d. 24 June, b. 28 June; baptised while dying.
	Reynolds	Martin (Thomas), of Bedford, aged 40, d. 6 Dec, b. 10 Dec.
	Anon.	of Bedford, aged 50, d. 10 Dec, b. 13 Dec *[a strange entry, with no names entered; the person is noted as having received the last sacraments conditionally]*
1887	Lightfoot	William, aged 69, baptism and confession administered conditionally, d. 31 Jan, b. 5 Feb.

Year	Surname	
	Lightfoot	Beatrix Ellen, aged 3 months, d. 4 Feb, b. 8 Feb.
	Brady	Catherine, of Bedford, aged 68, last rites, d. 4 March, b. 9 March.

[The entries jump from March 1887 to July 1890; there are no entries for either 1888 or 1889]

1890

[The priest in charge from now on was Rev. Robert C. Middleton (1853–1906, ord. 1883); he remained in Bedford for the remainder of his ministry. He replaced Canon G. Osman, at Bedford December 1887–90 (see p. 152 above) who, strangely, does not feature in the registers.]

Year	Surname	
	McMahon	Isabel, of Bedford, aged 48, died suddenly, no sacraments, d. 23 July, b. 26 July.
	Higgins	Mary, from Kempston, aged 35, died suddenly, d. 27 July, b. 31 July in Kempston cemetery.
	Pillow	Rose Lilian, of Kempston, aged 8, baptised, d. 15 Oct, b. 18 Oct in Kempston cemetery.
1891	Woolton	John Henry, of Bedford, aged 32, died suddenly 16 May, b. 19 May.
	Breen	Bridget, of Bedford, aged 62, last rites, d. 28 May, b. 30 May.
	O'Connell	Catherine T. M. M., of Ramsgate, aged 2, baptised, d. 11 Sept, b. 12 Sept.
	Ryan	Beatrix, of Bedford, aged 3 months, baptised, d. 24 Dec, b. 28 Dec.
1892	Wheeler	William, of Bedford, aged 17 months, baptised, d. 17 Jan, b. 20 Jan.
	Unknown	*[in margin]* under the name of Mrs Newton, aged 42, d. 18 April, b. 19 April. From … kew(?)
	Bannister	Sarah, from Deptford, aged 67, last rites, d. 21 Oct, b. 26 Oct.
	Ryan	Francis Patrick, aged 2 months, baptised, d. Dec, b. 11 Dec.
	Fuller	George Augustus, of Bedford, aged 63, died suddenly 21 Dec, b. 24 Dec.
	Fuller	Geoffrey Cecil, aged 2 yrs & 11 months, baptised, d. 22 Dec, b. 24 Dec.
1893	Ryan	Lawrence Joseph, of Bedford, aged 45, confession and Holy Communion, d. 25 March, b. 30 March.
	Toole	James, of Kempston, aged 60, last rites, d. 24 April, b. 27 April.
	Lipney (?)	Mary, of Bedford, aged 8 months, baptised, d. 13 July, b. 15 July.
	Watkinson	Mabel Emma, aged 6 months, d. 25 July, b. 27 July.
	Blake	James, of Bedford, aged 67, last rites, d. 20 Aug, b. 23 Aug.
	Course	Joseph William, aged 5 weeks, baptised, d. 19 Sept, b. 23 Sept.
	Hewett	Kathleen M. M. H., of Kempston, aged 4 months, baptised, d. 19 Sept, b. 23 Sept in Kempston cemetery.
	Munt	Cecily Elizabeth, of Kempston, aged 5 months, baptised, d. 24 Sept, b. 30 Sept, in Kempston cemetery.
	Lightfoot	Louis G., of Bedford, aged 10 weeks, baptised, d. 3 Oct, b. ??
	Ryan	Agnes Cecily, of Bedford aged ?, baptised, d. 17 Nov, b. 21 Nov.
	Dillon	Joseph, aged 2, baptised, d. 11 Dec, b. 15 Dec (By Rev) J. H. Ashmole.
1894	Lennon	Arthur Victor, of Kempston, aged 3 months, baptised, d. 31 Jan, b. 3 Feb in Kempston Public Cemetery.
	McMahon	Daniel Edward, aged 68, died suddenly, d. 12 Feb, b. 16 Feb *[added in Latin:* 'from sudden death free us, O Lord'*]*
	Cunningham	Joseph, of Kempston, aged 25, last rites, d. 5 May, b. 7 May in Kempston cemetery.

Year	Surname	
	Moore	John Joseph, of Kempston, aged 65, Penance and Extreme Unction, d. 18 June, b. 22 June, in Kempston cemetery. (By) Robert C. Middleton, p.p. J. H. Ashmole.
	Corcoran	Edward de Vere, of Bedford, aged 47, after Penance and Extreme Unction, d. 22 Oct, b. 27 Oct in Glasnevin Cemetery, Dublin. *[added in Latin:* 'from sudden death free us, O Lord'*] [see p. 217 above]*
	Holden	Jonathan, of Bedford, aged 2 months, baptised, d. 3 Dec, b. 5 Dec.
1895	Ibbett	Clara N. M., of Bedford, aged 1¼ years (*sic*), baptised, d. 15 April, b. 18 April.
	Richardson	Mary, of Bedford, aged 32, last rites, d. 26 June, b. 29 June.
	Witherow	Catherine E., of Bedford, aged 10 months, baptised, d. 11 Nov, b. 13 Nov.
	Clifford	William, of Bedford, aged 6 weeks, baptised, d. 30 Nov, b. 3 Dec.
	Blake	Francis, of Bedford, aged 30, last rites, d. 11 Dec, b. 16 Dec.
	Swinson	Mary, of Bedford, aged 53, last rites, d. 20 Dec, b. 23 Dec.
1896	Noble	Theresa, of Kempston, aged 68, after Penance and Extreme Unction, d. 4 Feb, b. 8 Feb Kempston Cemetery.
	Brookes	Catherine, of Bedford, aged 90, last rites, d. 12 Feb, b. 15 Feb.
	Fuller	Phyllis B., of Bedford, aged 15, last rites, d. 13 Feb, b. 17 Feb.
	Harris	William, of Bedford, aged 67, last rites, d. 13 March, b. 17 March.
	Lever	Isabel, aged 6 months, baptised, d. 15 March, b. 17 March.
	Blake	Sarah, of Bedford, aged 68, after Penance and Extreme Unction, d. 31 May, b. 3 June.
	Toole	Rose Ann (*sic*) Nugent, of Kempston, aged 62, died suddenly 5 June, b. 10 June, Kempston cemetery.[25]
	Bonugli	Violet Louise, of Bedford, aged 5 months, baptised, d. 8 July, b. 11 July.
	Whelan	Nora, of Kempston, aged 27, last rites, d. 9 Aug, b. 11 Aug, Kempston Cemetery.
	Critchley	Leo Reginald, of Kempston, aged 6 weeks, baptised, d. 15 Aug, b. 18 Aug, Kempston Cemetery.
	Munt	Frederick James, of Kempston, aged 8 hours, baptised, d. 3 Sept, b. 5 Sept, Kempston Cemetery.
	Lightfoot	William, of Bedford, aged 40, after confession, d. 23 Sept, b. 26 Sept.
	Lavelle	Theresa, of Bedford aged 50, last sacraments, Penance & Extreme Unction, d. 22 Oct, b. 24 Oct.
1897	Shanahan	Mary, of Bedford, aged 28, last rites, d. 31 Dec 1896, b. 6 Jan.
	Kelly	James, infant, baptised, d. 31 Dec 1896, b. 4 Jan.
	Dillon	Michael, of Bedford, aged 72, last sacraments, d. 5 Jan, b. ? Jan.
	Sullivan	Thomas, of Kempston, died suddenly, d. 23 May, b. 25 May in Kempston Cemetery.
	Press	Helen J. Mary, of Bedford, aged 41, last sacraments, d. 1 June, b. 5 June.
	O'Connell	Daniel J., of Bedford, aged 80, last sacraments, d. 14 June, b. 18 June.

25 Possibly sister of Mgr Nugent, the well-known Catholic social reformer of Liverpool; he had a sister Rosanne (b. 1834).

Year	Surname	
	Munt	Teresa, of Kempston, infant, baptised, d. 22 Aug, b. 24 Aug in Kempston Cemetery.
	Bryant	Frederick G., of Bedford, aged 37, Penance & Extreme Unction, d. 1 Oct, b. 5 Oct.
	Moylan	Charles R. B., of Bedford, aged 14, sudden death, d. 6 Oct, b. 9 Oct.
	Hamblett	Sarah A., of Bedford, aged 23, last rites, d. 23 Nov, b. 27 Nov.
	Colbert	Richard, of Kempston, aged 47, last rites, d. 4 Dec, b. 9 Dec in Kempston Cemetery.
1898	Eardley	Nora M., of Bedford, aged 3½, baptised, d. 15 Feb, b. 18 Feb.
	Read	James Joseph, of Bedford, aged 51, last rites, d. 18 March, b. 22 March.
	Lever	Elizabeth A., of Bedford, aged 25, d. 31 March, b. 4 April.
	Hansom	Henry, of Ampthill, infant, baptised, d. 29 May, b. 2 June in Ampthill Public Cemetery.
	Holden	William Alfred, of Bedford, aged 6 months, baptised, d. 9 June, b. 11 June.
	Allen	Agnes Gertrude Mary, of Ampthill, aged 25, d. 7 Aug, b. 12 Aug in Parish Cemetery, Ampthill. *[By Rev.]* John Henry Ashmole.
	Huckle	William, of Bedford, aged 70, sudden death, d. 3 Sept, b. 6 Sept.
	Bonugli	Frederick J., of Bedford, aged 6 months, baptised, d. 7 Sept, b. 9 Sept.
	Goffer	Muriel G., of Bedford, aged 1¼, baptised, d. 15 Sept, b. 17 Sept, p.p. W. Cooper.[26]
	Nolan	Catherine, of Bedford, aged 25, sacrament of penance, d. 1 Dec, b. 5 Dec.
1899	Hinde	George, aged 38, last rites, d. 13 April, b. 14 April.
	Cherriffi (*sic*)	William, infant, baptised, d. 22 Sept, b. 23 Sept.
	Newland	Bridget, aged 55, d. 29 Sept, b. 2 Oct.
	Miller	William, aged 70, last rites, d. 30 Sept, b. 3 Oct.
1900	Bazzell	Hannah, aged 82, last rites, d. 13 Jan, b. 17 Jan.
	Mower	Mary, aged 59, died suddenly 16 Jan, no last sacraments, b. 20 Jan.
	Twidell	John Alphonsus, infant, baptised, d. 5 Feb, b. 8 Feb.
	Kenealy	Nora, of Kempston, aged 9, with last rites, d. 6 Feb, b. 9 Feb in Kempston Cemetery.
	Dickenson	Winefrid, of Ampthill, infant, baptised, d. 14 Feb, b. 19 Feb.
	Mansfield	Mary, aged 87, last rites, d. 7 March, b. 10 March.
	Schoedelin	Anne Mary, of Streatham, aged 62, last rites, d. 27 March, b. 30 March.
	Critchley	Daniel, of Bedford, aged 50, sudden death, d. 22 June, b. 30 June.
	McDermott	Kathleen, of Bedford, infant, baptised, d. 18 Aug, b. 22 Aug.
	Gorman	Harriet, of Bedford, aged 47, last rites, d. 12 Oct, b. 15 Oct.
	Loftus	Frederick, of Kempston, aged 7, baptised, d. 29 Nov, b. 3(?) Dec in Kempston Cemetery.

[End of entries for 1900 in register]

[26] Rev. William Cooper (1869–1927, ord. 1897).

Leighton Buzzard registers, 1894–1900

Introduction

Current location of registers
These registers, currently in the diocesan archives in Northampton, cover baptisms and funerals for 1895–1900. There were no Catholic marriages in the area until 1902.

Format
The register entries are in a standard Latin format. They have been translated and abbreviated here.

A Latin example:

> Die 30th Octobris 1894 natus et die 20th Decembris 1895 baptizatus fuit Jacobus Smith filius Gulielmi et Agnis (*sic*) Smith (olim Ellaway). conjugum a me Carolo Reilly Misso.
> Patrinus fuit ... Matrina fuit Esther Maria Rouse

See entry no. 1, 1894, below for working translation.

Ministering priest
Unless otherwise noted, the ceremonies were performed by the Rev. C. Reilly, (1864–1916, ord. 1894). He died a priest of the Southwark diocese where he had worked since 1908.

Baptisms
All the nine individuals baptised were infants; one of the five burials was of an infant who had been baptised seven weeks earlier, the rest were of adults.

Godparents
There are proxy godparents noted in two cases, presumably because of the difficulties that the actual godparents faced in travelling.

Marriages
One baptismal entry has a later marriage notice added (1895); this was officially the canonical practice, to avoid bigamous marriages.

Addresses
Unusually, each entry includes the address of the person concerned, providing some limited idea of the area covered by the church.

Baptismal register, 1895–1900

Year	Entry no.	Surname	
[1895]	1.	Smith	James, b. 30 Oct 1894, bp. 29 Dec 1895, s. William and Agnes (nee Ellaway). Gm: Esther Mary Rouse. 27 Lammas Close, Leighton.
[1896]	2.	Thomas	John Lionel Llewellyn, b. 19 Oct 1895 bp. 19 Jan 1896, s. of Llewellyn and Cecily (nee Croker). Gf: Lawrence Joseph Smith; gm: Celestine Mary Smith. (p.p. Llewellyn and Cecily Thomas). Woburn Sands. *[Marginal note]* In the church of St Raphael, Kingston upon Thames, 3 April 1918 married Mary Bentam.
[1896]	3.	Bates	Patrick Thomas, b. 4 Aug 1896, bp. 4 Oct 1896, s. of William and Mary Anne (nee Taaffe). Gf: Maurice Shelton Reilly. 44 Regent St., Leighton.
[1896]	4.	Wilcox	Wilfrid Joseph, b. 18 Nov 1896, bp. 6 Dec 1896, s. of Augustus and Agnes (nee Wilcox (*sic*)). Gf: George Cheadle Wilcox; gm: Mary Teresa Fleming. (p.p. Maurice Shelton Reilly and Mary Emily Smith). Fullers Earth Lodge, Woburn.
[1897]	5.	Norman	Isabel Margaret, b. 23 Oct 1896, bp. 9 May 1897, d. of Alfred and Margaret (nee Hafenegger). Gf: Joseph Savin. Leighton St., Woburn.
[1898]	6.	Lawrence	Ada Rose, b. 24 Sept 1898, bp. 30 Oct 1898, d. of Abel William and ? (nee Shirley). Gf: Maurice Shelton Reilly. 53 Old Rd., Linslade, Bucks.
[1899]	7.	Cole	Eveline Mary, at home, b. 31 March 1899, bp. 11 April 1899, d. of John and Margaret Isabel (nee Blenkinsop). Rev. Henry James Hardy (p.p. CER) *[presumably Charles Reilly, no godparents are mentioned]* *[address illegible]*
[1899]	8.	Bacon	Mary Jessie (?), b. 22 June 1899, bp. 5 Aug 1899, d. George and Marina (nee Slattery). Gm: Mary Emily Smith. 22 St. Andrew St., Leighton Buzzard.
[1900]	9.	Appleton	Rene David Christopher, b. 1 March 1900, bp. 3 June 1900, s. of David Joshua and Zelia Marcllina (nee Dupont). Gf: Charles Tinger; gm: Alphona Cone. 14 George St., Woburn, Beds. *[This is entry no.10; but no.9 only has the name Bacon, crossed through.]*

Burial register, 1897–1898

There was no Catholic cemetery within reasonable distance, hence the use of local Anglican churchyards; the place of burial is noted in each entry.

'Last sacr(ament)s' or 'in communion with the church': the full range of 'last sacraments' consisted of confession, holy communion and last anointing; if for any reason these were not able to be administered, but the person had been a regularly practising Catholic, then they were said to be 'in communion with the Church'.

The register was completed in Latin: for example, entry 2 below reads:

ANNO 1897, die 1 mensis Maii Elizabeth White ex Leighton Buzzard, aetatis 55, in communione S. Matris Ecclesiae animam Deo redidit Sacramentis munita, cujus corpus die 5 mensis Maii sepultum est in cemeterio Leighton Buzzard. Carolus Reilly Miss°

Full translation: IN THE YEAR 1897, on 1st May Elizabeth White of Leighton Buzzard, aged 55 and in communion with Holy Mother Church, gave up her soul to God, fortified by the Sacraments; her body was buried in Leighton Buzzard cemetery on 5th May. Charles Reilly, Missioner.

Year	**Entry no.**	**Surname**	
[1897]	1.	Wilcox	Wilfrid Joseph, of Woburn, aged 7 weeks. Buried 8 Jan 1897 in Woburn churchyard. *[see baptismal entry above, 6 Dec 1896]*
[1897]	2.	White	Elizabeth, of Leighton Buzzard, aged 55. Died 1 May 1897 having received the last sacraments; buried 5 May, in Leighton Buzzard churchyard.
[1897]	3.	Duddy	James, of Redborough, aged 24. Died 8 June 1897 in communion with the Church; buried 10 June, in Mentmore churchyard.
[1897]	4.	Reilly	Harriet Charlotte, of Leighton Buzzard, aged 72. Died 31 Oct 1897, having received the sacraments; buried 5 Nov in Leighton Buzzard churchyard. Rev. J. H. Ashmole.
[1898]	5.	Dahoney	James, of Leighton Buzzard, aged 43. Died 4 Aug 1898, in communion with the Church; buried 6 Aug in Leighton Buzzard churchyard.

Bibliography

Archives

Archives of the Archbishop of Westminster (AAW)
'A' Series, vol. 42, no. 88, Bp Talbot to Rome 1786
'A' Series, vol. 42, nos 163, 165, Taylor to Bp Talbot
'A' Series, vol. 42, no. 166, James Barnard VG to Bp Talbot
'A' Series, vol. 42, nos 159, 160, 162, 164, Letters re Shefford Mission
'A' Series, vol. 42, no. 168, Taylor to Rev. Barrow, 1809
B 1536, Challoner's Ledger
Z 71, Undated list of addresses in Challoner's hand
Z 73–5, Mayes' Roman Agency (1706–48)
Z 74, no. 81, Report to Rome on English Catholicism, c.1716
Z 74, no. 102, Howard's 'Memorial on the State of Catholics in England' c.1718
Bishop Griffiths' Papers, 2/17, 'Confirmati apud Shefford, die 25 Oct. 1835'
Douglass III.L.35, Bp John Douglass, VA London District, 1790–1812
'A Joint Pastoral Letter of the Cardinal Archbishop and the Bishops on the Catholic School Committee', 5 June 1898

Bedfordshire Archives (BA)
ABP/W1743/62, Will of William Noddings of Campton Kiln …1743
J1255–6, Codicil to will of Oliver St John, esquire, made at villa of Prattelina, Florence
RO5, Conquest Bury Estate
X89/1, John Noddings
X525, Blunham Baptist Church
X627/13, Financial Record Book St Francis' Home, Shefford, Bedfordshire 1875
X627/32 & 33, Bound volumes of St Francis' Home Reports containing Annual Reports, 1870–1904
X627/41, Annual Diaries kept by Canon William Collis of St Francis' Home
X627/42, St Thomas' Seminary, Shefford, February 1884. Catalogue of Books
X627/43, Seminary of St Thomas Aquinas, Shefford. Ledger 1893
X847, Bedford, St Joseph's RC Church

British Library (BL)
Add Mss 5811, Notebooks of Rev. William Cole, 1714–82

Northampton Diocesan Archive (NDA)
Box 144, Early Registers, including three Shefford sets, 1787–1858
Box 157, Bp Riddell's Assorted Papers (uncatalogued)
Box 161, F iv 15, Collis to Bishop, July 1881
Coll. A. 3. 3. The Seminary of St Felix … latterly at Northampton

Coll. A. 3. 18 & 19, Pastoral Letters of Bishop Wareing 1840–50
Coll. A. 6. 7, Wrigglesworth's Appeal, January 1886
Coll. A. 6. 16, Assorted Papers concerning St Francis' Home
Coll. A. 6. 17(c), Bishop Riddell's Correspondence, 1881–92
Coll. A. 6. 17(d), Canon Collis' correspondence with Bishop
Coll. A. 6. 19, Pastoral Letters, Bishop Riddell
Coll. A. 6. 20, Diocesan Synod, Visitation of Bedford, 1898
Coll. A. 6. 21, Confirmations in Luton, Visitation of Leighton Buzzard
Coll. B. 5. 1, Church of the Holy Child & St Joseph, Bedford
Coll. B. 5. 11, Leighton Buzzard Mission
Coll. B. 5. 12, Luton Churches
Coll. B. 5. 14 (2), Rev. Potier and others
Coll. B. 5. 14 (4), Chronological Material, Shefford, 1: 1715–1850; 2: 1850–1933

Prerogative Court of Canterbury
PROB. 6/1776/152, Estate of John Noddings, d. August 1776
PROB. 11/1110/575, Will of Mary Noddings, d. October 1783
PROB. 11/1534/298, Will of Rev. Christopher Taylor, d. June 1812

Newspapers and periodicals

The following lists are intended only as introductory guides. Where local newspapers were concerned, titles changed from time to time as publications amalgamated or were replaced by rivals. The Northampton Diocesan Archives contain a large selection of cuttings from these publications, normally included in the relevant local accounts. (The definite article has been omitted from the titles.)

Catholic publications
Catholic Herald
Catholic Times
Catholic Times and Catholic Opinion
Northampton Catholic Magazine
Orthodox Journal and Catholic Monthly Intelligencer
Tablet
Universe
Weekly Register

Local publications
Bedford Bee
Bedfordshire Mercury (formerly Bedford Mercury)
Bedfordshire Times & Independent
Biggleswade Chronicle
Dunstable Chronicle
Dunstable Gazette
Leighton Buzzard Observer
Luton News

Luton Recorder
Luton Times

National/professional journals
Architect
Builder
Building News
Gentleman's Magazine

Websites

https://www.sacredheartlb.org.uk/parish-history/early-days/, Sacred Heart Catholic Church – Leighton Buzzard; accessed online September 2021

Hunter, Philippa and Richard Barton, 'Gilbert Blount: A Victorian Architect through his diaries', docslib.org, accessed online 22 September 2020

Secondary sources

Agar, N. E., *The Bedfordshire Farm Worker in the Nineteenth Century*, BHRS, vol. 60 (Bedford, 1981)

Allsopp, Anne, *The Education and Employment of Girls in Luton, 1874–1924: Widening Opportunities and Lost Freedoms*, BHRS, vol. 84 (Woodbridge, 2005)

Allsopp, Anne, *A History of Luton: From Conquerors to Carnival*, 2nd ed. (Andover, 2018)

Anon., *Centenary Book of the Diocese of Northampton, 1850–1950* (London, 1950)

Anstruther OP, Godfrey, *Seminary Priests: 1, Elizabethan 1558–1603* (Ware and Ushaw, 1968); *2, Early Stuarts 1603–1659* (Great Wakering, 1975); *3, 1660–1715* (Great Wakering, 1976); *4, 1716–1800* (Great Wakering, 1977)

Antrobus, Stuart, 'Robert Bloomfield (1766–1823): the self-taught rural poet', in Bedfordshire Local History Association newsletter, *History in Bedfordshire*, vol. 9 (Spring, 2022), pp. 5–8

Atkinson, Reginald, *The Shefford Catholic Mission, 1728–1823* (Shefford?, 1978)

Bartlett, Thomas, '"The Abominable Catholic Quest". Catholic Emancipation, 1820–1829', in *The Oxford History of British and Irish Catholicism*, vol. 3 (Oxford, 2023), pp. 85–103

Beales, David, *Prosperity and Plunder: European Catholic Monasteries in the Age of Revolution, 1650–1815* (Cambridge, 2003)

Bean, Adrian (ed.), *Bedford's Victorian Cemetery* (Bedford, 2021?)

Beck, Rt. Rev. George Andrew (ed.), *The English Catholics 1850–1950: Essays to commemorate the centenary of the Restoration of the Hierarchy of England and Wales* (London, 1950)

Bell, Patricia L., *Belief in Bedfordshire* (Bedford, 1986)

Bell, Patricia L. (ed.), *Episcopal Visitations in Bedfordshire 1706–1720*, BHRS, vol. 81 (Woodbridge, 2002)

Bellenger OSB, Dominic Aidan (ed.), *English and Welsh Priests 1558–1800* (Downside Abbey, Bath, 1984)

Bellenger OSB, Dominic Aidan. *The French Exiled Clergy in the British Isles after 1789* (Downside, 1986)

Bossy, John, *The English Catholic Community 1570–1850* (London, 1975)

Bouscaren, T. Lincoln and Adam C. Ellis, *Canon Law; A Text and Commentary*, 3rd rev. ed. (Milwaukee, USA, 1957)

Bradley, George T., 'The Leeds Seminary – An Experiment in Clerical Education', in R. Finnegan and G. Bradley, *Catholicism in Leeds, 1794–1994* (Leeds, 1994), pp. 57–70

Brady, W. Maziere, *The Episcopal Succession in England, Scotland and Ireland A.D. 1400–1875*, 3 vols (Rome, 1876; repr. London, 1971)

Brown, Paul, *Leighton Buzzard and Linslade: A History* (Chichester, 2008)

Brown, Paul & Delia Gleave, *Sand, Planes and Submarines: Leighton Buzzard and the First World War* (Stroud, 2017)

Bunker, Stephen, *Strawopolis: Luton Transformed 1840–1876*, BHRS, vol. 78 (Bedford, 1999)

Burton, Edwin H., *The Life and Times of Bishop Challoner, 1691–1781*, 2 vols (London, 1909)

Bushby, D. W., 'Elementary Education in Bedford 1868–1903', in BHRS, vol. 54 (Luton, 1975), pp. 1–107

Bushby, D. W., 'The Ecclesiastical Census, Bedfordshire, March 1851', in BHRS, vol. 54 (Luton, 1975), pp. 109–200

Bushby, David (ed.), *The Bedfordshire Schoolchild: Elementary Education before 1902*, BHRS, vol. 67 (Bedford, 1988)

Butler, David, 'The Catholic London District in the Eighteenth Century', in *RH*, vol. 28, no. 2 (October, 2006), pp. 245–68

Chambers, Betty, *Printed Maps and Town Plans of Bedfordshire 1576–1900*, BHRS, vol. 62 (Bedford, 1983)

Champ, Judith, *The Secular Priesthood in England and Wales: History, Mission and Identity* (Oscott, 2016)

Champ, Judith, *William Bernard Ullathorne 1806–1889: A Different Kind of Monk* (Leominster, 2006)

Chinnici, Joseph P., *The English Catholic Enlightenment: John Lingard and the Cisalpine Movement, 1780–1850* (Shepherdstown, WV, 1980)

Colley, Linda, *Britons. Forging the Nation* (New Haven and London, 1992)

Cosin, Charles, *The Names of the Roman Catholics, Nonjurors, and others, who refus'd to take the oaths to his late Majesty King George* (London, 1745; repr. for John Russell Smith, London, 1862)

Cottrell-Boyce, Aidan, 'Scandal in Somerstown: Conspiracism and Catholic Schools in Early Victorian England', in *BCH*, vol. 35, no. 4 (October, 2021), pp. 415–39

Cross, F. L. and E. A. Livingstone (eds), *The Oxford Dictionary of the Christian Church*, 2nd rev. ed. (Oxford, 1982)

Cunningham, Jack P., 'Fr Simon Bordley: eighteenth-century recusant priest, schoolmaster and trader in "two-legged cattle"', in *BCH*, vol. 36, no. 3 (May, 2023), pp. 280–308

Cwiekowski, Frederick, *The English Bishops and the First Vatican Council* (Louvain, 1971)

Decreta Quatuor Conciliorum Provincialium Westmonasteriensium 1852–1873, 2nd ed. (London, no date)

Devany, F. J., *The Faithful Few: A History of Norfolk Roman Catholics 1559–1778*, 2nd ed. (Norwich, 2010)

Donovan, Robert Kent, 'Sir John Dalrymple and the Origins of Roman Catholic Relief, 1775–1778', in *RH*, vol. 17, no. 2 (October, 1984), pp. 188–96

Doyle, Peter, 'Charles Plater S.J. and the Origins of the Catholic Social Guild', in *RH*, vol. 21, no. 3 (May, 1993), pp. 401–17

Doyle, Peter (ed.), *The Correspondence of Alexander Goss, Bishop of Liverpool 1856–1872*, CRS, vol. 85 (Woodbridge, 2014)

Doyle, Peter, 'The Education and Training of Roman Catholic Priests in Nineteenth-Century England', in *JEH*, vol. 35, no. 2 (April, 1984), pp. 208–19

Doyle, Peter, 'Leaders and Leadership', in *Oxford History of British and Irish Catholicism*, vol. 4 (Oxford, 2023), pp. 36–55

Doyle, Peter, *Mitres and Missions in Lancashire: A History of the Roman Catholic Diocese of Liverpool 1850–2000* (Liverpool, 2005)

Doyle, Peter, '"To Whom Should We Turn?" Aspects of the Relationship between the English and Welsh Hierarchy and Rome, 1880s–1920s', in *RH*, vol. 29, no. 4 (October, 2009), pp. 523–39

Doyle, Peter, *Upholland College: One Hundred and Fifty Years of Priestly Training* (Wigan, 2018)

Duffy, Eamon (ed.), *Challoner and His Church. A Catholic Bishop in Georgian England* (London, 1981)

Duffy, Eamon, '"Poor Protestant Flies": Conversions to Catholicism in Early Eighteenth Century England', in *SCH*, vol. 15 (Oxford, 1978), pp. 289–304

Estcourt, E. and John Orlebar Payne (eds), *The English Catholic Nonjurors of 1715: Being a Summary of the Register of their Estates, with Genealogical and Other Notes* (London, 1885)

Finnegan, R. and G. Bradley, *Catholicism in Leeds, 1794–1994* (Leeds, 1994)

Fitzgerald-Lombard OSB, Charles (ed.), *English and Welsh Priests 1801–1914* (Downside Abbey, Bath, 1993)

Flanagan, Thomas, *History of the Church in England: From the Earliest Period to the Re-establishment of the Hierarchy in 1850*, 2 vols (London, 1857)

Foley, Brian Charles, *Some Other People of the Penal Times* (Lancaster, 1991)

Foster, Stewart, '"In sad want of priests and money": Bishop Amherst at Northampton, 1858–1879', in *RH*, vol. 25, no. 2 (October, 2000), pp. 281–93

Fraser, Antonia, *The King and the Catholics: The Fight for Rights 1829* (London, 2018)

Furnival, J., *Children of the Second Spring: Father James Nugent and the work of child care in Liverpool* (Leominster, 2005)

Gandy, Michael, *Catholic Missions and Registers 1700–1880*, vol. 2, *The Midlands and East Anglia* (London, 1993)

Glickman, Gabriel, *The English Catholic Community 1688–1745: Politics, Culture and Ideology* (Woodbridge, 2009)

Godber, Joyce, *History of Bedfordshire 1066–1888* (Luton, 1969)

Godber, Joyce, 'Elizabeth Brown of Ampthill, 1778–91', in *Some Bedfordshire Diaries*, BHRS, vol. 40 (Streatley, 1960), pp. 110–29

Gooch, Leo (ed.), *The Revival of English Catholicism: The Banister-Rutter Correspondence 1777–1807* (Wigan, 1995)

Gooch, Leo, '"The Religion for a Gentleman": The Northern Catholic Gentry in the Eighteenth Century', in *RH*, vol. 23, no. 4 (October, 1997), pp. 543–68

Gregory, L. R., 'Saving Bishop Riddell', in *Catholic Archives, The Journal of the Catholic Archive Society*, vol. 41 (n.p., 2021)

Hadland, Tony (ed.), *From Country House Catholicism to City Church: The Registers of the Oxford Catholic Mission 1700–1875*, Oxfordshire Record Society, vol. 75 (Oxford, 2023)

Hardy, Mary, 'The seventeenth-century English and Scottish reception of Francis de Sales. An Introduction to a Devout Life', in *BCH*, vol. 33, no. 2 (October 2016), pp. 228–58

Heimann, Mary, *Catholic Devotion in Victorian England* (Oxford, 1995)

Hemphill OSB, Basil, *The Early Vicars Apostolic of England 1685–1750* (London, 1954)

Henington, J. F., *The Merchants Miscellany and Complete Compendium, containing a mercantile state and public view of the county of Bedford for 1785* (Bedford, repr. 1885)

Hill, Rosemary, *God's Architect: Pugin & the Building of Romantic Britain* (London, 2007)

Hilton, J. A., *Catholic Lancashire: From Reformation to Renewal, 1559–1991* (Chichester, 1994)

Hilton, J. A., *The Cockpit of Conscience, Society, Politics and Religion in Stuart Lancashire 1603–1714* (Carlisle, 2020)

Hilton, J. A., *Occasional Papers. Post-Reformation Catholic History* (Wigan, 2020)

Hilton, J. A., 'The Rise and Fall of the Catholic Mortuary Chapel', in *NWCH*, vol. L (2023), pp. 5–10

Holmes, J. D., *More Roman than Rome* (London, 1978)

Holt, T. G., 'An eighteenth century chaplain: John Champion at Sawston Hall', in *RH*, vol. 17, no. 2 (October, 1984), pp. 181–8

Hughes, Philip, 'The English Catholics in 1850', in G. A. Beck (ed.), *The English Catholics 1850–1950* (London, 1950), pp. 42–85

Kelly, Bernard W., *Historical Notes on English Catholic Missions* (London, 1907; repr. London, 1995)

Kelly, James E. and John McCafferty (eds), *The Oxford History of British and Irish Catholicism*, 5 vols (Oxford, 2023)

Kelly, Wilfred, *Liber Ruber Venerabilis Collegii Anglorum de Urbe, Annales Collegii, I. A.D. 1579–1630*, CRS, vol. 37 (Leeds, 1940)

Kelly, Wilfred, *Liber Ruber Venerabilis Collegii Anglorum de Urbe, Annales Collegii, II. A.D. 1631–1783*, CRS, vol. 40 (Leeds, 1943)

King, Henry E., *An Ancient Catholic Mission and its Modern Development* (Shefford, 1896; repr. 1918)

Kirk, John, *Biographies of English Catholics in the Eighteenth Century. By the Rev. John Kirk, D.D., being part of his projected continuation of Dodd's Church History* ed. by J. H. Pollen SJ and E. Burton (London, 1909)

Knight, Edmund, 'Family Notes of the Knights of Lincolnshire', *Miscellanea IV*, in CRS, vol. 4 (London, 1907), pp. 261–3

The laity's directory; for the church service on Sundays and Holy Days, for the year of our Lord MDCCXCIV (London, 1793); and *MDCCCXIII* (London, 1813)

Lance, Derek, *The Returning Tide: Northampton Diocese 1850–2000* (Northampton, 2000)

Lannon, David, 'Bishop Turner, the Salford Diocese and Reformatory Provision, 1854–1872', in *RH*, vol. 23, no. 3 (May, 1997), pp. 389–407

Lehner, Ulrich L., *The Catholic Enlightenment: The Forgotten History of a Global Movement* (Oxford, 2016)

Lindsay, Claud Reginald (ed.), 'Catholic Registers of Lincoln's Inn Fields Chapel, London', *Miscellanea XI*, in CRS, vol. 19 (London, 1917), pp. 202–368

Lock, Alexander, 'Catholicism, Apostasy and Politics in Late Eighteenth-century England: the case of Sir Thomas Gascoigne and Charles Howard, Earl of Surrey', in *RH*, vol. 30, no. 2 (October, 2010), pp. 275–98

Lysons, Samuel and Daniel, *Magna Britannia: being a concise topographical account of the several counties of Great Britain* (London, 1806–22), vol. 1

McClelland, V. A. (ed.), *By Whose Authority? Newman, Manning and the 'Magisterium'* (Downside, Bath, 1996)

McClelland, V. Alan and Michael Hodgetts (eds), *From Without the Flaminian Gate. 150 Years of Roman Catholicism in England and Wales 1850–2000* (London, 1999)

Manning, H. E., 'The Work and Wants of the Church in England', in *Miscellanies I* (London, 1877)

Marshall, Peter and Scott, Geoffrey (eds), *Catholic Gentry in English Society: the Throckmortons of Coughton from Reformation to Emancipation* (Farnham, 2009)

Milburn, David, *A History of Ushaw College* (Durham, 1964)

Morgan, Richard (ed.), *The Diary of a Bedfordshire Squire (John Thomas Brooks of Flitwick, 1794–1858)*, BHRS, vol. 66 (Bedford, 1987)

Morton, Adam, 'Anti-Popery', in *The Oxford History of British and Irish Catholicism*, vol. 2 (Oxford, 2023), pp. 170–88

Muldoon, A. R., 'Recusants, Church-Papists and "Comfortable Missionaries"', in *Catholic Historical Review*, vol. 86, no. 2 (April, 2000), pp. 242–57

Mullett, Michael, *Catholics in Britain and Ireland, 1558–1829* (London, 1998)

Mullett, Michael, 'Catholics in the United Kingdom, 1800–1820', in *The Oxford History of British and Irish Catholicism*, vol. 3 (Oxford, 2023), pp. 67–84

Norman, Edward R., *Anti-Catholicism in Victorian Britain* (London, 1968)

Norman, Edward R., *The English Catholic Church in the Nineteenth Century* (Oxford, 1984)

Northampton Diocesan Directory (Northampton, 2016)

O'Brien, Susan, 'French Nuns in Nineteenth Century England', in *Past & Present*, vol. 154 (February, 1997), pp. 142–80

O'Brien, Susan, 'Religious Life for Women', in McClelland, V. Alan and Michael Hodgetts (eds), *From Without the Flaminian Gate* (London, 1999), pp. 108–41

O'Sullivan, Patrick (ed.), *Religion and Identity*, vol. 5 of *The Irish Worldwide: History, Heritage, Identity* (London, 1996)

Parish Registers of Campton cum Shefford, Bedfordshire Parish Register Series, vol. 52 (Bedford, 1982)

Petti, Anthony G. (ed.), *Recusant Documents from the Ellesmere Manuscripts*, CRS, vol. 60 (St Albans, 1968)

Phillips, Peter, 'Catholic Belief and Practice', in *The Oxford History of British and Irish Catholicism*, vol. 3 (Oxford, 2023), pp. 122–41

Phillips, Peter (ed.), *The Diaries of Bishop William Poynter, V.A. (1815–1824)*, CRS, vol. 79, (London, 2006)

Phillips, Peter, *John Lingard: Priest and Historian* (Leominster, 2008)

Phillips, Peter (ed.), *Lingard Remembered: Essays to Mark the Sesquicentenary of John Lingard's Death*, CRS, Monograph 6 (London, 2004)

Phillips, Peter 'The English Secular Clergy, 1559–1829' in Robert E. Scully SJ with Angela Ellis, *A Companion to Catholicism and Recusant Studies* (Leiden and Boston, 2022), pp. 59–84

Pickford, Chris, *Bedfordshire Churches in the Nineteenth Century*, BHRS, vol. 73 (Bedford, 1994), vol. 77 (Bedford, 1998), vol. 79 (Bedford, 2000), vol. 80 (Bedford, 2001)

Pickering, W. S. F., 'The 1851 Religious Census – A Useless Experiment?', *British Journal of Sociology*, vol. 18 (1967), pp. 382–407

Pigot & Co.'s London & Provincial New Commercial Directory, for 1827–8 (London, 1827)

Pizzoni, Giada, 'The English Catholic Church and the Age of Mercantilism: Bishop Richard Challoner and the South Sea Company', *Journal of Early Modern History*, vol. 24 (2020), pp. 111–35

Plumb, Brian, *Arundel to Zabi: A Biographical Dictionary of the Catholic Bishops of England and Wales (Deceased) 1623–1987*, North West Catholic History Society (Wigan, 1987)

Quinn, Dermot, *Patronage and Piety: The Politics of Roman Catholicism, 1850–1900* (Basingstoke, 1993)

Robbins, Jack, *John Priestley Warmoll. Apostle of Bedford: His Life, Times and Family* (privately published, Downham Market, 2004)

Roberts, Jenifer, *Glass: The Strange History of the Lyne Stephens Fortune* (Chippenham, 2003)

Roberts, Jenifer, *The Beauty of Her Age: A Tale of Sex, Scandal and Money in Victorian England* (Stroud, 2016)

Rodell, Jonathan, *The Rise of Methodism: A Study of Bedfordshire 1736–1851*, BHRS, vol. 92 (Woodbridge, 2014)

Rowe, Joy, 'The 1767 Census of Papists in the Diocese of Norwich: The Social Composition of the Roman Catholic Community', in David Chadd (ed.), *Religious Dissent in East Anglia III* (Norwich, 1996), pp. 187–234

Rowlands, Marie B. (ed.), *English Catholics of Parish and Town 1558–1778: a joint research project of the Catholic Record Society and Wolverhampton University*, CRS, Monograph 5 (London, 1999)

Schieffen, Richard J., *Nicholas Wiseman and the Transformation of English Catholicism* (Shepherdstown, US, 1984)

Schofield, N. and G. Skinner, *The English Vicars Apostolic 1688–1850* (Oxford, 2009)

Scully Robert E. and Angela Ellis, *A Companion to Catholicism and Recusancy in Britain and Ireland: From Reformation to Emancipation* (Leiden/Boston, 2022)

Sheils, William, 'Catholics and their Neighbours in a Rural Community: Egton Chapelry 1590–1780', in *Northern History*, vol. 34 (1998), pp. 117–43

Sheils, William, 'Religious Divisions in the Localities: Catholics, Puritans and the Established Church before the Civil Wars', in Edward Vallance et al. (eds), *Faith, Place and People in Early Modern England: Essays in Honour of Margaret Spufford* (Woodbridge, 2018)

Skinner, John, Howard Coombs & Peter Coombs (eds), *Journal of a Somerset Rector 1803–1834*, 2nd rev. ed. (Bath, 1971)

Smart, Richard (ed.), *The Bousfield Diaries: A Middle-Class Family in Late Victorian Bedford*, BHRS, vol. 86 (Woodbridge, 2007)

Smith, Sr Hazel, *The Annals of St Etheldreda's*, 2nd rev. ed. (Bedford, 2020)

Stack, John A., 'The Catholics, the Irish Delinquent and the Origins of Reformatory Schools in Nineteenth-Century England and Scotland', in *RH*, vol. 23, no. 3 (May, 1997), pp. 372–88

Stonor OSB, Robert Julian, *Stonor. A Catholic Sanctuary in the Chilterns from the Fifth Century till Today* (Newport, Mon., 1951)

Swift, R. and S. Gilley, *Irish Identities in Victorian Britain* (London, 2011)

Uglow, Jenny, *The Lunar Men: The Friends who made the Future, 1739–1810* (London, 2003)

Ullathorne, W. B., *Ecclesiastical Discourses Delivered on Special Occasions* (London, 1876)

Vallance, Edward, Trevor Dean and Glyn Parry (eds), *Faith, Place and People in early modern England: Essays in memory of Margaret Spufford* (Woodbridge, 2018)

Vowles, Gordon, *Henry Clutton. Victorian Architect of Gothic Revival Churches and Country Houses* (Willington, 2022)

Vowles, Gordon, *The Reverend Augustus Orlebar: 'squarson', sportsman and 'father of the village', Vicar of Willington 1858–1912* (Willington, 2010)

Walsh, Michael, *The Tablet, 1840–1990: A Commemorative History* (London, 1990)

Ward, Bernard, *The Dawn of the Catholic Revival in England 1781–1803*, 2 vols (London, 1909)

Ward, Bernard, *The Eve of Catholic Emancipation, Being the History of the English Catholics during the First Thirty Years of the Nineteenth Century*, 3 vols (London, 1912)

Ward, Bernard, *The History of St Edmund's College, Old Hall* (London, 1893)

Welch, Edwin (ed.), *Bedfordshire Chapels and Meeting Houses: Official Registration 1672–1901*, BHRS, vol. 75 (Bedford, 1996)

Wellington, Arthur Wellesley, 2nd Duke of (ed.), *Despatches, Correspondence and Memoranda of Field Marshall Arthur, Duke of Wellington, K.G.*, vol. 4 and vol. 5 (London, 1873)

Whitehead, Maurice et al, 'Education and Schooling', in *The Oxford History of British and Irish Catholicism*, vol. 4, *Building Identity, 1830–1913* (Oxford, 2023), pp. 94–118

Whitehead, Maurice, 'The English Jesuits and Episcopal Authority: The Liverpool Test Case, 1840–43', in *RH*, vol. 18 (October, 1886), pp. 197–219

Whyte, J. H., 'The Vicars Apostolics' Returns of 1773', in *RH*, vol. 9, no. 4 (January, 1968), pp. 205–14

Wigfield, W. M. (ed.), 'Recusancy and Nonconformity in Bedfordshire. Illustrated by Select Documents between 1622 and 1842', BHRS, vol. 20 (Aspley Guise, 1938), pp. 145–229

Williams, J. Anthony, 'Change or Decay? The Provincial Laity 1691–1781' in Eamon Duffy, *Challoner and His Church* (London, 1981), pp. 27–54

Williams, J., 'The Distribution of Catholic Chaplaincies in the Early Eighteenth Century', in *RH*, vol. 12, no. 1 (1973–4), pp. 42–8

Worrall, E. S. (ed.), *Returns of Papists 1767*, CRS Occasional Publications, no. 2, 2 vols (n.p., 1989)

Worrall SND, Jennifer (ed.), *Jubilee: Sisters of Notre Dame de Namur Celebrate 150 years in Britain, 1845–1995* (privately published, 1995)

Young, Francis, 'Bishop William Poynter and exorcism in Regency England', in *BCH*, vol. 33, no. 2 (October, 2016), pp. 278–97

Young, Francis (ed.), *Catholic East Anglia: A History of the Catholic Faith in Norfolk, Suffolk, Cambridgeshire and Peterborough* (Leominster, 2016)

Young, Francis, 'Surveying a field come of age', in *BCH*, vol. 36, no. 2 (October, 2022), pp. 204–21

Unpublished sources

Collins, Fr Gerald Albert, 'An Ancient Catholic Mission, Shefford, Beds 1762–1869' (unpublished typescript in NDA)

McPhee, Constance C., 'Gilbert R. Blount (1819–1876). Catholic Gothic Revival Architect', unpublished thesis presented to the University of Pennsylvania, for the Degree of Master of Arts (1987)

Taylor's 'Notes on the Baptismal Register of the Catholic Chapel of Thorndon Park, nr Brentwood, Essex' (unpublished typescript in NDA)

Index of subjects and places

Page numbers in **bold** refer to illustrations and those in *italics* refer to tables.

Index of personal names

Page numbers in **bold** refer to illustrations.

Abbreviations

Christopher	Chris	James	Jas
Edward	Edw	John	Jn
Elisabeth	Elis	Margaret	Margt
Elizabeth	Eliz	Richard	Rich
Frederick	Fred	Robert	Rob
George	Geo	Thomas	Thos
Henry	Hy	William	Wm

www.ingramcontent.com/pod-product-compliance
Lightning Source LLC
LaVergne TN
LVHW052105180826
845923LV00004B/33